LAY PIETY AND RE
IN MIDDLE ENG

In late fourteenth-century England, the persistent question of how to live the best life preoccupied many pious Christians. One answer was provided by a new genre of prose guides that adapted professional religious rules and routines for lay audiences. These texts engaged with many of the same cultural questions as poets like Langland and Chaucer; however, they have not received the critical attention they deserve until now. Nicole Rice analyses how the idea of religious discipline was translated into varied literary forms in an atmosphere of religious change and controversy. By considering the themes of spiritual discipline, religious identity, and orthodoxy in Langland and Chaucer, the study also brings fresh perspectives to bear on *Piers Plowman* and *The Canterbury Tales*. This new juxtaposition of spiritual guidance and poetry will form an important contribution to our understanding of both authors and of late medieval religious practice and thought.

NICOLE R. RICE is Associate Professor of English at St. John's University.

CAMBRIDGE STUDIES IN MEDIEVAL LITERATURE

GENERAL EDITOR
Alastair Minnis, *Yale University*

EDITORIAL BOARD
Zygmunt G. Barański, *University of Cambridge*
Christopher C. Baswell, *University of California, Los Angeles*
John Burrow, *University of Bristol*
Mary Carruthers, *New York University*
Rita Copeland, *University of Pennsylvania*
Simon Gaunt, *King's College, London*
Steven Kruger, *City University of New York*
Nigel Palmer, *University of Oxford*
Winthrop Wetherbee, *Cornell University*
Jocelyn Wogan-Browne, *University of York*

This series of critical books seeks to cover the whole area of literature written in the major medieval languages – the main European vernaculars, and medieval Latin and Greek – during the period *c.* 1100–1500. Its chief aim is to publish and stimulate fresh scholarship and criticism on medieval literature, special emphasis being placed on understanding major works of poetry, prose, and drama in relation to the contemporary culture and learning which fostered them.

A complete list of titles in the series can be found at the end of the volume.

LAY PIETY AND RELIGIOUS DISCIPLINE IN MIDDLE ENGLISH LITERATURE

NICOLE R. RICE

CAMBRIDGE UNIVERSITY PRESS
Cambridge, New York, Melbourne, Madrid, Cape Town,
Singapore, São Paulo, Delhi, Tokyo, Mexico City

Cambridge University Press
The Edinburgh Building, Cambridge CB2 8RU, UK

Published in the United States of America by Cambridge University Press, New York

www.cambridge.org
Information on this title: www.cambridge.org/9781107404656

First published 2008
First paperback edition 2011

A catalogue record for this publication is available from the British Library

Library of Congress Cataloguing in Publication Data
Rice, Nicole R., 1973–
Lay piety and religious discipline in Middle English literature / Nicole R. Rice.
p. cm. – (Cambridge studies in medieval literature)
Includes bibliographical references and index.
ISBN 978-0-521-89607-8 (hardback)
1. English prose literature – Middle English, 1100–1500 – History and criticism.
2. English poetry – Middle English, 1100–1500 – History and criticism.
3. Religion and literature – England – History – To 1500.   4. Spiritual life in literature.
5. Spiritual life – Christianity – History of doctrines – Middle Ages, 600–1500.
6. Religious thought – Middle Ages, 600–1500.   I. Title.   II. Series.
PR275.R4R53   2008
820.9′382 – dc22   2008033467

ISBN 978-0521-89607-8 Hardback
ISBN 978-1-107-40465-6 Paperback

For my parents, for Howard, and for Lana ז"ל

Contents

Preface

In later fourteenth-century England, the persistent question of how to live the "best life" preoccupied many pious Christians, and new answers proliferated for enterprising laypeople. The literate might read the catechism or monastic meditations translated from Latin into English; the prosperous could participate in administering religious guilds and chantries or perhaps retire to monasteries. During this period, religious reformer John Wyclif argued controversially that perfection was to be found in the life of biblical reading, preaching, and teaching, a priestly discipline that should be accessible in some measure to every Christian. Meanwhile the instabilities and contingencies of religious identity offered ready material for poetic satire. *Piers Plowman*, Langland's great, inconclusive meditation on the complexity of Christian life, begins as narrator Will dons a shepherd's clothes, "in habite as an heremite, vnholy of werkes," assuming a new religious role even as he acknowledges its falseness. In Chaucer's *Canterbury Tales*, monks persistently flout the Benedictine vow of stability, appearing in taverns, manors, and ladies' beds: everywhere but in their cloisters.

During a period when many forms of professional religious life were subject to lay interest and emulation, as well as doubt and critique, vernacular authors responded in varied ways to the question of how lay Christians should seek spiritual fulfillment. This book analyzes some of these textual formations of lay piety in an age of social change and religious upheaval, drawing upon a largely neglected body of religious guidance together with reformist discourses and contemporary poetry.[1] At the heart of my study lie five late Middle English prose spiritual guides – the anonymous *Abbey of the Holy Ghost, Fervor Amoris, Book to a Mother, The Life of Soul*, and Walter Hilton's *Mixed Life* – that propose to define and routinize religious life for lay readers wishing to move beyond catechism to explore the ordered practices and contemplative experience traditionally associated with life in religious orders.[2] I argue that these guides, written between the beginning of Wyclif's career and the flowering of "vernacular Wycliffism" in the fifteenth century,³ must be newly understood as culturally central texts whose new literary popularizations of the religious life mediate between the requirements of orthodoxy and the impulses of reform. Prose spiritual guidance, which has recently begun to receive critical notice commensurate with its importance in the late medieval period, proves a flexible and innovative literary mode that can be most profitably studied in conversation with poetic and polemical visions of the religious life. This study also brings fresh perspectives to bear on selected works of Langland and Chaucer, poets alternately skeptical and hopeful about the future of religious discipline.

I have selected these particular guides based on their claims to offer plans for devout living to spiritually aspirant lay readers.⁴ The five works considered here are united by similar constructions of their audiences: they posit readers, whether known or imagined, ambitious to move beyond basic religious competence toward fuller dedication to religious life, perhaps even contemplative experience.⁵ Walter Hilton ascribes to his addressee a wish "to serue our lord bi goostli occupacioun al holli, wiþoute lettynge or trobolynge of wordeli bisynesse."⁶ The author of *Fervor Amoris* solicits a wider group of lay readers who "al day askin how þei schul loue God, and in what maner þei schul liue to his plesaunce for his endles goodnes."⁷ In response to this perceived demand, each of the guides proposes techniques for transforming lay existence into a form of "goostli occupacioun," a dedicated religious life in which the reading subject might "serve" and "love" God without undermining priestly intellectual, pastoral, and penitential power.

The key to this balancing act is the careful transformation of religious discipline into textual form. These guides translate contested religious roles into new written models of self-regulation and self-assertion for lay readers, exploiting the overlapping senses of discipline (a system of correction or mortification; a process of education; a branch of learning) to encourage readerly self-regulation and expand possibilities for lay identification with the disciplines of monastic, anchoritic, fraternal, and secular clerical life. These are guides written for readers in the world, and this fact is critical. Their authors endeavor to draw readers *back* to the world on newly rigorous terms, constructing new modes of lay religious conduct to be explored under the careful supervision of clerical authority.⁸

In addition to being linked by their shared concept of audience, these five guides deserve particular attention because they illuminate some of the most significant uses of literary form to shape lay religious knowledge and practice at the end of the fourteenth century and into the early fifteenth.⁹ In the first part of the study, I treat guides that reimagine cloistered modes of religious discipline as textual frameworks for lay self-regulation in the world. The monuments of professed religious life – cloister and rule – become literary forms for redefining lay religious practice within the social structures of penance and lay community. In the second part of the book, I explore spiritual guides that present priestly life and the Bible as model and rule for lay Christian conduct, encouraging their lay readers to imitate clerical modes of biblical study, preaching, and pastoral care without encroaching on priestly prerogatives. While the first group of texts is cautious in its textual and ideological strategies, drawing upon cloistered forms of religious life to mediate between powerful lay desires and the actual requirements of penitential discipline, the second group proves reformist,[10] mediating between Wycliffism and orthodoxy to accommodate new forms of lay spiritual authority within the boundaries of ecclesiastical hierarchy.[11] In my concluding chapter, I show that circulation of these works in the fifteenth century both complicates their messages and suggests important continuities between fourteenth- and fifteenth-century literary practices, with implications for our larger narrative of Middle English literary history.

The claustral and clerical categories that I am positing describe ways of transforming religious disciplines into didactic literary forms.[12] To create this distinction for texts is not to imply that these categories were distinct in the realm of professional religious practice (for example, monastic and priestly status nearly always overlapped for monks in later medieval England). Nor do the clericalizing texts I consider necessarily disparage the monastic life or contemplative life more broadly. For both groups of guides, the multiple meanings of religious discipline suggest strategies for the formation of lay religious identity on numerous fronts. In the *Abbey* and *Fervor Amoris*, monastic enclosure and contemplation reinscribe pastoral penitential discipline and collective social regulation. In *The Life of Soul*, *Book to a Mother*, and Hilton's *Mixed Life*, reading, preaching, and pastoral care become literary realms in which apostolic life is posited as a site of lay–clerical cooperation rather than a threat to ecclesiastical hierarchy.

Placing spiritual guidance in conversation with reformist discourses and contemporary poetry reveals with new clarity a set of common concerns about lay piety's challenges to contemporary religious roles. As David Aers and Lynn Staley observe in *The Powers of the Holy* – one of few full-length studies to consider canonical poetry together with religious prose – Chaucer, Langland, and Julian of Norwich are all engaged in a "submerged conversation regarding the boundaries between lay and clerical activities" in the period.[13] By constructing this "conversation" in a new way, in terms of relations among lay piety, religious discipline, and literary form, I show how these texts work to investigate, cross, and even redefine lay–clerical boundaries during a particularly fraught period for these categories. Chaucer and Langland share a preoccupation with the status of religious figures as models for laity, and both explore extreme scenarios that the spiritual guides wish to avoid, the crossing of social and disciplinary boundaries that didactic texts strive to reconfigure.[14] Rather than arguing for poetry as "simply another form of vernacular theology,"[15] I suggest that poetry and devotional prose may illuminate each other, for Chaucer and Langland often ask the very questions that didactic authors seek to answer. Chaucer's response to monastic imitation and clerical impersonation exposes the dangers that exist at both ends of the disciplinary spectrum, while Langland's work functions both as analogue and counterpoint to the reformist works of spiritual guidance. Where *Piers Plowman* remains theoretical in its approach to diffusing "clergie" among laity and pessimistic about the state of pastoral care, the guides in question attempt to carve out a textual middle ground, reimagining certain intellectual and pastoral aspects of clerical discipline as tools for practical lay use.

The book unfolds as follows. The Introduction establishes a cultural matrix for the readings to come. In the post-plague period, amid institutional readjustments and the expansion of lay religious education, privileged elements of professional religious reading and practice became increasingly available to pious laity. In this section I consider the extension of different forms of religious discipline into the lay world, examining laypeople's efforts to accrue spiritual capital through affiliation with contemplative religious orders, investment in corporate organizations such as religious guilds and chantries, and use of texts including monastic rules, liturgical books, and books of hours. During the same period, John Wyclif's polemical writings interrogated the relation between religious discipline and perfection. Asserting that perfection lay in adherence to the dictates of scripture, Wyclif challenged the validity of the religious orders and advocated a radical form of identity between lay and priestly practice. In orthodox lay efforts to participate in and cooperate with clerical practices, I suggest we see an attraction to priestly culture that the authors of spiritual guidance exploit in their efforts to shape acceptable forms of religious practice.

Chapter 1, "Translations of the cloister: regulating spiritual aspiration," argues that *The Abbey of the Holy Ghost* and *Fervor Amoris* imagine lay pious aspiration as a potentially disruptive social force, a means of evading clerical authority or seeking spiritual transformation that might threaten existing categories of religious status. These works reimagine cloistered modes of discipline as ways to inculcate independent lay modes of self-control, returning readers to the supervision of confessors and the social structures of the larger lay community. By analyzing these texts as newly disciplinary translations of older works (for the *Abbey*, a French precursor, and for *Fervor Amoris*, Richard Rolle's anchoritic *Form of Living*), the chapter illuminates the literary workings of their cautious clerical ideologies. When considered alongside these two spiritual guides, Chaucer's *Shipman's Tale* is freshly seen as a knowing response to intersections of lay spiritual desire and monastic discipline, as it registers the confusions of material and spiritual capital that result from bourgeois lay identification with flawed rather than idealized claustral discipline.

While the guides considered in Chapter 1 look to the cloister and rule to construct new modes of lay spiritual discipline, the texts considered in the book's second part simultaneously imagine the pious lay public and confront the Wycliffite challenge as they fashion new orthodox modes of lay apostolic life. Chapter 2, "Dialogic form and clerical understanding," argues that *The Life of Soul, Book to a Mother*, and Hilton's *Mixed Life* adopt dialogic forms to posit the sharing of "clerical understanding" between priestly authors and lay readers.[16] This chapter charts the construction of the inscribed lay reader as a textual interpreter who moves toward an individual understanding of the Bible, in conversation rather than in competition with the priestly advisor. Techniques of reading, writing, and emendation become implicated in lay addressees' reform in the image of Christ, and the Bible is treated as a source to be consumed in the movement toward a simultaneous *imitatio clerici* and *imitatio Christi*. The emphasis these guides place on Christ as identical with scripture, and on unmediated contact with "holy writ," align them with Wyclif and the later Lollard Bible translators. But in highlighting the materiality and permeability of the Bible, they work – as does *Piers Plowman* – to resist insistence upon the Bible as a transcendent textual entity, refusing to privilege the text at the expense of the reader.

In Chapter 3, "Lordship, pastoral care, and the order of charity," I show that Hilton's *Mixed Life*, written for a wealthy lay lord, engages with contemporary controversy over the meanings of pastoral care and the clerical life in an effort to reform rather than reject the link between temporal and spiritual authority. The chapter explores Hilton's vision of a lay pastoral *imitatio clerici* that assimilates the lives of lay lord, prelate, and Christ, in juxtaposition with moments from Wyclif's writings and *Piers Plowman* that expose the costs to charity of clerical greed and lay spiritual pretension. By examining Hilton's advice on ordering charity in

tandem with some of Langland's meditations on the elusiveness of this
virtue, I show that Hilton's advice to a particular addressee also represents
an important response to the broader contemporary crisis over clerical
discipline and authority.

Chapter 4, "Clerical widows and the reform of preaching," focuses on
the transmission of preaching power, a contested aspect of clerical identity
during a period when lay aspiration and heterodox pressure forced the
serious evaluation of lay rights to public spiritual authority. The chapter examines selected Wycliffite arguments on lay and female preaching
alongside *Book to a Mother*'s widowed addressee, who is constructed as a
Christ-like teacher, and Chaucer's resistant female preacher, Alison of the
Wife of Bath's Prologue. Placed in conversation, these texts render the clerical preaching widow possible and problematic, exemplary and satirical at
this fraught moment in religious history. *Book to a Mother* offers a polemically orthodox vision of lay *imitatio clerici* as *imitatio Christi*, proposing
to empower the reader and condemn mendicant corruption much as some
Wycliffites did, but without abandoning sacramental authority or priestly
voice to lay readers.

The Conclusion, "Spiritual guides in fifteenth-century books: cultural
change and continuity," considers the circulation of some of these guides
in the fifteenth century, in the years after Arundel's Constitutions, written in 1407 and published in 1409, designed to restrict the circulation of
biblical translations made since Wyclif's time. The decades following the
Constitutions have been characterized as an anxious time for the composition of new religious works, but a period when fourteenth-century works
continued to move freely among elite readers.[17] Indeed, I argue, we find
affinities between the guides of Chapter 1 and Nicholas Love's *Mirror of
the Blessed Life of Jesus Christ*, which, in explicit response to Lollardy, looks
to the cloister to propose a limited view of the lay reader's capacity for
understanding and fitness for public spiritual authority. By considering the
circulation of some of the guides in fifteenth-century books, I show that
numerous and often surprising varieties of orthodox practice persisted into
the fifteenth century.

By considering religious prose together with poetry, as works produced
in a shared context of religious ferment, this study will enrich our understanding of how devotional prose mattered to later medieval readers and
how it might figure in our own narratives of Middle English literary history. Two abiding questions – what is the best life for the layperson in the
world? How might that life take textual shape? – powerfully link didactic
prose with canonical poetry.[18] These questions connect to a broad textual

system of lay religious discipline and self-transformation, in which literary compromise and hybridization become key to shaping new forms of lay spiritual life. By pursuing the complex affiliations of these works as they traveled to fifteenth-century readers of diverse religious statuses, I also hope to expand our understanding of how texts shaped the many varieties of orthodoxy that circulated in late medieval England.

Acknowledgments

This study began with a dissertation; I warmly thank Robert Hanning, Margaret Pappano, and Michael Sargent, who helped me to frame the project and continued to offer guidance as it evolved. I am grateful to Sandra Prior and Jocelyn Wogan-Browne for their astute early suggestions on revision, and to the members of the Columbia Medieval Guild for their collegiality and friendship.

Many other generous medievalists read parts of this work as it developed in articles and book chapters. For their thoughtful comments, I am indebted to Jessica Brantley, Donna Bussell, Michael Calabrese, Lisa Cooper, Elisabeth Dutton, Moira Fitzgibbons, Alfred Hiatt, Matthew Giancarlo, Lana Schwebel, and Nicholas Watson.

I also wish to thank colleagues who provided key suggestions and materials as I revised the manuscript for publication. They include Jennifer Brown, Margaret Connolly, Mary Erler, Roberta Frank, Vincent Gillespie, Langdon Hammer, Marlene Hennessy, Rebecca Krug, Traugott Lawler, Pericles Lewis, and Christopher Miller. I am grateful for the support I have received over the past six years from the members of Yale's English Department.

The readers from Cambridge University Press offered incisive reports, and the General Editor, Alastair Minnis, supervised the revision process with great care and efficiency. Many thanks are due to editors Linda Bree and Maartje Scheltens for bringing the project to completion, to Diane Brenner for indexing, and to Ann Lewis for copy-editing.

For invaluable research help, I gratefully acknowledge the archivists of the British Library and the Bodleian Library and my research assistants at Yale, especially Denis Ferhatović.

Financial support for this project was provided by fellowships from Columbia University, the Huntington Library, and Yale University. A generous subvention from Yale's Frederick W. Hilles Publication Fund offset costs associated with production and indexing.

Portions of this study have appeared in earlier forms in *Viator, The Journal of Medieval and Early Modern Studies*, and *Leeds Studies in English*. I express my thanks to the editors of these journals for permission to include that material here.

Translations are my own unless otherwise noted.

Abbreviations

EETS   Early English Text Society (OS, Original Series, ES, Extra Series)
MED   *Middle English Dictionary*
MLQ   *Modern Language Quarterly*

Introduction

Material success and the search for spiritual certainty often went hand in hand for the lay faithful in later medieval England.[1] Acts of endowment such as chantry foundation and donation to monasteries, where masses were said periodically for the benefit of individual souls, enabled the laity to benefit from the activities of religious professionals, tapping into the network of services dedicated to amassing and distributing the treasury of spiritual merit.[2] For some fortunate laity, earthly life may have presented greater time and opportunity not only to cultivate the active penitential life, but also to pursue the "spiritual life": what P. S. Jolliffe calls "the whole of a Christian's life insofar as it is directed towards that perfection which God demands from him, in which prayer is central and in the course of which sins are purged and virtues implanted."[3] But as numerous scholars of the period have observed, living a life of perfection was easier said than done, and "the desire to meld an authentic spiritual life and a prosperous worldly existence constituted a site of genuine cultural struggle in late-medieval society."[4] Texts written to transform this struggle into productive modes of practice are the subject of this study.

In a late medieval English culture characterized by the frequent "intersection of piety and prosperity," some prosperous laity looked to religious professionals for models of the religious discipline that might eventually lead to perfection. In this introduction, I look first at the venerable monastic idea of *disciplina* as a fundamental plan for perfect living and then at its radical late fourteenth-century rejection by Wyclif, who argued for secular clerical life (i.e., non-vowed clerical life in the world) as the most perfect form of apostolic religious practice.[5] Although Wyclif viewed the religious orders as lacking scriptural justification and argued for the superiority of secular clerical models, I contend that contemporary practical and textual evidence suggests lay interest in multiple and overlapping various forms of religious discipline, an interest upon which the authors of spiritual guidance would capitalize.

Scholars who approach medieval courtesy literature with the aid of Pierre Bourdieu's theory of practice have noted that conduct guides aided their readers in the attainment of "symbolic capital," defined as "the prestige or renown attached to a family and a name" in return for material and symbolic investments such as protection and economic aid.[6] Bourdieu argues further, "symbolic capital is always *credit*, in the widest sense of the word, i.e., a sort of advance which the group alone can grant those who give the best material and symbolic *guarantees*."[7] We might begin to conceptualize the lay search for spiritual self-improvement as in part defined by a search for spiritual capital: a fund of credit for salvation and a repertoire of techniques leading to personal perfection, available in return for financial investment.[8] For some laypeople in late fourteenth-century England, success in the mercantile economy may have facilitated pursuit of "the disciplined development of the self," freeing up the time and material resources necessary to seek the spiritual "guarantees" available to those in professional religious life.[9]

The required practice of penance linked all Christians, regardless of status, as a minimal religious discipline. From the fourth to the twelfth century, penance had gradually been transformed from a public, one-time act to a private and repeatable practice of confession, contrition, and satisfaction. The Fourth Lateran Council of 1215 obligated all to engage annually in confession, mandating a form of self-discipline, in cooperation with clerical authority, that would become fundamental to late medieval religious mentalities.[10] The penitent, having expressed contrition for sin, was required to accuse herself and then, separately from the priest's absolution (increasingly given before any satisfaction was performed), to reform her own internal dispositions in order to produce a reformed self.[11] Thus, as Asad observes, "[t]he outstanding feature of penance is not merely its corrective function but its techniques of *self*-correction."[12] In a culture where penitential practice was the entry point to religious expression, those individuals who devoted themselves professionally to "self-correction" may have offered the most visible examples of how religious life could lead to personal perfection. On practical and textual levels, the disciplines of regular and priestly life were privileged sites for laity to begin accumulating spiritual capital.

The chance to live according to professional "ritual discipline" was a privileged option available only to a few, and the late fourteenth century witnessed animated conversation over the best version of religious *disciplina*.

Latin patristic writers had first adopted *disciplina* to represent the Greek term *paideia*, meaning education in its fullest sense, "not only the intellectual element of education, but also its moral aspect... the method, its precepts, the *rule* that the master imposes upon the student."[13] Synonymous with a "rule of faith," discipline thus referred both to the act of teaching and to the subject matter taught: "under Saint Augustine's pen, *disciplina christiana* is the *rule of Christian life*, the law that dictates in every case how to conduct oneself according to the faith."[14] Another key sense of *disciplina*, arising from this nexus of teaching and learning, denotes its corrective function: "a penalty inflicted to warn and amend the guilty person."[15]

During the early medieval period, the monastery was the site where these meanings of discipline – as educational process, body of knowledge, and technique of correction – had coalesced most clearly into a specific Christian way of life, organized by the *Rule of Benedict* (*Sancti Benedicti Regula Monachorum, c.* 593–94), which quickly became the most widely used monastic rule in the West. The *Rule* defines religious discipline as an exercise in submission to and praise of God, admonishing the reader,

[l]isten carefully, my son, to the master's instructions... This is advice from a father who loves you; welcome it, and faithfully put it into practice. The labor of obedience will bring you back to him from whom you had drifted through the sloth of disobedience. This message of mine is for you, then, if you are ready to give up your own will, once and for all, and armed with the strong and noble weapons of obedience to do battle for the true king, Christ the Lord.[16]

The *Rule*, largely devoted to explaining the performance of the *Opus Dei* (the monastic liturgy),[17] uses the term *disciplina* to refer to many aspects of monastic life: to the "good order" the *Rule* establishes in the monastery, to the *Rule* itself, to the proper ways of chanting the psalms or receiving new brothers, and to the "penalties and corrections" imposed for infractions of the monastic discipline.[18] According to the *Rule*, collective prayer, ordered practice, private reading, and meditation should combine to promote each monk's spiritual return to "him from whom you had drifted through the sloth of disobedience." This complex of meanings became common to medieval monastic authors who treated discipline as a system of practices both mandated by authority and self-imposed, always undertaken in a spirit of radical humility.[19]

The monastery remained throughout the Middle Ages the most privileged site for the strictly supervised "disciplined development of the self," even as monks began to share the laity's esteem with the new regular orders of friars. The friars became more visible in England after the plague of

1348–49 and its consequent clerical mortality, for they were permitted to supplement the confessional and preaching duties of secular priests.[20] For many late medieval laity, the cloister still represented the most "powerful *symbol* of the mental aspiration toward heaven that defined the ideal spiritual life."[21] But in later medieval England, the arguments of theologian John Wyclif on the superiority of priestly discipline in the world offered a radical alternative to the vowed religious life of monks or friars as the ideal site for lay religious identification. Although Wyclif's positions may not have been shared by most pious laity, his views on priestly discipline have important implications for vernacular texts written to guide lay readers and negotiate boundaries between lay and clerical authority. I consider Wyclif's arguments here in order to set the scene for the interventions of Middle English spiritual guidance.

Wyclif's arguments for the superiority of secular clerical life, and against the regular religious orders, built upon his vision of Christianity as a communal practice with the unadorned biblical text as its only legitimate source. The idea of priestly discipline as the ideal form of religious life was hardly novel: as the contemporary priest's guide *Speculum Christiani* proclaims, "as gold es more preciose than al other metal, so es prestehode more excellent than al other diuine office3 and dignites."[22] But rather than emphasizing that priestly worth derived from "office," Wyclif argued that the priest's dignity lay in his literal imitation of Christ's preaching and adherence to his words as recorded in the Bible. Although the monastic order had traditionally viewed its own discipline as the ideal imitation of the apostolic life, as did the friars after them, Wyclif's vision left no room for the religious orders.[23] As Wyclif argues in *De Civili Dominio* (*c.* 1375–76), a treatise concerned preeminently with the *lex Christi*, the only source for all human law, true religious life must be based only on Christ's example, for no rule should be added to the precepts that Christ taught and embodied. Turning the vocabulary of the religious orders against them, he writes, "the rule of religion that Christ instituted is the most perfect possible, therefore if an extraneous thing were added, it would be impious."[24]

The mandate to adhere to biblical precedents made any additional rules suspect, particularly those involving "private" observances not dedicated to "edifying" the Church. In developing the contrast between novel, "superadded" private forms of religion and the evangelical model that demands only the performance of virtue, Wyclif casts the cloister as a dangerous place where material goods are mistaken for spiritual, as opposed to the "pure" clerical life in the world, where goods are communal and evangelical movement unfettered. This contrast is expressed in the difference between the providential movement of preachers, identified as the "militia Christi," and the pointless self-restraint of those in the cloister. In Wyclif's idealizing view, true secular clerics are those who "profess poverty, chastity, and obedience to our mother the church and not to the convent":[25] they actively battle the world, the flesh, and the devil, working to edify the church, while those who "retreat foolishly into the cloister" are tempted by the physical ease of the cloistered life.[26] In contrast to those who "bind" themselves to such self-serving observances, St. Paul, next to Christ in exemplarity, steadfastly resisted the torpor of the cloister. Wyclif approves the Apostle's avoidance of degenerate fellowship, "lest in being bound to any private profession he should be delayed from the work of the gospel, for as Gregory says, the strong athlete of Christ refused to be enclosed in the cloister, in order that he might earn more for his God."[27] Here a very different notion of spiritual capital appears: in Wyclif's view, merit is amassed to be given back to God in evangelical practice rather than hoarded in the cloister for the sake of individual or communal "spiritual security."

With his conviction in preaching as the most fundamental aspect of priestly discipline, and his concern about the degeneracy of the contemporary priesthood, Wyclif manages to be pro-clerical in theory but anti-clerical with regard to contemporary practice. In extending his evangelical vision to lay practice, he begins to imply a breakdown between the categories of clerical and lay status, a dissolution that would become more extreme in the theories of his followers and in vernacular Lollardy.[28] While forms of religious life lacking scriptural bases are unacceptable accretions to Christ's "rule," Wyclif argues that the "religious life" may be lived most genuinely by simply avoiding sin and behaving virtuously.[29] Indeed, all Christians should be engaged in some measure in spreading the gospel: "spreading God's word toward the edification of the church" is for Wyclif the very definition of religious discipline.[30] Wyclif's philosophy, with its emphasis on simplifying the life of pastoral service and evangelism, had much in common with that of the friars, although he came later in life to condemn the mendicants for their entanglement in church property and politics.[31] In *De Veritate Sacrae Scripturae*, his treatise on the literal interpretation of the Bible, Wyclif goes further to blur the line between priestly and lay responsibilities. His radical interpretation of Christ's command to Peter to "feed my sheep" requires both priests *and* laity to teach the gospel, for in his view all fathers are priests: "if the fleshly father and elders are required by both testaments to teach God's law to their sons, how much more must spiritual fathers, in such a way that they should all be priests! Every faithful person has the power spiritually to generate children for the church out of the seeds of the strength of faith."[32]

Wyclif's view of the Bible as the only true "rule" for Christian practice[33] and his arguments for the possibility of shared lay–clerical intellectual, evangelical, and pastoral practice implied a challenge to the entire late medieval system of religious discipline, which depended for its coherence upon the maintenance of distinctions between clerical and lay "officez and dignites." For Wyclif, these distinctions became unimportant, as in the case of penance, which was a departure from the gospels and therefore unnecessary. In any case, his belief that God alone could evaluate contrition rendered priestly absolution irrelevant.[34] If priest and layperson ultimately possessed the same biblical mandate and the same "power spiritually to generate children for the church," then the only form of "self-correction" necessary for clergy and laity was absolute conformity to "God's law."

SPIRITUAL CAPITAL AND RELIGIOUS DISCIPLINE IN PRACTICE

In later medieval England, laypeople's practical engagements with religious professionals – monks, friars, secular clergy, and others – suggest sustained lay interest in the disciplines of religious life in many quarters. Practices including confraternity and corrody at religious houses may have offered personal ways for prosperous, pious laity to engage with the religious orders. Others in search of the spiritual capital to be gained through charity and intercessory prayer sought out contact with the practical liturgical aspects of secular clerical discipline, while still apparently respecting the priestly "officez and dignites" that Wyclif wished to sweep away.

The varieties of semi-religious life remain more elusive for late medieval England than for the Continent where, since the twelfth century, many types of lay practice had appealed to laypeople who, in André Vauchez's terms, "aspired to perfection while not desiring or being able to enter monastic life."[35] Such options included membership in third orders associated with the friars[36] and the custom of abiding by a strict devotional program within the lay household. The lay third orders associated with the Franciscans and Dominicans left few traces in England, although a few scattered references to *sorores minores* may allude to Franciscan tertiaries rather than Franciscan nuns.[37] Moreover, almost no mention exists from England of beguinages, the female lay religious communities that flourished in northern Europe in the thirteenth and fourteenth centuries, although there is evidence of two "communities resembling beguinages" in early fifteenth-century Norwich.[38]

Given what may have been the relative dearth of such forms of lay religious organization, lay confraternity with religious houses, as well as the practice of corrody (retirement at a religious house), were two practices whose popularity in later medieval England implies lay interest in regular religious discipline and its attendant spiritual benefits.[39] In the case of the letter of confraternity, the lay benefactor donated money or land to a religious house, in return for which the house agreed to distribute alms and perform liturgical commemorations on the donor's behalf. By this means the donor fulfilled the active duty of charity, which was expected as an act of justice and stewardship to the poor and also functioned as a means of penance, to alleviate purgatorial suffering.[40] Not only did entry into confraternity with a religious house, a ritual that originally involved the ceremonial acceptance of the order's rule, entitle the *confrater* or *consoror* to individualized spiritual capital, but the status of *confrater* or *consoror* might also have given donors an increased sense of participation in the life of a religious house.[41]

Letters of confraternity speak a language of spiritual entitlement, explaining that the donor's material gifts will be transmuted directly into spiritual capital, promising, in one typical formulation, "full participation in all the good things, by the tenor of these presents, that the mercy of our savior may grant to be performed by our brothers."[42] Those in receipt of letters of confraternity could be buried in the habit of the order: this ceremonial garbing ushered deceased members into the "guarantees" afforded to full members.[43] In June 1377, John de Meaux, a knight of York diocese, asked to be buried in the church of Saint Bartholomew in Aldeburgh, in the Franciscan habit. His will reads, "I wish my body to be buried in the habit of the Friars Minor, for I am a member of that same order, and I wish my body to be covered by a black rag on the day of my burial."[44] The combination of habit and black rag seems paradoxically to signify his financial investment in the spiritual rewards of asceticism and humility.

Like lay confraternity with religious houses, with which it may often have overlapped, the practice of corrody offered the promise of spiritual capital in return for material outlay. A corrody, essentially a pension given for cash or a grant of land, comprised a "bundle of privileges" granted to a lodger or non-resident of a religious house.[45] Corrodies often generated considerable income for late medieval religious houses,[46] yet in official documents, the practice was sometimes described in spiritual terms suggesting it served as a way for well-off, pious laity to participate in the *habitus* of a chosen religious house, accruing spiritual capital while organizing their religious lives in terms of ritual regulation and ordered contemplation.[47]

Those who retired to a religious house were entitled to share in all of its material and spiritual benefits, "participating in its religious life, sharing its merit and enjoying the provision of all their physical needs."[48] The 1378 *Corrodium Paynot* grants corrody to Thomas and Johanna Paynot, a burgess and his wife, at the house of the Carmelite Friars of Lynn. After describing the details of their food and lodging, the document grants the couple free access to the spiritual spaces and practices of the friary, permitting them to enter "into their [the friars'] church through the cloister at all hours of the divine office."[49] Without obligating them to follow the rule of the order, this agreement suggests that Thomas and Johanna will agree to submit to the friary's particular "logic of practice." To borrow from Bourdieu's formulation, in the system that this document lays out, "the whole social order imposes itself at the deepest level of the bodily dispositions through a particular way of regulating the use of time, the temporal distribution of collective and individual activities and the appropriate rhythm with which to perform them."[50] This clause suggests that the couple may be engaged, potentially for much of their day, in observation of the *Opus Dei* with the friars, not just as onlookers but as participants. Along with the right to this flexible engagement in the order's *habitus*, the corrody also grants Thomas and Johanna the same right to "participation" in spiritual benefit, from the friars' prayer and other activities, that the above letter of confraternity granted to its *confratri* and *consorores*.[51] This brief look at the evidence of wills, letters of confraternity, and corrodies suggests that a sense of possibility existed at the end of the fourteenth century for privileged laity to enter in practical ways into regulated and introspective religious lives.

While the cloister attracted some who sought daily access to the rhythms of its "spiritual life," the parish was the most immediate and primary site for the expression of devotion by most laity. Lay investments and limited participation in clerical discipline, understood both as a "body of knowledge" and as "physical and spiritual practice," were basic features of late fourteenth-century parish life. Even had they been able to navigate Wyclif's academic Latin, it is uncertain whether many devout laypeople of the late fourteenth century would have been receptive to his conviction that lay fathers should be considered "presbyteri" or that all Christians could eschew the requirements of the confessional. The ecclesiastical condemnations of some of Wyclif's views on preaching, the eucharist, and auricular confession in 1382, however much they distorted his actual positions, further removed him from the mainstream of piety.[52]

However, in parallel with lay participation with religious institutions through practices of confraternity and corrody, collective modes of lay practice such as membership in religious guilds and supervision of chantry foundations do suggest quite well-developed lay interest in understanding, superintending, and cooperating with clerical liturgical practices. Religious guilds, perhaps the best known of English lay religious organizations, were "brotherhoods" organized according to *regulae* that probably derived ultimately from monastic sources yet existed to enable lay individuals, male and female, "to participate more fully in the rituals and sacraments of the church."[53] In their church-based activities, focused on securing intercession for deceased members and supporting clerical liturgical practice, guild-members also shared in the spiritual capital to be gained from clerical functions.

Although guilds were usually associated with parishes, a guild's association with a given parish might be shifting, and its social influence, especially in the case of later urban guilds, could transcend parish boundaries.[54] Overlap between religious and craft guilds was common: although religious fraternities did not usually restrict their membership to people in specific professions, urban craft guilds were always fundamentally religious organizations. As Caroline Barron argues, "[e]very craft association in London, as elsewhere, had at its core a fraternity or religious brotherhood."[55] In the diocese of Salisbury, to take another regional example, membership in the tailors' guild also entailed being "parterie of the praiers and suffrages of . . . [the] fraternitie of Seynt John the Baptist."[56] The tailors considered themselves a religious community bound to maintain divine service for their members, both living and dead.

In addition to administering charity to living members who had fallen upon hard times,[57] the religious guilds' most important church-based activities focused upon intercession for souls in purgatory: attendance at members' funerals and the financing of prayers and masses performed by guild chaplains. The paramount guild duty of light-keeping, the maintenance of candles in the church, was a constant at all liturgical occasions.[58] The London Guild of the Light of St. Mary, dedicated to the Assumption of the Virgin, maintained a perpetual light before Mary's image, observed a solemn mass on her Assumption day and required the lighting of candles at funerary masses: "thei ordeigne of here comone box v tapres and foure torches for to brenne a boute the body at first dirige and o the day . . . at messe at which dirige . . . is asaiyng, and at morwe fro the begynnyng of the first messe to all the messe be sayd."[59] In a particularly resonant ritual, the Holy Sepulchre Guild of Chatteris in Cambridgeshire observed Christ's death on Good Friday by entering the sepulcher set up in the church carrying thirty tapers, which were set to burn from Good Friday noon until

Easter matins.[60] Thus in celebrating its main liturgical occasion, the guild managed to perform intercession for the buried Christ, its own deceased members, and the larger body of all the faithful. With their intense liturgical and sacramental focus, these organizations provided opportunities for close practical cooperation with priests: lay guild members were frequently involved in appointing and maintaining guild chaplains, and in many cases, priests and laypeople founded religious guilds together and cooperated in their administration.[61] In providing charity under the auspices of the church, religious guild members engaged in a heightened expression of the active life that enabled supervision, if not full participation, in clerical liturgical practice.

For laity with more significant funds to invest, chantries (temporary or perpetual) represented another appealing means for procuring the spiritual capital available through intercessory masses and clerical prayer. In later medieval England, the chantry, an endowed chapel employing a priest (or group of priests, in the chantry college) to perform masses for the benefit of founders and patrons, supported a greater percentage of the clerical population than any other intercessory institution.[62] In the course of the fourteenth century, chantries came to be founded in urban areas not only by wealthy merchants but also by "more obscure craftsmen" wishing particular prayers.[63] Although lay chantry founders and patrons may have had less involvement in day-to-day liturgical practice than religious guild members, with their lighting of candles, attendance at funerals, and co-administration with clergy, the foundation and support of a chantry entailed a number of other ways of engaging with clerical discipline. Lay individuals may have founded chantries and supported stipendiary priests primarily for the sake of securing their own immortal souls, but these priests also contributed to meeting liturgical needs and pastoral demands that had developed in the wake of the plague. As Clive Burgess has shown for Bristol, many chantry priests participated in and augmented the daily liturgy of parish churches, and benefactions recorded in the All Saints' Church Book discuss chantries not only as engines of individual prayer but "in terms of the contribution that each made to the 'increase of the Divine Service' within the church."[64] Founding a chantry often meant taking an active role in supporting liturgical practice.

Chantry foundation and the support of stipendiary priests also enabled laity to superintend and participate vicariously in other clerical functions with wider effects on the surrounding community. Some chantry founders directed their gifts not only toward liturgical activity but also toward "such vital tasks as serving as assistants in the cure of souls, teaching

children, or presiding at the charitable doles to the poor."[65] In providing
for the ministration of pastoral care, these founders were in some measure
participating in another aspect of priestly activity. Thus, without necessarily
mounting visible threats of intellectual usurpation or damage to the clergy's
official distinction, many prosperous late fourteenth-century laity showed
their desire to procure spiritual capital, both individual and collective, via
investment and limited participation in clerical discipline.

TEXTUAL FORMATIONS OF LAY PIETY: DISCIPLINE AND DEVOTION

The Latin and vernacular texts produced from the thirteenth century
onward as adjuncts to penitential practice and public worship depended
on the requirements of the confessional and translated monastic and clerical
modes of knowledge and practice, encouraging lay textual engagement as
means to "self-correction" and devotional practice. After the Fourth Lateran
Council, the syllabus for lay education in England was standardized over the
course of the thirteenth century, culminating in England's own Lambeth
Council of 1281. Canon 9 of the Council, known as known as *Ignorantia
Sacerdotum*, required parish clergy to preach at least four times per year
on the articles of the faith, the ten commandments, the two evangelical
precepts, the works of mercy, the seven deadly sins, the seven virtues,
and the seven sacraments.[66] Canon 9 was a list rather than an exposition,
and much-needed teaching aids for the clergy proliferated throughout
the thirteenth and fourteenth centuries, primarily in Latin.[67] As Middle
English began to come into its own as a literary language, some works
originally written for clerics to aid in preaching and confession became
available in translation to literate laity.[68] Archbishop Thoresby of York's
1357 Latin text of the standard syllabus was translated into Middle English
as *The Lay Folks' Catechism*.[69] In a measure that probably added to its
popularity, the translated formula came with an indulgence of forty days
for everyone who learned it or taught it to others.[70]

The production of vernacular works of religious instruction coincided
with and indeed depended upon increasing and varied levels of lay literacy. From the thirteenth century onward, the written word had become
increasingly important for bourgeois laypeople in "pragmatic" realms such
as administration and the law, and that growing experience with texts may
have facilitated a transition from purely pragmatic to more "cultivated"
reading practices in Latin and increasingly in French.[71] Along with bureau-
cratic culture as a spur to literacy, religious initiative may have played
an equally foundational role, particularly among women. For well before

the development of vernacular texts of religious instruction, lay people had begun to engage textually with religious disciplines by using books of hours, Latin prayer books adapted from monastic and clerical liturgical practice.[72] As Eamon Duffy argues, "Because [the primers'] essential core was liturgical, and the visual conventions which governed their production were derived from liturgical books, they formed an important bridge between lay piety and the liturgical observance of the church, for they enabled lay people to associate themselves with the prayer of the clergy and religious."[73] The devotions of the book of hours, which had at its core the Little Office of the Virgin, the Office of the Dead, Psalm 118 (119), and the Penitential and Gradual Psalms, reciprocally influenced the public worship of the church as its devotions became popular among lay users.[74] By the fourteenth century, regular monastic or clerical performances of the hours usually included some elements from the book of hours. The Office of the Virgin was regularly recited as an addition to the *cursus* of the canonical hours, and laity often used an abbreviated form of this text (the version found in the primer) while in church.[75] Some lay guilds required members to recite the prayers for the dead at funerary observances.[76] For many lay readers, whatever their command of Latin, the book of hours occupied a significant role both in public and private prayer life. It was said of Margaret Beaufort in the fifteenth century that "she had a lytell perceyuynge specyally of the rubrysshe of the ordynall for the sayeng of her seruyce which she dyde well vnderstande."[77] While her Latin literacy may have been limited, the "rubrysshe" provided a way into developing a practical "understanding" of the service.

In addition to making modes of liturgical prayer accessible to laypeople, the private use of psalters and books of hours might well have encouraged some to aspire to contemplative transformation. Paul Saenger has argued that the proliferation of small portable books of hours coincided with and may have contributed to the privatization of reading practices in the fourteenth through the sixteenth centuries.[78] In arguing for a shift of emphasis from vocal prayer to silent prayer or "prayer of the heart," Saenger suggests that private, contemplative prayer was increasingly made available and recommended as conducive to a "higher state of spiritual awareness" for a greater range of readers.[79] The content of the Office of the Virgin lends itself as well to private *lectio* as to public recitation: it consists primarily of psalms, each hour beginning with the psalm that also opens the monastic *cursus*: "Lord, open my lips, and my mouth will announce your praise. Lord, stretch out to help me. Lord, hurry to my aid" ("Domine, labia mea aperies et os meum annunciabit laudem tuam.

Deus in adiutorium meum intende. Domine ad adiuvandum me festina").
This phrase evidently became a kind of emblem for lay devotional reading.
In the image of Nicholas Blackburn and his wife Margaret that appears in
an early fifteenth-century window at the church of All Saints, York, this
phrase is legible in the open prayer book that Margaret carries.[80]

By the mid-fourteenth century, a growing body of Middle English didactic works had begun to supplement the devotions of the book of hours,
defining the requirements of the active penitential life for a broader reading population. Middle English works of "basic moral instruction" are
precursors to the lay spiritual rules I consider in this study, for they construct active, literate laypeople as members of an order who might use
texts to facilitate penitential self-discipline, or "self-correction." As Parkes
has shown, by the fourteenth century, vernacular texts were becoming a
medium of teaching and entertainment, and religious didactic texts tended
to be the first priority, with catechetical texts often appearing as the first
contents in a family's composite manuscript.[81]

Parkes names *The Prick of Conscience* as his primary example of one of
the most popular fourteenth-century "guides to godliness."[82] This ency-
clopedic work, which has been called the most popular English medieval
poem based on its survival in over 100 manuscripts,[83] not only teaches the
basics of catechism through narrative[84] but also explicitly views pious laity
as deserving of their own system of religious discipline. In keeping with a
catechetical regime that emphasizes penance and the need for self-scrutiny,
conscience lies at the center of this work, as the agent that cleanses the soul
through penance and continually disciplines the reader.[85] In this sense,
conscience is the "prick" or *stimulus* that governs both the obedient and
the recalcitrant. At doomsday, the conscience accuses the wicked and then
gnaws within them once they are sent to hell. But if the conscience rules
people properly, they will enjoy the joys of heaven, which are described
in detail alongside the pains of hell. Thus the reader's conscience, itself a
goad, is also a sentient force subject to the goading of the text:

> For if a man [this book] rede and understande wele,
> And þe materes þar-in til hert wil take,
> It may his conscience tendre make,
> And til right way of rewel bryng it bilyfe,
> And his hert til drede and mekenes dryfe,
> And til luf and yhernyng of heven blis,
> And to amende alle þat he has don mys.[86]

If all goes well, the experience of reading *The Prick of Conscience* may
tenderize the reader's conscience into such a state of receptivity that he

will feel compelled to follow this "right way of rewel," the way of "drede" and "mekenes." Like a monk, the layperson is deemed worthy of a "rewel," and like the monastic rule, this work makes the mandate to "amende alle þat he has don mys" a precursor to achieving spiritual "bliss." To borrow from Asad's theory of discipline, the work produces a "desire for obedience to the law" that should become intrinsic to the reader's idea of him- or herself.[87] The reader's conscience is ultimately the force in control, but this text (much like the book of hours in a private setting) purports to make that conscience a vehicle for spiritual elevation, however far away "blis" might seem from the sinful lay reader.

Even as it locates the lay reader firmly within the penitential nexus, in need of assistance and frequent recourse to the clerical advisor, *The Prick of Conscience* offers a certain independent literary access to means of "self-correction." Likewise, it has been argued, pastoral guides designed for priests and translated into the vernacular were beginning to spread some of the intellectual aspects of clerical discipline (the wide range of knowledge captured by the Middle English term "clergie"). "Clergie" is a slippery term that might be status-related (meaning "non-lay"), or possess meanings traditionally related to that status (meaning "learning," "body of knowledge").[88] Pantin has argued for significant overlap in content and readership between "manuals of instruction for parish priests, mainly though not exclusively in Latin," and "vernacular religious and moral treatises, some in prose, some in verse, dealing with the vices and virtues, the ten commandments, and so forth, and intended for the laity as well as for the less educated clergy."[89] As the slippage between these two categories of works suggests, both may have begun to spread "clergie" beyond the ranks of the clerical class.[90]

The Lay Folks' Catechism, translated into English in 1357, is a pastoral text that combines the improvement of lay knowledge with the examination of clerical *authority*, preparing the ground for more extensive dissemination of "clergie." Noting that *The Lay Folks' Catechism* includes criticism of incompetent priestly advisors,[91] Fiona Somerset contends, "[i]t is a short step from allowing that criticism of clerical insufficiency concerns the laity, and providing them directly with pastoral materials in the vernacular that acknowledge that fact, to employing this rhetoric of clerical critique to justify writing vernacular tracts capable of conveying far more 'clergie' than the minimum the laity are strictly said to require."[92] Alluding to the *Prick of Conscience*, Wendy Scase implies that the *Lay Folks' Catechism* might even have had the potential to spark lay subversion: "With the spread of devotional literacy, books intruded into private homes and the writer gained direct access to the conscience of the lay reader. Affective strategies especially could prick conscience. Thus 'clergie' may be thought of as the new usurper of priestly power."[93] While Somerset's observation points to the potential of pastoral works to engage with lay demand and, in so doing, invite readers into the specialized knowledge of the clerical class, Scase suggests that such knowledge might even lead to the evasion of priestly authority.

Although *The Lay Folks' Catechism* implies that potential for lay–clerical antagonism was certainly present, I contend that the use of actual clerical books by laity suggests more strongly the possibility for practical cooperation and identification among parishioners and their priests. Since the thirteenth century, laity had been charged with the upkeep of their parish churches. By the fourteenth, as these expenses only increased, lay involvement became more highly organized in the forms of vestry committees and the new office of churchwarden. Laypeople were responsible for the books, vestments, and vessels used in parish worship,[94] and although the sharing of devotional books with regular religious may have been a practice with greater spiritual prestige,[95] lay ownership of traditionally clerical books indicates "the extent to which [laity] had access to what might be thought to have been the parish clergy's intellectual preserve."[96] Ecclesiastical registers and lay wills show that laypeople used books to participate vicariously in liturgical procedures traditionally thought to be the "preserve" of the clergy. In York diocese, Archbishop Neville's register for 1374–88 shows that out of thirteen bequests of service books (many of them in the vernacular), the majority were given or received by laity.[97] Moran's study of York wills from 1370 to 1510 demonstrates lay interest not only in liturgical books but also in the "professional" literature of the clergy: among the titles commonly bequeathed by laity to clergy during this period, a range of priestly guides appear, including the Latin *Oculus Sacerdotis*, *Manuale Sacerdotis*, and *Speculum Christiani*, as well as the English *Lay Folks' Catechism*.[98] We cannot know what use each testator made of his books during his lifetime, but the prevalence of such bequests in York suggests that devout urban laity were exploring the intellectual aspects of clerical discipline, notably sermon construction and penitential theory, and perhaps using them in personal ways for their own techniques of "self-correction." In these cases it seems unlikely that this newfound lay "clergie" functioned as "usurper of priestly power," since the final bequests of these books to the church suggest lay recognition of parish priests as the most fitting owners of such literature.

Working in what James Clark has aptly called "an increasingly crowded spiritual marketplace," the authors of vernacular lay spiritual guidance responded to the initiative that they perceived to be mounting with acute awareness of the complexity of lay religious affinities and practices.[99] The texts considered in Chapter 1, *The Abbey of the Holy Ghost* and *Fervor Amoris*, reach for the literary languages of the cloister to contain lay evasion of clerical authority, while working to relocate lay practice in the context of collective social self-regulation. The guides of this book's second part (*Book to a Mother*, *Life of Soul*, and the *Mixed Life*) will exploit the possibilities that I have considered for cooperation between lay and clerical practice, responding to Wyclif's challenge with new, orthodox translations of clerical discipline for lay readers.

CHAPTER I

Translations of the cloister: regulating spiritual aspiration

In the late fourteenth century the religious orders, with their textually mandated forms of ritual regulation and ordered meditation, maintained privileged claims on earthly contemplation and eternal salvation. They continued to garner the respect of many laypeople who pursued the "spiritual life" through affiliation with them. But relatively few laypeople could seek the rewards of the cloister by combining the practices of emulation and devotional reading considered above. Perhaps they lacked the means to enter into confraternity or were unable to retire; perhaps they did not have the time or patience to sort through the lengthy Latin programs of the books of hours. Sensing a demand for new texts of spiritual advice, a number of clerical authors addressed the demands of lay piety by translating the most iconic structures of monastic life (rule and cloister) into literary form for the guidance of lay readers.

If linguistic translation responds to what Roger Ellis calls "a perceived intellectual/cultural lack, which the translator hopes the translation will make good,"[1] then these spiritual rules respond to a perceived lack of appropriate guidance material for pious laity. In this chapter I consider two guides, *The Abbey of the Holy Ghost* and *Fervor Amoris*, which encourage their lay readers to imagine themselves part of an order of spiritually committed laypeople, while recognizing that the transformation of laypeople's internal, spiritual status could have implications for the transformation of external social and religious roles. The *Abbey* and *Fervor Amoris*, both courting an interest in "para-monastic forms of spirituality," translate monastic models of regulation, stability, and enclosure for their anticipated lay readers, while carefully discouraging the detachment from the world that actual cloistered life (at least in its ideal form) would entail.[2] The authors of these works posit lay spiritual enthusiasm as a potentially disruptive force, elusive to clerical authority because it may be intertwined with readers' material ambitions and involve unchecked desire for contemplative experience, social transformation, or both.³ Thus texts must mediate between desire and discipline, negotiating, in Bourdieu's terms,

the dialectic of the objective chances and the agents' aspirations, out of which arises the *sense of limits*, commonly called the *sense of reality*, i.e. the correspondence between the objective classes and the internalized classes, social structures and mental structures, which is the basis of the most ineradicable adherence to the established order.⁴

By translating female monastic and anchoritic forms of life into new vernacular rules mandating social and spiritual steadfastness, these guides provide new "mental structures" within which readers may voluntarily enclose themselves in "adherence to the established order" of existing social roles and penitential discipline. In their proposed textual systems, the lay subject remains firmly in the world and the confessor retains his central position as a figure of "broad social power and profound spiritual authority."⁵

In the first part of this chapter, I analyze these texts as newly disciplinary translations of prior works (for the *Abbey*, its French precursor, and for *Fervor Amoris*, Richard Rolle's English anchoritic guides), in order to unpack the workings of their cautious clerical ideologies. In the final section, I show that these reinventions of female cloistered discipline as a literary technique of lay self-correction can shed new light on Chaucer's *Shipman's Tale* (c. 1390), the fabliau of a merchant deceived financially and sexually by his wife and his friend, a dissolute monk. When considered together with the *Abbey* and *Fervor Amoris*, the *Tale*, which enacts its own uneasy translation of the cloister for a spiritually inclined merchant, can been understood as Chaucer's own response to the intersection of bourgeois spiritual aspiration with monastic discipline. Chaucer's comic vision of inchoate lay spiritual ambition and dubious monastic example offers insight from a different angle into the stakes involved, for laity and clergy alike, in the negotiation of lay spiritual aspiration through the adaptation of regular discipline.

REGULATION AND STABILITY: DEFINITIONS AND EVOLUTIONS

The terms "reule"/"reulen" and "stable"/"steadfast" had gathered a range of meanings in the cloister and the world by the later fourteenth century. The *Abbey* and *Fervor Amoris* exploit the monastic origins and the contemporary secular resonances of these terms, using the frame of the cloister to enclose the requirements of the active penitential life. In later medieval England, these terms had particularly salient connections to the women's religious disciplines and lay religious organizations. The social locations of cloistered religious life and communal lay practice will both be critical for evaluating the literary workings of these two spiritual guides, for as Helen Barr has argued, "[l]anguage use in literary texts can also be seen as material form of social practice in the way that writers deploy marked vocabulary whose significance would have been apprehended by audiences who belonged to a similar social matrix."[6] While the audiences imagined by these guides may have aspired to the "social matrix" of the monastery, they were more likely to belong to organizations such as the religious guilds that I have discussed in the Introduction.

The monastic ideas of rule and stability (*regula* and *stabilitas*) required vernacular equivalents early on to express these concepts for the professional religious of medieval England. As I discussed above, the *Rule* of Benedict provided one dominant plan for monastic discipline, and in fact the term "reule," in the sense of "regulations governing a religious order," first appears in the early Middle English translation of Benedict's *Rule*.[7] The earliest instance of the verb "reulen" with the sense of "direct," though not "regulate,"[8] appears in the women's anchoritic guide *Ancrene Wisse* (*c.* 1230). The anchorite was the medieval version of the desert saint, a solitary enclosed in a cell adjoining a church. In this role, the anchorite, or female anchoress, "liturgically and psychologically dead to the world," pursued an ascetic life with the support of the surrounding community.[9] It is therefore notable that the author of *Ancrene Wisse*, stressing that the work should not be understood precisely as a rule in the monastic sense,[10] argues that the first and most important rule is the inward rule, which directs the heart: "Þe an riwleð þe heorte & makeð efne & smeðe… þeos riwle is chearite of schir heorte & cleane inwit & treowe bileaue."[11] The "outer rule," governing conduct and practice, exists to serve that inward rule, and must be practiced according to the dictates of the heart: "ʒe schulen alles weis wið alle mihte ant strengðe wel witen þe inre. & þe uttre for hire sake. þe inre is eauer ilich. þe uttre is mislich. for euch schal halden þe uttre efter þ[et] ha meibest."[12] The *Abbey* and *Fervor Amoris*, in translating the terms of regulation from the cloister to the world, transform earlier, more flexible structures of guidance into more strictly disciplinary "rules" for lay use.[13]

The idea of *stabilitas*, likewise complex in its array of literal and moral meanings, proved productive for writers of vernacular spiritual guidance as they exploited the dual senses of Middle English "stable" – morally steadfast and literally fixed – to elicit lay obedience to familiar social and penitential structures.[14] The term *stabilitas* appears in the *Rule* of Benedict as an element of the monk's solemn vow: the novice to be received "promises stability, fidelity to monastic life, and obedience."[15] Although its most fundamental meaning is "perseverance,"[16] the term also denotes physical permanence in the cloister, originally expected of every monk.

While later medieval male monastic life tended to privilege this moral meaning of the term, allowing increased movement out of the cloister, female monastic life required ever-stricter forms of literal *stabilitas*, enforced through enclosure. Later medieval English monks enjoyed many relaxations from "observance *ad literam*" of the *Rule*, including the mandate to physical stability in the *coenobium*.[17] Chaucer's "outridere" Monk of the General Prologue may be extreme in his contempt for the "reule . . . of Seint Beneit – / By cause that it was old and somdel streit," but he is nevertheless a recognizable monastic officer of the later fourteenth century.[18] In contrast to monks, with their expanded opportunities for mobility, nuns were subject to a renewed mandate to enclosure that enforced their roles as contemplative brides of Christ rather than evangelical imitators of Christ.[19] The papal bull *Periculoso* of 1298, ostensibly written in response to scandals caused by nuns traveling outside their abbeys and admitting inappropriate guests, requires all nuns to remain perpetually enclosed and restricts outsiders from entering abbeys.[20]

Despite this renewed requirement of female monastic enclosure, late fourteenth-century nuns' complex engagements in their larger communities often hampered them from observing this mandate to the letter.[21] The one religious figure who was, however, almost certain to remain enclosed was the anchoress. Although *Ancrene Wisse* stresses the importance of its "inner" over its "outer" rule, the guide offers the anchoress no choice about *stabilitas* in the literal sense, mandating "obedience. chastete. & stude steaðeluestnesse. Þ[et] ha ne schal þ[et] stude neauer mare changin bute for nede ane. as strengðe & deaðesdred."[22]

Having originated in the realm of the cloister, the terms of regulation and stability not surprisingly also came to be applied in the sphere of collective lay practice, specifically in religious and craft guild ordinances. In its Middle English certificate, the London fraternity of St. Nicholas uses such language in formulas that inscribe its own system of discipline. The document claims, in typical language, that the brotherhood was founded in 1369, "of gode men of Colmanstrete in noresshyng of loue & of charite amonges hem and in helpe to hem that falleth in pouert of the brothirhed thoruy auenture of godes sonde. And also in other dedes of Charite that be worsschepe to god."[23] The goals of collective support combine with praise of God, even though "goddes sonde" (what God has sent) might bring poverty. This guild return outlines the duties of pious light-keeping, mutual support in life, and solemn liturgical observance after death. The document culminates by invoking the language of regulation to ensure compliance, warning that anyone who "wil nouth be reuled bi the wardeynes ne by his bretheren, he schal ben put out of oure paper and i holde for non brother in to the time that he wil be reulid and make amendes of his rebelhed."[24] Thus in this collective context, members can expect to "be reuled" both by the text of the ordinances and the authority of the wardens, officers chosen, like the monastic abbot, by the "bretheren." In turn, members of the guild are expected to hold the above points, or any that should be added in the future, "*ferme & stable* . . . and ther to god yeue us alle grace wel to holden hem with alle oure power."[25] Here stability is transposed into the world as a discourse of collective lay obedience to regulation. In translating the spaces and discourses of female cloistered discipline for male and female readers into terms legible to a range of lay readers in the world, the *Abbey* and *Fervor Amoris* create newly bounded definitions of the "stable," enclosed religious subject, using literary form to enforce a self-imposed "sense of limits" on lay religious identity and practice.

The Abbey of the Holy Ghost *and the discipline of the cloister*

As this study's only translation from one language to another, and likely its earliest lay spiritual rule,[26] *The Abbey of the Holy Ghost* requires attention to its function in an English social context. The *Abbey* is a short allegorical meditation originally written for aristocratic laywomen in French, later translated and transformed to attract a spiritually inclined English readership. The story of this work's development is one of adaptation for a growing audience in need of rules for the spiritual life: an imagined "lay readership striving to realise and fulfill its spiritual potential."[27] In and through this changing text, the English adaptor expresses optimism and growing concern about lay spiritual life, changing the work to appeal to a wider, more diverse audience, while circumscribing the universe of practices and identifications that it offers to readers, increasingly imposing a "sense of limits" on lay spiritual autonomy.

This work began its life as a meditation in French (*L'Abbaye du Saint Esprit, c.* 1300) and was translated into English, probably in the last quarter of the fourteenth century, as *The Abbey of the Holy Ghost*. This new work offers English readers a guide more explanatory, more concrete, and more detailed than its French precursor, designed to reach a wider audience while at the same time leaving less room for the "regulated improvisations"[28] that the French text had encouraged.[29] A pronounced reliance on female monastic models enables the *Abbey* adaptor to translate the tradition of *stabilitas* and the mandate of enclosure, still in place for nuns and anchoresses, into virtues simultaneously spiritual and social, for both men and women.[30] As Warren has aptly noted in reference to the translation of monastic rules, translation functions simultaneously to "shift boundaries and to shore them up."[31] In the case of the *Abbey*, the new allegorical boundaries of the cloister encourage monastic personifications while shoring up priestly control over the terms of religious discipline.

A linguistic translation from the *Abbaye du Saint Esprit* and a cultural translation from an aristocratic female readership to a socially broader, mixed-gender English readership, the *Abbey* uses monastic discourses to reinforce familiar penitential structures in a "transformed form."[32] The adapted text features a much stronger emphasis on the link between religious discipline and textual and practical self-containment for English lay readers. The *Abbaye* offers a vernacular version of a monastic building meditation,[33] a "tour"[34] that superimposes a monastic map over the space of the aristocratic household.[35] This text, which the English translator follows closely in its outlines and trajectory, describes the foundation, raising, and enclosure of an imaginary abbey in the conscience of the reader, under the supervision of the Holy Spirit. The *Abbaye* describes the rooms and the inmates of the abbey: some are virtues (e.g., Charity is the abbess), and some are practices (e.g., Meditation is the granarer). The meditation ends with a sudden incursion into the abbey by the Devil and his four daughters, Envy, Presumption, Detraction, and False Judgment, who are finally repelled by the monastic inmates with the help of the Holy Spirit.

The French meditation also draws upon the discourses of the semi-religious beguines, the thirteenth-century *mulieres religiosae* who lived communally under the direction of a confessor, combining collective and private prayer, and sometimes-mystical devotion, with active works such as nursing and teaching.[36] But where a beguine text called the *Règle des Fins Amans*, a source for the *Abbaye*, organizes religious practice by mandating a collective stability of the heart, agreeing "that our hearts should be stable and joined together in the love of Jesus Christ,"[37] the English *Abbey* imposes a "religion of the heart" that in attempting to appeal to a wider audience, individualizes and internalizes the idea of religious discipline.[38] More than "joining together" with other subjects, the *Abbey* emphasizes individual stability as a prelude to effective self-regulation.

Although it is common for monastic authors to describe the heart as an inner, textual space to be inscribed with the "writing" of thought,[39] the Middle English *Abbey* inscribes a new "religion of herte" that revises its French original in subtle but significant ways.[40] The *Abbey* carefully targets a wide range of lay readers, those who enthusiastically sought spiritual capital through affiliation with religious houses, with a guide that offers them a chance to engage in independent self-discipline and meditation without causing social disruption or evading clerical mediation.

ESTABLISHING THE *ABBEY*

In contrast to the French text from which it was translated, *The Abbey of the Holy Ghost* targets this expanded audience with a concrete vision of the text's disciplinary function for a new English "order" of laity. The source text, *L'Abbaye*, opens thus: "Many people would like to enter into religion and cannot, either for poverty, or because they are restrained by the bond of marriage, or for some other reason. Therefore I have made this book, so that those who cannot enter into temporal religion may be in spiritual religion."[41] Although poverty could present a barrier to entering monastic life (postulants were expected to bring donations upon joining an order), poverty was likely not a significant concern for the wealthy intended readership of *L'Abbaye*. Marriage, however, might have presented a more significant obstacle to the pious desires of wealthy ladies.

The Middle English translator performs significant changes to render the English *Abbey* more accessible and more authoritative for a broader social range of female and male readers. The *Abbey* opens:

Mi deore breþren and sustren, I seo wel þat monie wolde ben in religion but þei mowe not for pouert or for age or for drede of heore kin or for bond of mariage. And þerfore, I make her a book of religion of herte þat is of þe abbeye of þe Holi Gost, þat alle þo þat mouwe not ben in bodi religion, þei mowe ben in gostly.[42]

This newly intimate opening leaves the realm of theory to address readers directly, recalling *Ancrene Wisse*, whose author acknowledges, "Ant 3e mine leoue sustren habbeþ moni dei icrauet on me after riwle."[43] This revised opening declares priestly insight and authority, significantly expanding the inscribed audience of the work to include male as well as female readers, demanding that potential readers recognize themselves as the subjects being addressed. As Anne Bartlett argues about devotional literature generally, "[t]his creation in the text of exemplary readers... activates personifications that actual readers must imitate or resist, in order to access the devotional material."[44] Showing an interest in appealing to a more diverse audience, the translator acknowledges a greater variety of potential obstacles to religious profession: not only poverty and marriage, but also "age"[45] and "drede of heore kin" (fear of familial opposition).[46] In addition to welcoming a more diverse audience, the revised address formula presents the English *Abbey* as a more comprehensive guide to a more circumscribed and established form of devotion. What was before simply a "book" (livre), is now "a bok of religion of herte," a definitive guide to "gostly" religion that will take place in an internalized religious establishment, the abbey of the Holy Ghost, in which vaguely defined "spiritual religion" will take on a newly institutionalized form.

As the *Abbaye* progresses, the author continues to pay lip service to "poverty," but the foundation of the allegorical abbey presents an appealing hybrid of the spiritually humble and the physically sumptuous. The French abbey is established in a place called "Conscience" by the damsels Poverty and Humility. Once this place has been purged by confession, it appears quite idyllic, situated

> on a good river, that is, of tears and of weeping, because the city or abbey that is located on such a good river is very comfortable and pleasant. The Magdalene was founded on a good river, from which great good came . . . For the good river makes the city clean and joyous, safe and abounding with commerce.[47]

The "good river" on which the abbey is situated is made of the tears of contrition ("lermes de contricion") necessary to the penitential process, but this river of tears is not painfully wrung from the reader. This "Magdalene" is a place of penitential pleasure: a spiritual abbey with an air of luxury, an attractive retreat for an aristocratic woman.[48]

The intended wealthy female readers of the French *Abbaye* might have imagined themselves insulated from "commerce," though they probably were not, given the deluxe manuscripts in which this text often traveled. But the English *Abbey* author shows a heightened concern to make his new "mental structure" compatible with the established social and penitential orders in which his imagined readers live: thus, he acknowledges the material realities faced by an English readership intent on accruing spiritual capital while remaining in the world. After translating the above passage exactly, the *Abbey* author adds a reminder of the gospel's emphasis on spiritual poverty, warning readers not to focus unduly on the fact that the allegorical city just evoked is "riche of alle good marchaundises" (4). For adhering to the "religion of herte" means practicing spiritual poverty in the construction of the abbey's "foundement":

> Pouerte . . . casteþ out of þe herte al þat is of eorþliche þinges and worldliche þouhtes, þat þei þat haue erþliche goodes, with loue, þei faste not heore hertes þeron. And þeose ben cleped pore in spirit. Of wȝuche, God spekeþ in þe godspel and seiþ þat heoren is þe kindom of heuene. Beati pauperes spiritu quoniam ipsorum est regnum celorum. (3)

The new image of poverty "casting" out worldly things and thoughts from the heart, which recalls Christ ejecting the buyers and sellers from the temple at Jerusalem,[49] attempts to ensure that the purifying foundation of the interior abbey will be compatible with a worldly life of commercial activity and modest acquisition.[50]

By making strict enclosure into a mental requirement for both male and female readers, the *Abbey* fits this personal technique of self-discipline into the larger penitential system of self-correction overseen by each reader's confessor.[51] The heart becomes a space to be kept clean of sin and sealed off against tempting elements: in the process, it begins to bear a striking resemblance to the native disciplinary space of the anchorhold rather than the luxurious French aristocratic household or the socially fluid beguinage.

In the translation from a French to an English context, *The Abbey of the Holy Ghost* evokes *Ancrene Wisse*'s penitential associations while leaving behind that work's confidence in individual readers to negotiate textual and practical regulation for themselves. Whereas the French source simply advises, "keep yourself closed up and guard your cloister" ("tien toi close et garde ton cloistre"), the English *Abbey* instructs its "deore bretheren and sustren" more emphatically: "ʒif ʒe wollen holden ow in gostlich religion, holdeth ow withinne and stekeþ or ʒates and so warliche kepeþ þe wardes of ʒor cloistre þat *non otter fondinges non innore* mowe haue eny entre to maken þi sylence to breken or sturen þe to synne" (7–8, emphasis added).[52] With the reference to "otter fondinges non innore," the *Abbey* alludes economically to several parts of *Ancrene Wisse*'s "rule of the heart," which deal with the outer and inner senses, and temptation. Yet in adopting a more deliberate stance than its French source toward the prevention of sin, the *Abbey* propounds a more limiting discipline than *Ancrene Wisse*. For *Ancrene Wisse*'s fourth part undertakes not only to warn but to explain the nature of temptations, so that readers may effectively "understand" and thus protect themselves against them.[53] The *Abbey*, in contrast, suggests that it cannot be understood or put into practice without resort to further explanation and disciplinary interventions by priestly advisors.

STABILIZING CONTEMPLATION

Just as the Middle English translator replaces the French *Abbaye*'s looser form of self-discipline with a model of more explicit enclosure, the treatment of contemplative practices changes considerably in the translation from French to English, suggesting that as much as readers may wish to rise up to contemplative heights, they must take care not to leave the cloister that has been so carefully constructed in their hearts.

Where the French text borrows images of contemplation from the mystical beguine *Règle*, the English translator courts spiritual aspirations by echoing the privileged idioms of the native hermit-mystic Richard Rolle (*d.* 1349), then proceeding to promote an internalized form of contemplation that remains inward and strictly regulated, never threatening social disruption.

Although at the outset of the allegory, *L'Abbaye* mentions contemplation only briefly ("Contemplation will make the dormitory"),[54] the English *Abbey* draws upon a prestigious Middle English source to describe contemplation as a opportunity for spiritual elevation and pleasure: "Contemplacion is a deuout risynge vp of þe herte with brennynde loue, in God to dwellen, and of his delyces forto heeren and of his halewes [and] sumdel tasten of þe swetnesse þat Godes ichosene schul hauen in heuene" (8–9). As H. E. Allen remarks, this passage bears a striking resemblance to Richard Rolle's description of the higher part of contemplative life.[55]

But after luring readers with this initial rapturous evocation of Rolle, the English *Abbey* turns to the internalization and stabilization of contemplative joy, revising the practice of contemplation to promote spiritual stasis as itself potentially pleasurable, as opposed to the rapid upward movement that might exceed the disciplinary control of a reader's clerical advisor. This new emphasis becomes clearer upon comparing the treatments of "Jubilation" in the French *Abbaye* and English *Abbey*. In the *Abbaye*, once the cloister has been constructed and the good deeds of the active life put in place, the reader is encouraged to succumb to flights of contemplative elevation. The sensation of "Jubilation," which follows immediately after prayer, causes the allegorical nuns to lose control over their bodies: "sometimes the tongue cannot restrain itself from singing . . . nor can the feet restrain themselves from dancing and frolicking."[56] A further description of bodily abandon strongly recalls the beguine *Règle*: "some were so ravished there where they were, that their spindles fell down on one side and their distaff[s] on the other, or their book[s] or psalter[s], and they fell down in a faint."[57] The French *Abbaye* reader is thus encouraged to experience such intense contemplative pleasure that, like the beguines, only after exhausting herself with joyful movement does she drop her spinning tools and her prayer books.

In marked contrast to the contemplative abandon of the French text, the *Abbey* depicts God's English lovers experiencing "Jubilacion" in a restrained, passive mode that stresses their location in a single place:

after þat þei han beon in orisoun, þei ben so likyng in God, þat wherso þei ben, heore hertes syng[en] mornynge songes of loue-longynge to heore leof, þat þei ʒeornen wiþ armes of loue semeli to cluppen, and, with gostly moones of his goodnesse swetely to cussen, and, sumtime so deeply þat wordes hem wonteþ for loue-longynge. (18–19)

Drawing on the Middle English tradition of religious love lament, to be found both in *Ancrene Wisse* and in Rolle's *Form of Living*,[58] the *Abbey's* love-longing passage rewrites the French original to internalize the performance of rapture. Where in *L'Abbaye*, "spiritual people" ("genz espiriteus") sang and danced loudly, in the English *Abbey*, song is located only within the stable, still "herte." Instead of giving themselves over to uncontrolled singing and physical movement, these ideal lovers move from singing, to moaning, to silence. Even as they sing, yearn, and moan, they never move from "wherso þei ben," experiencing rapture of the spirit and the "herte" rather than of the body and its constituent parts.

REINFORCING REGULATION

These suggestions of more thoroughgoing conformity to what Bourdieu calls an "established order," one now firmly installed in readers' hearts, are confirmed at two further moments that stress the English *Abbey's* new function as a founding document for a new religious order, based upon internalized "mental structures" that discourage readerly transgression. Near the end of the *Abbey*, the adaptor abandons the last vestige of the loosely organized beguine community evoked in the *Abbaye* in favor of a more clearly delineated "religion" to be followed carefully by a range of pious readers. A passage near the end of the French *Abbaye* describes the internal "clock of contemplation and of the holy beguinage; it is zeal and love of contemplation."[59] In contrast, the English *Abbey* describes an "*orlogge in religion* þat wakeþ þe couent to matyns, and þat is þe ouerlogge of contemplacion, And þat is of þe *holi religion* þat is foundet of þe Holi Gost" (35–36, emphasis added). This removal of the French text's only explicit reference to the beguines not only reflects the probable absence of beguinages in England, but also sums up the major transformation that has occurred in the text's cultural function.[60] Whatever the *Abbey* translator knew of the beguine movement, the beguinage (a place either unknown or undesirable) has become an established and strictly regulated abbey, with a known founder: the Holy Ghost. As Christiania Whitehead argues, the appearance of the Holy Ghost at the end of the allegory suggests that the "text wishes to promulgate the necessity of episcopal or other male oversight."[61] Moreover, the repetition of "religion" and introduction of the term "foundet," with its combined architectural and moral associations, reinforce the concrete presence of the abbey in the reader's heart, driving home the new work's attempt to create an official form of religious life for laity who might desire one.

The *Abbey*'s final passage, original to the translation, emphasizes the conjunction of two elements critical to the work's unique new form of spiritual guidance: the need for obedience to this internalized male authority, and the new function of the revised *Abbey* as a rule to be obeyed. This authority figure, the Holy Ghost, serves as proxy for the author, who begins by interpellating "my deore breþren and sustren": he is the figure of inspiration and teaching who has overseen the building and will remain to ensure that all the text's directives are carried out. After the incursion and repulsion of the devil and his daughters, the translator admonishes all those reading or hearing to be "buxom" (obedient) to the allegorical ladies of the abbey, "And loke vchone bisyliche þat ȝe *don no trespas aȝeyn þe reule* ne þe obedience of þe religion" (41–42, emphasis added). The text has become a "reule" for its inscribed lay readers. Moreover, "trespas," which echoes the Middle English *Pater Noster*, returns readers to this essential prayer as a penitential rule for the laity, assimilating the "reule" of the abbey to the regulation imposed by the reader's confessor, the father in careful control of this new lay religious order.[62]

Fervor Amoris: *regulating the fire of love*

The Abbey of the Holy Ghost trades on the cultural prestige of monastic life to install a "religion of herte" as a literary extension of priestly social and spiritual authority, proposing to discipline lay material ambition and rein in potentially disruptive desires for contemplation. The author of the spiritual guide *Fervor Amoris* shares his contemporary's preoccupation with creating new literary forms of religious regulation and spiritual stability for lay readers. But rather than framing the text as a response to pre-existing lay desire to be "in religion," *Fervor Amoris* posits a more complex relation between desire and discipline, acknowledging that potential readers who urgently wish to develop their love of God may not yet even be receptive to the construction of a "mental structure" like the abbey of the Holy Ghost. *Fervor Amoris* is a longer, more complex text, dated between 1375 and 1425, which has been accurately characterized as a devotional compilation.[63] Bringing together disparate sources with the stated purpose of inducting aspiring readers into a new system of love of God, the work also undertakes to build a regulatory structure. Rather than using the form of the building meditation, as the *Abbey* does, *Fervor Amoris* gradually constructs a rule, which in its series of explanations and exhortations more closely resembles a monastic rule or the ordinances of a religious guild.

Although *Fervor Amoris* appears as a title in only two manuscripts featuring the work,[64] the phrase "Ardeat in diuini feruor amoris" heads or follows the text in seven of sixteen extant manuscripts, thus functioning more as "epigraph" than as title.[65] This phrase seems carefully chosen to appeal to aspiring lay readers,[66] for the author explicitly proposes to channel readers' burning love for God, addressing "men and women, wiche haue ful gret liking to speke of þe loue of God, and al day askin how þei schul loue God, and in what maner þei schul liue to his plesaunce for his endles goodnes."[67] Thus in Gillespie's phrase, the text solicits an audience of "eager but unskilled lovers."[68]

With the phrase *Fervor Amoris*, whether title or epigraph, and this early focus on "loue of God," the work announces early that it too is a translation: not an adaptation from French, but a work indebted to the language of spiritual love made famous by fourteenth-century England's most celebrated spiritual writer, Richard Rolle.[69] The term "fervor amoris" directly echoes Rolle's *Incendium Amoris*, an account of his own contemplative life, in which he uses the term *fervor* to describe the first stage of mystical experience.[70] But the lay guide *Fervor Amoris* is more profoundly indebted to Rolle's vernacular works intended for women religious, most notably his anchoritic guide *The Form of Living*.[71] *Fervor Amoris* cites, modifies, and disciplines its contemplative predecessor in order to fashion a new "reule" for lay devotion in the world, a journey of four degrees that will not culminate in the solitary union with Christ that Rolle's *Form of Living* envisions, but will rather return readers to active penitential life in the world, observed in conformity with priestly guidance and the social structures of lay community.

As Nicholas Watson has shown, the idea of "love of God" could in some cases have radical implications for fourteenth-century Middle English spiritual writing. Richard of St. Victor's highest degree of love (*amor insatiabilis*) and presentation of God as himself a passionate lover offered later English writers such as Langland and Julian of Norwich "a radicalized image for preaching or writing as imitative forms of kenosis [incarnation]" with implications for the "revalorization of passion meditation, the role of the vernacular writer, the 'uneducated' reader, and the vernacular itself."[72] But in developing its own system of lay spiritual guidance around a scheme of four degrees of love,[73] *Fervor Amoris* enters into sustained engagement with Rolle's degrees of love to transform them to more conservative pastoral purposes. Written at the end of the fourteenth or start of the fifteenth century, *Fervor Amoris* is not a reactionary text, not visibly concerned about lay readers appropriating preaching or writing techniques. If the author is aware, for example, of Wyclif's arguments for lay evangelism or critique of confessional dogma, he does not engage with them. Instead, *Fervor Amoris* is concerned with responding carefully to lay attraction to contemplative life and mystical experience.

In *The Form of Living*, the highest degree of love entails a union with Christ in which the soul feels itself "as a brennynge fyre, and as þe nyght-galle, þat loueth songe and melody, and failleth for mykel loue" (17). This description of perfect love evokes the promise and danger of all mystical writing, "heady and potentially uncontrollable, always in a position to lay powerful claims to an authority which lies outside and above ecclesiastical institutions, even to deny the authority which inheres in those institutions."[74] *Fervor Amoris* is concerned to appeal to all potential lay readers and to discourage those who, fueled by a sense of material entitlement, might attempt to rise above priestly authority seeking the feelings that Rolle describes. The work thus offers literary forms that carefully shape lay devotion according to disciplines holding recognized places within "ecclesiastical institutions." Even more intricately than *The Abbey of the Holy Ghost*, *Fervor Amoris* exploits a perceived lay desire for contemplative life, as championed by Rolle, in order to channel this desire into self-regulation and safely disciplinary meditation, activating mystical schemes to produce regulatory results.

"REULING" AND "STABLING" IN ROLLE'S ENGLISH WORKS

The conservatism of *Fervor Amoris*'s adaptation comes into focus when the text's literary and didactic strategies are considered together with Rolle's own treatments of regulation and stability. Rolle's *Form of Living* and *Ego Dormio* trace trajectories of mystical progress that promise to lead his enclosed female readers' progressive absorption into Christ. Rolle treats the idea of a "reule" as an elementary literary form to be transcended and envisions stability as a desiring attitude, a state of mind that changes subtly as readers progress upward in their love of God. The first part of *The Form of Living* sketches for the newly enclosed anchoress an outline of her active duties, combining formulaic litanies of the sins and virtues with more personalized warnings about overdoing penitential abstinence. It is revealing of Rolle's attitude that he uses the term "reule" only twice in the *Form*, first to characterize this part of the text even as he moves beyond it to his true interest: love of God. The second part of the guide begins, "Now [h]as[t] þou herd how þou may dispose þi lyf, and reul hit to Goddes wille. Bot I wot wel þat þou desirest to hyre sum special poynt of þe loue of Ihesu Criste, and of contemplatif lif þe which þou hast taken þe to at mennys syȝt. As I haue grace and connynge, I wil lere þe" (15).[75] The tedious business of "reuling" can only be preliminary to the anchoress's true goal: learning how to advance in "þe loue of Ihesu Crist," the essence of her contemplative vocation.

In Rolle's *Form of Living*, however, the concept of stability can expand to accommodate the reader's anticipated progress in "contemplatif lif." Borrowing his system of degrees of love from the twelfth-century canon Richard of St. Victor,[76] Rolle posits the trio of "insuperabile," "inseparabil," and "synguler" for Margaret.[77] As he summarizes, "loue is insuperabile when no thynge that is contrarie to Goddis loue may ouercum hit, bot hit is stalworth agayns al fandynges, and stable, wheþer þou be in ese or in anguys, in heel or sekenesse" (16). In turn, "[i]nseparabil is þi loue when al þi hert and þi þoght and þi myght is so hooly, so entierly and so perfitly fasted, set and stablet in Ihesu Criste þat þi þoght cometh neuer of hym, neuer departeth fro hym" (16). In the first instance, the anchoress's stability of heart complements her stability of abode, as she remains steadfast against temptations, as *Ancrene Wisse* had directed. In the second degree, her stability is a dynamic, desiring attachment enabling the perfect focus on Christ that is the contemplative's main duty. The term returns to characterize the experience of "perfect love" in *Ego Dormio*: in this state, "al worldes solace þe behoueth forsake, þat þi hert be holdynge to no loue of any creature ne to any bisinesse or erth, þat þou may in silence be euer stabily, and stalworthly in hert and mouth loue God" (32). While physical stability is ensured by the monastic or anchoritic enclosure, mental and spiritual stability take on increasingly complex meanings as the reader shuts out all bodily sensations to ascend toward contemplative perfection.

FERVOR AMORIS: A "REULE" FOR THE ACTIVE LIFE

In adapting Rolle, *Fervor Amoris* revises these discourses to negotiate carefully between readers' inner and outer states, requiring readers to remain stable – both steadfast and immutable – in their social positions and internal dispositions, constructing the text as means not to solitary bliss but to a form of self-regulation in obedience to existing social and religious structures.[78] Although *Fervor Amoris* makes initial gestures toward personalization and pleasure, inviting readers to imagine themselves the privileged recipients of spiritual guidance like the anchoress Margaret Kirkeby, the text's monumental form reveals a more pressing drive toward developing readers' "desire for obedience to the law": that is, to the discipline of a rule. Literally organized to resemble a rule, *Fervor Amoris* is divided into a series of chapters, with a table of contents preceding the main text. The text is prefaced with this advertisement: "This schorte pistel þat folewith ys diuided in sundri ma[t]eres, eche mater bi himself in titlis as þis kalender scheweþ. And þat þou mowe sone finde what mater þe pleseþ, þese titles ben here and in þe pistil marked wiþ diuerse lettres in manere of a table" (3).[79] Although "pistil" evokes a tradition of individual spiritual guidance, the rest of this briskly welcoming introduction emphasizes the text's high degree of structure. The finding aids might facilitate the easy use of the text by busy readers in the world, those lacking the monastic or anchoritic *otium* necessary to read an entire text from start to finish.[80]

Fervor Amoris is patently a rule for readers in the world: for this author's projected readership, the search for "spiritual fulfillment" must be located within the main disciplinary matrices of the active life: penitential relations with the confessor and communal relations with fellow lay Christians. By beginning the guide with tantalizing references to Rolle, *Fervor Amoris* openly solicits spiritual aspiration, widening readers' awareness of spiritual possibilities even as it limits the horizons of possible lay practice to the requirements of the active, penitential life.[81] Although lay readers may not be able to follow the example of "oure holi fadres in old time," some "ful holi men of riȝt late time" (i.e., Richard Rolle) have already begun to channel spiritual ambition into fruitful forms of expression. These "holi men . . . were visitid bi þe grace of God wiþ a passing swetnesse of þe loue of Crist, wiche swetnesse, for ensample, þei schewid afturward bi here writing to oþer men folewing, yif eny wold trauaille to haue þat hie degre of loue" (5–6). Thus seizing the chance to reproduce Rolle's scheme of three degrees, *Fervor Amoris* does so with a difference: subtly rewriting Rolle's degrees to begin to emphasize love of God as a process of penitential "trauaille," inscribing desire for God while insisting upon imperatives to "self-correction" not present in Rolle's text.[82]

In Rolle's *Form of Living*, the first degree of love is described thus:

Thi loue is insuperabile when no thynge that is contrarie to Goddis loue may ouercum hit, bot hit is stalwarth agayns al fandynges, and stable, wheþer þou be in ese or in anguys, in heel or in sekenesse, so þat þe þynke þat þou wil nat for al þe world, to haue hit withouten end, wreth God oo tyme; and þe ware leuer, if au[þ]er shold be, to suffre al þe peyne and woo þat myght cum to any creature, ar þou wold do þe þynge þat myght myspay hym. (16)

In its rendition of the first degree of love, *Fervor Amoris* makes these degrees theoretical for its novice readers and introduces changes highlighting not the passionate quality of this love, but the disciplinary requirements for worldly readers who might consider attempting it:

The ferste loue is so *feruent*, þat noþing whiche i[s] contrarie to Godis wil may ouercome þat loue, *welþe ne wo*, helþe ne sekenesse. Also *he þat haþ þis loue* wol nat wreþe God enytime, for to haue al þe world witouten ende, but raþer suffre al þe peine þat miȝt come to any creature þan onis willfulliche displese his God, *in þoȝt or in dede*. (6, emphasis added)

Fervor Amoris simplifies Rolle's florid language and alters the *Form of Living*'s pronouns from second to third person, suggesting the distance still to be traveled between readers' present active state and their hoped-for union with God.[83] Even with a degree of remove, this love is potentially dangerous, "so feruent" that it requires a carefully penitential orientation. The new phrase "welþe ne wo" reminds readers that to embody this love, they must strive to disentangle financial from spiritual fortunes: even though the likelihood of angering God seems remote, the final warning not to "displese his God, in þoȝt or in dede" raises the need for confession, which necessitates the revelation of both thoughts and deeds.[84]

As I noted above, in his *Form of Living*, which assumes that the contemplative reader will eschew all contact with the outside world, Rolle moves his addressee quickly past vices, virtues, and how to "reul" her life, to focus on "love of God" as a separate topic. But having courted spiritual desire with echoes of Rolle, *Fervor Amoris* reveals "reuling" to be its main concern, inscribing a connection between self-regulation, active service to God, and penitential practice in the world. Whereas in *The Form of Living*, Rolle had worried that too-harsh penance would weaken the anchoress's contemplative love for God,[85] *Fervor Amoris* explains its own third degree ("stedefast") using similar language to express the opposite fear: that excessively fervent love will overcome the duties of active life and the proper performance of penance and work. The essence of proper self-discipline, for the guide's inscribed readers, lies in the balance between the work of the active life and moderate penitential discipline:

Yif þou take for þe loue of God so muche abstinence, wakinge, oþer oþir bodiliche penaunce, þat þou may not for feblenes *continue to trauaile in þe seruice* of God, þan is þi wil to feruent.[86] For be þi loue neuer so gret, God is not plesed whan þou *reulest* þe in suche maner þat þou mowe not *abide in his seruice* þoru þi *mysreule*. Therfore be war and *reule* þe uppon resoun; take no more uppon þe þan þou maist bere, besie not þe to folewe oþer strong men or women of old time in doynge penaunce oþerwise þan þi streynþe wol aske. (20, emphasis added)

Although "bodiliche penaunce" may be a component of the active life, for those who may not leave the demands of the world, "seruice of God" involves outward-looking good works, which will be rewarded at the final reckoning.[87] Rather than fanning the flame as Rolle does, so that the contemplative reader might "wix euer more" in love, *Fervor Amoris* argues that "stedefast" love resides not in extreme shows of piety but in the commitment to spiritual moderation in the active life. While the guild ordinance considered in the Introduction exhorted readers to "be reuled" by wardens and brethren, *Fervor Amoris* places the reader in charge of his own self-regulation, warning that punishment for misrule will be the displeasure of God himself.

SOCIAL AND SPIRITUAL STABILITY

Even as they attempt to move upward through the four degrees of love, the imagined readers of *Fervor Amoris* must likewise submit to the discipline of vocational and economic "degre": social structures which, in tandem with penance, continue to regulate every interaction in the world. The mandate to conserve social degree was a familiar commonplace: in religious guild regulation, the language of "degre" marks social hierarchy as integral to the practice of communal regulation. For the Pouchmakers, a London craft guild with a religious dedication to the Annunciation, "degre" defines hierarchy within the guild as necessary to social and spiritual unity. The guild's ordinances end with the following statement, framed as an expression of collective desire: "we wilen this that alle these poyntes ben wel & trewely holden among al our bretheren with oute any withseyeng eueri brother in his degre with his gode wyl ther whiles god yiueth us grace of stat & of power."[88] Assent and adherence to the rules of the ordinance are thus made inseparable from each brother's maintenance of his rank within the guild.

The language of degree, so central to the didactic plan of *Fervor Amoris*, and its main textual link to Rolle, can thus be deployed to mandate that readers observe a link between social stability and spiritual moderation. Because the first three degrees of love cited were unattainable, *Fervor Amoris* offers "oþer þre degres of loue, þat þe same holi men wrot in here tretis, whiche be nat of so hie degre as þo þat be rehersed bifore" (7). These three "oþer" degrees are also based on Rolle's models, taken from *Ego Dormio*, with revealing changes that introduce a new alignment of religious progress with social stability in the world. Rolle describes the first degree of love as one in which the loving subject follows the commandments, avoids the deadly sins, and *"wil nat for any erthly þynge wreth God, bot trewely standith in his seruice, and lesteth þerin til his lyves end. This degre of loue behoueth euery man haue þat wil be saued"* (27, emphasis added).[89] But *Fervor Amoris* changes the central phrase of Rolle's text in a revealing way, to read, "whan a man wolde nat for any erþeliche þyng wraþ God, *bot treweliche stondeþ in his degre weþer he be religious or seculer*. In þis manere eche man bihoueþ to loue his God þat wol be sauid" (7, emphasis added). In addition to these basic catechetical requirements, remaining steadfast in one's social "degre" becomes a basic requirement for not angering God. The reference to "religious" and "secular" reminds readers in no uncertain terms that spiritual aspirations do not license laypeople to encroach on the vocational territories of priest or monk.

From the first degree ("ordeine") onward, the business of loving God requires an ordered engagement with the world, in which consciousness of one's social position, and satisfaction with it, are requirements for advancing any further toward perfection. The author admonishes readers

Þou knowest wel in þi biginning what þou art, lord or suget, pore or riche; holde þe apaied wiþ þi degre, so þat þou haue þi sustinaunce and desire to be no gretter, but onlich at Godis wil as he wol dispose for þe. Yif þou holde þe not paied wher God haþ sent to þe and to þyne a resonable liflode, but euer disirest to be gretter and gretter in þe world, þan þou louest to superfluite. . . and bi þat foule desire þou fallest into þe vice of couetise, wiche is repreued bi al Godis lawe. (13)

Although he holds out the possibility of increasing individual spiritual capital, the author makes no claim to transform the reader's social "degre," warning that undue worldly ambition will surely ruin any chance to realize spiritual aspiration and may indeed cause readers to "fall" back into the most wretched of sins. Spiritual ambition is not a license to rise in the world: readers may only advance spiritually by maintaining consistency in their "ordeined" state of life.[90]

SPIRITUAL STABILITY AND PRIESTLY AUTHORITY

In *Fervor Amoris*, stability of internal dispositions and external state is the very goal of the guide, which replaces Rolle's "euer clymynge to Ihe-suward" with a careful process of self-correction in the world. Rather than a disposition that the anchoress has no choice but to embody physically, stability may itself be an elusive goal for the untutored reader. Thus even in recruiting Rolle to encourage the reader, *Fervor Amoris* eschews Rolle's characteristic confidence in his reader and places the reading subject at the mercy of guide and spiritual advisor:

> But for as muchil as þer be many þat haue nat a sad grounde, ne but litel feling what maner þei scholde drede and loue God (wiche is ful spedful and nedful for alle men to knowe), þerfore to suche þat be nat knowinge y wol schewe ferst in what maner þei schul drede and loue, þat þei mowe be þe more stable in þe loue of God. Aftur þat y schal schewe, bi þe grace of God, foure degrees of loue wiche eche Criste[n] man, religious and seculer, scholde holde and kepe, and may performe for þe more partie, yif his wil be feruentliche yset to the loue of God. (7–8)

Readers may not even claim the virtue of stability until they have been inculcated into the founding values of dread and love, for dread, the "beginning of wisdom," is a disposition critical to the penitential tradition that expanded upon this resonant biblical phrase.[91] As in *The Abbey of the Holy Ghost*, where "Drede" serves as porter of the abbey and stabilizes the cloister of the heart, in *Fervor Amoris* dread of God provides the first stone for the foundation, the "sad grounde" necessary for progress in the love of God. The phrase "feruentliche yset to the loue of God" strongly recalls Rolle's "set and stablet in Ihesu," but here, although this fervent attachment must be present for progress beyond the penitential minimum, the ominous string of conditionals calls into question any reader's ability to conceive of such a love, let alone to "holde," "kepe," or "performe" these four degrees.

Moreover, although the reader may begin to achieve stability, s/he cannot fully execute the text's demands without priestly intervention to ensure that stability is maintained. The hierarchy of knowledge and practice separating lay readers from priestly teachers, which forms a crucial component of lay readers' "objective" social situations, must be recalled even as they are welcomed into the higher reaches of self-administered devotional practice. To those who might be afflicted by "temptacions þat scholde be letting," the author exhorts

> chaunge not þerfore þi wil, but stond sadli, and schewe þi diseise to þi gostliche fadur, asking of him to yeue þe suche counseil þat mai be most helping to þi soule . . . þe grace of þe Holi Gost wol fulfille boþe him and þe, him for-to teche, þe for-to lerne; and taak of him such counseil þat schal be most streinþe and confort to þe and confusion to þe deuil. (22)

Although the text of *Fervor Amoris* represents a preliminary tool for stabilizing and encouraging the reader, healing of the actual "diseise" must be left to the priest, the reader's spiritual physician. This passage enforces a hierarchical division of spiritual labor: the priest is the teacher, the reader the learner and receiver of the priest's wise "counseil." The scenario envisioned here thus exploits the contemporary overlap in the mentalities of confessional and classroom: as Curry Woods and Copeland observe, "[t]he confessional also operates in the manner of the classroom: the priest-confessor, as teacher, instructs and examines the penitent, to produce in him or her an internalized system of self-regulation."[92] This characterization seems especially apt for *Fervor Amoris*, which offers itself as the rule that will help to install these proper penitential dispositions.[93]

CONFESSIONAL CONCLUSIONS

When Rolle's anchoress attains to "parfit love," she sits, physically stable, indeed immovable, rapt in her focus on Christ and unconscious of the outside world: "Fro þou be þerin, þou hast no nede afterward of no lykynge, or no liggynge, ne of bed, ne of worldes solace, bot euer þe wil list sit, þat þou be euer louynge thy Lord" (*Ego Dormio* 32). But the intended reader of *Fervor Amoris* will likely not be able to sit in such leisure: s/he must remain in this world in order to attempt a newly disciplined response to it. This imagined reader need not "fle bodili fro the world or from þi worldli goodis," but must still "fle al suche vanities, for þay þou be a lord or a laidi, housbond-man or wif, þou maist haue as stable an herte and wil as some religious þat sitteþ in þe cloistre" (40). As suggested by this specific list of worldly states, which echoes the lists offered earlier in the text and contrasts with the vague phrase "some religious," *Fervor Amoris* endeavors to make its own rule a concrete and accessible response to the desires of many laypeople, to offer a clear channel for the undefined hopes that might lead readers to try to transcend their social or spiritual "degres," potentially evading structures of ecclesiastical mediation.

Ultimately, the idea of "stable herte and wil" does refer back to the discipline of the cloister, and *Fervor Amoris*'s culminating penitential meditation offers readers a chance to enclose themselves for a private confrontation with the sinful self through the spectacle of Christ's Passion. This sequence of reading, meditation, and prayer is orchestrated to issue not in spiritual elevation and sight into heaven, as at the end of Rolle's *Form*,[94] but in a private "devotional confession" designed to promote compunction.[95] Locating these texts at the end of *Fervor Amoris* makes visible the long distance that readers must still travel, even after reading this entire "reule," in order to achieve the stability needed for spiritual progress. The meditation begins with an exhortation to privacy: "Whan þou schappest þe to preie or haue eny deuocion, fond to haue a priue place from all maner noise, and time of reste wiþoute eny letting" (41).[96] Once she has tucked herself into a private place, the reader must reflect that "þer is no more sinful þan þou art. Also yif þou haue eny vertu or grace of god liuinge, þenke it comeþ of Godis sonde and noþing of þiself" (41). To the end of making God's mercy visible and promoting readerly compunction, nearly all manuscript copies of the work contain a final "schort meditacion of þe passion," perhaps adapted from Rolle's Passion meditations, which were themselves indebted to the *Meditationes Vitae Christi*.[97] In *Fervor Amoris*, this meditation on Christ's suffering promotes self-disciplinary remembrance of one's own misdeeds through a process of devotional confession. The confessional script includes the following admission:

Now, Lord, wiþ soreful hert y knoweliche to þi godhed þat falsliche y haue spended and wiþoute profit al myn wittis and vertuis whiche þou hast yeue me in helping of my soule, alle þe time of my lif in diuerse vanites, alle þe lymes of my bodi in sinne and superfluites . . . Of þi grete suffraunce y had ful litel knowing, of þi grete riʒtwisnes y had but litel dred. (43)

This confrontation with misguided spiritual spending, which in turn echoes language from one of Rolle's Middle English Passion meditations,[98] adding the emphatic "wiþoute profit," returns lay readers to the discourses of the market in order to stress the need to consolidate and discipline these errant wits, virtues, and limbs.

This final confession offers a window into the capacities and limitations that *Fervor Amoris* has attempted to install with its literary translation of the cloister. Readers are exhorted to say further to God, "And sende me þat grace of þin Holi Gost to liʒtne myn herte, to confort my spirit, to stable me in þe riʒt wey, to performe þin hestis, þat y mowe haue perseueraunce in þat y haue bigonne, and þat y be departid no more now from þe bi my unstabilnes or bi temptacions of myn enemy" (43). By virtue of this specially designed rule, complete with final meditation, the reader is now acquainted with the "riʒt wey" and knows, in theory, how to fend off the "temptacions" that might intervene to derail progress up the ladder of four degrees. But even at the end, the reader has not attained "stabilnes": spiritual "unstabilnes" defines her present reality, and it will take the constant presence of the disciplinary text, along with the aid of confessor and "Holi Gost," to ensure that she will be able to "perform" the techniques that this "reule" has taught.

Lay spiritual aspiration and monastic instability: Chaucerian response

Having redefined to his own satisfaction the terms of regulation and stability for lay use in the world, the anonymous clerical author of *Fervor Amoris* can finally gesture to the contemporary "religious" as a vague and fleeting image, implying that the layperson's stability of "herte and wil" will be superior to those professed by this imaginary figure.[99] Given *Fervor Amoris*'s multiple efforts to define its prospective readers by status categories, the term "religious" is left intriguingly undefined here: it might refer to an anchoress, a monk, or a nun. This ambiguity seems productive for a devotional author wishing to gather in readers of as many classes and genders as possible. In this final section, I show that Chaucer, like the anonymous authors of the *Abbey* and *Fervor Amoris*, is well aware of the contemporary urgency to define appropriate points of identification between spiritually inclined laity and "religious," real or imagined. In view of the two translations of the female cloister that we have just examined, it is possible to appreciate Chaucer's poetic response to lay spiritual aspirations, real or imagined, as he intervenes in the *Shipman's Tale* with his own translation of the male cloister. Here Chaucer suggests that imagining oneself "in religion" or "as stable an herte and wil as some religious þat sitteþ in þe cloistre" (40), might not be the smooth or inevitable process that these guides suggest. The religious that Chaucer's merchant emulates is neither sitting "in a cloistre" nor "stable" of heart and will: the *Tale* registers the mishaps that result from lay identification with a flesh-and-blood monk rather than an idealized system of cloistered discipline.

In the *Shipman's Tale* the poet's concern about what Staley calls "an endemic mercantilism that threatened finally to meld all degrees of social distinction into a disorderly, self-interested, and finally unworkable unit" is expressed humorously in response to the prevalence of lay spiritual aspirations.[100] In the *Tale*, the merchant's religious inclinations are stymied both by the requirements of his own "degre" and by the mercantilism of the monk, who inspires stirrings of lay religiosity but fails as a model of religious discipline. Lay spiritual aspiration and monastic discipline are compromised by the very elements that the *Abbey* and *Fervor Amoris* strive earnestly to redirect and compensate for with the resources of literary form: lay materialism, monastic instability, and priestly incompetence. These failings come as no surprise in a Chaucerian fabliau, but considering the *Tale* in light of these particular spiritual guides provides new perspectives on Chaucer's humor and on the potential consequences of undisciplined lay spiritual desires.

If one considers the *Shipman's Tale* in light of patterns of contemporary religious life rather than in terms of hidden biblical contexts or "exegetical strategies" that result in moralizing readings,[101] then it becomes possible to detect a fresh sense of Chaucer's skeptical engagement with contemporary piety. For Lee Patterson, resistance to this moralizing tendency means reading the *Tale* in recognition that its pervasive terms of commercial exchange are not just a reflection of human fallenness but simultaneously a means to "recover the kind of innocence that protects the merchant,"[102] who ultimately emerges unscathed from wife's and monk's betrayals, inviting a similar generosity from the *Tale's* readers. In his argument that the *Tale* thus obliges us to understand bourgeois life "not as a specific historical form of social life but as life itself," Patterson recalls John C. McGalliard's earlier grounds for resisting moralizing readings of the *Tale*.[103] McGalliard argues

I do not believe that Chaucer intended to present the merchant as wanting in insight into spiritual values, that is, spiritual values relevant to the content of this narrative . . . There is no outline of a different way of life with which we are tacitly invited to compare his way. If the story juxtaposed to the merchant, say, a devout Franciscan friar or a scholastic philosopher, who came and went in some kind of parallel movement in the narrative, and who acquired a spiritual good – or conspicuously avoided a loss – we might need to interpret it as an exemplum showing the folly of seeking material goods.[104]

However, I suggest that the *Shipman's Tale* does present an alternative "way of life" – monastic life – as object of the merchant's spiritual ambition, while refusing, as McGalliard rightly notes, to provide an "outline" of this life, as spiritual guidance claims to do. On the contrary, the *Tale* offers an odd "parallel movement," whereby the merchant in his desire for brotherhood with the monk, in his impulses to introspection, and in his upright conduct as a merchant, demonstrates an inchoate desire for a religious "way of life" that the monk himself refuses. Thus, I argue, much of the *Tale's* humor derives from the fact that although the monk's "way of life" (*disciplina*) is subject to desire by the merchant, the monk is himself unstable, failing to serve as example or guide to the merchant's "spiritual longings,"[105] which in the absence of guidance prove weaker than his mercantile instincts.

The problematic intersections of lay spiritual desire and monastic discipline produce not a "role reversal," but an uneasy hybrid of the monastic and the mercantile, an unsuccessful translation of the cloister that renders the return to bourgeois life inevitable (though not necessarily culpable) and offers a skeptical perspective on the possibility of converting material to spiritual capital. If the tale's "unstable verbal texture"[106] is considered in view of the instability of spiritual ambition and religious discipline, then one can perceive the *Tale* as satiric response to the very religious climate in which lay spiritual guidance was being written.[107]

Many critics have observed that the monk Daun John imitates the merchant in his worldliness and may thus been seen as a religious figure of social ambition. One also notices from the beginning of the *Tale* that the merchant is a lay figure with spiritual aspirations.[108] Although the monk is first described, not very promisingly, as a "fair man and a boold," a hanger-on at the merchant's house whose motives may be questionable ("in his house as famulier was he / As it is possible any freend to be"),[109] the *Tale's* introduction suggests that the monk's presence provides a catalyst for the merchant's desire to imagine *himself* as part of an idealized monastic order. A hint of this desire surfaces in the opening description of their relationship, which suggests that their easy friendship stems from a shared origin, having been "bothe two yborn in o village" (35). The merchant warmly embraces this fact:

> The monk hym claymeth as for cosynage,
> And he agayn; he seith nat once nay,
> But was as glad thereof as fowel of day,
> For to his herte it was a greet plesaunce.
> Thus been they knyt with eterne alliaunce,
> And ech of hem gan oother for t'assure
> Of bretherhede whil that hir lyf may dure.
> (36–42)

Despite the monk's dubious piety, the terms "eterne alliaunce," "bretherhede," and "lyf" have religious overtones.[110] While the monk ingratiates himself at the merchant's household for the sake of secular good cheer and access to the merchant's wife, the merchant can hope for no material gain from the monk. His desire to be the monk's "brother" recalls the many laypeople seeking to emulate and even live among religious in the fourteenth century, attempting to trade material for spiritual capital in the process. Richardson captures the poignancy of this desire though in a moralizing vein: "[i]n this 'bretherhede' there is apparently no buying and selling, only mutual love, and with pathetic eagerness the merchant grasps at this fulfillment of his spiritual need."[111] According to Richardson, the merchant fails in his effort to attain a spiritual goal because "[h]e has blindly and unknowingly accepted a worldly standard of values in place of spiritual truth."[112]

But the *Tale* offers a more complex perspective on the fulfillment of lay "spiritual need." Having established the merchant's desire for "bretherhede" with the monk, the narrative repeatedly hints that the merchant's behavior might conform (partially and even perhaps "unknowingly") to a *spiritual* "standard of values" – that is, the standard of monastic life – even in the absence of a constructive example or guidance from his avowed "brother" Daun John. In the light of these concerns, then, the phrase "hir lyf " takes on a new significance. Its grammatical oddity is striking: it should be translated literally as "their lives," but the singular "lyf " implies that a hybrid is formed here between the monastic and the mercantile ways of life, a hybrid unfortunately founded upon the volatile conjunction of lay desire and monastic vice.

As the *Tale* makes clear, the monk has little interest in exemplifying monastic conduct for the merchant: he is received as an honored guest, and they "ete and drynk and pleye, / This marchant and this monk, a day or tweye" (73–74). Nevertheless, having given this early hint of the merchant's desire for monastic "bretherhede," the *Tale* draws attention to his desire, in his restless introspection and anxiety over his material situation, for the tranquility that might be available, even if only in the imagination, from "a different way of life." Even before voicing discontent with his status, the merchant cloisters himself in his counting house, in a scene suggestive not only of monastic practices but of the stabilizing spiritual practice that a worldly layperson might engage in, were he to recognize his "spiritual need" and seek help for it.

> The thridde day, this marchant up ariseth,
> And on his nedes sadly hym avyseth,
> And up into his countour-hous gooth he
> To rekene with hymself, wel may be,
> Of thilke yeer how that it with hym stood,
> And how that he despended hadde his good,
> And if that he encressed were or noon.
>
> (75–81)
>
> . . .
>
> Ful riche was his tresor and his hord,
> For which ful faste his countour-dore he shette,

> And eek he nolde that no man sholde hym lette
> Of his acountes, for the meene tyme,
> And thus he sit til it was passed pryme.
>
> (84–88)

Remarking that this scene contains "echoes of the monk's world," Woods notes that the merchant "reckons solemnly ('sadly') with himself, as though he were meditating."[113] But Daun John has not offered an example of meditation to his merchant brother, much less given guidance on how to transform mercantile leanings in a spiritual direction: at this very moment he is in the garden below, propositioning the merchant's wife. Despite the scene's heavy eschatological overtones, the merchant's "rekening" remains resolutely material. He misses the opportunity to perform a "devotional confession" of the sort constructed in *Fervor Amoris*, shutting the door to hide material gains from others rather than opening his heart to reveal spiritual losses to himself. The fact that he "sit til it was passed *pryme*" registers a missed opportunity to profit spiritually from this rare moment of mercantile *otium*.[114]

The speech that follows this tableau in the counting house shows the merchant to be grappling with the difficult question of how to reconcile spiritual ambition with material status in the absence of guidance. When the merchant does give voice to his insecurity, speaking to his wife (apparently through the counting-house door, which reinforces the confessional association), he reveals himself to be a prime candidate for "spiritual self-help," in Margaret Aston's phrase.[115] For he voices the sort of tension between outward prosperity and inward instability that spiritual guidance strives so hard to reconcile with its new mental structures. The merchant admits his inability to convert "drede" into a spiritual disposition as *The Abbey of the Holy Ghost* and *Fervor Amoris* so carefully exhort, and it becomes clear that this inability is compounded by a lack of advice.[116] Lamenting the uncertain lot of "us chapmen," he complains

> We may wel make chiere and good visage,
> And dryve forth the world as it may be,
> And kepen oure estaat in pryvetee,
> Til we be deed, or elles that we pleye,
> A pilgrimage, or goon oute of the weye.
> And therefore have I greet necessitee
> Upon this queynte world t'avyse me,
> For everemoore we moote stonde in drede
> Of hap and fortune in oure chapmanhede.
>
> (230–38)

Despite appearances to the contrary, the chapman's constant oscillation between concealing riches and evading detection has taken a heavy spiritual toll. Given the insecurities of his social life, he reveals himself to be in need of a "stable herte and wil," lacking the means to build an internal cloister on the stabilizing foundation of dread. For the merchant's life has no spiritual center or place of reflection except the "countour-hous," a private location in which *self-*"avysement" generates helpless reflections generating further "drede / Of hap and fortune." Without a clerical figure "t'avyse" him, he indulges his fear of chance and market forces instead of developing the ability to "stonde in drede" of God, the disposition that even a minimally competent confessor could tell him constitutes "the beginning of wisdom."

In attempting to "avyse" himself "upon this queynte world," the merchant understands his "necessitee" as material rather than spiritual. Chaucer's wink at the devotional confession genre suggests the practical difficulty that the layman faces in bringing himself to spiritual "rekening" when faced with a favorable balance sheet and a pile of "tresor." But the desire for "bretherhede" earlier hinted at and the lay/monastic hybridity suggested by the phrase "hir lyf" are partially realized in the *Tale*'s final sequence, which offers a comical scene of monastic guidance taken by the layman and flouted by the monk. In his display of "personal probity and moral integrity" during his business trip, the merchant embodies not only mercantile good conduct but a lay version of monastic discipline based on brief hints he has received from the monk.[117] As the merchant leaves on his journey, Daun John invokes one of the fathers of religious discipline to see him off:

> God and Seint Austyn spede yow and gyde!
> I prey yow, cosyn, wisely that ye ryde.
> Governeth yow also of youre diete
> Atemprely, and namely in this hete.
> Bitwix us two nedeth no strange fare;
> Farewel, cosyn; God shilde yow fro care!
>
> (259–64)

Under the "guidance" of "God and Seint Austyn,"[118] the merchant shows uncommon sobriety in his personal conduct: even as he buys and sells "faste and bisily" (302), he "neither pleyeth at the dees ne daunceth, / But as a marchaunt, shortly for to telle, / He let his lyf, and there I let him dwelle" (304–06). Prudence and particularly abstention from gambling were generally exhorted of merchants, but this refusal of secular pastimes may stem partially from the merchant's desire to follow the monk's advice, to imagine himself part of an order of monks, a brother to St. Augustine, St. Benedict, and Daun John as well as to his fellow "chapmen."[119] He is living his "lyf" "as a marchaunt," but this "lyf" also puts into practice his longing for monastic "bretherhede."

The inverse is true of Daun John, whose "lyf" comprises a sinful rather than a virtuous hybrid of the monastic and the mercantile, as he appears to the merchant's wife "with crowne and berd al fressh and newe yshave" (310) and engages "That for this hundred frankes he sholde al nyght / Have hire in his armes bolt upright" (315–16). The *Tale* comes uneasily to rest in this shared hybridity, these partial transformations of "ways of life" that seem not altogether intentional in either case, and short-lived in both, as the merchant ultimately returns to his role as demanding husband while the monk returns to the monastery once his transactions with the wife are complete. The fabliau form demands that the merchant-husband be reduced to a figure whose sexual appetite revives when his debts are cancelled: "His wyf ful redy mette hym atte gate, / As she was wont of oold usage algate, / And al that nyght in myrthe they bisette; / For he was riche and cleerly oute of dette" (373–76).[120]

CONCLUSION

In his own response to a culture of bourgeois spiritual aspiration, Chaucer hints at the layman's budding desire for spiritual transformation and then comically draws his own intended readers' attention away from such matters. The merchant's spiritual ambition is inchoate and fleeting, trumped by his material aspirations, but in his fondness for "bretherhede," his impulse to introspection, and his demonstration of probity in a religious vein, he shows hints of the desire to be "in religion" that was circulating so widely in the late fourteenth century. The beginnings of his spiritual aspirations are at odds with his social situation, as he himself seems to realize – a version of the dissonance that the spiritual guides anticipate – but in the absence of a fully conscious desire for spiritual transformation, or a model of guidance that might reconcile his "mental" structures with his "social" ones, he returns to his old ways. The merchant remains "stedefast in his degre," true to his social rank as "chapman," and that very steadfastness, which requires that he privilege material over spiritual concerns, prevents him from beginning to construct a cloister in his heart or endeavoring to embody the "stable hert and wil" that might dispose him to disciplined spiritual progress in the world.

Scrutinizing the *Shipman's Tale* through the lens of lay piety need not result in the conclusion feared by McGalliard, that it offers "an exemplum showing the folly of seeking material goods." On the contrary, the *Tale* registers an awareness that for this merchant, as for the bourgeois population at large, the seeking of material profit enables the seeking of spiritual profit in the first place. Even if never fully realized, expressed, or disciplined, spiritual aspiration contributes to the *Tale's* narrative energy, and the monastic "way of life" informs the merchant's practice even if he remains unaware of its influence.

Although the merchant does not find himself able to rise above his "drede of hap and fortune," his wife's angry words from outside the counting-house door suggest that the "countour" might function as a private space of religious discipline as well as of financial "rekenynge":

> What, sire, how longe wol ye faste?
> How longe tyme wol ye rekene and caste
> Your sommes, and your bookes, and your thynges?
> The devel have part on all swiche rekenynges!
> Ye have ynough, pardee, of Goddes sonde,
> Com doun to-day, and lat your bagges stonde.
>
> (215–20)

"Goddes sonde," relatively unusual in Chaucer's lexicon,[121] rings familiar from *Fervor Amoris's* meditation on personal sinfulness.[122] But God's gift is misrecognized here as the rhyme converts it back into inert moneybags. The *Shipman's Tale* shows with a light touch, and, for the amusement of upper-class readers, the missed opportunities that might result when bourgeois lay spiritual ambition to be "in religion" is weak, unsupervised by clerical authority, and subject to dubious monastic example. Ultimately, Chaucer's depiction of the mercantile/monastic hybrid suggests a knowing, if harsh, perspective on the possibilities and limits of spiritual advice. The *Tale's* merging of monk and merchant, money and God's gifts, exposes a mercantile mentality that enables and endangers the burgeoning literature of spiritual guidance. Thus spiritual guides can show Chaucerian satire in a new light: in some respect, the *Tale's* "loss of social distinction" (Staley's phrase) humorously parodies lay efforts to achieve spiritual distinction through imitation of those "in religion." By dramatizing the absence of guidance in the very language these texts use to proffer advice and shape lay practice, Chaucer's satire offers unexpected insight into why *The Abbey of the Holy Ghost* and *Fervor Amoris* insist upon their textual regimes of regulation and stability.

CHAPTER 2

Dialogic form and clerical understanding

LAITY AND CLERGY IN CONVERSATION

Catering to an expanding marketplace of spiritually inclined lay readers, *The Abbey of the Holy Ghost* and *Fervor Amoris* offer stabilizing literary forms designed to promote obedience to structures of clerical mediation and awareness of assigned religious and social degrees. In *Piers Plowman*, Passus 12, we find an argument for clerical intellectual and social privilege that would perhaps have found favor with the authors of those guides.[1] Arguing for the need to respect clerks as the chosen conduits for God's wisdom and ultimately for salvation, Ymaginatif, Will's interlocutor, posits "clergie" as a quality to be shared secondhand by clerks with laymen, who should be subject to rather than participants in clerical intellectual discipline:

> Ne countreplede clerkes, I counseille þee for euere.
> For as a man may noȝt see þat mysseþ hise eiȝen,
> Na moore kan no Clerk but if he cauȝte it first þoruȝ bokes.
> Alþouȝ men made bokes [þe maister was god],
> And seint Spirit þe Samplarie, & seide what men sholde write.
> [And riȝt as siȝt serueþ a man to se þe heiȝe strete]
> Riȝt so [lereþ] lettrure lewed men to Reson.
> And as a blynd man in bataille bereþ wepne to fiȝte
> And haþ noon hap wiþ his ax his enemy to hitte,
> Na moore kan a kynde witted man, but clerkes hym teche,
> Come for al his kynde wit to cristendom and be saued;
> Which is þe cofre of cristes tresor, and clerkes kepe þe keyes
> To vnloken it at hir likyng, and to þe lewed peple
> ȝyue mercy for hire mysdedes, if men it wole aske
> Buxomliche and benigneliche and bidden it of grace.[2]

The status of these "lewed" learners as objects in the verse draws attention to their passivity, as the monumental structures of "samplarie" and "cofre" stand carefully guarded and unopened to those lacking clerical privilege.

Rather than a quality available to those who seek it, "clergie" will only be distributed vicariously, for, as Fiona Somerset points out, "if the clergy did in fact diffuse the benefits of their 'clergie' to all, then a learned person would not be better off than a 'lewed' one."[3] But as Ymaginatif's first words, intended to cut off Will's argument, imply, clerical authority is not untroubled here. The very need for a warning shows that these idealized boundaries between "lewed men" and clerks are unstable.

That first line also reveals that this passage is a dialogue of sorts, one that began with a sharp challenge to the clerical privilege that Ymaginatif defends here. Will has already heard Clergie and Scripture lecture on the definitions of Dowel, Dobet, and Dobest (believing in Holy Church; suffering for Christ's teachings; preaching and teaching, to summarize Clergie's account). After suffering through it, Will complains, "'litel am I þe wiser; / Where dowel is or dobet derkeliche ye shewen'" (10.377–78). Defining these modes of life theoretically, as Will's protest makes clear, has failed to reveal their location or make their practices accessible. Will angrily indicts "clergie," arguing that the learned man's salvation is no more assured than the ignorant's:

> Right so lewed [laborers] and of litel knowyng
> Selden falle so foule and so fer in synne
> As clerkes of holy [k]ir[k]e þat kepen cristes tresor,
> The which is mannes soule to saue, as god seiþ in þe gospel:
> *Ite vos in vineam meam.*
>
> (10.478–82)

Even as he attacks the cultural privilege of "clerkes of Holy Kirke," Will appropriates the language of the Bible, alluding to the parable of the vineyard (Matthew 20:1–16), which suggests the equal legitimacy of the "lewed laborers'" work.

In *Piers Plowman*, dialogues between Will and his interlocutors both demonstrate and widen the gap between "lewed" and clerical subjects, embodied or theoretical. But in the second group of lay spiritual guides to be considered in this study – *The Life of Soul, Book to a Mother*, and Hilton's *Mixed Life* – dialogue becomes a medium for positing the extension of intellectual privilege from clerical authors to lay readers. In contrast to the guides considered in Chapter 1, these works critically examine relations among religious status, spiritual discipline, and literary practice, suggesting that the proper imitation of Christ can only be performed with skills borrowed from the realm of clerical learning. By constructing open-ended and expandable works (a dialogue, a "boke" with proliferating meanings, a "form" lacking clear boundaries), these three authors create literary matrices into which Christ appears in multiple forms as well: as interlocutor, text, and model for lay readers.[4] These forms thus begin to suggest a textualized process of *imitatio Christi* involving clerical techniques of reading, writing and theological understanding, a process in which the Bible becomes what Bakhtin calls an "internally persuasive discourse" – that is, a discourse that advertises "its capacity for further creative life in the context of our ideological consciousness . . . and the inexhaustibility of our further dialogic interaction with it."[5]

By arguing for these three guides as dialogic texts, I am proposing a new way of connecting them to each other and to broader questions within late medieval English religious culture. Although *Book to a Mother* and *The Life of Soul* are works whose didactic priorities link them more obviously to early Wycliffite writings,[6] Hilton has often been viewed as a stodgy vernacular theologian intent on reproducing traditional models of religious discipline.[7] But in these three works, I argue, formal commitment to dialogue reveals shared concern to reform the terms of lay engagement with professional religious life and offer new models of orthodox spiritual authority to lay readers.[8] For Hilton in particular, a position within the hierarchical church makes him all the more conscious of the need to appeal to lay readers attracted to the spiritual life while keeping them in productive conversation with clerical figures. Unlike the texts of Chapter 1, which translate the stabilizing forms of the cloister to fashion lay methods of individual and collective self-regulation, these works use dialogic forms – whether actual dialogue, or forms that overtly privilege "the dialogic orientation of discourse"[9] – to model strategies for readers to engage with the world on clerical terms.

In Middle English, as is well known, "clerc" is a vocational term with numerous overlapping meanings: "a member of the clergy"; "a person in minor orders"; "a learned person, scholar, master"; "a man of letters, writer, author."[10] In view of this definitional complexity, *Book to a Mother*, *The Life of Soul*, and Hilton's *Mixed Life* are best investigated together and in conversation with Wyclif, early vernacular Lollardy, and *Piers Plowman*, in their use of literary means to extend what Steven Justice has called "clerical understanding" from priestly authors to lay readers. Justice writes

the sermons, tracts, devotional treatises, handbooks, autobiographical accounts – the whole literature of vernacular Lollardy – are *clerical* works, all of them, in the banal sense that they were written by clerics and in the more interesting sense that they, like more orthodox manuals of devotion and belief for the laity, were meant to shape and inform the lay mind with clerical understanding.[11]

By emphasizing "clerical understanding" as a technique of lay engagement with authors, texts, and the outside world, these works avoid fostering the lay self-isolation that some other Middle English spiritual guides
encourage.[12] Their authors insist that clerical skills equip readers not only
for intellectual and practical self-discipline, but also for lay forms of pastoral
care and preaching, practices that I consider in detail in Chapters 3 and 4.

Book to a Mother, *The Life of Soul*, and Hilton's *Mixed Life* posit flexible, dialogic relations between writers and intended readers, attempting
to develop cooperative strategies of spiritual guidance. These three guides
share common strategies with some of Wyclif's writings and early vernacular Lollard texts in their efforts to diffuse to laity clerical techniques of
reading and interpretation, promising new access to the definition of *clerc*
captured by "scholar, author, man of letters." The pedagogical approaches
of these spiritual guides thus overlap in some respects with Lollard educational ideology, notably the effort to break down strict hierarchies between
teachers and learners and make "the learners' own political and material
situation . . . the object of their own reflection and inquiry."[13] These works
of guidance encourage critical reading and writing, practices culturally
marked as "intellectual," but with their premises of fostering cooperation
between academically enfranchised teachers and lay readers, they expand
the boundaries of orthodoxy without breaching them.

The question of how to define points of contact between lay and clerical
knowledge in an expansively orthodox vein was a critical one for teaching
texts of the period, one that became increasingly urgent as the Wycliffite
movement coalesced. The impulse to construct orthodox forms of *imitatio
clerici* for lay learners was not isolated to spiritual guidance: it appears in a
public form in later medieval sermons from before and after Wyclif's career.
The Middle English prose sermon cycle known as the *Mirror*, translated
c. 1310–20 from Robert of Gretham's Anglo-Norman verse, adapts its source
to emphasize the shared Christian duties of cleric and layperson. In noting
the importance of this theme throughout the sermon cycle, Ralph Hanna
observes

> The Christian responsibilities of cleric and lay person are identical; the former has
> merely provided the information that allows the latter to behave properly, as he
> has done . . . The translator will undo the letter, "þat men wel vnderstonde hem,
> and forto schewe vche man his lyf and hou he schal take ensample of holy men
> hou he schal ȝelde God his soule and reden his book for to amenden hemseluen
> and for to techen oþere."[14]

Thus clerical advisor inducts lay listener/reader, through textual means,
into forms of self-reformation and teaching that reproduce the cleric's

own virtuous practices. Similar dynamics of teaching and learning obtain in the sermon cycle *Jacob's Well*, dated from the late fourteenth or early fifteenth century. Although the *Well* author is concerned to distinguish between acceptable and excessive theological knowledge, perhaps due to anxiety over Lollardy, he strongly encourages readers to seek knowledge and understanding of the faith under clerical supervision. As Moira Fitzgibbons puts it, he shows himself "open to intellectual and pedagogical activity on the part of lay people themselves."[15] On the topic of "knowynge of þe-self" the *Well* advises, "vnderstondyth þanne weel what þis knowyng is! it techyth þe to lyven ryȝtfully a-monge euyll lyuerys, & to teche ryȝtly, & to defende þi feyth wyth resouns fro inpugnyng of heretykes."[16] While these sermons hint at possibilities for practical and intellectual overlap between clerics and laypeople, spiritual guidance puts these hints into practice. Dialogue offers the literary technique for keeping clergy and laity in cooperative conversation.

As seen above, dialogue provides Langland with an important formal resource for the poetic interrogation of lay–clerical relations: Will's conversations with clerical, in some cases scholastic, figures occupy much of the third dream of *Piers Plowman*.[17] But there is a critical difference between the way dialogue conveys the elusiveness of clerical privilege in *Piers Plowman* and the way spiritual guides deploy dialogic form to posit the sharing of clerical understanding. In the central books of *Piers Plowman*, the idea of "clergie" is understood primarily in terms of competition (by lay or ambiguously clerical figures) or condescension (by legitimately clerical figures). But in these didactic texts, dialogue becomes a resource for attempting to clarify connections between the theory of the best life and the actual practice of religious discipline.

By inducting readers into a textualized process of self-reform, *Book to a Mother*, *The Life of Soul*, and the *Mixed Life* define "clerical understanding" as a shared intellectual process for priestly author and lay reader. In order to shape themselves in the image of Christ, readers of these texts must engage dialogically not only with the author and the guide at hand, but also, and through it, with holy writ, that fundamental yet carefully guarded clerical resource.[18] In each of these guides, the dialogue and the Bible – whether alluded to, incorporated in, or added to the guide – comprise part of the same textual process, so that although the Bible possesses and provides superior authority, it does not have the "separate hermeneutic status" insisted upon by Wyclif in his Latin writings and by the translators who produced and annotated the Wycliffite Bible.[19] In their insistence on the identity of Christ with "holy writ," these three guides recall Wyclif's views on Christ as *scriptura*, while in their eclectic vision of textuality they reject Wyclif's impulse to downplay non-scriptural forms of guidance. Promoting engagement with Christ on a textual level, they work to induct readers into clerical skills of reading, emendation and "accord" with his model, keeping this process orthodox by remaining on an abstract level, discouraging lay competition with priestly advisors.

These guides posit clerical understanding as a course of study to which texts contribute and during which they must also be consumed. In this conviction, their attitudes to the biblical text run in parallel with *Piers Plowman*, whose dreamer is carried forward by the ambivalent desire for clerical knowledge and self-transformation, in the process of which he processes the Bible in an "accretive, dialogic way."[20] In the course of this chapter, I will suggest connections between the didactic process of *imitatio clerici*, with its combination of textual work and physical embodiment, and Will's attempts to achieve "kinde knowinge," the experiential knowledge needed to internalize intellectual formulations. But whereas Will's fulfillment as a reader ultimately demands profound change in the hierarchical Church,[21] *Book to a Mother*, *The Life of Soul*, and the *Mixed Life* attempt to find literary means to an even more difficult goal: the reformation of lay spiritual authority within existing religious roles.[22]

DIALOGIC FORM AND SPIRITUAL REFORM

Understanding the dialogic investments of orthodox spiritual guidance is essential to evaluating the cultural work of the texts examined in this chapter and mapping their relations to late fourteenth-century English literature more broadly. I offer the term dialogic in the Bakhtinian sense, to describe a form that resists "unitary language" and monumentality in favor of flexible exchange between teacher and learner. These guides propose to induct lay readers into new varieties of textual work and confident use of the biblical text, attempting to realign what Copeland calls "pedagogical" with "hermeneutical" priorities.

Although Bakhtin would surely classify *The Life of Soul*, *Book to a Mother*, and Hilton's *Mixed Life* as "rhetorical" rather than "artistic" prose works, they are dialogic in form and in the relations they posit between authors and readers, teachers and learners. Unlike the regulated, meditative, or confessional scenarios of *The Abbey of the Holy Ghost* and *Fervor Amoris*, these other works acknowledge that, in Bakhtin's words, "[r]esponsive understanding is a fundamental force, one that participates in the formulation of discourse, and it is moreover an *active* understanding, one that discourse senses as resistance or support enriching the discourse."[23] In the spiritual guides I examine, dialogic form creates a new matrix for literary discrimination and mutual imitation among clerical author, lay reader, and Christ.

The anticlerical or controversial dialogue was a familiar feature of the late medieval English literary landscape; such fourteenth-century dialogues often emphasize the transferability of intellectual authority from clerical to lay figures. For example, in translating Ralph Higden's *Polychronicon* and its preceding *Dialogue* between a Lord and a Clerk, John Trevisa exploits the form to show the Lord teaching and the Clerk learning in a manner that gives the Lord rhetorical advantage.[24] In Trevisa's translation of the pseudo-Ockham *Dialogus Inter Militem et Clericem*, the lay Knight becomes rhetorically dominant, first arguing at length against clergy holding temporal lordship, later switching his arguments to emphasize that the clergy's temporal power should be limited and subject to the power of secular rulers.[25] In conversation, these lay figures not only gain the upper hand but do so by appropriating traditionally clerical modes of discourse.[26] In the frankly dissenting Lollard literary milieu, textual authority might travel even more dramatically from clerical author to lay reader/s. Lollard pedagogy emphasized non-hierarchical relations among teachers and learners, and, as Copeland has argued, "texts used for instruction invite dialogic participation in the activity of teaching."[27] In a case in point, one Middle English Lollard sermon writer ends his work by humbly asking readers to "ouerse" it in order that he might later "wiþ beter will come and amende my defautis."[28]

Such conjunctions of dialogism, clerical humility, and lay power to "amend" didactic texts may also be found along the spectrum of orthodox devotional guidance. Without overtly radicalizing the acquisition of clerical textual skills, *The Life of Soul*, *Book to a Mother*, and Hilton's *Mixed Life* posit dialogue as a collaborative mode in which authors and readers may undertake a shared search for knowledge and perhaps realize shared forms of intellectual authority.[29] As in the dialogues of Boethius and Augustine,[30] these texts imagine instructional conversation as a way of answering troubled, questioning spirits, a form that may convert "instruction into the experience of the growth of understanding."[31] In addition to providing formats for confession or catechism, monastic dialogues had since the twelfth century demonstrated the dynamic nature of instruction and highlighted ways for interlocutors to teach and learn simultaneously without antagonism.[32] In the three spiritual guides in question, dialogic form invites a reformist overlap between intellectual and spiritual purposes in the world rather than the cloister, proposing *imitatio clerici* as a means to *imitatio Christi*, creating textual conditions that may have encouraged new forms of spiritual authority for lay readers.

The Life of Soul

In *The Life of Soul*, which literally takes shape as a dialogue between two speakers of different statuses, form signals the possibility for a horizontal sharing of knowledge, rhetorical authority, and practice. The devotional manual takes the definition of the immortal "lyfe of soule" as its task and proceeds to relate this definition to the needs of its learner figure.[33] Rather than offering a set of precepts illustrated by examples, the treatise unfolds according to the rhythms of conversation, continually relating belief, works, and the life of Christ, depicting him as the soul's "liflode" and interweaving catechetical information with illustrative narratives from Christ's life and other biblical stories. The latter half of the guide particularly emphasizes the virtues of meekness, patience, poverty of spirit, truth, and chastity, and is replete with original scriptural paraphrases, many seamlessly incorporated into the main text. As I will show, this treatment of the Bible as an integral part of the treatise links the work's didactic practice to *Book to a Mother* and Hilton's *Mixed Life* as well as to controversial biblical versions of roughly the same period.[34]

The Life of Soul's learner figure quickly becomes an active participant in conversation with the teacher, who appears as a sympathetic figure of authority. In the three extant texts, the names that these figures give each other suggest that mutual affection or institutional closeness might mitigate imbalances in material or religious status. The two interlocutors are styled as "Frend" and "Sire" (Oxford, Bodleian Library, MS Laud Misc. 210), "Fader" and "Suster" (San Marino, Huntington Library, MS 502), and "Fader" and "Sone" (London, British Library, MS Arundel 286).[35] In the context of that intimacy, whether between the imagined figures of wealthy male penitent and clerical advisor, or woman and spiritual father, the conversation begins abruptly, without an authoritative framing gesture. Quite differently from either *The Abbey* or *Fervor Amoris*, which announce clerical authors' desires to respond to perceived lay demand, *The Life of Soul* opens with an assertive request from the learner, whose precise relation to clerical authority remains undefined:

Frend in Crist, as Seynt Poule seiþ, we ne hauen here no cyte þat is dwelling, but we sechen on þat is to com hereafter. And þerfore me þinkeþ þat we schulden ben longyng þiderward alle þe tyme of oure lyf wiþ al oure power . . . But more harme is, I knowe noȝt ariȝt þe weye toward þis place. And þerfore I preye þe þat þou telle me þe weye toward þis place.[36]

Rather than priestly figure interpellating lay reader, here the learner, speaking first, interpellates the teacher as "Frend"/"Broþer"/"Fader," as the request for guidance is written into the guide itself. Even in claiming ignorance of "þe weye toward þis place," the learner's oblique reference to Hebrews 13:14 shows that he or she possesses enough biblical knowledge to desire more: this lay spiritual "seeking," "thinking," and "longing" will structure the work to come.[37]

The learner's use of "we" as he refers obliquely to the Bible and sets out a course for learner and teacher not only affirms that both are Christians hoping for salvation, but also claims a share in clerical ways of achieving this goal. As the dialogue unfolds, *The Life of Soul* suggests that the layperson's bold question deserves a serious, even deferential response that likewise announces clerical pedagogical priorities. The "Frend" responds, "Dere frend, oure Lord and oure Mayster, Ihesu Crist, seyde to his disciples þat he hymsiluen is þe weye toward heuene, and he is truþe þat ledeþ vs sikerly in oure weye, and he is lyf þat makeþ vs lyue in soule whyles we ben in þis world" (1.9–13). With his own biblical reference, the teacher combines Christian universality with spiritual privilege, suggesting that the "dere frend" who spoke first (who in this text, taken from MS Laud Misc. 210, subsequently begins to be called "sire") may also be included in the fraternity of Christ's "disciples" even as he, like all Christians, must strive to adhere to the life of Christ as "weye toward heuene."[38] Thus *The Life of Soul* shapes dialogue to suggest that layperson and clerical advisor might position themselves to take similar "weyes" to the "place" of salvation. Rather than offering to construct a stable structure *within* the soul like *The Abbey of the Holy Ghost*, this text treats the soul itself as a mobile vehicle toward lay perfection "in þe world."

Book to a Mother

Although the speakers of *The Life of Soul* are indeterminate, the work's dialogic form grows out of and in turn reinforces affective relations between them. These relations become a family affair in *Book to a Mother*, a long spiritual guide written by a priestly son for his widowed mother but explicitly also aimed at a wider audience of lay Christians. Though the work's dating is unclear, the editor, Adrian McCarthy, locates *Book to a Mother* in the 1370s or early 1380s, noting that while it offers access to vernacular scripture and harshly criticizes the religious orders, there is no mention of Wyclif or anxiety that these views might be controversial, as they may well have been after the 1382 Blackfriars Council, which in addition to condemning Wyclif's views also contained an order against unauthorized explication of scriptures in Latin or the vernacular.[39] As Elizabeth Schirmer notes, if we can accept this early dating, the *Book* "epitomizes in many ways the potentials of vernacular theology before the crisis over Lollardy."[40] The *Book* survives today in only four copies, sometimes in the company of theologically controversial works: this dearth of copies may be due to regional isolation or to the work's potentially controversial contents.[41]

The possibility that *Book to a Mother* saw only limited circulation should not keep us from taking this idiosyncratic work seriously as an innovative piece of spiritual guidance written at a critical juncture in English religious history. The anonymous author of *Book to a Mother* employs an epistolary, conversational form to combine priestly authority with familial intimacy in a long guide that blends catechism, homely advice, polemic, and biblical paraphrase into a "boke" with proliferating meanings and unclear textual boundaries, a work whose open-ended form both asks and teaches its reader/s to practice clerical skills of interpretation. *Book to a Mother* resists neat distinctions between lay and clerical *personae*, devotional guide and Bible, but the work refuses to dissolve these categories as Wyclif does in his arguments for fathers as preachers and the Bible as sole "rule" for Christian life. The work addresses a reader who has expressed the desire to be "in religion," but *Book to a Mother* does not privilege the contemplative life: anticipating some aspects of Lollard ideology, the author insists upon an active form of *imitatio Christi* in the world.[42] Although *Book to a Mother* reserves a place for contemplation of Christ's Passion, the work's attention to Christ as "teacher and doer of good," rather than primarily as suffering body, incorporates particular aspects of clerical learning and teaching that the author wishes to extend to the lay reader, while remaining well within the bounds of orthodoxy.[43]

It is perhaps not surprising, given its similarities of approach and form to those of *The Life of Soul*, that *Book to a Mother* (which travels with the former in MS Laud Misc. 210), also constructs author and addressee as privileged disciples of Christ in their shared dedication to a spiritual life.[44] That the author of the *Book* should pointedly set himself and his mother apart from others who fail in their religious roles is also typical of this sometimes-polemical work.[45] Lamenting contemporary lapses in piety, the author alludes to the positive spiritual role he and his addressee share and lambasts fathers who fail to teach their children properly "to drede and worschupe God in holdinge his hestis, and to despise þe world and forsaken hemself and do penaunce, as Crist techiþ and seiþ we mowe not ellis be his disciples."⁴⁶ In a move that becomes familiar as the text unfolds, the author uses a moment of critique to allude to the priorities that link himself and the mother/addressee to Christ.

Book to a Mother is not a dialogue *per se*, but the text's conversational form invites inscribed readers into dialogic participation in the reformation of self-discipline and self-understanding.⁴⁷ Establishing an intimate rhetorical relationship between himself and motherly reader, the author extends this familiarity to a wider set of lay readers, advertising the book as a guide to achieving a uniquely profound form of access to Christ. Initially sounding more like the narrator of *The Abbey of the Holy Ghost* than the first speaker of *The Life of Soul*, the *Book* author focuses first on his own aims: "[t]o knowe þe bettere my purpos in þis boke, wite ȝe wel þat I desire eueryche man and womman and child to be my moder, for Crist seyþ: he þat doþ his Fader wille is his broþer, suster and moder" (1.1–4). By positing an analogy between his own "desire" for the transformation of all readers into his "modur" and Christ's promise to believers of kinship with himself (cf. Matthew 12:50), the author invokes the triple valence of his role: he is fleshly son and spiritual father, mediating Christ's desires to the reader. The imagined role of mother, extended to readers beyond the author's actual mother, becomes a conduit to the roles of brother and sister, as familial imagery activates as many identifications as possible.

Rather than promising that this "boke" has already been "lerned" or possesses a known, set form, the author shapes his inscribed reader as a particularly privileged kind of learner, inviting her into a shared interpretive search for the meaning of this "boke." The author deftly combines literary *personae* and form to initiate a shared narrative of learning that should culminate in their mutual assimilation to Christ. Anticipating the long spiritual journey to come, he warns

my leue dere moder, holde we vs komelynges and pilgrymes in oure prysoun, straynyng oure loue withinne þe hestes of God. And for we ben heuy þorow erthly loue, nayle we vs with foure nayles vp þis cros: loue we Crist aboue alle þyng, for oure hed of þe cros; oure frendes as vs self, for þe right half . . . And þus bigynne we to lerne oure a.b.c., eiþer of [vs] seyinge, "Cros Crist me spede," and hauyng lamentaciouns for oure synnes, and seynge with þe prophete Ieremye: "A, a, a; Lord, I cannot speke . . . for I am a childe." (23.15–24.3)

As "komelynges" (newcomers to religion) and "pilgrymes," author and reader are portrayed as beginning their journey with a shared conversion.⁴⁸ Using the abc and the charm "Cros Crist me spede" to posit a shared literary childhood of author and reader, casting it as a state of spiritual and intellectual promise, *Book to a Mother* mobilizes familiar devotional images to express reforming impulses.[49]

In keeping with more conservative modes of meditative devotion, "An ABC Poem on the Passion of Christ," perhaps a source for the *Book*, combines the ABC and the image of Christ's body to set the child apart from the teacher:

> In place as man may se,
> Quan a chyld to scole xal set be,
> A bok hym is browt,
> Naylyd on a brede of tre,
> Þat men callyt an abece,
> . . .
>
> Wrout is on þe boke with-oute,
> V. paraffys grete & stoute
> Bolyd in rose red;
> Þat is set with-outyn doute,
> In tokenynge of cristis ded.[50]

Offering the familiar image of Christ's crucified body as text or charter to the youngest of learners, the poem makes the child passive in the face of Christ's immeasurable sacrifice.[51] Having been "to scole . . . set," the child does not precisely read this book: it stands before him, its "V paraffys grete & stoute" (Christ's wounds) requiring no interpretation.

In stark contrast to this use of the "ABC," the schoolroom and charm are used to radicalize childhood learning in the Lollard poem *Pierce the Plowman's Creed*. Here, rather than standing in silent reverence, a lay learner invokes the ABC to express hostility toward a clerical teacher. This work begins with the learner bemoaning the incompetence of his teacher:

> Cros, and Curteis Crist this begynnynge spede
> For the faderes frendchipe that fourmede Heuene,
> And thorough the speciall spirit that sprong of hem tweyne,
> And alle in on godhed endles dwelleth.
> A. and all myn A.b.c. after haue y lerned,
> And [patred] in my pater-noster iche poynt after other,
> And after all, myn Aue-marie almost to the ende;
> But all my kare is to comen for y can nohght my Crede.[52]

Copeland argues that these lines advertise the speaker's failure to find any friar to teach him "the principles of true belief," and that in the course of the work, "the lowly primer itself becomes a mechanism for the highest aspirations of reformism."[53] The lay learner goes on to learn his creed from the humble plowman, as teacher and student plunge together into the unglossed scripture.[54]

Positioning itself ideologically somewhere between the hierarchical pronouncement of "An ABC Poem on the Passion of Christ" and the anticlerical complaint of *Pierce the Plowman's Creed*, *Book to a Mother* uses the ABC, creed, and schoolroom charm and its particular sequence of images to construct the process of clerical understanding as ongoing and difficult but still open to creative use of traditional imagery and biblical text alike.[55] The passage from *Book to a Mother* is dialogic in its inscription of both voices into the text, with "eiþer of [vs] seyinge: 'Cros Crist me spede,'" effectively blurring distinctions between son and mother (23.24–25). The form of this sequence offers mother and son a chance to witness the crucifixion, merge with the suffering Christ, and share Jeremiah's paradoxical persona of the priestly child. This tour de force of literary pastiche combines allusions to I Peter 2:11, Galatians 2:19, and Jeremiah 1:6 with schoolroom rhythms and familiar charms, to narrow the gap between clerical author and unlearned reader and suggest a shared physical and literary conversion from "erþly" to spiritual love, in a series of bodily humiliations that give a disjunctive literary form to spiritual desire. The contingent experience of a pilgrimage offers an ideal image for how to "best bigynne to [lerne] oure forseide boke" (24.10–11). The "boke" to be sought continually resists a unitary definition: it can only be defined by its need to be opened and understood through the process of penitential renunciation, literary interpretation, and somatic incorporation that author and reader will undertake together.

Walter Hilton's Mixed Life

Like *Book to a Mother*, Walter Hilton's *Mixed Life* claims to address a specific person: not a humble widow, but a powerful lord. Unlike the secular clerical author of *Book to a Mother*, Hilton was himself a member of a religious order, an Augustinian canon, both priest and adherent to a rule.[56] He was a seasoned writer of spiritual guidance, including most famously *The Scale of Perfection*, intended for an anchoress. Given these differences in context, it is the more noteworthy that Hilton should share certain didactic priorities and literary commitments with the *Book* author.[57] Writing as an advisor offering a series of suggestions to a powerful man, rather than as a father confessor and parish priest writing a comprehensive guide for his pious mother, Hilton also transmits clerical understanding through dialogue. Although his epistolary form does not permit the imagined verbal interchange on display in *The Life of Soul*,

Hilton proffers his text as part of a cordial relationship of guidance in which the addressee's apparent desire for spiritual self-improvement complements his own impulse to teach. In the opening moments of the guide, Hilton prepares the ground for his addressee's *imitatio clerici*, encouraging the reader to seek new forms of clerical understanding, even as he keeps his own priestly authority intact.

Hilton's careful rhetoric of guidance is characterized by suggestions, rather than binding rules, as he intervenes with the text into a devotional life that he has apparently been supervising for some time. As he describes the reader's "turning" or conversion to a more dedicated religious life in the hope of attaining the spiritual privilege and contemplative experience available to professed religious, Hilton posits fluid and reciprocal relations between learner and teacher. He opens the text with thanksgiving and congratulations:

Grace and goodnesse of oure lord Ihesu Crist, þat he haþ schewid to þe in wiþdrawynge of þyn herte fro loue and likynge of wordeli vanite and vse of fleschli synnes, and in turnynge of þi wille entierli to his seruice and his plesaunce, bringeþ in to [my] herte moche matier to loue him [in] his merci. And also it stireþ me greteli to strengþe thee in þ[i] good purpos and in þi worchyng þat þou hast bigunne, for to brynge it to a good eende ȝif þat I coude, and principalli for God, and siþ for tendre affeccioun of loue whiche þou haste to me, if I be a wrecche and vnworþi. (6.63–7.72)[58]

Although the impetus for the reader's "wiþdrawynge" from the world and "turnynge" toward God must be located with Christ's grace, Hilton's description of this process borrows phrases ("loue and likynge of wordeli vanite and vse of fleschli synnes") familiar from the confessional mode in which he and the addressee may be accustomed to conversing. The reader may be ready to move beyond basic penitential requirements, but he needs guidance for this progress to be successful. Just as Hilton may have played a role in encouraging this "turnynge," he casts himself as a humble but necessary helper in the reader's search for a more spiritual life. Emphasizing the relations of "tendre affeccioun" that draw them together, Hilton's rhetoric of humility offsets his claim for the necessity of his guide and works, in Copeland's terms, to "elide the sense of magisterial academic hierarchy,"[59] writing mutuality into the text. The carefully calibrated language of turning, stirring, strengthening, and bringing anticipates a literary process in which reader and author will continually cooperate.

Hilton claims to create his text not simply out of social deference but also out of belief in the possibility that the reader's understanding will grow through engagement with this text. Having begun to show that the reader's "medled liyf" must balance the power to regulate others with personal meekness, Hilton describes growth in the spiritual life as a process of self-discipline that the reader should control for himself:

Now ȝif þou aske hou þou schalt kepe þis desire and norisch it, *a litil* schal I telle þee, nouȝt þat þou schalt vse þe same foorme alwei þat I seie, but þat þou schulde haue þerbi, ȝif nede be, *sum warnynge and wissynge for to rule þee* in þin occupacioun. For *I mai not, ne Y can not, telle þee fulli what is beste* [euere] to þee for to vse, but I schal seie *sumwhat* to þe as me þenkeþ. (50.587–93, emphasis added)

As he draws attention to the partial, contingent quality of his advice, Hilton resists codifying the text into a single "foorme" or list of binding prescriptions but offers suggestions to be used according to the reader's "nede." Thus he offers not a rule but "warnynge and wissinge" whereby the reader may learn to "rule" himself. This phrase, in which the term "wissynge" appears most consistently in the manuscripts,[60] implies that relations of authority move on a horizontal rather than a vertical axis, that the clerical author serves as spiritual consultant rather than as "spiritual director."[61]

Indeed, the *Mixed Life* unfolds not according to a regulatory logic but through a dialogic sequence of exhortation, explanation, and interpretation, in which Hilton advertises the virtues of the "medeling" of action and contemplation by inviting the reader to organize his own activities as he sees fit. Hilton endeavors to elicit a "responsive understanding," in Bakhtin's terms, from the reader, to make him understand and therefore desire the mixed life:

Þis ensample I seie to þee, not for þou doost not þus as I seie, for I hoope þat þou dost þus and betere, *but I wolde þat þou schuldest doo þus gladli*, and not þenke looþ for to leve sumtyme goostli occupacion and entirmete þe wiþ wordli bisynesse . . . but þat þou schuldest *doo boþe werkes in diuers tymes, and wiþ as good wille þat oon as þat oþir*, ȝif þou myȝt. As, ȝif þou hadde praied and been ocupied goostli, þou schalt aftir certayn tyme breke of þat, and þanne schalt þou bisili and gladli occupie þe in sum bodili occupacion to þyn euen-Cristen. (28.311–29.322, emphasis added)

Since the addressee's enterprise of self-discipline and holy living is a voluntary one, Hilton presents himself not as a figure of penitential surveillance, but as a fellow traveler offering his own forms of desire and equanimity as exemplary. He builds a dialogic rhythm into the text, constructing the reader's practice as a dynamic play of alternatives, in which his own desire ("I wolde") is answered by the reader's action ("þou schuldest doo gladli"), a back and forth between "goostli occupacion" and "wordli bisynesse." The reader thus receives a textual plan for engaging in dialogue with himself, a guide that will perhaps enable him to develop flexibility to "doo boþe werkes in diuers tymes" with equally good humor. In the *Mixed Life* as in *The Life of Soul* and *Book to a Mother*, spiritual progress depends upon conversation, in which dialogic relations, growing from mutual affection, may begin to foster the growth of clerical understanding.

CHRIST THE BOOK AND LAY SELF-EMENDATION

The ultimate purpose of any Christian spiritual reading is to find and imitate Christ; therefore, in a profound sense, many medieval authors argued, Christ is identical with his words as recorded in the Bible.[62] But where Wyclif posits Christ's identity with scripture as a radically exclusive entity, the guides of this chapter preserve a flexible, eclectic approach to textuality, bringing techniques of reading, emendation, and writing into alignment with embodied efforts to reform the self and imitate Christ. Holy writ is posited as an integral part of this conversation rather than a separate text, as clerical techniques of "emendation," "accord," and "writing" are diffused to lay readers. The contrast between Wyclif on Christ as scripture and *Book to a Mother* on Christ as "holi writ" illuminates how reformist spiritual guidance subscribes to the textuality of Christ while keeping the Bible subject to negotiation with other complementary textual forms. The medieval commonplace that Christ was identical with his words and could by extension be figured as a book is implicit in John 10:35: "non potest solvi scriptura, quem pater sanctificavit et misit in mundum" ("the scripture cannot be broken, which the father sanctified and sent into this world"). In his thirteenth-century *Lignum Vitae*, under the title "Jesus, liber signatus," St. Bonaventure affirms, "And this wisdom is written in Jesus Christ, as in a book of life in which God the Father hid all the treasures of wisdom and knowledge."[63]

Although Wyclif grappled throughout his youth with the considerable textual complexity of the medieval Bible, by the time he wrote *De Veritate Sacrae Scripturae* (*c.* 1378) he invoked the Christ-book metaphor in support of his belief in God's unchanging *intentio* as the *auctor* of the biblical text, and the text itself as conveying a single essential meaning identified with the literal sense.[64] Wyclif's discussion of Christ as book cites John 10:35, presenting Christ/scripture in a perfect, indestructible form. He understands the words of scripture to signify "the sense of God," claiming

This book cannot be destroyed, precisely because the divinity and the humanity are insolubly united in the same person in a seven-fold manner. Every Christian should study this book, since it is all truth. Whereupon, in order that we should learn by this saying to understand that book, rather than the one which is product of human hands, the Holy Spirit ordained in the correct manuscripts the relative pronoun "whom" [quem] and not "which" [quam] . . . And it is evident from the faith of scripture that scripture must be supremely authentic, thereby surpassing sensible signs.[65]

Here Christ is assimilated with scripture in a monolithic textual form, for as Ghosh notes, "[i]f indeed scripture were to be identified with its material embodiments, it would be encumbered with all kinds of vulnerabilities and would consequently be of no authority."[66] Later in *De Veritate*, Wyclif alludes obliquely to the image of Christ, taken from Colossians, as the "book of life" in which "God the Father hid all his treasures of wisdom and knowledge." Elaborating on the need for laymen and priests to know scripture and for priests to understand preaching as their primary duty, he argues that all other liturgical books are superfluous for the "office of preaching"[67] and forcefully returns to the analogy between Christ and the Bible:

Christ is the strength of God and the wisdom of God, which no Christian can effectively know, except through knowledge of the scriptures, for every Christian is required to know the scriptures. For to be ignorant of the scriptures is to be ignorant of Christ, because Christ is the scripture, which we must know, and the faith, which we must believe.[68]

Positing "knowledge" of scripture as the only way to find Christ, hence a capability that no Christian can do without, Wyclif's negative formulation downplays the physical forms of the book or of Christ. Although he testifies elsewhere to having undergone this effortful process himself, Wyclif does not offer a textual strategy for achieving knowledge, nor a sense of how one might then move from *scientia* to *sapientia*, implying with the syntax of his sentence that this journey should be providential and effortless. Having stripped away traditional clerical teaching texts including the sacramentary, missal, psalter, and homilies, Wyclif offers the theoretical Bible as the only way for clerical teachers to achieve knowledge of a theoretical Christ.[69]

Book to a Mother shares Wyclif's preoccupation with the ethical, intellectual, and practical imperatives that priests and all Christians share. This guide was written contemporary with Wyclif's career and likely with some exposure to his theories, though none can be definitively proven.[70] In treating Christ as synonymous with his own guide and with the book of "holi writ," the *Book* offers access to Christ in a textual mode. But in refusing to elide Christ's embodied existence or the materiality of the book, the author offers the addressee suggestions for assimilating herself to Christ in a clerical mode without requiring her to abandon other models of textual guidance.

As seen above, Ymaginatif's remarks in *Piers Plowman* make the unlocking of the "cofre of cristes tresor" subject to the whims of clerical "likyng" while withholding specific insight into how to gain access to the "lettrure" that might enable laypeople to develop "Reson" for themselves. In contrast, *Book to a Mother*'s shifting form encourages the reader to use her literary skills not only to venerate but also to imitate Christ by assimilating her textual skills to those of the clerical author. As Watson notes, the work "announces itself as a composite text that both uses and deconstructs several genres of didactic writing by showing how they find their summation in Christ."[71] The author begins early to suggest how this book, Christ's life, and the mother's life may coalesce:

> Mi leue dere modur, to speke more opunliche to þe of þe bok þat I ches bifore alle oþire, for þe moste nedful, most spedful and most medful: þis bok is Crist, Godis Sone of heuene, wiþ his conuersacioun þre and þrytti wyntur, iwrite wiþinne and wiþoute with humilite to hele Adames pride and oures . . . And so he wiþ his conuersacioun is to alle þat wollen be saued þe beste remedie and þe beste rule and þe beste mirour þat mai be to ouercome synne. And þerfore furst studefastliche þenk þou to rule þine þou3tes and þine wordis and werkis aftir his; and specialli þat þou be write wiþinne and wiþoute wiþ þulke þre as Crist was, for wiþoute hem mai no man holde Cristes religioun. (31.1–14)

The assertion that "þis bok is Crist," as well as the statement that without assimilating oneself to Christ-book, one may not "holde Cristes religioun," recall Wyclif's formulations of Christ as scripture and his imperative to know this "book" inside and out. But the difference is critical: here, the book's materiality remains vital for understanding it even though, as Schirmer observes, "the internally written Word . . . must first subsume *and* supplant all other modes of religious writing."[72] Unlike Wyclif's textualization of Christ, which results in disembodiment, *Book to a Mother* gives textual life to Christ's earthly life, his embodied "conuersacioun" or conduct. Although the narrative of Christ's "conuersacioun" supersedes the didactic genres of remedy, rule, and mirror for those in search of guidance, these genres have not been erased: they remain to provide vehicles for understanding the textual forms that Christ's life may encompass.

Thus, where Wyclif strips away, the *Book* author augments, even as he proclaims the radical self-sufficiency of his guide. This "conuersacioun," which will be the essential content of the *Book*, will teach the mother to practice the same form of absolute self-consistency as Christ, who like the book of Revelation is "iwrite wiþinne and wiþoute with humilite." The repetition of that phrase as applied to the mother models in the text the act of "ruling" oneself according to Christ's example. But the slight change from exemplar to copy ("iwrite wiþinne and wiþoute with humilite" to "write wiþinne and wiþoute *with þulke þre*") demands vigilant reading. With this small textual change, *Book to a Mother* revises the idea of the "rule" to emphasize self-discipline as a process requiring and teaching skills of textual criticism and synthesis. Rather than appealing to abstract ideas of *scientia* and *sapientia*, *Book to a Mother* writes an experiential understanding of Christ into this passage, so that by the end, although the warning resembles Wyclif's, the reader, by practicing the recommended "thoughts, words, and works," may begin to feel entitled to "holde" a place in Christ's fellowship.

As *Book to a Mother* repeatedly shows, the effort of self-improvement is a textual process requiring constant vigilance:

And ȝif þou wolt knowe sikerliche þi soule and þi lif þat þou be not bigiled, þenke ofte and loke inwardlich in Crist wiþ his conuersacion and his techinge. For þat is þe bok and þe mirour wiþouten wem, in þe whiche ben hid alle tresoures of wisdom and conninge of God. And in þe gospel Crist clepiþ himself Holi Writ þat his Fadur halewide and sende into þis world, þat men schulde amende her false bokis bi him. (38.2–9)

Bringing back the image of the "mirrour," a form both visual and literary, the author explicitly equates Christ's "conuersacioun" with "Holi Writ" as a guide sent from heaven, a template for human self-correction and a trove of "wisdom and conninge."[73] Alluding to John 10:35 with an original addition ("þat men schulde amende here false bokis bi him"), he predicates the passage from hiddenness to openness not only on *reading* the narrative of Christ's life, but on careful *comparison* of the "false bok" of one's own life with the examples found in "Holi Writ."

In *Book to a Mother*, if Christ is the copy text with which to compare the "false bok" of one's life, then it seems logical that the lay reader should be further invited into clerical techniques of emendation and even of writing, in cooperation with her priestly advisor. In contrast to the confessional process modeled in *Fervor Amoris*, where the confessor's role is strictly to "teche," and the reader's strictly to "lerne," in *Book to a Mother* confession is presented as a collaboration between the author's priestly power and the reader's developing clerical skills. In the process, the mother becomes a reader of her own life and of Christ's life, as well as the writer of a new, corrected text. She should compare her "liuinge" to Christ's and when it does not "accord" scrape it out wiþ sorew of herte and schrift of mouþe and satisfaccioun . . . And þat þat þe lackeþ, þat þou most nedis haue to holde Goddis hestis, writ in þi soule. Þy penne to write wiþ schal be þi loue and þi wil ymad scharp wiþ drede of sharp peyne of helle; and þis is a kene knyf ynow to make þi penne scharp, cordinge holliche wiþ Cristes liuinge, and ȝif þou scaue þi penne and make hure feir and loueliche, noþing larger wilnynge in þouȝt, word and dede þan God wol þat þou wilne. (38.21–39.5)

Mention of the "sharp peyne of helle" reminds the reader in no uncertain terms that the author maintains priestly powers of binding and loosing, but the emphasis on the reader's own "penne" is the more striking. The *Book*'s exhortations to "scrape" and "scaue" (sharpen) allegorize traditional scribal methods of preparing parchment and stylus to give this metaphorical form of "writing" a lay apostolic meaning.[74] Penance becomes a writerly, self-transformative process critical to the reader's active *imitatio Christi*.

The notion of inscribing God's commandments on the heart and soul is altogether orthodox,[75] and a similar outline of the necessary sequence of "sorew . . . schrift . . . satisfaccioun" appears in many vernacular religious works, including *Piers Plowman*, in which penance is allegorized in Passus 14 as the scraping, washing, wringing, dyeing, and bleaching of a dirty coat. But Langland, highlighting the lay subject's distance from the privileges of "clergie," presents this sequence as one performed upon the penitential subject, in this case Haukyn the Active Man, an embodiment of sinful humanity. The once-yearly confessional process affords him glimpses of Dowel, Dobet, and Dobest: Haukyn stands by as his filthy coat is removed and Conscience begins to teach him,

> "And I shal kenne þee," quod Conscience, "of Contricion to make
> That shal clawe þi cote of alle kynnes filþe:
> *Cordis contricio &c.*
> Dowel shal wasshen it and wryngen it þoruȝ a wis confessour:
> *Oris confessio &c.*
> Dobet shal beten it and bouken it as bright as any scarlet
> And engreynen it wiþ good wille and goddes grace to amende þe,
> And siþen sende þee to Satisfaccion for to [sonnen] it after:
> *Satisfaccio.*
> Dobest [shal kepe it clene from vnkynde werkes]."
>
> (14.16–21)

Although this extended allegory offers valuable insight into the phases of penance, Conscience's speech renders the penitential subject oddly passive, as Haukyn contemplates the purification of his "cote" by others, from a distance. In contrast, *Book to a Mother* uses the image of the "penne," which evolves in this passage into a sign for the reader herself, to suggest that "according" with Christ's life should be a carefully calibrated intellectual and textual process. The reader should strive for a state in which her desire absolutely accords with God in "þouȝt, word and dede," in which her own "writing" can accurately mirror God's "hestis."

Although Walter Hilton is neither as polemical nor as self-consciously textual as the author of *Book to a Mother*, he also constructs a vision of lay *imitatio Christi* that involves clerical techniques of self-scrutiny, accord, and emendation, in cooperation with rather than in submission to the priestly advisor. Hilton's position of deference toward his wealthy patron means that he must translate relations of textual accord in the opposite direction from *Book to a Mother*, to persuade the reader not how he can amend himself to fit Christ's model, but rather why Christ's mixed life "accords" with the reader's own needs. Hilton's addressee has apparently put himself in a difficult position: he rashly wishes to abandon his life in the world to "serue oure lord bi goostli occupacioun al holli, wiþoute lettynge or trobolynge o[f] wordeli bisynesse" (7.74–75). But even with pious intentions, Hilton reminds him, fleeing from responsibilities to family, household, and other dependents would betray the very love of God that he seems to wish to express. Therefore Hilton recommends a "medeled liyf" combining the best of action and contemplation: "þou schalt meedele þe werkes of actif liyf wiþ goostli werkes of lif conte[m]platif, and þanne doost þou weel" (10.101–03). This is the very model that Christ established, alternating between active works and contemplative prayer: as Hilton describes, "he comouned wiþ men and medeled wiþ men, schewynge to hem his deedes of merci, for he tauȝte þe vncouþ and vnkunynge bi his prechynge . . . and wente into dissert upon þe hillis, and contynued alle þe nyȝt in praieres aloone, as þe gospel seiþ" (17.181–18.188). This summary of Christ's "medeled" life, taken almost verbatim from Gregory's *Regula Pastoralis*,[76] offers a convenient textual model of Christ's "conuersacion and his techinge," to use *Book to a Mother*'s terms. It is a model of active and contemplative practice that combines clerical teaching practice along with the prayerful rest that the addressee apparently desires.

But Hilton still faces the challenge of making this model appealing as an object of imitation. With strategic use of textual terms, he suggests that this Christ-like mixed life may be both an entitlement to clerical privilege and a mandate to spiritual work. His description of this life cautiously deploys the terms "accord" and "rule":

sooþli, as me þenkeþ, þis medeled liyf accordeþ moost to þee. [For] siþen oure lord haþ ordeyned þee and sette the in staat of souereynte ouer oþir men as moche as it is, and lente þe habundaunce of wordeli goodis for to rulen and sustene speciali alle þise þat arn vndir þi gouernaunce and þi lordschipe of þi my3t and kunnynge, and also wiþal þat þou hast receyued grace of þe merci of oure lorde for to [haue sumwhat knowynge of] þi self and goosteli desire and sauour of his loue, I hope þat þis lif þat is medeled is þe beste, and acordeþ moste to þee for to traueile inne. (22.240–23.249)

Having already constructed the "medeled liyf" as a textual means of access to Christ, Hilton activates the technical meaning of "accordeþ," its sense of offering a verbal correspondence to an existing thing,[77] proffering the "medeled liyf" as the textual form that may best express the reader's particular combination of material power and spiritual privilege. Already possessing material powers of "souereynte" and "wordeli goodis," as well as grace and "knowynge of [him]self," the reader need only recognize "þis lif" as the ideal role for a man in his situation. Repeating his own language with a difference, recalling *Book to a Mother*'s repetition and alteration of the phrase "iwrite withinne and wiþoute," Hilton's "accordeþ most to þee for to traueile inne" suggests that this form of life will fit the reader and create a textual mode to which he must now "traueile" to match his own conduct to Christ's.

HOLY WRIT, OPEN UNDERSTANDING, AND LAY SELF-REFORMATION

Converging with Wyclif in their emphasis on Christ as book, Hilton's *Mixed Life* and *Book to a Mother* imply that lay readers should study scripture in order to "amend" their lives and thus embody Christ's "conuersacioun" as closely as possible. Having argued that the present "bok" lies within the motherly reader and need only be recognized, then externalized as Christ's "liuinge," the *Book* author lends the addressee further scholarly and moral authority: he contends that by understanding her imitation of Christ as a combination of textual accuracy and intense love, she may go on to embody the true meaning of the term "clerk":[78]

þou maist lerne aftir þi samplerie to write a feir trewe bok and better konne Holi Writ þan ony maister of diuinite þat loueþ not God so wel as þou; for who loueþ best God, can best Holi Writ. For bokis þat men wryten ben not Holi Wryt, but as ymages ben holi, for þei bitokeneþ holi Seintes; but Crist, Godis Sone, he is uerreiliche Holi Writ, and who þat louiþ him best is best clerk. (39.7–13)

Whereas the university-trained "maister of diuinite" may be able to pen a sterile commentary on Holy Writ, the mother, through imitation of

Christ's "samplerie" (a nice textual pun) can combine her literary acumen with the embodied "loue" that the worldly clerk lacks. Even as he uses the metaphor of writing to open up new intellectual possibilities to the reader, the author's subsistence in the realm of metaphor preserves his own authorial position and orthodox credentials. "Holi Writ" is essential to furthering the mother's *imitatio clerici* as *imitatio Christi*, a means to making the reader see the current book as well as the Bible as mere "pointers to Christ" that must be consumed and exceeded.[79]

In their views on the uses and meanings of the biblical text, *Book to a Mother*, *The Life of Soul* and Hilton's *Mixed Life* must be seen together and from a new perspective, not among works that take a condescending approach to lay learning,[80] but among contemporaries, including *Piers Plowman*, that insist upon readers' encounter with the Bible as a malleable entity, at once personal resource and in Simpson's words part of "the communal institution of the Church, even if in some cases they refigure the Church at the same time."[81] In their views on the biblical text in particular, these guides reveal their capacity to be both "devotionalist" and "reformist" at the same time.[82] Including significant portions of biblical paraphrase in their guides, these authors participate in the robust orthodox tradition of "Englishing the Bible" responsible for myriad prose and verse works in the later medieval period.[83] This tradition viewed the Bible as multiple and unbounded, not (as in Wyclif's view) an inviolable entity to be read as a whole[84] but a series of books to be used as needed for liturgical, homiletic, or devotional purposes.[85] Although these guides recall Wyclif on the need to study and translate scripture[86] and anticipate full biblical translation with their expansive paraphrases, their dialogic approaches to the Bible and emphases on cooperation between lay readers and clerical teachers are at variance with the views expressed in the Wycliffite Bible Prologue – a very different sort of devotional guide – which touts a bounded biblical text that laity should consult in defiance of clerical authorities.

As I noted above, along with condemning some of Wyclif's theological positions, the 1382 Blackfriars Council prohibited unauthorized explication of scriptures in Latin or the vernacular, probably with little success given the popularity of vernacular biblical texts among orthodox and dissenting readers alike.[87] After several decades, which had witnessed the translation and copying of the Wycliffite Bible[88] and the heated Oxford translation debates of 1401–07,[89] translation was regulated by Archbishop Arundel's Constitutions, written in 1407, published in 1409. Article Seven prohibited the translation of scripture or use of translations made since Wyclif's time.[90] Thus by the fraught early fifteenth century, biblical translation had become associated in England with the Wycliffite movement, though there was nothing objectionable in the translations themselves.

The Life of Soul, Book to a Mother, and *Mixed Life* suggest how fully, in the last quarter of the fourteenth century, scripture might form the subject of orthodox spiritual conversation, providing the very medium of dialogue between clerical advisors and lay addressees. Given the uncertainty in the dates of these guides, they were either written before or untroubled by the possibility that their biblical paraphrase might run afoul of the 1382 Blackfriars decree, and they were certainly composed before Arundel's wider censorship came into effect. In their insistence on scripture for use, incorporation, and self-reformation, their authors make encounter with holy writ a tool for promoting collaboration between clerics and lay seekers poised to gain clerical tools through reading.[91]

This contrast becomes visible in uses of the term "open" and its variants in the Prologue to the Later Wycliffite Bible and in *The Life of Soul.* This Prologue, which Dove has recently dated to *c.* 1387, polemically relates scriptural study to Wycliffite ecclesiology for the benefit of readers preparing to encounter the whole Bible in the vernacular.[92] A critical term in the Wycliffite lexicon, "open" as used in the Bible meant "readily comprehensible" or clear[93] and was linked to the Wycliffite agenda of making the literal sense of the Bible accessible to all readers.[94] As Ghosh observes, "the adjective 'open' was habitually used by the Lollards to emphasise their direct access to a divine intention informing a scriptural text which offers to its readers meanings of unmediated clarity."[95] Though this "unmediated clarity" might not come easily, requiring careful translation and techniques of exegesis "grounded opynly in þe text of hooli writ,"[96] the Prologue connects the idea of openness to the rejection of clerical advice in the process of coming to know the Bible. In the Prologue, even as the term "open" offers access, it also fosters antagonism between clerical and lay subjects, constructing the Bible as a text that will end conversation between them. At the start of the Prologue, in the determination of canonical books, the author asserts that all the books of the New Testament are

fulli of autorite of bileue; therfore cristen men and wymmen, olde and ȝonge, shulden studie fast in the newe testament, for it is of ful autorite, and opyn to understonding of simple men, as to the poyntis that be moost nedeful to saluacioun; and the same sentence is in the derkiste placis of holy writ, whiche sentence is in the opyn placis; and ech place of holy writ, bothe opyn and derk, techith mekenes and charite; and therfore he that kepith mekenes and charite hath the trewe vndirstondyng and perfectioun of al holi writ, as Austyn preuith in his sermoun of the preysing of charite . . . And no clerk be proude of the verrey vndirstonding of hooly writ, for whi verrey vndirstonding of holy writ with outen charite, that kepith Goddis heestis, makith a man depper dampned, as James and Jhesu Crist witnessen; and pride and couetise of clerkis is cause of her blindenes and eresie, and priueth hem fro verrey vndirstondyng of holy writ, and maken hem go quyk into helle, as Austyn seith on the Sauter, on that word, *Descendant in infernum viventes*.[97]

Just as the Prologue refuses a distinction between the "open" and "derk" places of holy writ on the grounds that both will be equally transparent to the person living in charity, in the service of making the Bible "open" to "simple men," the writer eliminates clerical help in the process of inter-pretation, offering this prologue as a key to independent lay reading of the Bible. Recalling Wyclif's attitude toward *sapientia* – that one either possesses wisdom or not – the Prologue implies that meekness, charity, and effort will lead to "trewe vndirstondyng and perfectioun of al holi writ": no special preparation or techniques of interpretation are needed.[98] By making conduct more important than cognition for purposes of developing "verrey vndirstondyng of holy writ," the Prologue pre-empts conversation between clerks and lay readers, engendering suspicion of clerical reading because of suspicion about clerical conduct, guilty as clerks may be of "pride" and "couetise," leading to "blindenes and eresie."

For the author of *The Life of Soul*, the terms "open" and "openliche" refer less to the text of scripture than to the *relation* between lay learner and clerical teacher, to the way in which Christ's teachings may be absorbed, digested, and performed. In this work, most strongly among the guides under consideration here, biblical reading and dialogue are made comple-mentary, and "open" is used to characterize the shared effort of reader and teacher as they seek and explain biblical ideas through the medium of the guide itself. The terms "opun" and "opunliche" are first used by "Frend" and are soon picked up by learner figure ("Sire"), who repeats them obses-sively, first complaining that the answers of "Frend" are inadequate to his needs: "Frend, þi answere þat þou ȝeuest in my axyng is ful schort and ful derk also for me. And þerfore, I preye þe ȝif me a more open answere" (18.13–15). Not unlike Will, complaining to Scripture that "Where dowel is or dobet derkeliche ye shewen" (10.378), "Sire" does not hide his distaste for abstractions, later demanding

I preye þe þat þou write to me *more opunliche* of þe liflode of my soule to kele þe hungur and þe þrist of my soule, and telle me *opunlyche* þe virtues þat Crist techiþ to cloþe wiþ my soule, þat I be not naked in þe comyng of my Lord, but be wil icloþed in my weddyng cloþ. And *tel me opunliche* wordes þat I mow fulfillen hem in dede . . . And *wryte to me opunliche* þe techynge of Crist þat I mowe ben iheled þerby of þe sekenes of my soule, and þat I mowe ben icounforted þerby whyles I am in prysoun of þis world and in a strange lond as a pylgrym far fro myn owene cuntre. And siþe my soule is derk þoru vncunnynge, for I knowe not parfiȝtliche þe liȝt of Cristes wordes, I preye þe þat þou *write hem opunliche* and ne hyde hem not from me. For þere ne is no man þat tendeþ a candel and setteþ hit vndur a buschel, but vpon a chaundeler þat hit ȝeueþ liȝt to alle hem þat ben in þe house . . . And þerfore ne hyde hit not from me but *tell openliche þat I axed raþer*: Whyche is þe lyflode of oure soule . . . [Frend responds paraphrasing Christ's words]: herefore Crist seyde to his disciples: It is igraunted to ȝow to know the priueytees of þe kyngdom of heuene, but to oþere men it is not igraunted . . . And þerfore I speke to oþere men in parables þat ben derk speches, for þei seyn and seiþ nouȝt . . . And sire, siþe Good of his goodnesse haþ ȝeue sum knowyng of his wordis, preyeth hym tristyliche þat he ȝeue ȝow more knowyng, and I wil do my trauayle þoru þe grace of God to make ȝow knowen *þat ȝe axeden raþer.* (20.4–22.17, emphasis added)[99]

Here the active lay learner uses "openliche" to refer to the quality of the teacher's instruction, not precisely to describe the scripture itself but the way it should be imparted and paraphrased in conversation and writing. For the learner, Christ's teachings will function simultaneously as text and as physical embodiments of the works of mercy, nourishing and clothing him. A seamless transition occurs between the process of learning these lessons through demonstration and performing them "in dede": this presentation suggests that the "wordes" will be useful to the reader only as a guide to performance of the works of mercy. The learner anticipates that as they are imparted "openliche," the textual virtues, words, and teachings will become embodied, satiating "þe hungur and þe þrist," or will be performed ("þat I mow fulfillen hem"), as textual understanding blends into somatic experience.

The dialogic passage itself becomes exemplary in the words cited by "Sire" on the candle under the bushel, and in Christ's speech to the disciples from Matthew 13:11–18, an almost uninterrupted biblical paraphrase. In creating this dialogue of paraphrases, the clerical author of *Life of Soul* does not mark out "holy writ" as separate from the conversation between teacher and learner, but frames the reader's encounter with scripture in terms of cooperation between the two speakers and the two biblical passages. Thus, the guide invites readers into "more knowyng" by encouraging them to consider the progression between these two passages, and view themselves as disciples offered the privilege of this "knowing."

There are revealing parallels between this passage from *The Life of Soul* and the dialogic Passus 17 of *Piers Plowman*, part of the "Vita de Dobet" that takes as its subject Will's search for the best way "to leue [on] for lif and for soule" (17.27). In Will's conversation with the Good Samaritan, however, understanding of Christ's words is set in motion by a non-clerical teacher, the Good Samaritan, who provides a model of virtuous action in offering to be "þi frend and þi felawe" (17.89) after Will's learned interlocutor Spes has fled from the horrible sight of the wounded man on the road. Will does not *demand* to be taught in the same fashion as *The Life of Soul*'s "Sire," but submits himself faithfully to the Samaritan as spiritual teacher. As the Samaritan explains the need for the wounded man to incorporate Christ in order to be spiritually whole, he comes to embody Christ's struggle with the devil, paraphrases Christ's words, and promises his return:

> Ac er þis day þre daies I dar vndertaken
> That he worþ fettred, þat feloun, faste wiþ Cheynes,
> And neuere eft greue gome þat gooþ þis ilke gate:
> [*O Mors ero mors tua &c*].
> . . .
> And alle þat feble and feynte be, þat Feiþ may noȝt teche,
> Hope shal lede hem forþ with loue as his lettre telleþ,
> And hostele hem and heele þoruȝ holy chirche bileue
> Til I haue salue for alle sike; and þanne shal I turne
> And come ayein bi þis contree and conforten alle sike.
> (17.112–23)

Will's response shows that the process of the dialogue has fulfilled his desire to be instructed "for life and for soule." He has assimilated the Samaritan with other teachers and begun actively reflecting upon the mystery of the trinity and the lesson of the double commandment:

> "A, swete sire!," I seide þo, "wher I shal bileue,
> As Feiþ and his felawe enformed me boþe,
> In þre persones departable þat perpetuele were euere,
> And alle þre but o god? þus Abraham me tauȝte;
> And Hope afterward he bad me to louye
> O god wiþ all my good, and alle gomes after
> Louye hem lik myselue, ac oure lord abouen alle."
> (17.127–33)

In a dialogic process similar to that depicted in *The Life of Soul*, though here with partial independence from clerical teachers, Will enters into conversation with Christ through the medium of the biblical text. The process of "understanding," though not yet complete, becomes evident in Will's own reflection on Abraham's lesson and his *ad hoc* scriptural paraphrase in the final line. In *The Life of Soul*'s terminology, Will moves from "sum knowynge" to "more knowynge" over the course of this short dialogue.

In connection with this comparison, I suggest that Walter Hilton's approach to the Bible is also akin to Langland's in its flexibility and emphasis on dialogic participation. Despite arguing for Hilton's essential conservatism, Simpson concedes Hilton's emphasis on a variety of devotional practices:[100] specifically, where Hilton recommends "stikkes of o þing oþer of oþer, eiþer of preieres or of good meditaciouns or reding in hooli writte, or good bodili worchynge, for to norische þe fier of loue in his soule" (38.443–39.446). For Hilton, I suggest, this recommendation to read "hooli writte" separately from the guide is not a departure from his usual didactic stance but is in keeping with the dialogic nature of his work as a whole. Hilton builds a process of active selection into his guide, which, like *Piers Plowman*, remakes "holi writ" into a script for the reader to enter into, paraphrase, and perform in the manner best suited to the development of a personal religious discipline.

Offering an interpretation of the Rachel and Leah story for his reader, Hilton fashions a clerical "ensample" of the mixed life and prepares the reader for his own independent use of the Bible. With the story of the two sisters, he invites the reader into one of the oldest authoritative, clerical explanations of active and contemplative life, offering this "ensample" as a way for the reader to imagine an unmediated relationship to Christ as advisor.[101] The reader should reimagine himself as a second Jacob, his two wives representing active and contemplative life respectively:

Bi Jacob in hooli writ is vndirstonde an ouergoere of synnes. Bi þise two wymmen are vndirstonden, as Seynt Gregor seiþ, two lyues in hooli chirche, actif liyf and contemplatif liyf. Lia is as moche to seie as trauelous, and bitokeneþ actif liyf. Rachel is as moche for to seie as siȝt of bigynnynge þat is God, and bitokeneþ liyf contemplatif. (30.338–31.343)

Modeling a form of allegorical interpretation that initiates the reader into this practice, Hilton mediates the Bible to fit its story to the reader's life, proposing an "accord" that offers a form of guidance.

By proposing this "ensample" to the reader, Hilton extends techniques for "reading" and governing his own life, a complex existence lacking the predictability and harmony of the iconic story. The reader may expect to be interrupted in his prayer and contemplation "[bi] þi children or þi seruauntes, or bi ony of þyn euene-cristene" (34.384–85), but he should use his "understonding" of the Jacob story to preserve equanimity:

be not angri wiþ hem, ne heuy, ne dredefulle ... Leue of liȝteli þi deuocioun, wheþir it be in praiere or in meditacioun, and goo doo þi dette and þi seruice to þyne euene-Cristene as redili as oure lord him silf badde þee doo so, and suffre mekeli for his loue, wiþouten grucching if þou may. (34.386–35.392)

Thus Hilton's addressee, who should consider duty to his family and servants to be as holy as Jacob's own "dette" to God, is encouraged to internalize the principles of the mixed life for use now and in the future, even after Hilton is no longer there to advise him. Although the lay reader may eventually encounter the Bible without his clerical teacher, Hilton (unlike the Wycliffite Prologue writer) imagines that his pupil will always keep their conversation in mind as a guide to practice.

HOLY WRIT, JUDGMENT, AND UNDERSTANDING

In these three guides the Bible functions as a tool in the textualized process of self-reformation, "judgment" and understanding, as scripture literally becomes part of the dialogue between clerical teacher and lay learner. Lay readers are encouraged to develop new understandings of how parts of scripture might be pieced together and used in personally efficacious ways. In the passage considered above, the Wycliffite Bible Prologue invokes the judgment of Jesus Christ and James to criticize clerics ("verrey vndirstonding of hooly writ with outen charite, that kepith Goddis heestis, makith a man depper dampned, as James and Jhesu Crist witnessen"). By contrast, the Epistle of James is incorporated into *The Life of Soul* and *Book to a Mother* to highlight the qualities of knowledge, judgment, and action that clerical authors and lay readers might share. *The Life of Soul*, whose latter half incorporates extensive biblical paraphrase in order to impart the lessons of the soul's "liflode," arranges sections of New Testament antiphonally, demanding synthesis of the text into new forms of self-judgment and regulation. The author juxtaposes St. John and St. James in order to create a dialogue between them on the need for "mesure" and charity and the avoidance of "coueytise." The section begins with a condemnation, arguing that keeping any "goodes" to oneself beyond need constitutes an affront to "Goddis wille," for "God ne ȝeueþ nouȝt to oo man more richesse þan to anoþer oonliche for hymseluen, but for he schulde departen it among his nedy breþeren. And but a man do þus, he nis not in charite" (59.6–9). John's exhortation not to close one's heart from one's brother – "Ne loue we not in wed, ne in tunge, but in dede and in treuþe" – is followed by "a ful hard word" from James, who proclaims, "[w]epe ȝe riche men and make ȝe sorewe for þe wrechednes þat schal come to ȝow hereaftur" (59.13–18). Just as the boundaries between these two epistles are blurred to bring a theory of charity into relation with a theory of damnation, the reader is encouraged to embody charity to avoid such a fate, working with the author to understand these epistles as flexible guides to knowledge and practice. Although the voices of teacher and learner, which spoke in the first part of the work, have now disappeared, these unmediated biblical paraphrases preserve the interplay of voices and suggest that multiple interpretations might be possible.

The final section of *Book to a Mother*, which consists largely of paraphrase from six "justices" of the New Testament, finally invites the inscribed reader to encounter (almost unmediated) the original "boke" of Holy Writ and exercise (almost independently) the Christ-like and clerical powers of interpretation and judgment that the author has encouraged throughout.[102] The author has repeatedly emphasized the importance of understanding Christ as judge, and a harsh one when necessary. Just as in both *Piers Plowman* and *Book to a Mother* the learner's induction into the use of scripture is wrapped up with a critique of the friars as inadequate counselors, in both texts the proper use of judgment is contrasted with the friars' oft-repeated dictum "Nolite iudicare quemquam" (do not judge any man). Where the figure of Lewte argues immediately following Will's attack on the friars that "It is *licitum* for lewed men to [legge] the soþe / If hem likeþ and lest; ech a lawe it graunteþ" (11.96–97), the author of *Book to a Mother* makes an almost identical argument in prose, less to level a clerical critique than to argue for lay readerly judgment as integral to the larger project of *imitatio Christi*. He argues that Christ's exhortation not to judge (Luke 6:37) should be understood not as a prohibition on judgment so much as a warning not to judge "foliliche, wiþouten certeyn euidences . . . For Crist iuggede and cursede muche in þis world, and tauȝte forte iugge to destruye sinne þer as hit is opene aȝenus his hestis" (72.22–26). In essence the entire *Book* is designed to teach the mother how to "iugge forto destruye" her own sins and to use her increasingly acute judgment to propel herself closer to the "rule" of Christ's life. And "judgment," broadly conceived, is the theme of the final section:

Lo, my dere modur, here I shewe to þe sixe hiȝe iustices of þe heiest King, Fadur and Emparour of heuene, erþe and helle: Crist, Ion, Iude, Iame, Petur and Poul, wiþ here sentence and dome þat þei leften write wiþ men in þis world . . . For alle þat holliche and finalliche acorden wiþ þes sixe shullen be saued fro honginge of helle and be deliuered out of prisoun on þe dredful dai of dome. (191.1–8)

To invoke the author's own textual metaphor, the reader's final task is to compare her own deeds and the advice of these "justices," to work toward "according" herself in order to avoid damnation.

The last section of *Book to a Mother* stresses the reader's obligation to use her skills of interpretation independently, to discern the difference between godly and ungodly conduct using the tools that the guide has offered. Stripping away almost everything except the scriptural text, the author lays out alternatives: in the section taken from James, he proposes, "Be ʒe doers of Godis word, and not onliche herers, deseyuinge ʒouself. For he þat is herer of Godis word, and not doere, he shal be likened to a man lokinge his face in a myrour: he lokede himself and passede, and anon he forʒat whuche he was" (170.9–12). This image places the mother back into the familiar position of parishioner hearing "Godis wordis" from an authoritative source as well as referencing the image of Christ as mirror "wiþouten wem" into which the reader must look to assess the progress of her own life. She must rely on her own judgment to understand the difference between being a "herer" and a "doer," striving for a correspondence between the image in the mirror and the ideal of Christian life.

HOLY WRIT, CONSUMPTION, AND *IMITATIO CLERICI*

As I have suggested, for these three guides, the Bible is not a stable textual entity but a set of texts to be consumed in order to effect a personal *imitatio clerici*. This conviction is especially palpable in the argument for ingestion of the Bible, a venerable monastic metaphor that in Hilton and *Book to a Mother* takes on a newly urgent connection to *imitatio Christi*. Whereas in *Piers Plowman*, the feast of Scripture, at which Will is "served" various biblical texts, offers an opportunity for rumination on the need for repentance (the texts he ingests include, "Miserere mei Deus, et quorum tecta sunt peccata"), in these guides the clerical discipline of reading is offered as a means to ingest scripture and in the process, perhaps to be transformed into Christ's image. Hilton proposes an unmediated encounter with "holy writ" in order to nourish the love of Christ; *Book to a Mother* goes further to connect ingestion of holy writ to embodiment of Christ's own "living." Hilton argues

A man þat is lettered and haþ vndirstondynge of hooli writte, ʒif he haue þis fier of deuocioun in his herte, it is good vnto him for to gete him stikkes of hooli ensamples and seiynges of oure lord bi redynge in hooli writte, and norissch þe fier wiþ hem . . . And so it is good þat eche man in his degree, after þat he is disposid, þat he gete him stikkes of o þing oþer of oþer, eiþer of preieres or of good meditaciouns or reding in hooli writte, or good bodili worchynge, for to norische þe fier of loue in his soule þat it be not quenchid. (38.434–39.446)

By "a man þat is lettered," Hilton probably means a reader of Latin. Although we cannot know whether his addressee was Latin-literate, such literacy would certainly be imaginable for a person of the status Hilton implies: it would indeed be a milestone if, as Margaret Deanesly claims, "Hilton . . . was the first English religious to recommend the laity to read the Bible at all."[103] However, more noteworthy for my purposes is Hilton's placement of "hooli writte" among complementary forms that might be in English, Latin, or wordless: prayer, meditation, and good works. Holy writ, moreover, is posited as useful only insofar as it can be consumed: in this description, the object to be incorporated is mentioned even before being identified as a textual entity (*"stikkes* of hooli ensamples and seiynges of our lord bi redynge in hooli writte"). In keeping with the work's constant play of alternatives, the text of the Bible offers a source of "ensample" for the reader, but rather than preserving the text as a stable entity, the addressee is encouraged to consume and incorporate the wisdom of scripture into his own burning love for Christ.

In *Book to a Mother*, since the Bible is identical with Christ's life, the current book, itself identical to holy writ, must be incorporated by the reader who desires a simultaneous *imitatio clerici* and *imitatio Christi*. The author lends the reader a form of vernacular literary authority that approaches and might exceed that of actual "clerkes," proposing that she move beyond textual knowledge to understand and embody Christ's "liuinge." He exhorts her

lerne þis bok, as I seide, raþer; þat is, know þou þe liuinge of Crist and ofte chew hit and defie [digest] hit wiþ hot brennynge loue, so þat alle þe uertues of þi soule and of þi bodi be turned fro fleshliche liuinge into Cristes liuinge . . . Þerfore, modir, þat þou be siker, leeuinge more his liuinge whanne his wil and his liuing acorden togedere þanne alle þe clerkes of þe world þat seien þe contrarie, haue þis for a general rule profitable to þe . . . whanne þou wolt knowe þe wil of God, bi his werkes þou maist know his wil. Þerfore þenk inwardli hou Crist com into þis world, hou he liuede in his myddul liuinge, and hou he endede; and euere þou maist fynde þat he was humble, pore and chast. (32.12–33.4)

In a passage whose syntax creates a fluid relationship between reading, analysis, and practice, the author suggests that now that his mother has learned the "uertues" through the catechism, she may begin to turn her skills of reading and interpretation into an active, literary *imitatio clerici*.[104] The eucharistic valence of this "chew[ing]" and digestion reinforces the author's priestly authority, but at the same time, the passage constructs the reader's love of Christ in a strikingly clerical way, offering the "bok" as the means by which she may read, digest, and in the process literally embody "Cristes liuinge." This process will not necessarily be easy and smooth: she must use her clerical skills to guard against "clerkes of þe world," reading the *Book* and assessing the written evidence to base her own actions upon Christ's "werkes" against the "contrarie" evidence that others may produce. Despite the textual emphasis of the passage, with its focus on learning to determine when Christ's "wil and his liuing acorden togedere," ultimately, as in *Life of Soul*, that textualization yields to physical embodiment and the evidence of "werkes." Once the reader has chewed and digested the textual evidence of Christ's life, she may be able to look inside herself to see the contours of his life – its beginning, middle, and end – without needing further recourse to the "bok."

Book to a Mother's idea that the mother's "love" makes her a better "clerk" than actual "clerkes of þe world" is strongly reminiscent of comments made in the dialogic Prologue to a roughly contemporary translation of the Pauline and Catholic epistles, which survives (in varying forms) in five manuscripts.[105] The work may be an early vernacular Wycliffite production, by virtue of its aim to make scripture available to "lewid" readers and its controversial comments on matters such as confession and grace.[106] Not unlike the *Life of Soul*, the text's prologue takes the form of a dialogue between a "broþer" and another "broþer," who is later called "suster." Although these appellations could indicate monastic provenance, Deanesly argues persuasively that they are a literary fiction designed to suggest a religious community, perhaps a Wycliffite conventicle.[107]

One speaker occupies the role of teacher, and the other that of learner, the latter styling himself as the "lewid" interlocutor. Although there is no indication that the "learned" speaker should be read as a priestly figure as in *Book to a Mother*, we may profitably compare the tone and content of the dialogue to the guides considered in this chapter. Early in the dialogue, the learner figure tests the teacher by displaying biblical knowledge, saying

3ef oure Lord putte his soule for his serfauntes, it is skylful þat on broþer putte his soule for his breþeren: For þat axeþ þe lawe of charite þat Crist tau3te here on erþe, boþe in word & dede . . . & broþer, y preye þe for þe loue þat þou schuldest haue to God & to þi breþeren, þat þou answere trewelyche to þinges þat y wole axen þe to hele of my soule & of oþer mennes soules þat beþ lewedere þan þou art. & 3if þou ne wylt no3t, oure hope is þat God wole enformen ous by sum oþer trewe seruaunt of his. (7.16–33)

As if giving a sermon himself, the "lewed" persona presents himself as desperately in need of "hele . . . of soule" that only the learned brother can offer, yet also able to evaluate critically the teacher's performance based on his own knowledge of the Bible. This combination of necessity and criticism is encapsulated in the final words quoted, which threaten the teacher with the loss of patronage: if the "lewed" person does not feel adequately informed, he will have to seek spiritual guidance elsewhere.

In the comment that follows, the teacher figure constructs the "lewed" brother as clerical, but by virtue of the power of love rather than schooling: "Broþer, þou hast a-gast me sumwhat wiþ þyn argumentys. For þouȝ þou ne hafe noȝt y-ben a-mong clerkes at scole, þi skelis þat þou makest beþ y-founded in loue þat is a-bofe resoun þat clerkes vseþ in scole: & þer-fore it is hard for me to aȝeynstonde þyn skyles & þyn axynges" (8.1–5). This passage and the section that follows it show the power of the "lewed" persona's goadings to restart the biblical narrative: love takes over as a driving force and theme of the narrative, propelling the "lerned" persona into the biblical paraphrase.

Even if we understand this conversation to be taking place between two lay speakers, we can see how dialogue systematically and polemically dismantles the categories "lerned" and "lewed," clerical and lay. Like the Lollard poem *Pierce the Ploughman's Crede*, this (probably) Wycliffite text takes the idea of lay "clerical understanding" in a radical direction. But in its preoccupation with biblicism and concern to reshape traditional relations between learners and teachers, the text overlaps in content and form with the dialogic spiritual rules *Book to a Mother*, *The Life of Soul*, and Hilton's *Mixed Life*. As such it reveals the care with which the authors of these guides exploit textual form to shape the idea of lay "clerical understanding," expanding the potential for lay intellectual and spiritual transformation while maintaining the distinctiveness of their own priestly authority. The next chapter will consider the most critical social aspect of priestly discipline – pastoral care – to demonstrate how Hilton negotiates lay access to this practice while avoiding the social dissolution and spiritual antagonisms threatened in *Piers Plowman* and Wycliffite writings.

CHAPTER 3

Lordship, pastoral care, and the order of charity

Walter Hilton and William Langland, rough contemporaries writing hundreds of miles apart, in Nottinghamshire and the West Midlands respectively, viewed the question of lay religious life from rather different vantage points. As S. S. Hussey noted fifty years ago, Hilton was the sober "Augustinian canon and director of souls seeking mystic union with God," Langland "the wanderer, the talker, dealing primarily with Heaven as reflected in the things of this world."[1] But Hilton's *Mixed Life* and Langland's *Piers Plowman* target readers with similar social backgrounds and responsibilities: speaking of these intended readers, Anne Middleton notes, "[w]hether laymen or ecclesiastics, their customary activities involve them in counsel, policy, education, administration, pastoral care – in those tasks and offices where spiritual and temporal governance meet."[2] In one case Hilton and Langland also shared an actual readership: the Vernon manuscript (Oxford, Bodleian Library, MS eng.theol.a.1), probably copied in the late 1380s, contains the *Mixed Life* (*c.* 1380–85) together with the A-Text of *Piers Plowman* (*c.* 1370). This monumental collection of religious prose and verse, whose index proclaims its purpose to be "Salus Anime" or "Sowlehele," was compiled for public reading in a religious house, probably a community of nuns. The conjunction of the *Mixed Life* and *Piers Plowman* here suggests that at least one early compiler found the two works complementary.

When the Vernon collection was being compiled, Wyclif's views defining the church as the community of those predestined to salvation and condemning clerical endowment were spreading, in part due to Wyclif's own preaching, which gained him supporters at court and more widely among the London population.[3] Thomas Heffernan has even asserted that the Vernon anthology represents "the values of a resurgent orthodoxy under siege."[4] Although it seems unlikely that a rural convent would have been seriously threatened by heterodoxy, Heffernan's remark suggests another rationale for bringing together works very different in scope and form but linked by shared interest in the complexities of *imitatio Christi*, spiritual privilege, and temporal authority. In this chapter I consider the *Mixed Life* in light of *Piers Plowman* and Wyclif on "spiritual and temporal governance" to offer new perspectives on the reformist translation of professional religious discipline.

In response to the pressing question of how to reconcile spiritual aspirations with material circumstances, Hilton activated the idea of the mixed life to construct a pastoral form of *imitatio clerici* as a template for lay self-transformation. He defines hybridity as a necessary condition of lay religious life, merging the politically problematic hybrid of the cleric and lord with the Christ-like hybrid of the active and contemplative lives. Hilton thus strives to make these two forms of "medling" positively dependent upon each other and desirable to the lay reader. In focusing primarily on Hilton's didactic strategies, with selective reference to Wyclif's writings and *Piers Plowman*, I am not aiming to show that Hilton read Langland's work[5] nor proposing to revive the debate over whether Langland's Dowel, Dobet, and Dobest represent Hilton's active, contemplative, and mixed lives.[6] Instead I bring the *Mixed Life* and *Piers Plowman* into conversation in a different way, juxtaposing their sanguine and skeptical perspectives on charity, lay–clerical relations, and pastoral care in order to lay bare the social and spiritual stakes involved in the creation of the mixed life.

Where Langland depicts the mutual imitation of laymen and prelates as contributing to a major crisis in clerical discipline, Hilton's guide translates the pastoral model of the bishop for the wealthy layman, offering the mixed life as a way to integrate worldly status with spiritual desire. Hilton uses spiritual guidance to transform *imitatio clerici* from suspect impersonation into legitimate practice, recuperating the idea of the prelate as "spiritual gentleman" and so providing a model for the lay gentleman.[7] Others have noted that Hilton attempts to dissuade his addressee from pursuing contemplative solitude by emphasizing the similarity of the reader's duties as lord and estate manager to the pastoral responsibilities of a prelate, curate or bishop, thus encouraging the lord to persist in his caretaking role while understanding it as an imitation of Christ's "mixed life."[8] Ruth Nisse argues, "For Hilton, the rhetorical and political challenge of the 'mixed life' is how to govern spiritually those who must govern others bodily and who furthermore understand devotion in those terms."[9] In this chapter, I am interested in the forms of lordship Hilton constructs for his reader, and in the broader implications, for lay religious identity and discipline, of this positive combination of spiritual and temporal governance. Imagining the life of the prelate as an ideal *imitatio Christi* for the reader to emulate by virtue of his own worldly power and material wealth, Hilton endows the materially privileged layman with pastoral power and implicitly defends the contemporary clerical *status quo*. As he turns the temporal/spiritual hybridity that Wyclif and Langland perceive as a problem into an opportunity for his reader and himself, Hilton brings spiritual guidance into conversation with the broad ethical concerns of poetry and reformism.

PRELACY, PASTORAL CARE, AND *IMITATIO CHRISTI*

Although the *Mixed Life* originates as an epistle to a particular individual, I want to stress that Hilton's private extension of pastoral authority to his lay reader also contributes to a broader conversation that cuts across genres and continues through the fourteenth century and into the fifteenth. Lay pastoralism was Hilton's signature concern well before it was overtly politicized in the conflict over Wycliffism. In its constructive response to current views on the incompatibility of temporal and spiritual lordship, the *Mixed Life* anticipates and may even influence the arguments of the Dominican Roger Dymmok, who employs Latin to diffuse clerical authority in his own response to Wycliffite anticlericalism. Writing against the Lollard *Twelve Conclusions* of 1395, especially the Lollard critique of clergy who took part in civil administration, Dymmok produced the lengthy *Liber Contra XII Errores et Hereses Lollardorum*.[10] In his rebuff to Lollard "errors and heresies," Dymmok invites laymen as well as clerics to consider themselves as battling the heretics in a pastoral capacity, including under the rubric "shepherds of the church" not only "holy doctors" but also "kings and princes," implying that the category "pastor" can include, in Somerset's terms, "a mixed group of important laymen and clerics."[11] The Lollard passage in question angrily condemns hybridity:

a kyng and a bisschop al in o persone, a prelat and a iustise in temperel cause, a curat and an officer in worldly seruise, makin euery reme out of god reule . . . for temperelte and spirituelte ben to partys of holi chirche, and þerfore he þat hath takin him to þe ton schulde nout medlin him with þe toþir, *quia nemo potest duobus dominis seruire.* Us thinkith þat hermofodrita or ambidexter were a god name to sich manere of men of duble astate.[12]

This view had originated with Wyclif, who argues in several places against clerics holding secular office. In *De Officio Regis*, Wyclif writes, "Although [secular] office would be praiseworthy in a layman, it is nevertheless excessively unnatural in a cleric, repugnant to God's law and to his [religious] profession."[13] But in response to the Lollard complaint, Dymmok redefines the epithet "ambidexter" as an aspirational ideal for any holder of pastoral office, rehabilitating the word as a capacity to "bear both adversity and prosperity with equanimity, neither dejected by one nor elated by the other."[14] Thus Dymmok emphasizes pastoral care and the complementarity of spiritual and temporal responsibilities as the essential common ground between elite laymen and clerics.

Hilton, anticipating this approach to pastoralism by a decade or so, puts the idea of the lay pastor into vernacular circulation, intervening to shape this role in a particular way for his own lay addressee. Although Hilton's "medled lif" has analogues in Latin and vernacular writings, his particular vision of this life takes on Wyclif's concerns about clerical possession and administrative authority, positing a uniquely productive mingling, for the lay man, of material endowment, administrative responsibility, and fervent devotion.[15] Hilton conceives temporal and spiritual governance as outgrowths of devotion, proposing that the reader understand his "degree" as parallel to that of the prelate, whose regulatory authority over himself and others grows out of the desire to order charity.[16] Following Gregory the Great's *Regula Pastoralis* (as well as ideas from Gregory's *Moralia in Iob*), Hilton associates the lay imitation of Christ's own "mixed life" with the prelate's perfect balance between contemplation and engagement in worldly affairs. But unlike Gregory, whose pastor grudgingly endures worldly business, Hilton emphasizes the positive complementarity of temporal affairs and spiritual pursuits, depicting prelates as fruitfully engaged in both.

PASTORAL CARE AND SPIRITUAL ANXIETY

Unlike the anonymous authors of the spiritual guides *The Life of Soul* and *Book to a Mother*, Walter Hilton is a relatively well-documented figure. He seems to have been, in succession, a civil lawyer, a canon lawyer, a religious solitary, and for the last years of his life an Augustinian canon: he died in 1396 at Thurgarton Priory. It was probably during this final period that he wrote the *Mixed Life* for an addressee who is now unknown.[17] Hilton's movement through different religious and social roles informed his own writings, which consistently engage the question of how to integrate religious aspiration with the realities of status and grapple in the process with contemporary controversies over the religious life. Hilton frequently used his own experience as a touchstone for his advice to others, writing many of his surviving letters of guidance, including the *Mixed Life*, for individuals experiencing crises of vocation.

Hilton specialized in advising those who wished to pursue the elusive *vita contemplativa*. He often expressed the view that the monastic version of this life was not appropriate for everyone and that the spiritually inclined might engage in forms of contemplation without radically changing their social roles. In the early *Epistola de Utilitate et Prerogativis Religionis*, Hilton counseled Adam Horsley, an Exchequer official desiring to join the Carthusian order but hesitant to follow through on his intention. Even as he encourages Horsley to become a Carthusian, Hilton admits his own unreadiness for religious vows.[18] In a later letter, the *Epistola ad Quemdam Seculo Renunciare Volentem*, Hilton advises John Thorpe, a fellow lawyer and cleric who in the heat of conversion had made rash vows to enter religious life, not to abandon the world for solitary religious life, but to serve God while remaining in a secular state. As Nisse has noted, the *Epistola ad Quemdam* anticipates the *Mixed Life* in that it "attempts to define a 'mixed life' as Hilton simultaneously advises his friend against joining a religious order and persuades him to renounce wealth and ambition."[19] Here Hilton draws attention to the many religious roles in which an individual might serve Christ:

As the Apostle says, everyone has his gift from God, one such and another such . . . for the building of the mystical body of Christ . . . And so, as in the early church, he makes some active men, some contemplatives, some rectors, others simple priests, some monks, others hermits.[20]

Even as they emphasize flexibility and cooperation in the pursuit of the religious life, these Latin letters anticipate the political engagements of the *Mixed Life*, combining guidance with what may be anti-Wycliffite polemic.[21] In the *Epistola de Utilitate*, Hilton offers a defense of the religious life against "heretics," perhaps a reference to Wyclif and his followers. He then launches into an *apologia* for the monastic life, equating the vowed life with the life of Christ and the apostles.[22] Although Hilton never mentions Wyclif by name, his statement that anyone moved by the spirit should enter monastic or canonical life, because "private law is more worthy than public," recalls and implicitly rebuffs the propositions regarding "private religions" that had recently been condemned at the Blackfriars Council of 1382.[23]

Hilton's *Mixed Life*, though designed like his earlier Latin letters for a person poised between cloister and world, employs the vernacular to respond to a lay addressee in need of guidance. In this English epistle, Hilton proposes a more structured plan for achieving contemplative stillness and glimpses of "goostly þinges" while remaining in the world.[24] His earlier letters had grappled polemically with opposition to the religious orders, and the *Mixed Life* also engages, though more subtly, with current controversy. Hilton takes the complementarity of material and spiritual power as the basis for the layman's *imitatio clerici*, offering not a rule, but a lay form of pastoral care inspired by Christ and the earliest bishops.

Using his characteristic voice of suggestion, rather than command, Hilton makes a virtue of the combination of "goostli occupacion" with "wordli bisynesse": for his busy addressee, prayer must always alternate with "wise kepynge and spendynge of þi wordli goodes, in good rulynge of þi seruauntes and þi tenauntes, and in oþere good werkes wirkynge to alle þyn euen-Cristene of þi myȝt" (28.314–18). In these measured forms of "spendynge," "rulynge," and "wirkynge," all undertaken for the benefit of "euen-Cristene," the lay lord's "wordli bisynesse" and "goostli occupacion" meet. Making secular and spiritual authority mutually productive rather than contradictory, Hilton shapes a particular form of living for his wealthy addressee and answers widespread anxiety about the hybridity of contemporary lords and prelates, making it constitutive of the Christ-like mixed life of action and contemplation.

CLERICAL LORDSHIP AND DISORDERED CHARITY

Before tracing how Hilton reforms the clerical function and persona for the use of his lay reader, it is necessary to examine in more detail how his contemporaries defined the crisis in clerical performance. In Langland's bleak vision, the clergy is beset by innumerable errors that enfeeble its pastoral and exemplary powers. Clerical ignorance and materialism often go hand in hand, eliciting criticism from speakers whose "lewed clergie" empowers them to expose hypocrisy.[25] As Somerset has shown, in Will's fifth dream, the "extraclergial" figure of Anima accuses wealthy, pampered clergy of living in "lewed" fashion, "spending their tithes on clothes and building rather than the poor . . . Because the clergy live 'lewed'ly they deprive the people of a proper example, with the result that charity is widely disregarded."[26] Hilton's pastoral version of *imitatio clerici* proposes a corrective to such disorders in lay–clerical relations, positing the bishop as a "proper example" of charity for the wealthy layman once more. In Gregory the Great's *Regula Pastoralis*, the *locus classicus* for the pastor's duties and one of Hilton's favorite sources, Gregory defines the double commandment to love God and neighbor as the source and essence of pastoral care. Some, he notes, are drawn by love of neighbor to preaching in the world, while others, overcome by love of God, may resist episcopal office. Citing Isaiah and Jeremiah as examples of such eagerness and reluctance respectively, he writes, "a voice externally different hath come forth from the two, but it sprang not from a different fountain of affection. For there are two commands of charity, the love of God, that is, and of our neighbour."[27] Pulled by the irresistible strength of love of neighbor, both men ultimately take on the "sacred ministry" of pastoral office.

The pastor embodies in a heightened way the two-fold charity that should rule all Christian lives,[28] and the question of how properly to obey the law of charity is fundamental to all of Hilton's spiritual guidance.[29] In creating a devotional plan for his lay addressee, Hilton enters into a complex debate over proper relations of spiritual to temporal lordship, original to civil dominion.[30] Although their concerns are not identical, Wyclif and Langland both evoke pressing worries, of which Hilton was well aware, about clerics, lords, and the intersections of "spiritual and temporal governance," anxious about the way material possession threatens to blur boundaries between lay and clerical status and thus compromise pastoral authority.

Wyclif's argument for the separation of spiritual and temporal lordship developed from his particular combination of biblical literalism, contemporary papalist theory, and realist ecclesiology.[31] His belief in the Bible's sole authority as guide to Christian living led logically to a conviction that pastoral authority and temporal possession were incompatible. As radical adherence to I Timothy 6:8 ("And having food and raiment, let us be therewith content") would require, Wyclif held that clerics should possess only the minimum needed for daily survival.[32] This interpretation, combined with the theory that any form of dominion, or lordship, depended upon righteousness, implied that the sin involved in accepting superfluous goods condemned clerical possessions to disendowment.[33] In his conviction that the church of the elect, "the mystical body of Christ, gathered from all the predestined,"[34] was represented on earth by the lay prince, "the visible expression of the mystical entity of the 'State,'" Wyclif maintained that clerics were only stewards of the royal estates with no inherent civil dominion, or private property rights.[35] Although the argument for the disendowment of church temporalities predated Wyclif,[36] he embraced it with new fervor in the later books of *De Civili Dominio* (*c.* 1376), where he maintained that if "after the endowment of the church," clerics had paid attention to the words of John the Baptist, when he said, according to Luke 3:14, "be content with your stipends" (contenti estote stipendiis vestris), "they would never have torn apart the realm of Christendom by insinuating themselves monstrously and presumptuously into temporal and civil lordship. Thus the rules of the Baptist in I Timothy 6:8 were obliterated."[37] When clerics forget these biblical dictates and default on their duty to serve the king in simplicity as Christ's disciples, the lay power should remove temporal support, reminding clerics of their duty to follow the "lex Christi" and restoring the proper separation between lay lords, clerics, and the poor.[38]

Wyclif repeatedly suggests the difficulty of preventing the clergy's stewardship of temporalities from slipping into self-indulgent use of property, except through the separation of spiritual and temporal realms and responsibilities. He draws particular attention to the Donation of Constantine as the moment the church began its long decline into worldliness. In the process of distributing alms to the poor under the pretext of charity (*ex titulo caritatis*), corrupt clerics became obsessed with enjoying worldly goods rather than discharging their duties.[39] In his *Trialogus* Wyclif condemns endowment on grounds that clerics should keep their distance from worldly laws, management, and concerns.[40] Presenting Christ not as poor preacher but as feudal ruler committed to the perpetuation of secular dominion, Wyclif argues that the ruling classes sinned grievously when they endowed the church and must retake all temporalities from the clergy to avoid damnation.[41]

Langland, though not a revolutionary like Wyclif, nonetheless shares his anxiety and even anger about clerical possession as a threat to charity.[42] Traugott Lawler has argued that *Piers Plowman* posits such strong connections among the secular clergy, pastoral care, and charity that "the ideal of charity is primarily a priestly, pastoral ideal," albeit one repeatedly betrayed by priests failing to live up to it.[43] Though I would hesitate to associate charity primarily with the priesthood, I pursue this connection in the belief that *Piers Plowman*, in excoriating the clergy, embodies a reformist pastoral ideology rather than an anticlerical stance.[44] In his own vision of the danger priestly possession poses to pastoral care, Langland also depicts the donation of Constantine as the moment when the mutual imitation of clerics and lords becomes the source of disorders in charity. "Dos ecclesie" comes up in the midst of Anima's tirade on the wrong relation between temporal wealth and piety.[45] Here clerical lordship gravely threatens the proper order of society's resources:

> If knyghthod and kynde wit and þe commune [and] conscience,
> Togideres loue leelly, leueþ it wel, ye bisshopes,
> The lordschipe of londes [lese ye shul for euere],
> And lyuen as *Leuitici*, as oure lord [yow] techeþ:
> *Per primicias & decimas &c.*
> Whan Constantyn of curteisie holy kirke dowed
> Wiþ londes and ledes, lordshipes and rentes,
> An Aungel men herden an heigh at Rome crye,
> "*Dos ecclesie* this day haþ ydronke venym

And þo þat han Petres power arn apoisoned alle."
A medicyne moot þerto þat may amende prelates.
That sholden preie for þe pees, possession hem lettyþ;
Takeþ hire landes, ye lordes, and leteþ hem lyue by dymes.
If possession be poison, and inparfite hem make
[Charite] were to deschargen hem for holy chirches sake.

(15.553–66)

Appealing not to Christ as the model for the bishop, but to the Levite priests who survived on first fruits and tithes, Anima calls up the prophecy of God's angel that endowment would be the doom of the church to argue that now, "lords" must retake clerical possessions to return the church to apostolic standards.[46] The C-Text witnesses record "Charite were to deschargen," an emendation adopted by Kane and Donaldson for their B-Text edition.[47] In this compelling reading, the injunction to dispossess the clergy, though not unorthodox,[48] becomes much more pointed than in the B-Text's "Good were to deschargen," reminding bishops of charity as their primary duty and a charge to which they may be returned by force if necessary.[49] Crowding "knyghthod and kynde wit and þe commune [and] conscience" adversarially against the possessioner "bisshopes," Langland's verse drops rich prelates on the fringes of this loving community and threatens them with the loss of spiritual authority if they hold on to temporal possession. At this moment of crisis, the strict separation of social states and religious degrees, combined with a return to apostolic poverty, may offer the only hope for the reordering of charity.

Though Wyclif's call for disendowment stems from a more radical notion of priestly poverty and a more conservative view of lay power, Wyclif and Langland share a concern that clerical lordship is incompatible with charity, the basis of pastoral care. Into this broad field of complaint about clerical lordship and its distance from the apostolic model, Hilton will intervene to argue that for his reader, temporal lordship is precisely the element that links the lay lord to the bishop and thus to Christ's own example of charity, in the process recuperating *imitatio clerici* as a worthy endeavor. Making the argument for material possession and temporal authority as the bases for the layman's pastoral identity, Hilton will thoroughly "medle" the devotional and political realms, implicitly defending contemporary prelates in the process.

Mixed Life: *reforming regulation*

Writing for a layman wishing to abandon the world in search of contemplative life and responding to contemporary visions of lay lords and prelates as greedy, ignorant, and out of charity, Hilton positively connects the idea of self-regulation to the mingling of worldly and spiritual responsibilities.[50] His wealthy, responsible addressee, attracted as he is to spiritual pursuits, may bear a superficial resemblance to the lords Dame Studie complains about in Passus 10 of *Piers Plowman*. Her scathing speech implicates rich laymen and prelates in a shared cycle of gluttony, social pretense, and false piety:

> Elenge is þe halle, ech day in þe wike,
> Ther þe lord ne þe lady likeþ noȝt to sitte.
> Now haþ ech riche a rule to eten by hymselue
> In a pryuee parlour for pouere mennes sake,
> Or in a chambre wiþ a chymenee, and leue þe chief halle
> . . .
> I haue yherd heiȝe men etynge at þe table
> Carpen as þei clerkes were of crist and of hise myȝtes,
> And leyden fautes vpon þe fader þat formede vs alle,
> And carpen ayein cler[gie] crabbede wordes:
> "Why wolde oure Saueour suffre swich a worm in his blisse
> That bi[w]iled þe womman and þe [wye] after,
> Thoruȝ whic[h werk and wil] þei went to helle,
> And al hir seed for hir synne þe same deeþ suffrede?"
>
> (10.96–111)

On the one hand, self-consciously pious laity are isolating themselves, each in his or her own "pryuee parlour": the vogue for private devotion and proliferation of the personal "rule" have left dining rooms empty and the poor unfed, as rich people focus on spiritual self-improvement while ignoring their duty to give charity. On the other hand, as they "[c]arpen as þei clerkes were," the same lords also engage in vacuous after-dinner speculation, an ignorant form of *imitatio clerici* that broadcasts their own ignorance of theology and the negligence of their clerical teachers.

In his advice to the spiritually aspirant layman, Hilton offers an alternative to these extremes of pious self-absorption and indulgent speculation, both forms of uncharitable waste. Soliciting his own lordly addressee, Hilton posits life in the world as a potentially productive context for the expression of charity. In response to a personal piety that he seems to view as genuine, he writes, "Y knowe weel þe desire of þyn herte, þat þou ȝernest gretli to serue oure lord bi goostli occupacioun al holli, wiþoute lettynge or trobolynge o[f] wordeli bisynesse" (7.73–75). Pointing to the willful, all-consuming quality of his reader's "desire," Hilton suggests that his reader's interest in the spiritual life has caused him to imagine a barrier between "goostli occupacioun" and "wordeli bisynesse." But rather than faulting his charge for abandoning charity, Hilton strategically redirects his patron's "yearnings" toward a new religious discipline founded on the combination of "goostli occupacioun" and "wordeli bisynesse." Glossing the Song of Songs' signal phrase "ordinavit in me caritatem,"[51] he explains

> oure lord, ʒeuynge to me charite, sette it in ordre and in rule, þat it schulde not be lost þoruʒ myn vndiscrecioun. Riʒt so þis charite and þis desire þat oure lord haþ ʒeuen of his merci to þee is for to rulen and ordaynen hou þou schal pursue it aftir þi degree askeþ, and aftir þe lyuynge þat þou hast vsed bifore þis tyme. (8.82–87)

Bringing back the aforementioned "desire" in order to yoke it with the "charite" that must rule the Christian life, whether contemplative or active, Hilton makes the layman's personal spiritual ambition inseparable from his wider duty to love his neighbor. By furthermore defining this "charite and þis desire" as a form of responsibility – his duty is "for to rulen and ordaynen hou þou schal pursue it" – Hilton argues that this dual desire can only be fulfilled through the exercise of self-regulation.[52] He will not propose a self-isolating "rule" of the sort used by Langland's lonely diners: at the heart of this new discipline lies the reader's duty to reconcile his desire to "serve our lord" with his customary social "degree" and form of "lyuynge." Hilton uses "aftir" strategically here: not only to mean "according to," but also to stress that for his addressee the life of devotion comes belatedly and must be mingled carefully with the "lyuynge þat þou hast vsed *bifore* þis tyme." This prior "lyuynge" encompasses charitable responsibilities that the addressee may not simply shrug off for a life of contemplation.

In a small space, this passage reveals much about Hilton's strategy for bridging the gap between the cloister and the world. He characteristically insists upon the wisdom of mingling elements that his patron has tried to keep separate: "desire" and "charite," "wordeli" and "goostli," "bifore" and "aftir." This exposition posits a theory, but does not yet offer a plan, for how these combinations should take shape. Hilton's call to balance present spiritual desire with prior worldly life prepares the reader to emulate the role of the "spiritual gentleman," the prelate.

In his strategic bid to bring those elements positively together, Hilton argues that in fact the reader's material power entitles him to some of the same pastoral privileges as a prelate. The wealthy layman's responsibility for "keping" and "ruling" others closely recalls Gregory the Great's paradigm of the "third" life, which belongs, Hilton argues speciali to men of holi chirche, as to prelates and oþire curates which haue cure and souereynte ouer oþere men for to [kepe] and for to rule hem, boþe her bodies and principali heer soules . . . Vnto þise men it longeþ sumtyme [to] vsen werkes of actif lif, in help and sustenaunce of hem silf and of here suggettis and of oþere also, and sumtyme for to leuen al manere bisynesse outeward, and ȝeue hem vnto praieres and meditacions, redynge of hooli writ, and to oþere goostli occupacions. (14.144–53)

As Gregory had argued, the primary responsibility of the pastor (*pastor*, *rector*, *praelatus*, or *praepositus*) is balancing preservation and care of others with periods of contemplation: "Let the ruler be next to each one by sympathy, and soar above all in contemplation . . . that he may neither, while he seeketh things on high, despise the weakness of his neighbours; nor, being suited to the weakness of his neighbours, abandon the desire of things on high" (67–69).[53]

Hilton, however, places emphasis not only on "cure" and sympathy, but also on "souereynte," the ruling power that entitles the addressee to the privileged pastoral alternation of action and contemplation. For Hilton's addressee, a "temporal" man, sovereignty comes first, as a precondition to devotion, and in this "souereynte," the layman's status overlaps with the prelate's "degree." For as Hilton explains, the mixed life is proper not only to the rector in spiritual authority but also to

sum temporal men þe whiche haue souereynte wiþ moche auere [possession] of wordli goodis, and hauen also as it were lordschipe ouer oþere men for to gouerne and sustene hem, as a fadir haþ ouer his children, a maister ouer his seruauntes, and a lord ouere his tenantes, þe whiche men han also receyued of oure lord[is] ȝift grace of deuocion, and in partie sauoure of goostli occupacioun. Vnto þise men also longeþ [þis] medeled lif þat is boþe actif and contemplatif. (15.154–16.162)

Gregory is uneasy about prelates lowering themselves to deal with earthly matters, saying, "while the office of an earthly judge is exercised by the ruler of their souls, the care of the Pastor is set loose from the keeping of the flock" (91).[54] He also invokes Luke's warning that "no man can serve two masters" to stress the incompatibility of earthly and spiritual duties. In contrast, Hilton expands the "medeled lif" to the layman on the basis of his temporal possessions and responsibility to discipline others, making "souereynte" and "lordschipe" as well as care and teaching sources of the wealthy lord's entitlement and the ground for similarity among layman, prelate, and Christ. As Hilary Carey has noted, Hilton's passage takes a new position on lay spiritual life and religious discipline by implying that "secular authority can be considered as tantamount to a religious vocation."[55]

If the lay lord's authority, derived from property and "wordeli goodis," parallels that of a prelate, who derives his authority from Christ via the keys given to Peter, then the reader's model for identification must be a model of infinite power and humility: Christ himself. According to Gregory, Christ embodied the first mixed life, and Hilton borrows Gregory's portrait of Christ's life with some notable alterations. Hilton affirms that "oure lord, for to stire summe to vse þis medeled liyf, took upon him self þe persoone of sich manere men, boþe of prelates of hooli chirche and oþere sich as aren disposid as I haue seid, and ʒaue hem ensample bi his owen worchynge þat þei schulden vsen medeled liyf as he dide" (17.177–181). Hilton models this passage on *Regula Pastoralis* 2.5, where Gregory states, "the Truth Himself, manifested to us by taking upon Him our humanity,[56] in the mountain continueth in prayer, and worketh miracles in the cities, paving, that is, a way for good rulers to follow; that, although they even now long for the highest things through contemplation, they may, nevertheless, be mingled with the necessities of the weak by sympathy" (71).[57]

In altering Gregory's general "humanitas nostra" to the specific "persoone" of "prelates," or, as the Vernon manuscript group reads, "prelates & curatis,"[58] Hilton suggests that "prelates" might provide a direct and even accessible link to the ideal of the mixed life. No stranger to contemporary controversies over spiritual power, Hilton was surely aware of the contested meanings of "prelate" in the ongoing debate about pastoral care and clerical possession. If the text reads simply "prelates," it may be that Hilton is using the term expansively, as FitzRalph famously had, to refer to "all those with cure of souls, 'maiores atque minores' . . . curates, vicars, rectors and parish chaplains."[59] Scase argues that the term "prelate," though unstable in meaning, was often deployed anticlerically "to connote misused institutional power and, increasingly, wealth."[60] In the Visio section of *Piers Plowman*, prelates are implicated in the money economy as Mede links them to lay rulers in a chain of inescapable obligation: "Emperours and Erles and alle manere lordes / [Thoruʒ] ʒiftes han yonge men to [yerne] and to ryde. / The Pope [wiþ hise] prelates presentʒ underfonge[þ], / And medeþ men h[y]mseluen to mayntene hir lawes" (3.213–216). The parallelism between the reliance of "lordes" on "yiftes" and the dependence of "prelates" on "presents" speaks volumes about the way money has replaced charity in the performance of pastoral care for these two groups of rulers. Rather than a debased circuit of economic dependence, Hilton envisions a hopeful continuum of virtue among prelates, others with sovereignty, Christ, and the aspiring layman. The alternative reading "prelates & curatis," while de-emphasizing "prelate" as a universal term, encourages the layman to identify with pastoral care at all levels, pointing to a shared pastoral ethic between the higher and lower echelons of the clergy.

Seeking to return to the apostolic ideal and to suggest that it may still be possible to emulate in the present day, Hilton's vision of the life of Christ and the bishop posits the alternation of charitable action with God-loving contemplation as the duty of bishops and lay lords alike. First Hilton constructs a parallel between the life of Christ and that of the "holy bishop," showing Christ dividing his earthly life between public teaching and private contemplation. At one time he

> comouned wiþ men and medeled wiþ men, schewynge to hem his deedes of merci, for he tauȝte þe vncouþ and vnkunynge bi his prechynge, he vesited þe sike and heeled hem of here sooris, he fedde þe hongry, and he comforted þe sori. And anoþer tyme he lefte þe conuersacioun of alle wordeli men and of his disciples [also], and wente in to dissert upon þe hillis, and contynued alle þe nyȝt in praieres aloone. (17.181–18.188)

Without going so far as to assert that Christ had possessions, Hilton offers the life of the bishop, in which property and secular responsibilities play an integral part, as a reflection of Christ's harmonious alternation:

> This liyf ledden and vsiden þise *hooli bischopis* [here] bifore whiche hadden *cure of mennys soulis and mynistracioun of temporal goodes. For þise hooli men leften not vttirli þe ministracioun and þe lokynge and þe dispendynge of wordli goodes and ȝaf hem hooli to contemplacioun,* as moche grace of contemplacioun as þei hadden, but þei lefte ful ofte here owen reste in contemplacioun, whanne þei hadde ful lyuere haue be stille þerat, for loue of hire euene-Cristene, and entirmeted hem wiþ wordli bisynesse in helpynge of heer suggettis. And *soþeli þat was charite,* for wisili and discreteli þei departed here lyuynge in two. (19.196–206, emphasis added)

In contrast to Gregory, who had argued that when "any one after the habit of holiness mixeth himself with earthly business . . . the reverence that was paid to him is slighted and becometh pale" (95),[61] Hilton emphasizes the careful use and administration of "temporal goodes" as part of the unbroken continuum between Christ and these "hooli bischopes." The Vernon manuscript group depicts these bishops in the present tense ("leden and vsen") in what may be an effort to link these ancient exemplary figures to contemporary bishops. Hilton emphasizes "cure of mennys soulis and mynistracioun of temporal goodes" as continuous and constitutive of each other, implicitly countering the notion that spiritual and temporal duties and properties should be kept separate. By drawing three-fold attention to these bishops' exercise of "þe ministracioun and þe lokynge and þe dispendynge of wordli goodes," Hilton skirts the mention of clerical possession while implying that clerically managed "wordli goodes" are in safe hands. He implies that by looking after their temporal properties as commanded, in imitation of Christ's own activities, apostolic and contemporary prelates do nothing to disturb the order of charity, whatever Wyclif and his followers might suggest. The prelates' balance between active and contemplative forms of charity offers a model for the property-owning lay man who must balance his own devotional urges with administrative duty.

In *Piers Plowman*'s complex, shifting vision of prelates, the order of charity is palpably difficult either to maintain or to imitate. Langland's fleeting episcopal images, while they do not obviously refer to the Gregorian model, still less to Hilton, as Hussey has shown, present extremes of rigor and lassitude that call into question the very idea of lay imitation. How can one imitate a broken clergy? Langland must look to church history to find suitable models, albeit ones now neglected. Conscience's vision of Christ in Passus 15 as the "pastor bonus" whose model of giving his life for his sheep[62] is now disregarded by popes and prelates, briefly envisions Christ as archbishop.[63] But in decrying contemporary pastoral failure – "What pope or prelat now parfourneþ þat crist highte . . . ?" – this vision stresses the unrepeatability of Christ's story and sacrifice as he "bicam man of a maide and *metropolitanus*, / And baptised and bishined wiþ þe blode of his herte / Alle þat wilned and wolde wiþ Inwit bileue it" (15.516–18). The pastoral acts of baptism and preaching become inextricable from Christ's Passion, a self-sacrifice that may only be followed by saintly bishop-martyrs such as Thomas Becket, who died "for cristes loue . . . / And for þe riȝt of al þis reume" – specifically to resist the encroachments of civil authority upon the church.[64] Here the essential connection between Christ and the bishop lies not in the balance between self and other, worldly and spiritual goods, but in the *bonus pastor*'s fierce resistance to accommodate his own bodily needs or the demands of secular society.

While Christ's "episcopal martyrdom" embodies radical action that no contemporary bishop or worldly lord may even approach, *Piers Plowman* also shows bishops failing to embody the love of God that might flourish in an atmosphere of contemplative rest. Langland's bishops seem to have lost the ability to express either parts of the double commandment, and Wit's scathing remarks in Passus 9 provide an unexpected context for Hilton's recuperation of the episcopal life. Noting a generalized lack of clerical charity, Wit proclaims

> Bisshopes shul be blamed for beggeres sake.
> He is [Iugged wiþ] Judas þat ȝyueþ a Iaper siluer
> And biddeþ þe beggere go for his broke cloþes:
> . . .
> He dooþ noȝt wel þat dooþ þus, ne drat noȝt god almyȝty,
> [Ne] loueþ noȝt Salamons sawes þat Sapience tauȝte:
> *Inicium sapiencie timor domini.*
> That dredeþ god, he dooþ wel; þat dredeþ hym for loue
> And [dredeþ hym] noȝt for drede of vengeaunce dooþ þerfore þe bettre;
> He dooþ best þat wiþdraweþ hym by daye and by nyȝte
> To spille any speche or any space of tyme:
> *Qui offendit in vno in omnibus est reus.*
>
> (9.92–101)

The bishop's preference for an entertaining "japer" over one whose "broke clothes" announce his dire poverty marks an egregious failure of charity. This failure to show love to the beggar in the form of hospitality – one of the priest's key duties in canon law – is logically linked to a fundamental lapse in the "drede" of God that should stem from love rather than fear.[65] Although the sentence continues into the next line, we may also read the line "He dooþ best þat wiþdraweþ hym by daye and by nyȝte" as complete in itself, offering another fleeting suggestion of a contemplative withdrawal in which, far from the distractions of minstrels, love of God might grow.[66] In this passage appears a fragmented reflection of elements that if rejoined might make for an ideal bishop's life.

In response to his reader's desire for contemplation, and reflecting his own conviction in the superiority of contemplative life, Hilton does not hide the fact that the holy bishops he mentions would much rather have stayed in contemplative rest: they "ful lyuere haue be stille" (19.202–03). In fact he makes a virtue of their preference for contemplation, which resembles his addressee's own "desire" for "goostli occupacioun." As he declares after describing the bishops' alternation of action and contemplation, "soþeli þat was charite": charity lies in the combination of action and contemplation, which can only proceed, for this addressee, from a particularly episcopal overlap between temporal and spiritual obligations.

In his effort to posit the prelate's life as the model of Christ-like perfection, Hilton presses the parallelism between "spiritual souereynte" and "temporal souereynte" as a function of charity, emphasizing the public "cure and gouernance of oþere" as forms, above all, of pastoral work to which their practitioners are bound. He summarizes the mixed life of the bishop as an oscillation between the lower and higher works of charity, a combination that fulfills the double commandment to love God and neighbor and links the prelate positively to the lord:

O tyme þei fulfilleden þe lowere part of charite bi we[rk]es of actif lif, for þei were bounden þerto bi takynge of hire prelacies, and an oþir [tyme] þei fulfilleden þe hiȝere partie of charite in contemplacioun of God and of goosteli þynges bi praieres and meditacions, and so þei hadden ful charite to god and to hire euene-Cristen . . . þise men þat were in prelacie, and oþere also þat weren [hooli] temporal men. (19.206–21.220)

By adding "hooli temporal men," Hilton emphasizes that this conjunction is no paradox, attributing to the worldly men the same fullness of charity as the prelates described before. He further blurs the boundary between men in these two states by noting, "for siche a man þat is in spiritual souereynte as prelacie, in cure [and] gouernaunce of oþere as prelates and curates ben, or in t[em]poral souereynte as wordeli lordes and maistris aren, I hoolde þis liyf medeled best, and most bihoofful to hem as longe as þei are bounden þerto" (21.223–27). For men bound to remain in the world, these forms of service are the most crucial part of the "medeled" life: the discipline of the lord and prelate, following Christ.

SPIRITUALIZING COVETISE: THE END OF THE MIXED LIFE

Hilton's final step in the literary reform of the rich man into pastoral discipline is to reconfigure covetise (covetousness) as a spiritual desire, envisioning the reader's assimilation with Christ in a kingly/pastoral position at the "last ende." This rehabilitation draws upon a pastoral tradition stretching back to Matthew's gospel through John Chrysostom and into the fourteenth century. Hilton's vision resonates with new force when considered alongside Langland's ambivalent treatments of covetise, in which the impulse may be suppressed but cannot be fully spiritualized amid a wider crisis in clerical discipline. The sin of covetise, an excessive greed for material possessions, especially others' goods, holds obvious interest for any author interested in reconciling material with spiritual concerns. The fourteenth-century priest's manual *Speculum Christiani* features numerous warnings about covetise, beginning with commentary on the seventh commandment against theft. Of those who "for-saken rightwysnesse for temperal gudes," the author liberally renders Augustine: "O dampnable wynnynge of the! Thou couetouse wreche! Thou getest mone and leseste rightwysnesse, the which man oghte not to lese for any price of gude vndur heuen."[67] Somewhat less creatively, the text also translates patristic sayings about the incompatibility of wealth and spiritual pursuits, such as this passage from Ecclesiasticus: "[t]hat man is ful blessed that is founden wyth-oute spote of synne and that has not goon a-way aftyr golde bi couetise."[68]

In *Piers Plowman*, "covetise" possesses a remarkable capacity to degrade and to elevate depending on the circumstances.[69] Within Passus 15 alone, the term and its verb forms vacillate in their associations. Readers encounter Covetise as a bedraggled figure who confesses to dishonest work practices as well as theft (15.186–297), but the possibility for renovating covetise also appears. Earlier "Charite" has been as described as coveting not property or riches, but spiritual wealth: "alle manere meschiefs in myldenesse he suf-freþ. / Coueiteþ he noon erþely good, but heueneriche blisse" (15.174–75). This recuperation recalls the term's malleability in pastoral contexts, where coveting might be either a worldly or a spiritual act. In *Speculum Christiani*, anticipating Langland's declaration that Charite "chaffareþ noȝt" (15.165), the adaptor redefines "couete" in reference to the spiritual duties of curates:

He es a marchaunde [*mercenarius*] that holdeȝ place, office, or dignite of cure, and sekeȝ not wynnynge of soules. Thei be marchauntȝ that taken cure of soule not for thei couete to gouerne [*cupiunt regere*] and kepe the chirche in ryghtwysnes and holynes, bot for thei [couete] to be made rych and be honourde in worldly worschipe be-for other. Ther-for thei fallen in-to the trappe and temptacion of the deuyl. (170.26–32)

Although pastors should avoid using offices and power to aggrandize them-selves, the author implies that the highest form of clerical desire would be a *holy* covetise focused on "wynnynge of soules" and properly "governing" the church and its members.[70]

Hilton's *Mixed Life* culminates by exhorting the wealthy addressee to join those who embody charity by coveting "heueneriche blisse," to use Langland's terms. Hilton envisions the apotheosis of the mixed life as an assimilation of the lay lord with the good pastor, a transformation made possible by unstinting devotion to heavenly rather than earthly things. Like Hilton's earlier construction of the mixed life as a pastoral imitation of Christ and holy bishops, this vision of spiritual attainment not only offers a solution for his particular addressee, it also envisions a renewed order of charity in which worldly and spiritual authority resolve effortlessly into each other. In revealing contrast, the final passus of *Piers Plowman* shows covetise frustrating such resolution at every turn. Passus 15 offers fleeting possibilities for the ordering of charity through the mutual imitations of laymen, Christ, and prelates, and in Passus 19, the enigmatic hybrid figure of Piers demonstrates his own exemplary form of spiritual covetise. But as failures of clergy and laity to spiritualize covetise usher in Pride and Antichrist, the poem highlights the social crises and spiritual ambiguities that must finally be excluded from Hilton's vision if the wealthy layman's spiritual transformation is to be successful.

In Passus 15, which as Lawler notes "concerns itself almost constantly with the clergy, without quite achieving a clear theme,"[71] Piers Plowman reappears to offer what may be hope for a productive mutual imitation of layman and bishop.[72] Piers's lay–clerical hybridity at this moment seems critical to his ability to "knowe" charity, as Anima announces to Will,

> Therfore by colour ne by clergie knowe shaltow [hym] neuere,
> Neiþer þoruӡ wordes ne werkes, but þoruӡ wil oone,
> And þat knoweþ no clerk ne creature on erþe
> But Piers þe Plowman, *Petrus id est christus.*
>
> (15.209–12)

The riddling rapprochement of Piers, Peter, and Christ has been subject to much commentary and disagreement: I cite it here in order to register the suggestion, notably tentative in contrast to Hilton's confident assimilations, that the layman, the first bishop, and Christ must be connected in some way if the search for charity is to continue.[73] The implications of this grouping are of course ambivalent: Piers is cast as "vir apostolicus" even as his status as agricultural laborer, elaborated in earlier passus, separates him from the failings of the wealthy church.[74] In order to stand for the apostolic life and function, in Aers's terms, as a "lens through which Charity's 'persone' is finally disclosed,"[75] Piers must transcend earthly "clerks" while somehow embodying the best of clerical authority and lay industry.

But the virtue of charity cannot be limited to the realm of apostolic poverty: in typically protean fashion this virtue is embodied moments later in a prelate's dress, appearing in a new tableau that suggests even wealthy clergy and laity might embody a common charity if they avoid covetise. The unstable form of the following passage evokes the difficulty of grasping charity and the fleeting chance for cooperation between prelate and layman. Anima says

> I haue yseyen charite also syngen and reden,
> Riden and rennen in raggede wedes,
> Ac biddynge as beggeris biheld I hym neuere.
> Ac in riche robes raþest he walkeþ,

> Ycalled and ycrymyled and his crowne yshaue.
> And in a freres frokke he was yfounden ones,
> Ac it is fern [and fele yeer in] Fraunceis tyme;
> In þat secte siþþe to selde haþ he ben [knowe].
> Riche men he recomendeþ, and of hir robes takeþ
> That wiþouten wiles ledeþ [wel] hir lyues:
> *Beatus est diues qui &c.*
> In kynges court he comeþ ofte þer þe counseil is trewe,
> Ac if coueitise be of þe counseil he wol noȝt come þerInne.
>
> (15.225–36)

Here Charity appears in the prelate's tonsure, cap, and robe performing liturgical functions as a priest. In contrast to his very brief appearance in "freres frokke," he remains in the "robes" provided by "riche men" who also persist in holiness. In good pastoral style, Langland cites Ecclesiasticus 31:8, the passage featured in *Speculum Christiani* ("blessed is the rich man that is found without blemish: and that hath not gone after gold, nor put his trust in money nor in treasures"). Although this clerical figure is not above appearing in secular court, in his rejection of "coueitise" he mirrors the conduct of the rich man of Ecclesiasticus, to whom he provided a model. For the moment, the cycle of lay–clerical imitation seems harmonious.

Hilton manages, as I have shown above, to combine "temporal" lordship with "deuocioun" in his pastoral-sounding description of the lay man's "lordschipe ouere oþere men for to gouerne and sustene hem, as a fadir haþ ouer his children, a maister ouer his seruauntes, and a lord ouere his tenantes, þe whiche men han also receyued of oure lord[is] ȝift grace of deuocioun" (15.156–59). But wealth and pastoral capacity can coexist only briefly in *Piers Plowman*, as the vision of cooperation evaporates with the unsurprising revelation that bishops, who should combine the virtues of fathers, masters, and lords toward all their subjects, have let charity fall into abeyance:

> [Amonges erchebisshopes and bisshopes, [for beggeres sake],
> For to wonye wiþ hem his wone was som tyme,
> And cristes patrymonye to þe poore parcelmele dele;
> Ac auarice haþ þe keyes now and kepeþ for his kynnesmen
> And for his seketoures & his seruauntȝ, & som for hir children.]
>
> (15.244–48)

Having overtaken charity as the keeper of Christ's patrimony, Avarice has now established himself "Amonges erchebisshopes and bisshopes." In this final line Avarice embodies in a worldly form the very duties to dependents that Hilton exhorts his addressee to spiritualize.

Although Piers does not represent the mixed life that Hilton constructs for his addressee, the Plowman embodies a positive form of hybridity and becomes an exemplary practitioner of spiritual covetise, striving in the words of *Speculum Christiani* to "kepe the chirche in ryghtwysnes and holynes" until worldly covetise finally rushes back, a fact of life for laity and clergy alike (170.29–30). In Passus 19, taking on Christ's mandate to edify the church in the world, Piers embodies patient lay poverty and non-coercive clerical ploughing, seeking "wynnynge of soules" by instructing others in the critical tenets of the faith, administering the sacraments, and preaching. His spiritual form of covetise depends for its success on the commune's willingness to perform the mandate "redde quod debes" (pay what you owe). A command with a particular connection to restitution in the context of penance,[76] this motto also functions, as others have shown, to highlight Piers's role in ensuring that every Christian practices the most basic duty of justice, repaying the "debt of love to God and to his neighbor."[77]

Despite Piers's efforts, this passus demonstrates the fundamental difficulty of reconfiguring covetise on a broad social scale, as "redde quod debes" proves impossible for lay members of the commune, in the aftermath of the plague and government-imposed wage constraints, either to understand or to follow.[78] At the outset, even as Piers and Conscience receive their commission from Grace, they are warned that Antichrist waits with false prophets who "Shullen come and be curatours ouer kynges and Erles; / And Pride shal be Pope, Prynce of holy chirche, / Coueitise and vnkyndenesse Cardinals hym to lede" (19.222–24). When Pride's forces do attack, covetise infuses not only the church but the very fabric of daily life, muddling Conscience such that merchants become unable (or unwilling) to distinguish between "right," "wrong," and "vsure" (19.350). Though administration of communion is proposed as a sure defense for this attack on Christian Unity, the sticking point is widespread refusal to follow "redde quod debes," to offer restitution in the fullest sense of the word. Both the commune and the individual capitalist remain suspicious of this requirement. For the brewer aiming to profit in a tight market, there can be no contest between material and spiritual profit: "Thikke ale and þynne ale; for that is my kynde, / And noȝt hakke after holynesse; holde þi tonge, Conscience!" (19.401–02). This comment may emblematize spiritual "unkyndnes" (Covetise's partner), but the impulse is instantly recognizable as Langland exposes the toll that market realities may take on religious aspirations. In *Piers Plowman*'s final battle of Passus 20, Covetise, "armed" with Avarice, storms the scene followed by Simony, who convinces prelates to "holden wiþ Antecrist, hir temporaltees to saue" (20.128), as clerics reveal themselves to be past redemption and the entire penitential economy is thrown into question. Piers has disappeared from view, and Conscience must finally leave the edifice of the church to seek him.[79]

But the pursuit of "holynesse" is precisely the goal for Hilton's ambitious addressee, a lay man who, in his dedication to the life "þat is boþe actif and contemplatif," must somehow transcend the extremes depicted in *Piers Plowman*: the false religiosity of the rich lords seen earlier and the naked mercantilism of the individual capitalist. Reconfiguring the quality of covetise is, for Hilton, the means to usher his lay addressee into a final *imitatio Christi*. In contrast to Langland's vision of Antichrist, which plunges the fate of the conscience into peril and extends the search for charity into an uncertain future, Hilton's guide intervenes to preserve charity, spiritualizing covetise in order to fulfill the vision he has been developing of a lay pastoral *imitatio clerici*. If Langland threatens, in Aers's phrase, to make the "very possibility of the hierarchic, stable, authoritative and thoroughly spiritual church of received ideology, something irrelevant to the contemporary pursuit of holiness as his vision evokes it,"[80] Hilton's hopeful vision of "heueneli couetous men" assimilates rich lord, pastor, and Christ himself, emphasizing the relevance of that church to his own addressee's pursuit of holiness. Hilton's meditation on the joys of heaven and the pains of hell spiritualizes desire for acquisition to offer the lay reader a vision of a regal imitation of Christ "at the laste end," a bringing together of *imitatio clerici* and *imitatio Christi*.

Referencing the gospel and the homily tradition, Hilton rehearses the difference once and for all between earthly and spiritual forms of covetise, defusing the term's dangerous equivocality. He warns, "Many men aren couetous of wordli worschipes and erþeli richesse, [and þenken ny3t and day], dremyng and wakyng, howe and by what meenes þei my3te come þerto, and forþi þei forgeten þe mynde of hem self, þe peynes of helle [and] þe ioies of heuene" (59.711–60.715). But, he concludes,

I praie þee, be þou couetous of þe ioies of heuene, and þou schalt haue worschipes and richesses þat euere schal laste. For at þe last ende, whanne worldli couetous men bringen noo good in hire handes, for alle here worschipes and her richesse aren torned in to nou3t saue sorwe and peyne, þan schal heueneli couetous men, þat forsaken truli alle veyne worschipes and richesse of þis world, or ellis, 3if þei haue richesse and worschipes, þei setten not bi hem, ne here loue ne heer likynge in hem,[81] but leuen ai in drede and in mekenesse and in hope and in sorwe sumtyme, and abiden þe merci of God pacienteli, þei schullen þanne haue fulli þat þei heere coueitede, for þei schul be crowned as kynges, and stie [variants: set/sitte] up wiþ oure lord Ihesu in to þe blisse of heuene. (60.719–61.732)[82]

As Hilton suggests, fully pursuing the implications of this transformation of covetise from a vice to a virtue, right-minded individuals may be "heueneli couetous" even in the possession of "worschipes and richesses" if they renounce worldly desire and embody properly penitential virtues, including the "drede" of God that should be rooted in love rather than fear. As the "heueneli couetous" rise up to join Christ – briefly glimpsed in *Piers Plowman* retiring "an heigh vp into heuene" (19.191) to wait until judgment day when he would "rewarde hym right wel þat *reddit quod debet*" (19.193) – they will finally receive "þat þei heere coueitede": a recompense couched in the language of wealth as a moment of "having." This "having," which might be understood as the payment for a life of "redde quod debes," recalls and spiritualizes Hilton's original description of his addressee as one possessing "souereynte wiþ moche auere of wordli goodis," while extending the possibility of such reward to others.

In finally answering the question of how the rich man might be admitted to heaven, Hilton adapts the redemptions of covetise that formed part of its interpretation in the context of advice for pastors: not only the above passage from *Speculum Christiani* that considers "wynnynge of soules," but another idea from the *Speculum*, which may derive from Chrysostom's homily on Matthew 19: "He that coueteȝ glorie in heuen dredeȝ not aduersite in erthe" ("Qui gloriam concupiscit in celo, opprobria non timet in terris").[83] If this phrase seems familiar, it has already appeared above, as one of *Piers Plowman's* many fleeting definitions of charity ("alle manere meschiefs in myldenesse he suffreþ. / Coueiteþ he noon erþely good, but heueneriche blisse"). Where this vision of charity is one of many that must remain theoretical and unfulfilled in the teeming social world of the poem, it becomes a critical governing image for Hilton's *Mixed Life*. His image of a final endowment and "crowning" of the spiritually ambitious man, his transformation into a heavenly as well as an earthly lord, aptly concludes a text that repeatedly stresses the reconciliation of material and social responsibilities as a prelude to spiritual fulfillment. That this fulfillment is portrayed not in terms of feeling or knowing, but of *having* both material possession and spiritual lordship, underscores Hilton's larger argument that material power must be made complementary with spiritual desire if there is to be any hope of making *imitatio clerici* a viable mode of lay religious discipline.

Even Piers Plowman, a figure who encompasses past and present, laity and clergy, cannot finally mediate between Langland's uncompromising vision of the *bonus pastor* and his disillusion with contemporary clergy. Possession engenders failures of charity in the prelates who should be exemplars of that virtue, making them unsuitable as leaders of the faithful or as models of religious discipline. While covetise has the potential to be spiritualized, its transformation is continually frustrated by the vicissitudes of social life and clerical vice. But Hilton's *Mixed Life*, working in the mode of accommodation that defines his brand of lay spiritual guidance, salvages the bishop's role as viable for the eagerly pious lay lord, in the face of satire and polemic that pictured it as bankrupt. Responsive to the Wycliffite critique of clerical lordship, which cast the temporal and spiritual realms as radically incompatible, Hilton's vision of *imitatio clerici* promotes continuity of worldly and spiritual responsibilities as the key to imitating Christ's mixed life, as well as to deepening intellectual and practical mutuality between lay reader and priestly author. At least in the rarefied realm of guidance, the careful adaptation of clerical disciplinary categories manages to expand lay spiritual authority while defending clerical tradition.

In the next chapter, I return to the spiritual guide *Book to a Mother*, a work with a more vexed relation to hierarchy and less inclination to be accommodating. Yet this guide also performs a careful literary mediation between lay spiritual aspiration and the pressures of controversy, envisioning lay preaching as the terrain for the laywoman's *imitatio clerici* and reform into Christ-like exemplarity.

CHAPTER 4

Clerical widows and the reform of preaching

As the Wife of Bath concludes her *Tale*, Friar Huberd has some choice
words for her:

> Ye han heer touched, also moot I thee,
> In scole-matere greet difficulte,
> Ye han seyd muche thyng right wel, I seye;
> But, dame, heere as we ryde by the weye,
> Us nedeth nat to speken but of game,
> And lete auctoritees, on Goddes name,
> To prechyng and to scoles of clergye.[1]

It is not clear whether the friar is responding specifically to the *Tale*, with
its depiction of the hag's sermon on "gentilesse," or to the Wife's own
Prologue sermon on the "wo that is in mariage": he probably objects to
both. Either way, his comment not only implies that moral "scole-matere"
may be unfit matter for pilgrimage tale-telling, but more significantly
registers his resistance to the appropriation of clerical "auctoritees" and a
"prechynge" voice by this widowed "dame." Whether or not the Friar is
alluding to "[l]ate fourteenth-century Lollardly activities," it is clear that
"his comments read as a reaction to the Wife's words which threaten the
established monopoly of authorized men on religious interpretation."[2] The
authority to preach, a public form of "religious interpretation" and always a
contested element of clerical discipline, had rarely been more controversial
than during the last decades of the fourteenth century, when debate began
to rage over the proposition by some Wycliffites that laypeople, women
included, should be able to preach the gospel. In this chapter I consider
Book to a Mother together with dissenting discourses and the *Wife of Bath's
Prologue* to argue for the centrality of preaching to *Book to a Mother's* new
vision of lay religious discipline.

Andrew Galloway notes in connection with the Wife of Bath that
"[w]omen, excluded from learned culture even in the late Middle Ages,

are well suited to speak to the desires for intellectual authority felt by the whole class of those traditionally excluded, the 'educated or half-educated laity' emerging in the late Middle Ages."[3] Likewise, *Book to a Mother*, while intended for a specific woman, makes the author's mother stand for the larger body of laity desiring instruction. As the author announces, "I desire euerych man and womman and child to be my moder, for Crist seyþ: he þat doþ his Fader wille is his broþer, suster and moder" (1.2–4).[4] But while *Book to a Mother* thus begins to evoke the familiar medieval image of the laity as a symbolically "feminized entity," the author does not use this association with the feminine to raise insurmountable barriers between "clergy and laity, masculine and feminine . . . learned and 'lewd.'"[5] Instead, as already seen in Chapter 2, *Book to a Mother* invites the reader to understand her love for Christ in a particularly *clerical* way, while insisting on the specificity and unassailability of the author's own sacerdotal authority.[6]

Not only inducting the widow-mother and other potential lay readers into textual forms of "intellectual authority," but also offering access to evangelical teaching authority that shades into Christ-like forms of preaching, *Book to a Mother* operates in parallel with early Wycliffite arguments that the authority to preach resides not in ecclesiastical office but in personal virtue, as manifest in imitation of Christ and the apostles. But the subject of *Book to a Mother* is a figure of carefully crafted intellectual and spiritual authority who manages to be "clerical" without encroaching upon priestly terrain, to occupy as fully as possible the narrowing orthodox space for lay spiritual authority. The *Book* offers a reformist vision of lay *imitatio clerici* as *imitatio Christi*, proposing to empower the reader and criticize the corruptions of the mendicants much as the Wycliffites did, but without abandoning sacramental authority or priestly voice to lay readers.

By juxtaposing *Book to a Mother*'s clerical widow with Chaucer's threateningly textual female preacher Alison, the Wife of Bath, whose positions resonate with Wycliffite textual literalism and opposition to vowed chastity, I highlight the *Book*'s reformist view of the widowed mother as a figure for lay spiritual transformation under priestly supervision. Where *Book to a Mother* promotes readerly identification with female and male models whose teaching issues equally in imitations of Christ's preaching, Alison's public, textual preaching embodies a "self-interested" *imitatio clerici* that explicitly refuses Christ's example. The comparison will shed light on the capacity of spiritual guidance to reform, without fully radicalizing, the intersections of gender, religious status, and spiritual authority.

TEACHING, PREACHING, AND GENDER: A VOLATILE COMBINATION

Before investigating how *Book to a Mother* makes the clerical preaching widow, as opposed to the silent nun or anchoress, a figure of identification for women and laity more generally, it will be helpful to consider the inter-related prohibitions on lay and female preaching that came under attack during the last decades of the fourteenth century, roughly the period of the *Book* and the *Wife of Bath's Prologue*. Although the dating of both texts is uncertain, *Book to a Mother* was probably composed *c.* 1370–90, probably slightly earlier than the *Wife of Bath's Prologue*, which has been dated to the early to mid-1390s.[7] The text's editor, who locates *Book to a Mother* in the 1370s, claims that while the author likely had an acquaintance with Wyclif's thought, he remained "untroubled in his possession of orthodox teaching."[8] Nevertheless, as already seen in Chapter 2, the *Book* author's expression of reformist attitudes toward lay spiritual capacity and skepti-cism of many in clerical office show him turning this "orthodox teaching" in rather polemical directions.

An eclectic approach to devout practice also surfaces in the fifteenth-century manuscripts of *Book to a Mother*, all produced in the West Mid-lands, in which the work appears with a range of other religious texts, including catechetical material, contemplative guides, Wycliffite-sounding polemical works, and sometimes all of the above.[9] The only fourteenth-century witness to the work, also a Midlands production, is London, British Library, MS Egerton 826. In this volume, *Book to a Mother* (the codex's only text) is now incomplete, ending about a third of the way through.[10] Despite its incompleteness, this manuscript, copied by three scribes, offers a revealing contemporary response to *Book to a Mother* and its brand of orthodox reformism. Alan Fletcher has suggested that this manuscript may derive from a north-west Midlands scriptorium or center that produced an "ideologically mixed" output of books, some clearly Wycliffite, but others that combined controversial texts with unexceptional ones, its scribes working in "a context in which the boundaries of theological acceptability had not yet been tightly drawn, or at least, not yet legally enforced to any formidable extent."[11] The first scribe of MS Egerton 826 also contributed to a manuscript containing Wycliffite sermons, and he copied parts of the Wycliffite New Testament in another volume.[12] One of the two other MS Egerton 826 scribes added numerous red headings to the volume: these headings provide a running guide to important topics in the *Book*. I suggest throughout this chapter that MS Egerton 826's red headings, playing off the content of *Book to a Mother*, take advantage of the freedom this late fourteenth-century context afforded. The manuscript highlights the *Book*'s idiosyncratic combination of reverence for sacramental practice, angry critique of the religious orders, and pointed emphasis on the layperson's capacity to imitate the teaching and preaching of Mary, Tobias, and even Christ himself.

Book to a Mother may date from the 1380s, though its confident biblicism and willingness to probe the boundaries of lay and clerical practice suggest that it was written before Bible translation and lay preaching became subject to controversy and organized persecution. The most heated debate over lay preaching likely took place later than the composition of *Book to a Mother*, but I consider this debate first, to suggest that the work anticipates many of the same questions that would become critical to Wycliffite writers. *Book to a Mother* mediates between orthodoxy and Wycliffism in its careful deconstruction of traditional barriers between teaching and preaching, lay and clerical, female and male forms of authority.

Preaching was a jealously guarded privilege even before the early Wycliffite controversies made support for unauthorized preaching possible evidence of heterodoxy. The definition of preaching was fluid in the later Middle Ages and depended upon textual and practical traditions upheld by those in authority. As Claire Waters observes, "[w]hile the performance of preaching, like the performance of gender, has no explicit script, it draws on both Scripture and an authoritative lineage of performance, and those origins structured late medieval theorists' attempts to create and defend the boundaries of preaching."[13] Although the dominant definition of preaching was "the public explication of the sacred text,"[14] moral preaching of the sort first practiced by John the Baptist might involve non-textual exhortation "to restrain vices and add to faith and good morals."[15] Both were unequivocally forbidden to laity. The priest's guide *Speculum Christiani* distinguishes carefully between preaching as an official act and teaching as a work of mercy:

Grete differens es be-twene prechynge and techynge. Prechynge es in a place where es clepynge to-gedyr or foluynge of pepyl in holy dayes in chyrches or othe[r] certeyn places and tymes . . . And it longeth to hem that been ordeynede ther-to, the whych haue iurediccion and auctorite, and to noon othyr. Techynge es that eche body may enforme and teche hys brothyr in euery place and in conable tyme, os he seeth that it be spedful. For this es a gostly almesdede, to whych euery man es bounde that hath cunnynge.[16]

As Robert of Basevorn had earlier asserted in his *Forma Praedicandi* (1322), effective preaching depended upon the proper relation of three elements:

"purity of life, competent knowledge, and authority."[17] Of these, "authority" was the only objective standard, but the right to preach was not guaranteed even to those with priestly ordination. Basevorn begins his discussion in exclusionary terms:

No lay person or Religious, unless permitted by a Bishop or the Pope, and no woman, no matter how learned or saintly, ought to preach. Nor is it enough for one to say that he was commissioned by God, unless he clearly proves this, for the heretics are wont to make this claim. From this it appears that parish priests cannot preach unless permitted by the Bishop or the Pope, nor is it enough that they be allowed by the rectors.[18]

As Helen Spencer notes, according to Basevorn's view, which was finally codified by Arundel's 1407 Constitutions, even the seemingly intuitive notion that all priests should be able to preach was not upheld: "[e]ven before the alarm over Wycliffism, the reluctance of those who, like Basevorn, were unwilling to concede preaching rights *ex officio* to unbeneficed clergy, was rooted in fear that this less well educated, relatively mobile class would disseminate erroneous doctrine."[19]

The church's effort to limit preaching to beneficed priests ran directly counter to Wyclif's emphasis on preaching as the fundamental responsibility of every priest: this conviction soon drew ecclesiastical attention and condemnation. As I noted in the Introduction to this study, Wyclif maintained in *De Civili Dominio* that the most critical means to edifying "our mother the church" was to preach: for priests, "indeed to sow the word of God toward the building of the church is what pertains to the Christian religion."[20] But at the 1382 Blackfriars Council, the "fifteenth conclusion" culled from Wyclif's writings, that all secular priests were *missi* (sent) and should be allowed to preach, even without papal or episcopal approval, was declared erroneous, though not heretical, as were ten statements on topics including the eucharist, confession, and papal authority.[21]

In addition to arguing that all priests were commanded by Christ to preach, Wyclif more radically contended that no preaching authority existed other than personal righteousness. This Donatist conviction issued logically in the converse proposition, attributed in its most radical form to Wyclif's contemporary John Purvey, that any holy person in a state of grace had a right to preach by virtue of a good life. In addition to arguing, as Wyclif had, that all priests had the obligation to preach the gospel, Purvey reportedly claimed that official ordination and tonsure did not confer priestly authority unless Christ himself ordained those whom he wished "to live well and teach well his gospel, and minister all the necessary sacraments to the people. And whoever is a holy man, a member of Christ, and will be saved, is a true priest ordained by God."[22] In the wake of concerted prosecutions of Wycliffites during the last decades of the century, notably the attempts to extirpate Wycliffites from Oxford and the trials of accused Lollards in the Leicester area,[23] Purvey publicly recanted these views and condemned unlicensed preaching in 1401.[24]

Purvey had argued for the "holy man" as his example of the worthy preacher, but the question of women's right to preach could hardly be extricated from the broader argument for lay preaching, with its radical implications for the breaching of boundaries between "clergy and laity, masculine and feminine . . . learned and 'lewd.'" Although Wyclif himself expressed little interest in women's preaching,[25] the issue came to a head after his death, in the Hereford trial of the accused Lollard Walter Brut (1391–93). In remarks recorded in his trial transcript, Brut exposes the instability of the teaching/preaching distinction as well as extending to women, albeit cautiously, the priestly qualifications that Purvey had attributed to the "good man." The bishop's Register ascribes the following statement to Brut:

It is fitting for priests to teach and preach the word of God, and to this [duty] they have been ordained in the church as much by Christ as by the apostles. Paul teaches that women should learn in silence with all subjection, and does not permit a woman to teach or to exercise authority over men.[26] However Paul does *not* state that women are *not able* to teach or to exercise authority over men – nor do I presume to affirm it, since women, devout virgins, have steadfastly preached the word of God and have converted many people while priests dared not speak a word.[27]

Placing teaching and preaching in a paratactic relation, Brut admits no distinction between the two practices, treating female teaching and the exercise of "authority over men" as equivalent to the evangelical preaching of virgins. Moreover, Brut argues that women have the same capacity for edifying speech and spiritual authority as men and points to the arbitrariness of their exclusion from authority.[28] Objecting to the orthodox limitation on women "citing an authoritative lineage," he offers virgin saints as exemplary for women rather than, in the tradition of orthodox preaching guides, presenting such women as *non imitanda sed veneranda* (to be admired but not imitated).[29] Although Brut's reliance on the preaching of holy women such as Mary Magdalen and Catherine of Alexandria was potentially at odds with his own professed standard of *sola scriptura*,[30] his argument nevertheless demonstrates the urgency of the Wycliffite demand for public lay spiritual authority. Placing "devout virgins" in the category of apostolic preachers whose example might be emulated by contemporary laity was a move of questionable orthodoxy, for even if non-scriptural, such pastoral activity was still preaching, and a form of authority that laity were officially allowed to exercise only privately.[31] Here, indeed, women seem, in Galloway's words, to stand for "the whole class of those traditionally excluded, the 'educated or half-educated laity.'"

The energy expended upon refuting Brut's arguments reveals the threat they presented to the foundations of priestly authority, calling forth reiterations of traditional distinctions between teaching and preaching, female and male, lay and clerical forms of authority. The anti-Wycliffite compilation London, British Library, MS Harley 31 contains several responses designed to refute Brut's arguments, which in the process expand upon earlier canonical arguments against women's preaching.[32] The arguments included here work to reinforce the distinction between acceptable *private* and forbidden *public* "teaching," which might (as in Brut's discussion) encroach upon the realm of preaching. As traditionally argued, teaching is defined as a work of mercy acceptable for women to perform; however, it is established that women must be understood as "subjects," not as "leaders": as "subditos," not "prelatos."[33] Aquinas is cited to argue that women may teach other (young) women and children privately but may not teach in public.[34]

Most striking for my purposes, the *quaestio*, in its attempt to naturalize these distinctions, finally returns to the family and traditional gender roles, finding a biblical source for the idea of the mother as a source of limited spiritual authority. Referring to Proverbs 4:3 ("unigenitus fui coram matre mea et docebat me . . . "), the *quaestio* argues that on the one hand, this verse actually refers to the father teaching.[35] But if the mother is understood, it is necessary to see her as teaching privately.[36] Thus, Blamires argues, at this moment of cultural contest and clerical anxiety, for women who aspired to preach like Mary Magdalen or Catherine of Alexandria, "only two alternatives seemed open. They could teach within the cloister, discreetly, if they became abbesses: or they could become heretics."[37]

But I will show that *Book to a Mother*, whether written before the Brut trial or contemporary with it, argues that claustration and heresy are *not* the only two alternatives for eagerly pious women and laity more widely. These are the poles through which the work proposes to guide its reader, offering strategies of identification and spiritual authority that combine private with public, preaching with teaching, male with female, activating clerical associations for laity with spiritual aspirations.

As seen in Chapter 2, by constructing Christ as synonymous with "holy writ," accessible through textual study, *Book to a Mother* posits a process of "accord" that may enable the vigilant reader to be turned "fro fleschliche liuinge into Cristes liuinge" (32.5–6) and to embody his qualities of being spiritually "humble, pore, and chast" (33.4). The *Book* repeatedly suggests that this "accord" with "holy writ" will shade into a public, vocal form of spiritual authority, as when the author encourages his reader/s to move from learning the ABC, to lamenting sin privately, to "seyinge with þe prophete Ieremye: 'A, a, a; Lord, I cannot speke . . . for I am a childe'" (24.1–3). The guide connects clericalized modes of reading and "understanding" to vocal expression of this understanding, but laity and women lacked authorization for such speech. How then, once the lay addressee has been authorized to read and give voice to scripture, can her learning issue in a form of evangelical teaching that remains within the bounds of orthodoxy? In *Book to a Mother*, the identities of cleric and widow become reformist sites for lay identification. The guide begins by constructing chaste widowhood as an exemplary state for all pious laity, a potentially apostolic avenue to *imitatio Christi* that may be practiced in cooperation with priestly advisor within the setting of the parish, enabling the reader to avoid the corruptions of the monastery and the false counsel of the friars.

PIOUS WIDOWS AND PRIESTLY POLEMIC

In casting the motherly widow as a figure who may stand for all Christians, the *Book* author reimagines the widow's status as central rather than marginal, a way to avoid the feminized perils of lust, greed, and vanity that lurk in the woman's cloister and are typically associated with widowhood. The construction of the widow as an exemplary figure will prepare for the contrast between *Book to a Mother*'s subject and the preaching widow Alison, who embraces the feminine singularity and resistance to widowhood that *Book to a Mother* encourages readers to transcend.[38]

Although it might seem counterintuitive to posit widows as representing spiritually aspirant late fourteenth-century laypeople generally, the *Book* author suggests that his widowed mother might be a figure for wider identification and even emulation. During a period when marriage stripped Englishwomen of individual legal rights, widowhood offered a chance for some to escape the material limitations imposed upon adolescent and married women. But late fourteenth-century evidence suggests that the status of widow, which gave women rights over their property and bodies, was a legally privileged but often a materially insecure status for women of the middling and poorer classes.[39] Barbara Hanawalt notes that despite modern scholars' inclination to focus on "widows finally gaining independence from the legal and moral domination of men,"[40] the prospect of remaining a widow in male-dominated late medieval England was not always appealing, either materially or psychologically. Many late medieval widows were obliged to sue members of their families or tenants to obtain dower, the one-third of the husband's estate to which they were entitled, and many widows sought to remarry because of economic need.[41]

If they did not remarry, widows, as heads of their households, might be able to exercise greater self-determination in the realms of personal behavior and religious practice than had been possible during marriage. For some widows, mainly those from higher classes, the option of taking a vow of chastity in a public episcopal ceremony might promote both financial security and the realization of spiritual goals. Acknowledging that the widow's life was not always financially secure, Mary Erler notes, "in some cases taking the vow may have represented an attempt to establish publicly a permanent status and to claim the benefits it entailed, both financial and social."[42] In addition to ensuring control over material capital, Erler observes, "[s]piritually the vow placed a woman in the second most highly regarded female state, by formally recognizing her as chaste, though not virginal."[43]

Although the role of vowess was a fluid one, lacking a formal rule or specific requirements beyond chastity, some vowesses took the opportunity to emulate religious women and affiliated themselves with abbeys. The vowing ceremony for widows was similar to the ritual of profession for nuns, and some late fourteenth-century widows not only vowed perpetual chastity but also pledged to uphold other elements of the monastic vow of St. Benedict. In addition to chastity, in 1379 Isabel Burgh pledged "conversion of myn maners"; in 1399 Alice St. John went even further, promising "stabilitatem et conversacionem [sic] morum atque castatitem . . . [sic]."[44] Although most vowesses probably stayed in their own homes, a significant number occupied the precincts of women's religious communities.[45]

Little information survives about vowesses' daily practices, but their participation in the rituals of religious communities may have resembled the activities authorized in documents like the *Corrodium Paynot*, considered above in the Introduction. In a late example, the vowess Alice Hompton received a papal dispensation in 1484 to build and live in an oratory near Dartford Abbey, where she would hear Mass and *Opus Dei* daily.[46] This vowess's oratory, a space for daily life and prayer, thus literally functioned as an extension of the Dartford nuns' cloister.

By adopting the vowess status, well-off widows might embark upon holy lives in the world by bringing the gentry household into the monastery, in a process of translation that demonstrates the ready exchange and compatibility of material and spiritual capital, for a privileged few, during this period. Erler contends, drawing on Caroline Bynum's arguments about women's religious lives, that the most significant components of the vowess role were its "continuity" and "structurelessness."[47] It seems that personal property was crucial to achieving this continuity with one's former life, for vowess status both depended upon and safeguarded women's access to the material capital of their dead husbands. The author of *Book to a Mother*, keenly aware of the appeal of monastic life and by extension of the vowess role, responds to his mother's spiritual aspirations with an extended argument for a holy life in the world that promotes "continuity" with her domestic life through intimate links to fleshly son and spiritual father, but which does not depend upon access to material goods or property, which his own mother apparently lacked.

In her study of the ideological uses of female monasticism in later medieval England, Nancy Warren focuses on the gendered resonances of *Book to a Mother*, arguing that the work deploys monastic imagery, and particularly "nuptial discourses," to control the female addressee's body and subjectivity.[48] Warren draws attention to the author's persistent warnings against feminine frivolity in dress and furnishings, as well as to his connections between "maumetrie" (inappropriate worship, idolatry) and "lecherie."[49] In view of the author's recommendation, late in the *Book*, that those in danger of "maumetrie" should "holde Seint Benettis rule, faste iclosed in a cloister of foure stronge wallis, þat ben riȝtfulnes, strengþe, sleiþe and temperaunce" (120.26–121.2), Warren contends

[t]he priest's ultimate resolution to the problem of women's desires as such a socially corrosive force lies in an ideal version of female monasticism . . . he extols the value of claustration, which was for nuns (though not for monks) in effect a fourth substantial vow, and his treatment suggests that he has in mind not only "ghostly" claustration but also the bodily variety.[50]

Although *Book to a Mother* combines nuptial with monastic discourses to appeal to the tradition of enclosure as a privileged context for women's spiritual purity, I suggest that the work is more profoundly invested in reimagining virtuous widowhood as an avenue for a simultaneous union with and imitation of the "humble, pore, and chast" Christ who appears throughout the text. The *Book* de-emphasizes the reader's gendered identity to argue for a more widely available form of *imitatio Christi* available to the lay widow only *outside* the walls of the cloister.

By making his widowed mother stand for other Christians desiring spiritual instruction, the author of *Book to a Mother* offers all readers the combination of spiritual marriage to Christ with imitation of his example and words. The female addressee of this work stands not only for "euerych man and womman and child" but is also placed in a horizontal relation to the author, as his potential "broþer" or "suster." Just as the widow-addressee potentially figures every willing Christian, Christ is made available as a spiritual spouse to all who desire him, including the priestly author – he refers later to Christ as "oure Spouse" (89.12) – and marriage with Christ presents no threat of bigamy. The widowed addressee may, if she follows the *Book*'s guidance, anticipate an eventual reunion with Christ and her deceased husband: the author promises that she will "stie up wiþ angelis harpinge wiþ gret melodie, I hope, to þine two hosbondis – Crist and mi fadir" (30.5–6).

In a characteristic sign of his secular clerical orientation and social location, the *Book* author invokes monastic signifiers in order to emphasize the world over the cloister. He insists upon an apostolic meaning of "cloister" and "rule," instructing his mother to reimagine her rather marginalized existence in the world as a privileged form of membership in the original collectivity of the apostolic family, a religious community in which "propurte" (by which he means both "possessions" and, more fundamentally, any "private or individual ownership") should have no place.[51] The author proposes that his mother should recover the communal spirit of the apostles in the context of the parish, rather than seeking it through the imitation of actual monastic life, which has been compromised by the desire for "propurte." The *Book* appropriates Acts 4:32, traditionally used to justify monastic and fraternal life, to argue that the parish, not the cloister or the priory, should be the primary site for religious identity and practice.[52] The author assures his addressee,

þou hast þe blessynge þat Crist ʒeueþ to pore in spirit, and þe kyngdom of heuen is þyn; and so þe boke is lerned, bouʒt and sold, for þou hast boght God with forsakynge propurte, and þou art made anoon of Cristes religioun þat Holy Writ spekeþ offe: þat þer was "a multitude þat leued" [believed] in Crist her Abbot, "of oon herte and o soule." And þis is bettere þan forto haue þe mantel [nun's robe] and þe ryng and þe wympel and þe veil, with propurte: for Crist loueþ no propurte, and so Crist and þei haueþ not one herte and o soule. (22.14–23)

It is unlikely that the mother has given up all the material possessions necessary to sustain life. Rather, the author implies, as one of the truly "pore in spirit," she will have "boght God with forsakynge propurte" if she can manage to spiritualize whatever degree of real poverty she lives in with the correct desire for a truly apostolic religious life. By understanding her poverty spiritually and rejecting attachment to personal possessions, he posits that she will have joined the more inclusive "multitude" of the parish, instead of donning the nun's mantle, ring, wimple, and veil without a commitment to communal renunciation. By using the biblical passage in this way, the *Book* recalls Wyclif's own treatment of "true religion" in *De Civili Dominio*, where he refers to Christ as "the abbot of our order" and cites the same passage to hold up the early church as a model for all Christians.[53]

Redeploying monastic images to emphasize the superiority of life in the world, the author of *Book to a Mother* suggests that he has lost faith in the holiness of the monastic life. No supporter of the friars, either, the author constructs his mother as "clerk" to enhance the reader's knowledge and practice and to reinforce his own authority against the sacramental encroachments and intellectual pretensions of the mendicant orders, defending his own superior right to perform the sacraments, preach, and teach the faithful. Given the south-west Midlands provenance of all four surviving manuscripts of *Book to a Mother*, this author's advice to his mother can be located in the context of rural clerical life in the late fourteenth century, with its many economic, social, and educational hardships. In the West Midlands, the after-effects of the plague caused the secular clerical life to lose some of its previous appeal, as clerical livings were reduced and fewer dispensations given for priests to attend universities.[54] Although the author of *Book to a Mother* never reveals his precise position in the ecclesiastical hierarchy, his comments reveal frustration with the greed of fellow priests and indignation at corruptions and irregularities in the provision of benefices.[55] Although he may yearn for the security of a benefice, he has seen property turn clerics into "ypocrites" (57.3) and is anxious to distinguish himself from priests whose greed compromises their ability to minister to the faithful.

The *Book* author, perhaps a parish priest, is even more anxious about the incursions of regular religious into church management, incensed at the hypocrisy of groups whose members flout their official obligations to uphold rigorous standards of poverty and chastity. Recognizing the appeal of these communities to his reader, he does not condemn them outright, but argues that their restless search for material gain has vitiated their ability to offer models of spiritual community or individual self-regulation to laypeople. In many cases, religious houses held rights of patronage or received revenue from parish churches, and sometimes they were involved in the provision of pastoral care, particularly during the second half of the fourteenth century.[56] In the years following the plague in Hereford, the West Midlands diocese that was home to the Walter Brut trial and was perhaps near the *Book*'s place of composition, the religious orders became the most important patrons of the clergy, their dominance reaching a peak in the 1370s and 1380s.[57] This patronage did not necessarily point to the fact that religious houses were materially rich (many were not), but that they still retained the symbolic capital to support these ordinands.

Given this evidence from Hereford, it seems possible that the author was himself supported at one time by a religious order, but his references to these orders show his suspicion and disdain for the patronage system. His remark about personal experience with canons encapsulates his attitudes about the religious orders' involvement in the spiritual economy. The author bitterly reminds his mother, "Crist wiþ his couent axeþ not twenti marc, as þou woldest somtime haue ʒeue for me to haue ben a chanoun, and þei wolde not receiue me lasse þan twenti pound" (122.15–17). The greed of the regular orders, which once prohibited him from joining them, now prevents him from recommending the cloister as a viable setting for a holy life in retirement.

The author's accounts of presiding not only at confession, but also at marriage and baptism, strongly imply the experience of a secular priest rather than that of a friar, who would be canonically limited, except in special circumstances, to preaching, confession, and burial.[58] Although the *Book* explicitly mentions the friars only a handful of times, tensions with friars as confessors and competitors underlie this guide. As the author advises his mother to forsake "propurte" for a life that imitates the apostles in its purity, he is recapitulating the philosophy of St. Francis; he must therefore work throughout the text to differentiate the relationship between parish priest and penitent, son and mother, from the relation between friar-confessor and lay penitent.[59]

Since their arrival in England, and throughout the fourteenth century, the friars had represented a challenge to the control of parish priests over confession, preaching, and burial of parishioners.[60] Although early fourteenth-century papal legislation that roughly coincided with their arrival in England had attempted to mediate between the interests of the friars and the parish priests by giving friars limited license to perform only these three functions,[61] these efforts failed to avert many disputes between parish clergy and mendicants.[62] A well-known case from the Hereford diocese documents the bishop's use of mendicants to supplement the services of parish priests after the plague: this case may also testify to tensions between these hired penitentiaries and local members of the secular clergy. In 1351,

Bishop Trillek commissioned six Dominicans to travel to various parishes in the diocese hearing confessions, deploying an additional Austin friar and eleven Franciscan friars over the following two years. But in September 1355, just after commissioning several Austin friars, he suddenly revoked their licenses.[63] While this sudden revocation may have been part of an effort to stem the activities of unlicensed penitentiaries, no offenders were mentioned in the mandate, nor was a single reason given for the sudden order.[64] Perhaps the penitentiaries did not inspire complete confidence, but as Dohar speculates, "perhaps, too, Trillek had to consider the growing animosity between mendicants and secular clerics on matters of preaching, hearing confessions, and the general, if unsubstantiated, fears that parish revenues could be further lost in economically depressed times."[65]

Book to a Mother testifies to the author's considerable resentment of the mendicant orders, although this resentment surfaces explicitly only a few times, most notably in the indictment of "flateringe freres, oþer ony oþere þat wiþ false confessiouns and glosynge wordis disseyuen mennes soules" (194.5–7). Not only does this passage sound themes common to anti-fraternal literature, it also offers in English a criticism comparable to that found in Latin in a bill of clerical complaints issued to the 1356 Convocation of Canterbury. This bill decries "the confessors of such noble lords and ladies, nay rather the betrayers and notorious deceivers of their souls, they convert to their own gain the compensation for wrong-doing which by earthly and heavenly law ought to be restored to the injured parties."[66] In *Book to a Mother*, the author's invitation of the widowed reader into the clerical disciplines of reading, writing, and teaching paradoxically seems to follow from a sense of his own priestly authority. Protective of his sacerdotal privileges, the *Book* author blurs boundaries between the identities of cleric and widow, perhaps hoping that in so doing he will encourage his reader/s to eschew the lure of the monastery and the blandishments of the friars.

APOSTOLIC WIDOWHOOD

Book to a Mother constructs the layperson as a "disciple" of Christ's original "multitude" who lived communally and shared "oon herte and o soule": the author's advice to "lerne" the "book" who is Christ, forsake property, and pursue a poor apostolic life resonates with Wyclif's idealizing descriptions of Christ as *scriptura* and of secular priests as the true inheritors of the apostles. But by making chaste widowhood and marriage to Christ criteria for the pious subject's membership in the poor, apostolic family, the *Book* expresses a view that became anathema to the Wycliffite program as it coalesced in the vernacular. *The Twelve Conclusions of the Lollards*, published in 1395, denies that the categories of apostle and chaste widow could ever be embodied by the same person, for the very category of chastity had become, in Blamires's terms, "a casualty of polemic against vows *per se*."⁶⁷ This text, which airs the views of "pore men, tresoreris of Cryst and his apostelis," proposes to return the church to its primitive state of virtue, offering "certeyn conclusionis and treuthis for þe reformaciun of holi chirche of Yngelond, þe qwiche ha[þ] ben blynde and leprouse many ȝere be meyntenaunce of þe proude prelacye, born up with flatringe of priuat religion."⁶⁸ Having already condemned priestly celibacy as the cause of sodomy (the third conclusion), the work argues in the eleventh conclusion that

a uow of continence mad in oure chirche of wommen, þe qwiche ben fekil and vnperfyth in kynde, is cause of br[i]ngging of most horrible synne possible to mankynde . . . Þe correlary is þat widuis, and qwiche as han takin þe mantil and þe ryng [i.e., become vowesses] deliciousliche fed, we wolde þei were weddid, for we can nout excusin hem fro priue synnis. (28)

Book to a Mother harbors no illusions that adopting the status of vowess or nun will guarantee the reader's spiritual blessedness. But the *Book* author views widowed chastity as a valid mode of lay religious discipline even as he strives to separate it from the corruptions that he too deplores in the realms of "priuat religion." Acknowledging the possibilities for abuse when a corrupt cleric "weddeþ his soule to þe deuel bi dedlich synne, [whence] comen alle corsede popis, cardinallis, bishopis, prelatis, prestis, freris, monkes, chanouns, and alle manner sinnes" (90.14–17), he immediately touts the value of a spiritual form of married chastity practiced under priestly supervision (his own): "Þerfore, my leue dere modur, charge muche þe wedlac of Crist and þi soule. For ȝif Crist be þin hosbonde, þanne þou schalt bringe forþ children fre in trewe wedlac, þat ben chaste þouȝtes, clene wordis and goode werkes: and alle suche Crist wol knowe for his children" (90.18–22). Such a wedlock is the product of widowed "continence," whether vowed or not, and argues for the spiritual superiority of widowhood to remarriage.

In a strategy virtually opposite to the arguments of the *Twelve Conclusions*, *Book to a Mother* claims an apostolic precedent for the celibate life, arguing against those (Wycliffites?) who dismiss celibacy by "seiynge þat it is bettur to bringe forþ children" (91.20–21).⁶⁹ The *Book* argues, "Lo, here fadur of lesinges techiþ hem to lie, for þis is aȝenus Cristis conseil and holi Seintes doinge, þat leften þat lif and chosen chastite" (91.21–23). Thus the *Book* casts "chastite" as Christ's "conseil," a recommendation though not a requirement: a life promising the kinds of spiritual rewards that he has already enumerated. In reference specifically to women's "chastite" he cites saints Katherine, Cecilia, and Lucy, whose commitments to avoiding corruption offer models to "suche simple maidenes þat so clene kepen hem to Crist, here Spouse, schullen haue merci, as Holi Writ seiþ, and myȝti men to serue þe deuel myȝtiliche shullen suffre turmentis" (96.16–19). While the *Book*, in making the widowed "modur" exemplary for "euerych man and womman and child," cannot very well also demand that all its projected readers abstain from sex, these saintly models of "clene" marriage to Christ nevertheless provide exemplars of fortitude and spiritual purity that all reading subjects might internalize.[70]

Book to a Mother repeatedly encourages the reading subject to seek out spiritual marriage with Christ, but such a marriage does not involve the solipsistic self-enclosure that the author implies monastic life would entail. Rather, the *Book* posits the soul's marriage with Christ as a setting in which dutiful observation of sacraments might begin to issue in an imitation of Christ's ethical example in the world. The author finds in the marriage at Cana an appropriate site for this spiritual "wedlac." He exhorts

loue þou penaunce, and kep wel hereaftir þe furste robe of innocence unfouled, holdinge þi ring euermore in þin hond, and . . . þi schon: for ȝif þou haue þes þre wel, þou ert þe more able to þe wedlac þat I spac of er, of Crist and þi soule . . . And, as Marie and his disciples after þe wedlac foleweden Crist bodili, and Mari neuere failede, but euere was of trewe bileue, folewinge Crist to þe deþ whanne alle oþere failede . . . so, modur, folewe þou Crist in wei of uertues, þenkinge hou he prechede and what he tauȝte, furst doinge penaunce and alle þat he bad oþere do, and seþþe tauȝte and seide: 'Comeþ to me, alle þat trauelen and beren heuye, and I shal fulle ȝou.' (103.1–15)

This scene simultaneously inscribes the value of penance and posits this sacrament as both a technique of self-regulation and a point of entry into active virtue. The wedlock of Christ and the soul, in which the mantle ("robe") and ring take on new meaning as nuptial signifiers in the context of life among the disciples, draws the reader into an imagined emulation of Christ's virtuous example. By simultaneously imitating the Virgin Mary as an exemplar of "trewe bileue" and following "Crist in wei of uertues," the reader may perhaps begin to imagine herself as emulating Christ's virtuous acts of teaching and preaching. This scenario, in which Mary emerges from among the disciples and proceeds to merge with Christ, recalls Walter Brut's description of the early church, but it lacks the anticlerical charge or the explicit mention of women's preaching. Brut describes a community in which, Minnis notes, Jesus "did little to distinguish explicitly between the priests and the rest of the people; nor is the word 'priest' or the term 'preacher' used in the gospel; rather, he called some 'disciples' and others 'apostles' whom he sent to baptize and preach."[71] *Book to a Mother* thus constructs an imagined marriage to Christ as an avenue to membership in his original "multitude," who lived communally and shared "oon herte and o soule," while at the same time linking this apostolic identity to the practice of the sacraments under the author's own priestly guidance.

MOTHER AS TEACHER AND PREACHER

A traditional dichotomy persisted through the later Middle Ages in discussions of preaching, between the poles of women's bodily experience and male textual authority.[72] *Book to a Mother* both exploits and dismantles these associations to argue that female (motherly) teaching and male (fatherly) teaching may issue in virtually identical forms of *imitatio Christi* for the lay reader. By considering the *Book*'s vision of apostolic preaching together with Wycliffite views on preaching and the Wife of Bath's own sermon, I uncover the reformist implications of the moral "preacherly privilege" granted to the mother-reader.[73] Waters argues persuasively that the Wife of Bath, by co-opting a clerical preaching voice and textual authorities to uncover traditional links between antifeminism and anticlericalism (accusations of garrulousness, carnality, and greed), exposes all preaching as an essentially "self-interested discourse," a view characteristic of the *Canterbury Tales* as a whole.[74] *Book to a Mother*, while making some of the same anticlerical and misogynist assumptions, nevertheless envisions preaching as an extension of teaching, a practice not defined by "voice" or gender, nor limited to priests, but legitimate only for those practicing Christ-like virtue. In contrast to the Wife of Bath, whose appropriation of "auctoritees" and "prechynge" effects a "decentering of the priestly voice," the subject of *Book to a Mother* is invited into a method of "citing" Christ through virtuous conduct rather than scriptural repetition or explication.[75] In the process, the author responds to lay piety with a new religious discipline that expands the boundaries of lay spiritual authority, even as he preserves his own claim to priestly voice and sacerdotal power.

Book to a Mother offers a rare chance to see the Wife of Bath in a new light. In her singular embodiment of a widow's resistance to continence and in her textual opposition to Christ and his successors, Alison presents a revealing inversion of *Book to a Mother*'s spiritually fruitful chaste widow. Although it might appear that I am positing the Wife of Bath as a naturalistic "foil to the idealized views of femininity found in prescriptive texts of the period,"[76] I am actually suggesting the reverse: that looking selectively at the Wife of Bath's words can help illuminate *Book to a Mother*'s reformist vision of the widowed role as a locus of spiritual power.

Although the Wife of Bath loudly averts the possibility that the Parson might preach to the assembled company, it has been well established that her own *Prologue* is itself a sermon, delivered in playful violation of the prohibitions considered above.[77] As Blamires has noted, her "expres" textual literalism is reminiscent of Lollard textual sensibilities, as is her resistance to chaste widowhood.[78] The first part of the Wife's discourse, which concerns us here, is more precisely a short *sermon joyeux*, a mock sermon on the tribulations of marriage, based on I Corinthians 7:28.[79] The passage in question reads, "If however you take a wife, you do not sin. And if a maiden marries, she does not sin: but they will have trouble in the flesh because of this."[80] The Wife takes the opportunity afforded by this text to resist widowed chastity, seizing upon Paul's "conseil" for the "self-interested" aim of defending her multiple marriages, in the process dismissing as sterile female roles that do not serve her purposes:

> I woot as wel as ye, it is no drede,
> Th'apostel, whan he speketh of maydenhede,
> He seyde that precept therof hadde he noon.
> Men may conseille a womman to been oon,
> But conseillyng is no comandement.
> He putte it in oure owene juggement;
> For hadde God comanded maydenhede,
> Thanne hadde he dampned weddyng with the dede.
> And certes, if ther were no seed ysowe,
> Virginitee, thanne whereof sholde it growe?
>
> (63–72)

Striking a "warily poised attitude" at a historical moment when opposition to "maydenhede" and attachment to literal fruitfulness may have been viewed as signs of Lollardy,[81] Alison shows that like the author of *Book to a Mother*, she fully understands the distinction between "conseil" and "comandment." However, she uses her textual acumen to evade rather than fulfill the "conseil" to virginity that the *Book* attributes to "Criste" and views as a goal for all readers to aspire to, at least in spiritual terms. By exploiting textual specifics, she further "unlocks the letter to discover an irreducible carnality,"[82] treating "juggement" as a proxy for feminine preference rather than a tool for developing Christ-like powers of self-discipline and discrimination.[83]

Book to a Mother gathers together the seemingly incompatible roles of chaste widow and preacher to posit the conjunction as a productive one, compatible with clerical guidance rather than a rebuke to it. The *Book*, whose stated purpose is precisely "conseillyng" of the reader, not only treats "maydenhede" as compatible with "weddyng," but suggests that the Virgin Mary's example may adumbrate acceptable forms of lay female preaching. In order to make this suggestion, the author exploits the most familiar convergence of women's bodily experience and public speech, an association both orthodox and potentially radical: the notion that at the moment of chastely conceiving Christ, Mary was filled with divine wisdom and the power of prophecy. Though this power lay on the preaching continuum, it tended to be defined as distinct from preaching in order to prevent women from claiming evangelical authority.[84] In *Book to a Mother*'s domestic setting, the role of Mary, originating in the performance of penance, gradually transforms spiritual enclosure into evangelical agency. In the following long passage, this evolution occurs before the reader's eyes:

And ȝif þou wolt þou maist conceyue þe same Crist and bere him not onlich nine monþes but wiþoute ende; and þat is bettur þan to bere him bodiliche as oure Ladi dide . . . For Marie is as muche to seie as a bittur se or a sterre of þe see. Haue þou þanne a bittur sorwe for þi synnes, and wiþoute forþ ȝif good example to men þat þei mowen se bi þi liuinge hou þei mowen come to þe hauen toun of heuene; and þanne gostlich þou ert Marie for boþe skiles. And þis þou maist lerne wel of Marie ȝif þou wolt close þin herte fro þouȝtes and loue of þis world: for Marie was aschamed and troubled whanne she sai and hurde þe angel worshupinge hure and tellinge hure hou sche schulde be Godis modir, for sche desirede no worshup of þis world. Also ȝif þou wolt be angel Gabriel gostlich þou maist, for angel bitokeneþ a god m[e]ssanger, and Gabriel strenþe of God. Be þou strong þanne in þe loue of God, and so Gabriel; and be a good messanger, tellinge hem þat liueþ wiþ þe, wiþ goode desires of þin herte or wiþ goode wordis or wiþ goode werkes, hou ȝif þei wollen haue þe condiciouns of Marie þei schullen conceiue Crist. (44.23–45.17)

Initially, Mary's humble response to the annunciation gives the reader a model of spiritual enclosure that recalls *The Abbey of the Holy Ghost*'s exhortations to "close þin herte fro þouȝtes and loue of þis world." But unlike the *Abbey*, the *Book* suggests that Mary's example of good "liuinge" must complicate the idea of enclosure, for she also embodies a form of preaching by example. This example becomes more explicitly evangelical when the role of Gabriel, whose worshipful announcement gives expression to Mary's virtue, is offered as a means for the reader both to embody and *teach* virtuous conduct within the confines of female community, offering her authority that might lead others to similarly inspired "conception" of Christ. In MS Egerton 826, the smooth transitions from Mary to Gabriel, enclosure to preaching, are suggested by the successive red headings that highlight these critical examples: at the top of fol. 43v, "hou þou myȝt be marye," and on fol. 44r, "hou þou myȝt be gabriel." By remaining in the domestic sphere, these exemplary "desires," "wordis" and "werkes," though they invite conversion and distinctly recall the preaching of the "steadfast virgins" cited by Walter Brut, do not encroach upon the priestly privileges of the author nor activate suspicion of unauthorized textual activity.

By the same token, the *Book*'s exhortation to contemplation locates this spiritual goal within the realm of motherhood while refusing to separate contemplation from the evangelical work of preaching. The author exhorts, "Anon as þou hast conceiued gostliche Crist wiþ a stable desire, reise up bi þi loue fro worldlich þinges into contemplacioun and hiȝe þe into hilles, þat Dauid clepiþ holi seintes of heuene... And so gret Elizabet and serue hure and alle hure holi felouschup" (46.17–22). The parish and domestic settings are thus cast as productive places for the exercise of spiritual authority *and* the search for contemplative pleasure. Although these directives uphold "received ideals of female spirituality and suggest patterns of female conduct which do not threaten fathers, husbands and clerics,"[85] I contend that this traditionalism proves critical to the *Book*'s brand of reformism. By preserving these models and transforming them into subtle new modes of evangelism, the author steers a course between the poles of convent and conventicle.

In its treatment of Mary's example as powerfully generative for the pious reading subject, the *Book* not only negotiates these poles but offers a more penetrating critique than the Wife of Bath of the problem of preaching as a "self-interested" masculine practice. The Marian act of serving "Elizabet... and alle hure holi felouschup" is posited as more than simple domestic submission: as an emblematic act of humility, it becomes the entry point into an argument for humility as the *only* essential qualification for preaching. Mary's service to Elizabeth offers a model for Christ's humble submission to John when he "com to be fulled [baptized] of him" (60.19–20).[86] This image leads directly, even jarringly, into an argument for Christ's preaching as model to all good Christians. Mary's "þre monþes" with Elizabeth predict Christ's forty days in the desert, during which he "com into Galile prechinge þe euangelie of þe kingdom of God, seinge: 'Doþ penaunce, and þe kingdom of God schal neiȝe'" (60.2–4). In MS Egerton 826, the reader's eye is drawn to this exhortation by the red heading, "marke Cristys prechynge" (fol. 51v). And in imitation of Christ's preaching, the *Book* proposes

þus schulde we don: furst waschinge us of alle maner synne... and so go into desert – þat is, makinge al þis world to us a desert, wiþ alle unleful loues; and so fast til oure liues ende. And þus wiþ gode liuinge alle men and wommen ben holde to preche. For oure Ladi was þe beste prechour þat euer was, saue Crist; and ȝut sche spac but fewe wordis. Þus, modur, preche þou, desiringe alle men to do þus. Not as prechours prechen now, biddinge men do þat þei wollen not do hemself; þerfore here dede sedis growen not aftur hem for defaute of quikeninge wiþ þat goode liuinge. Not þus Crist, but furst he dide and seþþen he tauȝte. (60.22–61.12)

This passage, announced in Egerton by the bold heading, "How alle men schulde preche" (fol. 52v), imagines *imitatio Mariae* building into *imitatio Christi*, as the author blends a seemingly radical form of lay evangelism ("wiþ gode liuinge alle men and wommen ben holde to preche") with an orthodox devotion to penance and to Mary's humble silence as exemplary for women and men. In the process, an image taken from *Ancrene Wisse* (Mary's silence as a non-verbal means of preaching) is reshaped into public evangelism that stops short of threatening the clerically protected "chain of citation" upon which the Wife of Bath intrudes.[87] Although the author takes care to remind readers of Mary's famous forbearance, Mary is not a retiring figure here: she is a model of "trewe bileue," of a self-consistency and fruitfulness that too many contemporary preachers lack.

Moreover, in its rebuke to contemporary preachers whose words are as "dede sedis" without the example of "goode liuinge," the passage recalls Wyclif's call for Christians to generate spiritual children from the "seeds" of the faith, while arguing for virginity as compatible with preaching. Drawing once more upon the requirement of "accord" between words and deeds, Christ's life and the reader's life, the *Book* argues that preaching authority need not be wrested away from official authorities but may perhaps be fruitfully embodied alongside them. Depending upon whether priests manifest virtue or vice, the layperson's preaching "wiþ gode liuinge" will function as cooperation with or rebuke to the clergy. However, for the moment *Book to a Mother* is careful to locate the mother's imitation of Christ in the realm of analogy and in the context of deference to priestly authority.[88]

MOTHER, TOBIAS, AND CHRIST

Book to a Mother posits "preaching" as synonymous with "goode liuinge," the embodied result of "accord" between Christ's words and the actions of the pious subject, in which a spiritualized form of virginal conception may become manifest in cooperation with clerical spiritual advisor. It is remarkable, then, that the Wife of Bath's *Prologue* unfolds inversely with the growing momentum of *Book to a Mother*'s drive to assimilate the reading subject with Christ. If the Wife's *Prologue* ultimately reveals what Galloway calls the "failure – and her own unwillingness – entirely to embody the professional authority possessed by the traditions that she imitates and elaborates,"[89] then *Book to a Mother*, a guide for readers desiring spiritual progress, finally argues for the success of its paradigms of *imitatio clerici*, for the reader's capacity to embody, as far as orthodoxy will permit, the forms of "professional authority" that it has offered. Building on associations with the Virgin Mary and Christ, the *Book* pushes the reader toward this embodiment by assimilating the mother's active teaching and preaching authority to that of the Old Testament *paterfamilias* Tobias, and through him, the preaching of Christ himself.

For the Wife of Bath, in her refusal of clerical "conseillynge," preaching in the sense of "the public exposition of Scripture" becomes her vehicle for declaring "anti-perfectionist"[90] opposition to Christ's example rather than desire for apostolic "accord" with it. As she reminds her listeners

> Virginitee is greet perfeccion,
> And continence eek with devocion,
> But Crist, that of perfeccion is welle,
> Bad nat every wight he sholde go selle
> Al that he hadde, and gyve it to the poore,
> And in swich wise folwe hym and his foore.
> He spak to hem that wolde lyve parfitly;
> And lordynges, by youre leve, that am nat I.
>
> (105–12)

The Wife rejects precisely the advice that the *Book* offers the widowed addressee in its opening pages, when in the process of teaching the Decalogue, the author recounts the story of Christ and the rich young ruler, to whom he says, "'ʒif þou wolt be parfite, go and sell al þat þou hast, and ʒif hit to pore men; and come,' lyue as I do, 'and þou schalt haue tresour in heuene.' Þat is, first ʒyue þiself holly, bodi and soule, parseuerauntly to Crist þat was most pore for oure loue" (3.22–4.3). As Dutton has noted, "the subtle substitution of 'lyue as I do' for Christ's 'follow me' makes claims for this way of life as *imitatio Christi*, claims which are not inherent in 'follow me' as Christ's literal instruction to the rich young ruler."[91] This form of *imitatio* is exactly what the Wife of Bath wishes to avoid: returning to the rejection of virginity, she adds the rejection of poverty in an unsubtle jab at the friars, whose professed commitment to poverty is, she implies, honored more in the breach than the observance. In matters of sexuality and money Alison turns away from *imitatio Christi*: in her progressive diminution of the force and audience for her homiletic lesson, she backs down from her preaching stance with "myn entente nys but for to pleye" (192), further reframing her advice as intended not primarily for "lordynges" but meant to show "wise wyves" (225) how to conduct themselves with husbands. Although these rhetorical moves are certainly strategic, they draw attention both to the specificity of her speech and to its "self-interested" stance.

By shaping the story of Tobias (from the Book of Tobias or Tobit) as a narrative of following and teaching God's "hestes" as well as exercising forms of Christ-like judgment that look outward rather than inward as the Wife of Bath's form of feminine "juggement" does, *Book to a Mother* connects the mother's chaste widowhood with a privileged male version of self-regulatory and teaching power, citing a masculine model whose teaching will propel the reader non-threateningly toward the preaching example of Christ. The multigenerational story of Tobias is particularly appropriate to the didactic relation of son-author to mother-reader, useful for constructing the mother both as chaste widow and quasi-clerical teacher. Jerome's Vulgate, probably the source of the story for the *Book*'s author, assigns the name Tobias to both father *and* son, a suggestive correspondence for an author who was himself both spiritual father and fleshly son to his addressee.[92] In the biblical version, the younger Tobias marries the young widow Sara, whose seven previous husbands have been incinerated by the devil on successive wedding nights. Taking the advice of the angel Raphael, Tobias and Sara abstain from sex until three nights after their wedding, and Tobias is spared from death. A short section from the Book known as the "benediction of Tobias," in which Tobias's father-in-law marries the couple, was commonly used in medieval wedding liturgies.[93]

With its contemporary relevance to both female and male learners, the story of Tobias seems especially well suited to mediate between constructing the mother as an individual pious woman and encouraging her to embrace evangelical aspects of a traditionally male clerical role. In addition to the relevance of the Tobias text to the topic of marriage, in the later Middle Ages, the larger Tobias story had cultural currency for chaste women and for clerics. In a fifteenth-century book belonging to the nuns of Barking Abbey, now London, British Library, MS Additional 10596, the Book of Tobit was collected with the Book of Susannah and a series of prayers and meditations.[94] In the clerical realm, Matthew of Vendôme's version of the

Tobias story was often included in grammar school curricula: perhaps the author of *Book to a Mother* had encountered it in the course of his own early education.[95]

Book to a Mother features two installments of the Tobias narrative. The first version constructs a chaste form of desire for the reader to emulate in the context of parish life and practice; the complex second movement returns to the notion of the mother as "cleric," extending more direct access to an evangelical imitation of Christ. By manipulating the story of the pious father and chaste son with the same name, the author constructs multiple ways for his "clerical" mother to pursue spiritual aspirations while emphasizing the many layers of his own priestly authority.

The purpose of the first narrative is twofold: to teach "hou God in Holi Writ chargeþ fader and modur to teche here children to drede and worschupe God in holdinge his hestis, as Tobie tauȝt his sone," and to tell "of two parfite hosbondes: Tobie and his sone; of a parfite wif Sare; of cursede wed[l]ac, and a blessede; and hou þe angel techeþ to knowe þat on fro þat oþer" (69.22–70.2). These two didactic aims, signaled by the heading "Ensaumple of thobye" in MS Egerton 826 (fol. 57v), are interrelated, for the elder Tobias's perfect piety and capacity for moral teaching make him a model for his son, while the marital piety of Sara and young Tobias presents an even more focused model for the reader to emulate. For the elder Tobias, the transition between childhood perfection and exemplary fatherhood is seamless, and he shapes his son in his image. His perfection, marked by abstinence from unclean food and lack of concern for material gain, foreshadows the piety of Sara and Tobias the younger.

The unfortunate young widow Sara, despite her "cursede wedlac," epitomizes purity and embodies a model for the mother's own chaste widowhood. Fasting for three days and beseeching God to remove the curse that has claimed her seven husbands, Sara adumbrates the Virgin Mary when she claims, "I neuere coueitede man, and my soule haue kepte clene fro alle coueitise"; she desires only "[a] man wiþ drede of þe, not wiþ fleschli lustes" (67.27). Sara offers a model not only of bodily self-discipline and prayer, but also of chaste desire: desire for spiritual marriage that the widowed reader should seek with Christ now that her husband is no longer with her.[96] The angel Raphael constructs the marriage of young Tobias and Sara as a bond forged in chastity: their three nights of holy abstinence place union with God before the carnal union of man and woman. As Tobias exhorts Sara to rise and praise God after the third night, he explains, "For þes þre niȝt we ben oned to God, and aftur þe þridde niȝt we schullen ben oned. For we ben children of holi men, and we mowen not be oned as folk þat knowen not God" (69.11–14). Their premarital abstinence, issuing in continent marriage, fulfills the elder Tobias's teachings and holy example. The combination of chaste desire, spiritual union, and continent, productive marriage has specific relevance to the addressee of *Book to a Mother*, validating her former, current and future marriages: the continent marriage she once enjoyed, her current widowed chastity, and her desired spiritual union with Christ.

The second, more digressive and interpretive version employs the life of Tobias to demonstrate the importance of following God's "hestes" and the need to teach these precepts for the sake of spreading the gospel like the apostles.[97] Extending to the addressee an active and even evangelical form of teaching authority, the author nevertheless does not refer to it as preaching. In this version of the story, the elder Tobias's holiness stems from his fierce adherence to God's precepts and commitment to teaching them in the familial setting. Before introducing Tobias, the author laments that there are few fathers nowadays who teach their children correctly

to drede and worschupe God in holdinge his hestis, and to despise þe world and forsaken hemself and do penaunce, as Crist techiþ and seiþ we mowe not ellis be his disciples; but more bisiliche techiþ hem to despise God and his hestis, boþe wiþ grete oþis and lecherouse wordes and wickede werkes, charginge more siknes, parelis and schame of here bodies, lustis and likinges and londes lawes, craftus and bisinesse to gete wiþ richesse and worschupes of þis world, þan þei chargen sikenesse, parelis and schame of here soules, likinge of God or of gostlich þinges, in holdinge his hestis to gete rychesse and worschupes of heuene þat neuere schal haue ende. (71.7–19)

Renewing his exhortations to poverty and penance, the author implies that parents (both fleshly and spiritual) must "teche" these precepts as well. With the first-person plural, he manages to locate himself and his mother in the category of would-be "disciples" of Christ, a group to which Tobias (despite being an Old Testament figure) is understood to belong.

In its second rendition of the Tobias story, the *Book* invokes Christ's death not to inspire pity and sorrow but to encourage the addressee to embody an acceptable form of evangelical teaching in accordance with her son's priestly guidance. The *Book* connects Christ's teaching directly to his death on the cross, reminding the reader that Christ "ofte bad þat we schulde awake fro brekinge of his hestis, and so muche cride and bledde, honginge on þe cros, þat he þurstede... And his herte barst, and stones tobursten [burst open] and graues openden and dede men arisen, and þe soun of þe apostelis 'wente out into al erþe' to teche Godis hestis" (76.9–16). Combining elements of several biblical passages (Hebrews 5:7, Matthew

27:52, Romans 10:18), the author constructs a new narrative sequence, positing a direct continuity between learning Christ's "hestis," witnessing his death, and teaching those "hestis" to others. By crafting a continuous sentence that encompasses Christ's death and the immediate departure of the apostles, the author emphasizes the Passion not as an occasion for melancholy meditation, but as a spur to further teaching. Together with his earlier emphasis on himself and the mother as good "disciples" of Christ, this passage emphasizes the direct connection between reading Christ's life and performing imitative teaching (not yet preaching).

Like Mary's domestic teaching, which issues in preaching, Tobias's evangelical "teaching" provides models for the mother to internalize and attempt to imitate. In an extension of his mother's *imitatio clerici* into the realm of Christ-like preaching, the author finally offers Christ's own evangelism as the ultimate example. Recalling the story of Mark 3:21–22, in which Jesus demonstrates such "feruent" desire to teach the multitudes that the disciples "half helden him wod," the author repeats, "we alle ben holde to preche wiþ oure goode liuinge, aftur þe mesure of þe bileue, as Godis spensers [almoners] of þe seuenefolde graces of þe Holi Gost" (126.13–15).

In a series of recommendations that recall the earlier "preaching" of Mary as well as quite closely anticipating Walter Hilton's description of the "medled lif," the author explains that Mark's description of Christ

scheweþ foure nedful þinges to a good prechour. Þe furste: he ros erliche and wente into desert, makinge his preier; techinge us þerbi not to ligge [lie] idel in oure bed, as broþelis [rascals] þat hauen no sauour of heuene. Also, to fle preisinges of men, in þat he wente into desert. Þe þridde: þat we be occupied in preiers whanne we prechen not. Þe furþe: þat he wolde beningneliche, at þe preier of his disciples, preche to simple folk in litele tounes; techinge us to fle ueinglorie, not desire to preche in grete citees among grete lordis, to gete us a name, as mony don. (126.21–127.7)

This passage, which appears to be the author's own expansion of Mark 1:35–38, posits most radically a common ground of "preacherly privilege" between Christ, reader, and author, while reminding her not to emulate the corrupt friars. Assimilating the reader into a clerical "we," the author emphasizes the combination of prayer and preaching that connects him and his mother to Christ. By sustaining this "we" through the thinly veiled critique of the opportunistic friars, the author attempts to recruit the reader into a united front against the friars, suggesting that she has more right to preach with her humble, holy life than they do with their proud, corrupt ones.

As I have suggested of the Marian passage considered above, the author's phrase "preche with oure goode liuinge" sounds Wycliffite, resonating with Purvey's arguments for the "holy man" as priest and resembling the testimony of a Leicester Lollard who in 1388 wrote "whoever is a good man, whether or not he is literate, is a priest" ("quilibet bonus homo, licet literaturam nesciat, est sacerdos").[98] But while *Book to a Mother*'s use of this phrase is expansive, it is not heterodox. By arguing that holy living can be a form of preaching, the author invites the mother to share the fundamental standard of "living as one preaches" with the secular clergy, the group to which he belongs.[99] While the author controversially compares his mother's living to preaching, he qualifies this statement and never actually compares her to a "priest," reserving that role for himself. By suggesting that she, with all the faithful, is obligated to preach "after þe mesure of oure bileue," he locates the mother's "preaching" within his own pastoral supervision. If she is preaching, it is material that he has taught her through catechesis. She can be a "spenser" of the grace of the Holy Ghost, but only under his careful supervision.

By constructing the pious addressee as a clerical widow, the *Book* author proposes to enhance the mother's intellectual status and dignify her practice as moral and evangelical but non-textual, maintaining the separateness of and need for his own priestly authority. His arguments for the mother as teacher and even preacher work to assimilate her practice to Christ's own conduct and words without dismantling his own authority, admitting Wycliffite sympathies, or ceding disputed ground to the mendicants. Comparing this careful construction of the female reading subject to the Wife of Bath's appropriation of a clerical voice for purposes of resisting *imitatio Christi* gives us new insight into how the clerical widow might figure not only as an icon of resistant femininity, but also as a reformist emblem for all "hem that wolde lyve parfitly."

It has been observed that the Wife of Bath, in her control of her "verbal world and the tale-telling game itself . . . becomes a model for the poet."[100] In *Book to a Mother*, in a moral, spiritual, and even a rhetorical sense, the clerical mother becomes a model for the priestly author. Constructing his "leve dere modur" as a clerical reader, teacher, and preacher, the author fashions a polemical vision in which any aspiring layperson, in her or his *imitatio Christi*, may begin to lay legitimate claim to some of the clerical ground not covered by the sacramental office of the priesthood. Marshall Leicester has argued that in Chaucer's work the "act of storytelling" is "the encounter of a subject with an institution,"[101] and the same is perhaps more profoundly true for the act of spiritual guidance. In these texts, clerical and lay subjects are in a constant process of construction and encounter, with each other and with the ecclesiastical institution, whether the church is represented as a stabilizing structure in which lay readers must enclose themselves or, as in *Book to a Mother*, a process of relation pointing laity and clergy toward individual and collective reform.

Conclusion
Spiritual guides in fifteenth-century books: cultural change and continuity

During the final decades of the fourteenth century, lay spiritual aspirations presented clerical authors with a range of challenges and opportunities. For all of the authors whose guides I have considered, the first challenge was the danger of lay retreat from the world: the prospect that in desiring contemplative experience, readers might withdraw from social and sacramental responsibilities, beyond structures of priestly mediation. *The Abbey of the Holy Ghost* and *Fervor Amoris* show this danger to be their primary concern as they translate the cloister into a lay disciplinary structure, attempting to guard against the contemplative elitism that for lay readers might stem from a sense of material entitlement. *The Life of Soul*, *Book to a Mother*, and the *Mixed Life* also encourage their readers to return to the world on newly disciplined terms. But in responding to lay desire for contemplative experience, they tend to look away from the cloister, not denying the importance of contemplation, but stressing the active apostolate of Christ as they carefully extend clerical intellectual, pastoral, and teaching disciplines to lay readers. In doing so, these texts perform hard textual work to mediate controversial theological thought and construct orthodox strategies for devotional practice.

If one views Wycliffism, in Katherine Little's useful terms, "as an extreme example of the more general questionings and appropriations of the period,"[1] then the Chaucerian texts I have considered also suggest extreme scenarios, highlighting the social disruptions of monastic emulation and *imitatio clerici* when these forms of religious discipline are undertaken without the guidance or authorization that devotional texts provide. I have placed Chaucer at the margins, in the first and last chapters, and Langland in the center of the study, because, while Chaucer's commentary evokes the pitfalls that exist at both ends of the disciplinary spectrum, Langland's role is a more complex one. He is *himself* a clerical reformer, a writer of vernacular theology, and therefore engaged, though with different aims, in the same conversation as Hilton's *Mixed Life, Book to a Mother*, and *The Life of Soul.*

The intersections between orthodox didacticism and discourses already well on their way to becoming heretical testify to the hopeful possibility, near the end of the fourteenth century, of safely adapting texts and practices traditionally associated with the clergy for lay readers. But the translation of clerical religious discipline for laity, insofar as it involved translation of the Bible, a Wycliffite priority and *fait accompli* by century's end, was to become an officially forbidden prospect under Archbishop Arundel's Constitutions of 1409. Along with mandating newly stringent terms for licensing preachers and restricting preaching to preclude criticism of clerical vices or discussion of the sacraments, the Constitutions officially ended a lively academic debate over whether and how the Bible should be translated into English, forbidding translation of any biblical text into English or the copying or ownership of any such text made since Wyclif's time.[2]

At the start of the fifteenth century, the Oxford-based debate over biblical translation had shown it was still possible to advocate translation from a fundamentally orthodox position. Richard Ullerston's academic arguments share important features with the reformist spiritual guides I have considered, in their attitudes to lay engagement with the Bible and, by extension, to lay participation in clerical modes of teaching and practice. In response to his opponents, who argued that translation of spiritual texts would lead untutored laity into rebellion against ecclesiastical authority in pastoral and sacramental matters, Ullerston claimed that the laity should be recognized as the "'wise and understanding' people who follow God's laws" rather than considered to embody "stupidity and blindness," as the anti-translation party would have it.[3] In his conviction that Bible translation might actually foster cooperation between laity and clergy, Ullerston's positions resonate with *Life of Soul, Book to a Mother*, and Hilton's *Mixed Life*, although these works lie at varying places on the spectrum of orthodoxy.[4]

But after 1409, that common ground between moderate clerics and popularizing writers[5] became officially irrelevant, as the Constitutions attempted to shore up what Arundel perceived to be an unacceptably blurry boundary between lay and clerical prerogatives, prohibiting translation of the Bible into English or the reading of scriptural material translated since "the time of Wyclif" without official permission. It may be possible, as Nicholas Watson has argued, to detect a new conservatism in some of the first devotional works to take advantage of Arundel's official *imprimatur*.[6] Nicholas Love's *Mirror of the Blessed Life of Jesus Christ*, which presents a new translation of the pseudo-Bonaventuran *Meditationes Vitae Christi*, features significant anti-Wycliffite additions and posits a fairly circumscribed view of lay spiritual authority.[7] In his address to lay readers, Love quite literally translates the cloister for them, offering a work originally written in Latin for a Franciscan nun. Love installs hierarchical relations between clergy and anticipated readers, whom he calls "lewde men & women & hem þat ben of symple vndirstonding." These hierarchies become clear as Love justifies his translation:

Ande as it is seide þe deuoute man & worthy clerke *Bonauenture* wrot hem to A religiouse woman in latyne þe whiche scripture ande wrytyng for þe fructuose mater þerof steryng specialy to þe loue of Jesu ande also for þe pleyn sentence to comun vndirstonding [s]emeþ amonges oþere souereynly edifiyng to symple creatures þe whiche as childryn hauen nede to be fedde with mylke of lyȝte doctryne & not with sadde mete of grete clargye & of h[ye] contemplacion.[8]

This introduction is telling for its simultaneous rejection of the twin dangers of lay spiritual aspiration – desires for "grete clargye" and for "hye contemplacion" – inclinations that might well be subject to increased scrutiny in this period.[9] In rejecting these, the *Mirror* recalls the beginning of *Fervor Amoris*, although that guide acknowledges only the desire for "high contemplation," being either uninterested or unconcerned with lay desire for "grete clargye."[10]

In view of the changed ecclesiastical climate, Watson has influentially argued that anxiety over the production of new vernacular theology had the inadvertent effect of canonizing earlier works such as the devotional texts considered in this study, which became "staple reading" of the fifteenth century, though not necessarily for the wide swath of readers their authors had originally envisioned. While enforcement of the Constitutions tended to fall disproportionately upon those of lower social status, Watson contends, it was primarily in the houses of "professional religious and laypeople of rank" that these texts were read and the promise of cooperative modes of teaching among clergy and laity was kept alive.[11] These arguments, which have been salutary for establishing the vitality and range of fourteenth-century vernacular theology and highlighting the scope of the Constitutions, have been subject to helpful critique in recent years, as close attention to matters of dating and manuscript circulation has complicated Watson's claims about the quality and quantity of fifteenth-century religious works.[12] I conclude this study by considering four fifteenth-century manuscripts that transmitted some of the spiritual guides considered above, in order to nuance the picture further and suggest that cultural change and continuity went hand in hand during this period.[13] This material evidence suggests that the various modes of religious discipline I have examined continued to be translated, often conservatively and in elite settings, but sometimes in surprising ways even by "professional religious and laypeople of rank" during the decades after Arundel's Constitutions.[14]

The following discussion is intended to be suggestive rather than comprehensive, to gather some of the scattered insights that these books provide into the continuing value of lay spiritual guidance in the fifteenth century. I ask specifically how certain fifteenth-century compilers responded to the texts' emphases on monastic enclosure, lay pastoral care, and preaching and teaching. In considering these texts as integral parts of entire volumes, whether miscellanies or anthologies,[15] I bring to bear some of the strategies of what Stephen G. Nichols and Siegfried Wenzel have termed "materialist philology": the careful study of texts and volume as a cultural whole, with close attention to thematic and practical modes of organization.[16] During this fraught period for the negotiation of religious identities, the didactic impulses and formal qualities of spiritual guidance were exploited in ways that reflect conservative interpretations of religious discipline as well as continuing possibilities for the expansion of lay spiritual authority.

The four manuscripts considered below manifest a surprising range of techniques for configuring lay religious identity in relation to professional religious discipline. First, London, British Library, MS Harley 5272, a volume which places *The Abbey of the Holy Ghost* among other contemplative texts for women readers, suggests that the redirection of this text back to elite women, whether nuns or laity, worked to translate this socially engaged guide out of the bourgeois world and into a rarefied, meditative realm. Next, two manuscripts containing Hilton's *Mixed Life*, Lincoln Cathedral MS 91 (the Thornton manuscript) and Oxford, Bodleian Library, MS Ashmole 751, demonstrate that while a gentryman might have copied Hilton's work as part of a personal effort to construct a mixed life, a nearby priest carefully excerpted the same work to claim that life exclusively for the clerical class. Finally, in Oxford, Bodleian Library, MS Laud Misc. 210, which collects *Book to a Mother* and *Life of Soul* with a range of controversialist texts, we see perhaps the closest continuity between the aims of fourteenth-century reformism and fifteenth-century compilation. This collection polemically extends *Book to a Mother*'s lay preaching and teaching imperatives and tone of reformist clerical indignation into the fifteenth century.

RETURN TO FEMALE ENCLOSURE: BUILDING THE *ABBEY* IN LONDON, BRITISH LIBRARY, MS HARLEY 5272

Many of the guides considered in this study seem, perhaps counterintuitively, to have reached as many or more readers in religious life as they did readers in the world. Although it attained some degree of lay readership,[17] *The Abbey of the Holy Ghost*, likely the earliest of the guides and the one surviving in the largest number of copies, very often returned to the cloister.[18] The earliest extant copy survives in the compendious Vernon manuscript, along with Hilton's *Mixed Life* and the A-Text of *Piers Plowman*. And during the fifteenth century, when religious houses maintained their centrality as centers of copying and focal points for lay devotion and the exchange of books with laypeople, circulation of the *Abbey* demonstrates what A. I. Doyle calls "that close dependence on religious communities, in which all vernacular devotional works, even those addressed more inclusively [i.e., to laypeople], tended to remain."[19] One can readily see why the *Abbey* might be a welcome addition to an orthodox fifteenth-century devotional collection. The monastic conceit that organizes the text and its emphasis on the need for clerical mediation to establish the "religion of herte" place this composite work above theological reproach, certainly beyond suspicion of Lollardy at a moment marked, as Sargent has argued, by a "closing of ranks around precisely those kinds of literature to which the Wycliffites most objected."[20]

Although the *Abbey* was explicitly adapted for male and female readers in the world, its circulation was especially strong among vowed religious,[21] male and female, and among women readers in and out of religious life.[22] MS Harley 5272 is a neatly copied, carefully decorated mid-fifteenth-century parchment book, written by a single scribe who identifies himself as "Iohannes fforster" on fol. 98v.[23] John Lydgate's *Life of our Lady* is the longest work in the codex, occupying ninety-eight of the book's 137 total leaves; the volume then features a verse life of the fourth-century virgin martyr St. Dorothy and concludes with the *Abbey*, followed by *The Charter of the Abbey of the Holy Ghost*. Placed after these female saints' lives, the *Abbey* reinforces in a theoretical mode, in prose rather than verse, the emphasis of the *vitae* on contemplation, virginity, and enclosure.

During a period when the ecclesiastical establishment may have been eager to enforce boundaries between clerical and lay identities, the presence of the *Abbey* in this manuscript testifies to the contemporary blurring of boundaries between the reading practices and spiritual identities of nuns and well-off, pious laywomen. Numerous scholars have remarked upon the frequent practical and literary borrowings between these two female groups in the fifteenth century. Emulation traveled both ways: even as laywomen copied the practices of the cloister, the cloister increasingly resembled the upper-class world. Roberta Gilchrist has shown that in the course of the fifteenth century, female monasteries came to look like aristocratic and gentry homes, with greater partitioning of space and the division of the household into small groups called *familiae*.[24] Felicity Riddy argues that *familiae* may have constituted reading groups, and she argues that "the literary culture of nuns in the late fourteenth and fifteenth centuries and that of devout gentlewomen not only overlapped but were more or less indistinguishable."[25] The sharing of books was a primary way for these groups to participate in a shared religious practice.

By making the *Abbey* part of a contemplative program, this volume translates the guide back into the cloister, effectively removing the work from the world of bourgeois spiritual aspiration that called forth its translation and adaptation in the late fourteenth century. For enclosed female readers whose spiritual profession made them privileged figures of identification and placed them beyond the dangers of Lollardy, or for wealthy women whose social standing placed them above reproach, this *Abbey* text may have functioned in the fifteenth century to shape an introspective subjectivity, perhaps even encouraging the very spiritual elitism that the *Abbey*-adaptor had endeavored to contain.

In the absence of contemporary ownership marks, I speculate, as George Keiser does of London, Lambeth Palace, MS 432 (which also features the *Abbey* as well as a life of St. Dorothy), that MS Harley 5272 was written "for a pious lady either of the laity or in a monastic institution."[26] These lives of the Virgin Mary and of St. Dorothy present strong models of female contemplative practice, models cultivated both by nuns and by certain laywomen. David Bell's investigations of medieval English nunnery libraries have shown that female saints' lives (in both Latin and the vernacular) were popular reading material for nuns.[27] Likewise, lives of the saints are well-attested among the possessions of wealthy, pious, fifteenth-century laywomen.[28]

By placing Mary's life first in the manuscript, the scribe offers this vernacular *vita* as a kind of embodied rule for the contemplative female reader. Lydgate's *Life of our Lady* offers a portrait of the Virgin as a paragon of chastity and as the ultimate role model for women's contemplative life and devotion. Following the tradition of *Meditationes Vitae Christi* (which borrows from the *Revelationes* of Elizabeth of Hungary), Lydgate depicts the young Mary living in the temple pursuing proto-monastic devotions. Her body is a pure vessel, a kind of abbey in its own right: "ffor all þe tresoure of his sapience / And all þe wisdome of heven and erthe to / And all þe ryches of spirituall sciens / In hir were schitte and closed eke also" (fol. 19r).[29] Likewise, Mary's contemplative devotions bear a striking resemblance to the Rolle-inspired flights described in the *Abbey*. Lydgate remarks, "Of the ioy who couthe tell ary3t / Of thyne hevenly meditacions /

Assendyng vppe above the sterres bry3t / In thyne inward contemplacions"
(fol. 8v).[30]

The virgin martyr St. Dorothy is a particularly apt model for nuns and
would-be nuns, a paragon of sexual and spiritual inviolability whose spiritual marriage to Christ and concern for her sisters adumbrate monastic
values. Subject to repeated fleshly torments, Dorothy in her martyrdom
imitates Christ and prepares the reader for the meditations on Christ's
Passion that will follow in the *Charter*, the last text in the codex. Dorothy's
life offers both a rule and a meditation for the female reader. Although she
maintains her chaste body against sexual incursions, the extreme physical
torments that Dorothy suffers imitate those of Christ, and detailed descriptions provide graphic tableaux for meditation. Like Christ, she is scourged
and hanged, though in the opposite order:

> And in a Gybbet sche was nome
> Hir feet hangynge toward the skye
> And all to raced was hir body
> With hokys of yren and with roddis bete
> With fleylis brusched full cruelly
>
> . . .
>
> Brenynge fagottis ordeyned were
> Vn to hir pappes they did ham tye
> This to this virgyn they did there
> After this tormentrie and this fere
> Sche was put in prison half dede and more.
>
> (fol. 101v)

But as in many other virgin martyr's lives, after this "tormentrie,"
incarceration rejuvenates rather than further demoralizing her, and prison
provides a place of respite where Dorothy receives angelic feeding and
ministrations.[31] This portrait of the cell as haven promotes bodily enclosure as a technique of spiritual liberation for women. By placing *The Abbey*
and *Charter of the Holy Ghost* at the end of the codex, after the *vitae* of
Mary and Dorothy, the copyist Forster locates this composite work as a
theoretical "reule" that describes and reinforces the specialized contemplative patterns of an individual reader's life, whether she lived in a convent
or a pious lay household.

In this manuscript, the reader's interior cloister remains completely
inviolate, because the final episode of the devil's incursion into the abbey
is missing from the text. Instead, this particular *Abbey* text ends with the
description of Jelosie, "wiþ loue teris mornynge with longynge conceyved
in deuoute vppe risynge of the herte" (fol. 115r).[32] Rather than ending, as

we saw in Chapter 1, with the warning not to "trespass" against the "reule" of the abbey, this *Abbey* text concludes as follows:

Now haue I tolde ȝow what the abbey is of the holigost. And how hit schulde be foundid in clene conscience of sowle. Ffirste I tolde you þat ryȝtfullenesse and clennesse mote clansin þe place there þe abbey schulde be ybilde ... The fader of heuene is founder of þis holy abbey. And the holigost is wardeyne and visitoure as y tolde by fore. But nerethelesse thowȝ an abbey haue neuer so good a foundoure either visitoure. But he have also good dedis and chartres of hare placis. Where by they mowe kepe here londis rentis and franchesis. (fols. 115r–116r)

Lacking the episode of the devil's incursion into the abbey, the internal cloister becomes an unproblematically safe spiritual haven for the meditative female reader. Summarizing the rhythms of the contemplative life and suggesting a connection between bodily enclosure and mystical abandon, this collection reinforces a spiritual aspiration that women religious and elite laywomen might still safely pursue during an age of increased vigilance over maintaining disciplinary boundaries between laity and clergy in the world.

A GENTRYMAN'S *MIXED LIFE* IN LINCOLN CATHEDRAL MS 91 AND PRIESTLY CENSORSHIP IN OXFORD, BODLEIAN LIBRARY, MS ASHMOLE 751

The circulation of *The Abbey of the Holy Ghost* back to the cloister or the aristocratic household reinforces the text's emphasis on mental enclosure while moderating the principal source of anxiety for the original translator: that readers might, in retreating from the world, attempt to evade structures of clerical mediation and regulation. For nuns or would-be nuns, spiritual retreat entailed the observance of a rule or a closely supervised religious life.[33] More surprisingly, given its emphasis on the lay reader as involved in a form of active pastoral care, Hilton's *Mixed Life* also shows a high frequency of transmission among monks and nuns. The phenomenon of circulation back to religious houses was compounded, for the *Mixed Life*, by the fame of Hilton's *Scale of Perfection* and his attendant reputation as a writer of contemplative advice. The *Mixed Life* traveled with the second book of the *Scale* in London, British Library, MS Harley 2397, which belonged to an abbess of the London Franciscan house: she bought the book in London and in turn bequeathed it to her successors at the house.[34] The *Mixed Life* was copied as well in the parallel volumes Oxford, Bodleian Library, MS Rawlinson C.894 and London, British Library, MS Royal 17.C.xviii, which were probably made for London convents, the former for women and the latter for men.[35] Thus, despite the work's emphatic focus on the lay reader and explicit recommendation *against* entering religious life, the *Mixed Life* frequently returned to readers who might make use of its guidance in their efforts to practice contemplation in monastic communities.

Additional evidence shows that the *Mixed Life* reached varied audiences of non-monastic male readers. I consider two strikingly different collections here, one lay (Lincoln Cathedral MS 91) and one priestly (MS Ashmole 751). I analyze these manuscripts' differing uses of the *Mixed Life* to suggest that during the mid-fifteenth century, Robert Thornton, a Yorkshire gentryman, used his book to explore identification with the prelate and pursue multiple modes of religious discipline, while a nearby clerical compiler excerpted and copied the *Mixed Life* to reinscribe boundaries between lay and priestly knowledge and practice.[36]

Like the monastic volumes just mentioned, lay manuscripts featuring Hilton's *Mixed Life* tend to privilege contemplative contents, a pattern that suggests, above all, the continuing prestige and importance of meditative reading to readers of all statuses. This is true for two of the few *Mixed Life* manuscripts that can be reliably attributed to lay owners, London, Lambeth Palace, MS 472 and Lincoln Cathedral MS 91: while the first is a London "common profit" collection of Hilton's works,[37] the latter is the Yorkshire gentryman Robert Thornton's well-known "devotional book," covering fols. 179–279 of this large volume.[38] Thornton's book, varied in its contents, suggests that this fifteenth-century layman, whose devotional leanings and worldly responsibilities may have resembled those of Hilton's lay addressee,[39] used the book to structure his own moderate version of the mixed life of action and contemplation.[40] Thornton's copy of the *Mixed Life*, sandwiched between the devotional lyric "Þi Ioy be ilke a dele to serue þi godd to paye" and the prose treatise *An Epistle of Salvation*, lacks the first 218 lines, beginning abruptly but characteristically with a comparison of the layman to the prelate: "men þat ware in prelacye, and oþer also þat were haly temperalle men, had full charite in affeccione with-in, and also in wirkinge with-owtten: and þat is propirly þis mellide lyf, þat es made bathe of actyffe lyfe and of contemplatyfe lyfe."[41]

As George Keiser has argued, Thornton's combination of texts suggests that he was interested in educating himself in the essentials of the faith, especially in matters of "schrift," and in exploring contemplative practices that might enhance his devotion to Christ's Passion as well as give him a "foretaste of the eternal."[42] On catechetical matters, Thornton collected treatises on the *Pater Noster*, the ten commandments, the seven gifts of the

Holy Spirit, and John Gaytryge's sermon, the Middle English expansion of Archbishop Thoresby's Catechism.[43] Thornton also copied texts covering a wide range of contemplative activity: *The Abbey of the Holy Ghost* along with texts focused on the Passion, such as *The Previte of the Passion*,[44] and texts promoting somewhat more speculative approaches, including *The Mirror of St. Edmund*, originally written for enclosed religious. This last work offers guidance in affective meditation on Christ's life and on the Godhead, as well as theoretical discussion of contemplation. In treating questions such as God's "schewing" of himself to humanity, the work treats not only "reuelacyon" but also "resonn":

By resonn, commes He till þe knawynge of man one þis manere: – Ilke a man may wele see in hym-selfe þat at he es, and þat at he hase bene, bot he may wele wit þat he hase noghte bene ay, and for þat at he wate wele þat sume tym he be-gan for to be; þan was þaire sum tym when he was noghte. Bot when he was noghte, þan moghte he one na wyese make hym-selfe; and þis seghes man in his creature . . . For-þi, sen ilke thynges erre, and þay erre noghte of thayme self, þare-fore it behoues nede þat þare be ane to gyffe all thynges to be, þat is to saye of whaym alle thynges are; þare-fore it behoues of force þat He thurghe whaym alle thynges erre, be with-owtten begynnynge.[45]

Perhaps using the copying and compilation of his book to explore such questions as the proof of God's existence outside the boundaries of time, Thornton claimed access to some of the terms of clerical thought as well as to a wide range of penitential and contemplative modes. He was an exceptionally motivated lay reader "of rank," in Watson's phrase, one with the means and curiosity to search out and study a range of fourteenth-century spiritual writings. Thornton's book suggests that this particular fifteenth-century layman both desired contemplative experience and wished to remain within the bounds of orthodoxy. Unintimidated by Arundel's Constitutions, he appropriated multiple modes of religious discipline, perhaps in an effort to develop "full charite in affeccione with-in, and also in wirkinge with-owtten."

In few of these extant *Mixed Life* manuscripts, even those owned by priests, do the other contents reinforce the elements of teaching and pastoral care that Hilton had stressed in order to assimilate his addressee's life to that of the bishop. In fact, the only extant manuscript containing the *Mixed Life* whose contents might be called consistently "pastoral" is MS Ashmole 751, which did in fact belong to a priest. But in this volume, an extract from the *Mixed Life* has been censored to remove the reference to overlap between priest and layman. For all Hilton's attempt to restore equilibrium and present an orthodox vision of lay religious discipline for the aspiring layman, a vision that perhaps resonated with Robert Thornton, the Ashmole volume suggests that Hilton's vision of *imitatio clerici* may, for this priestly user, have had destabilizing implications for the actual relations of lay and priestly subjects.

MS Ashmole 751 is a large miscellany of Latin and a few English contents that clearly belonged to a priest, although his identity is unknown and it remains unclear whether he was a secular cleric or belonged to a religious order.[46] The contents cover a wide range of pastoral and devotional interests: the volume includes theological extracts attributed to Isidore, Hugh of St. Victor, and Innocent III, practical instructions on priestly duties such as composing sermons, administering extreme unction and confession, and devotional texts by Richard Rolle and St. Bernard, as well as excerpts from the *Meditationes Vitae Christi* and St. Edmund's *Speculum Ecclesiae*. In addition to these Latin contents, the volume includes an eclectic group of English texts: an extract from *Mixed Life*, penitential stories translated from Latin, excerpts from *Mandeville's Travels*, a tract explicating the ten commandments, and a twelve-stanza lyric, entitled "þo sauter of Jhesu" and "þo sauter of charite" in the manuscript.[47] While the vast majority of the contents are in Latin, these few English texts are mainly copied at the ends of quires.[48] This miscellany is highly idiosyncratic: its lack of finding tools and discontinuous copying of several texts mean that, as Hanna notes, "it is unlikely that anyone other than this scribe-owner could have moved through this personalized manuscript with facility."[49]

The English texts appear mainly near the middle of the manuscript, and the extract from Hilton's *Mixed Life* is the first among them. The extract, which runs from fol. 45r–v, is highly selective, covering only about thirty-four lines of the printed modern edition. This short piece, unique to my knowledge, combines two passages from the *Mixed Life* into a new form that offers a short definition of the priestly life in terms of the life of Christ, while excising any reference to the lay lord for whom the *Mixed Life* was originally composed. Here the compiler has taken a selection out of its original context and copied it into the codex as a way of defining his own life and role in contrast to those of the layperson. The extract begins abruptly on fol. 45r with the explanation of the three lives:

þer are thre <are> maner of lyfynges: on is actyfe; a noþer is contemplatyfe; þo thryd is made of bothe and is a melled lyfe. ¶Actyfe lyf al only longes to wordly men and wymen whyche are fleschly and boystes in knowyng of gostly ocupacion, for þai fele no sauour ne deuocyon by peynez of lufe, as oþer men dose, þai kan no skyl of it.[50]

The passage continues through the account of these three lives and through the description of those, especially "prelates and oþer curates," who combine doing "werkes of actyfe lyfe" with giving themselves over to "meditacions, redynge of holy wryt and to oþer gostly ocupacions, after þai fele þam disposed." But in a striking omission, the excerpt is missing the passage, considered at length in Chapter 3 above, which invites the lay reader into this privileged fraternity by virtue of his status as secular lord, extending the mixed life to

sum temporal men þe whiche haue souereynte wiþ moche auere [having] of wordli goodis, and hauen also as it were lordschipe ouer oþere men, for to gouerne and sustene hem, as a fadir haþ ouer his children, a maister ouer his seruauntes, and a lord ouere his tenantes, þe whiche men han also receeuyed of oure lord[is] ȝift grace of deuocioun, and in partie sauoure of goostli occupacioun. Vnto þise men also longeþ [þis] medeled lif þat is boþe actif and contemplatif.

Instead of including this passage (cited here from Ogilvie-Thomson's edition), the Ashmole selection proceeds directly into the discussion of Christ's alternation between preaching and meditation and its function as an example to "prelates and curates." It reads as follows:

Oure lord, for to styr sum men to vse þis melled lyfe, toke vpon hym self þo offys of men of holy kyrk as prelates and curates, and gaf to þaim ensaumple by his awen werkes, þat þai [fol. 45v] schuld vse þis melled lyf as he dyd. Ffor one tyme he comyned and meld, schewand to þaim his dedis of mercy, for he kynd þo vnkonyng by his prechyng; he vysyt þo seke and heled þaim of þair sores. ¶Another tyme he left þo conuersacion of all þo worldly men and of his disciples also, and went alon in to desert opon þo hyllys and continued al nyght in prayers as þo gospel sais.

In addition to omitting the first passage from his extract, the compiler of MS Ashmole 751 has altered parts of the second passage included in the extract, changing the description of Christ's practice to enhance its relevance to the priestly subject. While the full passage as reconstructed in the critical edition records that Christ "took upon him self þe persoone of siche maner men, boþe of prelates of hooli chirche *and oþere siche as aren disposid as I haue seid*,"[51] thus referring back to the layman in temporal "sovereignty," the Ashmole text reads "toke vpon hym self þo offys of men of holy kyrk as prelates and curates." In what appears to be a variant unique among manuscript witnesses, the compiler has changed "persoone" to "offys," making clerical status a requirement for the practice of the mixed life and rendering the exclusion of the layman complete. Just as the layman was removed from the first section of the extract, so "oþer siche" men have been removed from the second section, so that the notion of Christ providing an example to both "prelates and curates" and to pious laymen has disappeared.

I assume as Ralph Hanna does that the scribe, compiler, and user of this book were one and the same person, an individual whose shifting "sense of how much of any single text was wanted" resulted in his copying texts and then adding more of the same texts in later quires, in a process that "rendered the quires incapable of being bound in any rational manner."[52] This scribe was responsible for creating a unique extract of the *Mixed Life* to suit his own specifications, whether he was a priest in secular or religious life. In removing all references to the layman as addressee, as well as the related lay-oriented argument for the need to observe charity through a balance of "contemplacioun" with "werkes of actif liyf" and "bisynesse of þe world," this extract returns Hilton's Gregorian-inspired definition of the mixed life to the priest, shaping a definition of the priestly life that simply elides the overlap between priest, Christ, and layman that Hilton had emphasized in his guide.

It is telling, in light of Nicholas Love's construction of his projected fifteenth-century lay readers as "symple creatures," that Love, in his own borrowing from Hilton's *Mixed Life*, performs an act of clerical editing comparable to that of the Ashmole compiler.[53] Love's three-part scheme of active and contemplative lives, which is indebted, like Hilton's, to Gregory the Great, divides the active life into two "parts" and posits the contemplative life as a category lying between these two. The first part of the active life involves

amendyng of him self as wiþdrawing fro vices & profetyng in vertues . . . þe seconde parte of actif life is, when a mannus occupacion & bisinesse, stant in þat exercise þat longeþ to þe profite of oþer men principaly, þouh it be also þerwith to his owne mede þe more þerby. As it is in gouernyng of oþer men & teching, & helping to þe hele of soule, as done prelates & prechours & oþer þat hauen cure of soule. (118.26–35)

Love shows his indebtedness to Hilton's *Mixed Life* in defining the exercise of the second degree of active life as involving the "gouernyng of oþer men & teching, & helping to þe hele of soule, as done prelates & prechours & oþer þat haue cure of soule."[54] The fact that Love offers this elevated state to prelates and preachers only, leaving out the pious layman whom Hilton had included in the analogy, suggests Love's concern to make certain that the teaching and preaching of the mixed life remain the preserve of the clergy. As Sargent observes, the text "presents a more conservative treatment of the 'mixed life', here attributed to bishops and prelates... than does Walter Hilton, whom he cites below."[55] Given the overtly anti-Lollard stance of the *Mirror*, Love's conservative recruitment of Hilton may stem from a desire to distinguish carefully between clergy and laity. Love has read Hilton and, like the compiler of MS Ashmole 751, he has improved upon Hilton's mixed life by fully clericalizing it.

Although there is no evidence in MS Ashmole 751 of anxiety specifically about Lollardy, the parallel between the compiler's treatment of Hilton's work and the *Mirror*'s Hilton excerpt suggests that the Ashmole compiler's alterations to the *Mixed Life* may have been both practical and ideological. The compiler's desire to claim the mixed life as his own might reflect a more generalized fifteenth-century clerical concern to reassert boundaries between lay and clerical status in the hopes of suppressing the heterodox views of religious discipline considered in Chapter 4 with respect to preaching. Where the *Mirror* echoes and alters Hilton in a text explicitly adapted for lay reading, the Ashmole compiler fashions a conservative vision of the mixed life for his own use, a vision that might be transmitted to laypeople in a pastoral context.

This manuscript, with its practical aim of aiding the priest by improving his theological knowledge and supporting daily pastoral care and sacramental duties, includes other texts that restore the specific professional knowledge separating laity and clergy, so that here the layperson is implicitly understood as the object of penitential discipline and sacramental practice rather than the reading subject invited to engage in *imitatio clerici*. The unique extract of the *Mixed Life* heads a sequence of texts that focus attention on priests as powerful ministers of penance. The concomitant emphasis on the layperson as penitent subject is conveyed, in combination with an insistence upon the orthodox doctrine of confession, by the rest of this sequence of English contents, notably in the next set of texts, on fols. 45v–47v, a group of anecdotes excerpted from Caesarius of Heisterbach, James of Vitry, Innocent III, Chrysostom, and Bede. These stories, which would lend themselves readily to inclusion in sermons, focus on the effectiveness of penance, the necessity of clerical intervention, and the danger of falsifying contrition. As with the Hilton extract, context is crucial for attempting to gauge the possible function of these tales for a priestly user.

The first story, taken from Caesarius, also appears excerpted in Robert Thornton's manuscript (Lincoln Cathedral MS 91, fol. 194r), among a series of three tales relating to contrition. In the Thornton manuscript, compiled and used by a layman, the inclusion of this tale in a "Rolle-related cluster"[56] followed by the English *Mirror of St. Edmund*, reinforces the layman's appropriation of penitential and contemplative vocabularies. But in the MS Ashmole 751 sequence, the tales highlight the priest's sole control over the administration of penance. The first story (fol. 45v) tells of a scholar "at Paris" who

had don many foule synnes of þo whylk he had gret schame to schryfe hym. But at þo last gret sorw of hert ouer come schame, and when he was redy to schryfe hym to þo pryoure of þo abbay of Seynt Victor, so mykyl contricion was in his hert þat for sorow he myght [not] speke a word.

The wise prior advises the penitent to write his sins on paper; the prior reads them, understands their gravity, and proceeds to show the paper to the abbot. But the abbot sees only a blank page: the conclusion, voiced by the abbot, is that "God has sen his contricyon and has forgyfyn hym all his synnes." Although the power of God to forgive sins constitutes the story's miracle, the tale insists upon the intervention of the priestly figures, both for initiating the process and for confirming absolution.[57] The need for confession, in a written form if auricular confession is not possible, seems the critical lesson of the story from the priestly point of view.

Even more strongly than this first story, the other tale from Caesarius (fol. 47r) highlights the importance of special priestly insight and mediation for furthering lay spiritual purification. This anecdote also appears in the composite northern volume London, British Library, MS Harley 1022, a codex combining Latin and English pastoral materials with English texts such as Book I of Hilton's *Scale of Perfection*.[58] In this story, "a prest þat had cure of saules sagh a woman cled in diuers clothynges and had a longe tayle þat sche droght after hyr, in þo whylk he sagh a multitude of fendes blake and smale." In response to his vision, the priest

bad hyr stand styll, sythen he called þo folk and coniured þo fendes þat þai schuld fle, and prayed to god þat þo folk myght se þat, and so þai dyd. Þen þo womon sagh þat fendes dyssayued hyr in pryde of clothyng, scho ȝede home and chaunged hyr clothes and fro þat tyme scho was ensaumpell of mekenes.

This story emphasizes the superior discernment of the priest and the absolute necessity for detecting sin that remains invisible to those without the "cure of saules." One can see how readily these two English stories might be lifted and placed directly into a sermon to emphasize not only the requirement of confession but also the quasi-miraculous power of priestly insight.

There is a haphazard quality to the MS Ashmole 751 miscellany, and one should not overstate the logic of its compilation of English contents. However, the inclusion of these instructive texts after the *Mixed Life* extract argues for a degree of thematic unity in these pastoral selections, and for their particular relevance not only to the situation of a priest, but perhaps also to a particular clerical mood of the mid-fifteenth century. The material and social power enjoyed by Walter Hilton's late fourteenth-century addressee enabled Hilton to take spiritual and disciplinary chances, to construct his reader as a sort of prelate, and thus to enter into a wider debate about lay religious practice and clerical propriety. But this later priestly reader did not share Hilton's impulse to use spiritual guidance as an occasion for analyzing and expanding the boundaries of lay religious identity, as Robert Thornton continued to do with his own book.

REFORM CONTINUES: *IMITATIO CLERICI* IN OXFORD, BODLEIAN LIBRARY, MS LAUD MISC. 210

Examination of MS Harley 5272, Lincoln Cathedral MS 91, and MS Ashmole 751 reveals the appeal and accessibility of fourteenth-century spiritual guidance to elite laity and those in professional religious life, whether nuns or priests. But the uses of the *Abbey* and the *Mixed Life* were varied even among these readers. MS Ashmole 751 suggests that readers in positions of religious authority may have been uneasy about possibilities for overlap between lay and clerical identities. I turn finally to a curious compilation that cannot reliably be attributed to either group, a collection that suggests more boldly than the Thornton manuscript that the project of lay *imitatio clerici* continued into the fraught fifteenth century.[59] The contents of this book, Oxford, Bodleian Library, MS Laud Misc. 210, a mid-fifteenth-century codex of unknown origins and ownership, show that even in what has been characterized as an atmosphere of anxiety about heresy and a dangerous time for the composition of new vernacular theology, challenging combinations of texts were still being made in manuscripts. Whoever the compiler and whatever the rationale for this collection, which includes catechetical works, the guides *Book to a Mother*, *The Life of Soul*, and a Wycliffite tract, these contents combine to suggest a polemical vision of shared lay and clerical knowledge and practice.

The categories of orthodox and heterodox reading are notoriously slippery ones throughout the fifteenth century. Material from the English Wycliffite Bible frequently reached readers with little interest in heterodoxy; on the other hand, orthodox devotional texts were eagerly used by Lollards in the later part of the fifteenth and early sixteenth centuries.[60] MS Laud Misc. 210, a manuscript that combines aspects of traditional religious thought with quite controversial statements, might well have appealed to a range of readers, lay or religious, interested in interrogating the question of how religious life should be lived. Although the manuscript lacks any ownership marks or evidence of institutional provenance,[61] the codex can be considered an anthology by virtue of its careful organization. The collection was copied by one scribe with the exception of the last text, *The Abbey of the Holy Ghost*, which was added at a later date. This compiler was evidently more concerned with what Dutton calls "the Decalogue, the theology of love, and the necessity of resisting evil"[62] than with the orthodoxy of every single text: the book thus falls into Hudson's category of "manuscripts that appear to be orthodox in initiative [but] contain isolated Wycliffite texts."[63] This manuscript persistently emphasizes religious fundamentals and the importance of the active life in the world, although the presence of eremitic and monastically influenced works (Rolle's *Form of Living* and the *Abbey*, the first and final texts in the codex) suggests that this compiler, like Thornton, considered multiple modes of reading and guidance to be complementary. The inclusion of these texts, which encourage modes of life and practice criticized by the Lollards, offers another caution against assuming this volume to be a Wycliffite manuscript.

After the *Form of Living*, the rest of the book's early contents repeat and reinforce items basic to the Syllabus and emphasize the need for active imitation of Christ in the world.[64] *Book to a Mother* appears immediately after the *Form of Living* booklet, followed by several shorter texts that emphasize particular elements of the catechism, crucial aspects of the active life, and the benefits of tribulation in the world. As we have seen, *Book to a Mother* invokes and claims to transcend the image of the cloister to construct an approach to poverty, obedience, and humility in the world; the shorter texts immediately following it invite the male or female reader to develop the practice of these same active virtues.[65] The short text immediately after *Book to a Mother* begins, "Diliges dominum deum tuum ex toto corde. Yow schalt loue þe lord þi god of al þin herte of al þi lyf of al þi mynde and of alle þi strengþis or miȝtis, and þi neiȝebore as þi silf" (fol. 94r).[66] This text offers specific instructions on the care of neighbor, instructions that both recall the advice of *Book to a Mother* and augment the earlier text to suggest specifically how the reader's "good liuinge" might function as an example to others:

by holy counselyng, and techyng, and by ensaunple of þin owne good lyf, bi drede of grete peynes boþe in þis world in purgatorie and in helle, and by counfort of the endeles blis of heuene, hou soone he mai gete þat, bi goddis mersy and very repentaunce and amendyng of his wickid lyf. (fol. 95r)

This short text insists that the reader's "owne" mixed life, a combination of "preyer" and "counselyng and techyng," must be beneficial not only to him- or herself but also to the larger Christian community. This text is followed by three works, evidently copied to go together,[67] including an acephalous *Visitacio Infirmorum, De Utilitatibus Tribulationis*,[68] and *The Life of Soul*. The collection of this last text together with *Book to a Mother* may speak to the compiler's sense of the two works' shared commitment to the centrality of scripture and to the lay reader's continuing search for knowledge.

In the way that *Book to a Mother* expresses theologically orthodox ideas while adumbrating an uncompromising apostolic vision of *imitatio Christi*, this manuscript combines Syllabus items with a Wycliffite tract to offer an extremely rigorous view on holy living in the world.[69] As Hudson has argued, in examining manuscripts with uncertain affiliations, "it is easy for a modern critic to oversimplify – to demand doctrinal consistency where a medieval reader, Wycliffite or conventional, would have been less narrow-minded."[70] Although the Syllabus-related items are not otherwise controversial, in one of them, the exhortation to follow the ten command-ments and perform "þe seuene dedes of mercy bodily or ellus þe seuene goostly" is followed by familiar-sounding words that elevate the simple pro-fession of Christ over the various forms of vowed religious and even priestly life. This treatise advises serious devotion to the teachings of the catechism and condemns those who fail to keep its essential priorities foremost:

> Þis is cristes religioun þat iche cristen man mut kepe ȝif he wil be saued. And whoso kepeþ not þis religioun, be he lernd or leud monk or freere, fast he neuer so miche or were þe hayre [wear the hairshirt], he is a verray apostata, and brekeþ his ordre. And þerfore who so euer styreþ [commands] þe be word or dede to kepe þis ordre and þis relygioun þat crist ordeyned and kept hym self, leue hym and loue hym, and do blcþcly after hym, be he lewed or lernd . . . for oute of doute, þis lyf is beest, for mannes lyuynge in erþe and schortest to cunne and also lyȝtest to kepe, ȝif hit be kept in his owne kynde, as crist hym self tauȝt it, and not acombered ne clouted be cursed clerkes of anticristes couent. (fols. 167v–168r)

In a passage complementary to sentiments expressed in *Book to a Mother*, this author scorns the distinctions between religious states and degrees of learning for the more important criterion of faithfulness to Christ's "reli-gioun." As in *Book to a Mother*, the association of apostasy and Antichrist with monks, friars, and clerics suggests that the text's anonymous author retains faith in these representatives of religion only if they adhere strictly to their models.

The Lollard tract, even more frankly controversial, shares an interest with *Book to a Mother* and *The Life of Soul* in the shared teaching responsibilities of clergy and laity, and its inclusion here reinforces these concerns as central to the codex. A treatise on "maters of holy wryȝt þat is nedeful to be knowen," this text simultaneously upholds and criticizes the priesthood, arguably drawing an even closer analogy than these guides do between the clerical life and a layperson's mixed life. This work argues that the priestly life is holy so long as priests sustain themselves by necessary manual work. Adopting the clerical "we," a technique seen often in *The Life of Soul* and *Book to a Mother*, the author argues that if it is necessary to work in order to help others, then

whi schulde we not don þat þe apostle poule comaundeþ to us, þat is to seye wurche bodily werkes oþer whyle to wynne oure liflode bodily and giue god þe better gostly, for on preyere of him þat is obedient to godis hestes and his apostles schal sonner be herd þan a þousand of hem þat dispiseþ godis hestes and doþ not hem in dede. (fol. 169r)

This argument for manual work by priests, in order to "kepe hem fro nede and beggyng," demystifies priestly status by insisting upon the bodily need that priests suffer as much as laypeople. The text also narrows the gap between priest and lay reader with a final statement that might apply equally well to laypeople's religious life. For clerics and layfolk, the focus (as in *Book to a Mother*) is upon obedience to God's "hestes" and the performance "in dede" of the example of Christ and the apostles.

These texts repeatedly emphasize information vital to both lay and clerical readers, blurring rather than reinforcing distinctions between the two states. In its vernacularity, repetition of Syllabus items, and advice on forms of active life in the world, MS Laud Misc. 210 might have been intended for lay readers, but this combination of texts would also have been useful to the reform-minded cleric seeking private edifying reading or material for teaching the faithful. Like *Book to a Mother*, its longest single text, this codex is both didactic and polemical, narrative and regulatory. In a more strident vein than Thornton's book, this volume also suggests continuity between fourteenth-century reforming spiritual guidance and fifteenth-century compilers, even amid potential anxiety about how to define boundaries between lay and clerical prerogatives. By considering this manuscript through the lens of *imitatio clerici*, I suggest that even in the fifteenth century, it was possible for some to envision common ground between the reading and practices of the "modur" and the "clerk."

I have argued for significant literary and ideological distinctions between fourteenth-century spiritual guides that look to the cloister and those that find in the clerical life a model for lay religious discipline. But I have also suggested throughout this study the fundamental orthodoxy of both sets of texts (as well as of Chaucer and Langland), as these authors strive to reconfigure professional religious models for pious lay readers in the world. Surviving books demonstrate that fifteenth-century readers eagerly drew upon monastic and clerical forms of religious discipline alike. As I noted above, along with texts offering clerical models to laity, both Lincoln Cathedral MS 91 and MS Laud Misc. 210 also feature *The Abbey of the Holy Ghost* (albeit added by a later compiler in the Laud manuscript). The presence of the *Abbey* in these two compilations suggests not only that some fifteenth-century compilers imagined lay and priestly knowledge and practice as overlapping, but that they continued to embrace the monastic model, collecting as many "forms of living" as possible within the covers of their anthologies. These fifteenth-century readers, whether or not they lined up with the audiences sought by fourteenth-century authors of spiritual guidance, persisted in making use of religious discipline in all its complex literary variety.

Notes

1. Recent interest in this field owes much to Nicholas Watson, who has argued for the centrality of devotional literature to late medieval English culture and for considering contemporary poets as engaged in complex ways in the broad project of writing "vernacular theology." See for example "Censorship and Cultural Change in Late-Medieval England: Vernacular Theology, the Oxford Translation Debate, and Arundel's Constitutions of 1409," *Speculum* 70 (1995): 822–64; "Visions of Inclusion: Universal Salvation and Vernacular Theology in Pre-Reformation England," *Journal of Medieval and Early Modern Studies* 27 (1997): 145–87; "The *Gawain*-Poet as a Vernacular Theologian," in *A Companion to the "Gawain"-Poet*, ed. Derek Brewer and Jonathan Gibson (Cambridge: D. S. Brewer, 1997), 293–313.

2. With the exception of Walter Hilton's *Mixed Life*, all of the guides in this study are anonymous. It is clear from their content that they are clerical, almost certainly priestly productions, although the particulars of their authors' statuses remain unclear in most cases (the exception is *Book to a Mother*, which can be associated with a secular priest). For an excellent brief introduction to all the works in the study, including others that I do not include for reasons noted below, see Vincent Gillespie, "Anonymous Devotional Writings," in *A Companion to Middle English Prose*, ed. A. S. G. Edwards (Cambridge: D. S. Brewer, 2004), 127–49. I refer to the writers of these works as "authors" rather than "compilers," the term favored in the case of *Book to a Mother* by Elisabeth Dutton, on the grounds that much of that work is woven together from other sources. See Elisabeth Dutton, "Christ the Codex: Compilation as Literary Device in *Book to a Mother*," *Leeds Studies in English* New Series 35 (2004): 81–100. Each of these writers is invested in constructing himself, in Alastair Minnis's terms, as an *auctor*, "someone . . . to be respected and believed," rather than a *compilator*, who brings together sources but "add[s] no opinion of his own." A. J. Minnis, *Medieval Theory of Authorship: Scholastic Literary Attitudes in the Later Middle Ages* (London: Scolar Press, 1984), 10, 94.

3. Anne Hudson's phrase: *The Premature Reformation: Wycliffite Texts and Lollard History* (Oxford: Clarendon Press, 1988), 390. These works can all be

conservatively dated within the period *c.* 1375–*c.* 1425. *The Abbey of the Holy Ghost*, *Book to a Mother*, and Hilton's *Mixed Life* can be dated with certainty to the late fourteenth century, and it is likely that *The Life of Soul* and *Fervor Amoris* also date from before the turn of the century, although the evidence remains inconclusive. For a list of works of late fourteenth- and early fifteenth-century "vernacular theology" with approximate dating, see the Appendix to Nicholas Watson, "Censorship and Cultural Change," 861–62.

4. I have eliminated works not definitely written for lay readers (e.g., *The Holy Boke Gratia Dei*), or written later in the fifteenth century explicitly to confront Lollardy (e.g., Reginald Pecock's *Reule of Christian Religioun*). One work deserving of further study but which I have not included is *The Pore Caitif*, a compilation proposing to teach lay readers how to progress "fro the grounde of bileve in to the keping of Goddis commaundementes and so up fro vertu into vertu, til to he se God of Syon regnyng in everlasting blis." I do not include *The Pore Caitif* because it is a collection of treatises, often copied separately, rather than a unified guide. For discussion of *The Pore Caitif* and an excerpt from its Prologue, see *The Idea of the Vernacular: An Anthology of English Literary Theory, 1280–1520*, ed. Jocelyn Wogan-Browne *et al.* (University Park: The Pennsylvania State University Press, 1999), 239–41 (quotation above at 240). For a diplomatic edition, see Mary Teresa Brady, ed., "*The Pore Caitif*: Edited from MS Harley 2336 with Introduction and Notes" (Ph.D. diss., Fordham University, 1954). Also see Kalpen Trivedi, "The 'Pore Caitif': *Lectio* through *Compilatio*: Some Manuscript Contexts," *Mediaevalia* 20 (2001): 129–52.

5. Vincent Gillespie aptly characterizes such real or imagined readers in considering a passage from the compilation *Book for a Simple and Devout Woman*: this was "an audience aware of its own spiritual potential, eager to realise it, newly hungry for signs of divine grace and for communion with the deity" ("Anonymous Devotional Writings," 131).

6. S. J. Ogilvie Thomson, ed., *Walter Hilton's "Mixed Life" Edited From Lambeth Palace MS 472*, Salzburg Studies in English Literature: Elizabethan & Renaissance Studies 92.15 (Salzburg: Institut für Anglistik und Amerikanistik, 1986), 7.74–75. Further citations appear in the main text by page and line number.

7. Margaret Connolly, ed., *Contemplations of the Dread and Love of God* [*Fervor Amoris*], EETS OS 303 (London: Oxford University Press, 1993), 5. Further citations appear in the main text by page number.

8. As James Simpson notes, these guides "register and contain lay pressures to assimilate the religious practice of professional religious." See *The Oxford English Literary History*, vol. 2, 1350–1547, *Reform and Cultural Revolution* (Oxford: Oxford University Press, 2002), 435.

9. Treating slightly later English works, Rebecca Krug draws attention to the importance of literary form in devotional texts written by and for fifteenth-century women readers. Krug suggests that works such as *The Book of Margery*

Kempe convey women's "interest in the linguistic 'shape' of devotion." "The Comfort of Form: Prayer and Lay Women's Devotion in the Fifteenth Century" (Paper presented at the International Congress on Medieval Studies, Kalamazoo, MI, May 2007), 2. I thank her for permission to cite this paper.

10. I am using the term "reforming" and "reformist" to characterize works that shift boundaries without breaching them, in the tradition of suggestions made by Nicholas Watson: see "Fashioning the Puritan Gentry-Woman: Devotion and Dissent in *Book to a Mother*," in *Medieval Women: Texts and Contexts in Late Medieval Britain: Essays for Felicity Riddy*, ed. Jocelyn Wogan-Browne *et al.* (Turnhout: Brepols, 2000), 169–84. My use of the term is also indebted to James Simpson's arguments in *Reform and Cultural Revolution*: his account of *Piers Plowman*'s ecclesiastical critique captures the tension at work in these spiritual guides: "[t]he poem's satirical strategy is, however, reformist rather than damnatory: it circles back to revisit and reform institutions whose inadequacy has been exposed" (357).

11. In all of these texts, the "affective" approach to Christ is operative to varying degrees and is never abandoned. Even in the texts that I view as conservative, the humanity of Christ does not function to "abject" lay readers or encourage "a spirituality which would isolate or detach the individual from the daily concerns of her or his neighbors," as David Aers has argued traditional representations of the Passion do. See David Aers, "The Humanity of Christ: Representations in Wycliffite Texts and *Piers Plowman*," in David Aers and Lynn Staley, *The Powers of the Holy: Religion, Politics, and Gender in Late Medieval English Culture* (University Park: The Pennsylvania State University Press, 1996), 66.

12. My categories overlap to some extent with the various modes of "perfectionist" thought (themselves overlapping) that Nicholas Watson has recently posited: see discussion of "mixed life," "puritanical," and "affective" modes in "Chaucer's Public Christianity," *Religion and Literature* 37.2 (2005): 101–02.

13. David Aers and Lynn Staley, "Epilogue," in *The Powers of the Holy*, 268.

14. Watson suggests that Chaucer is a "mediocrist" who does not believe worldly laity capable of pursuing perfection, in contrast to Langland, for whom "seeking God comes to constitute the only valid form of living" ("Chaucer's Public Christianity," 104).

15. Jim Rhodes cautions against the "postmodern tendency" to view poetry as such: see *Poetry Does Theology: Chaucer, Grosseteste, and the "Pearl"-Poet* (Notre Dame: University of Notre Dame Press, 2001), 2.

16. I borrow this phrase from Steven Justice, "Inquisition, Speech, and Writing: A Case from Late-Medieval Norwich," *Representations* 48 (Autumn 1994): 20.

17. Watson, "Censorship and Cultural Change," 830–35.

18. I agree with Ralph Hanna that "our recovery of a historical sense of vernacular written culture in the Middle Ages depends heavily on rediscovering the connection of more minute works with what one is conditioned to admire as 'canonical Middle English literature.'" See "Notes Toward a Future History

of Middle English Literature: Two Copies of Richard Rolle's *Form of Living*,"
in *Chaucer in Perspective: Middle English Essays in Honour of Norman Blake*,
ed. Geoffrey Lester (Sheffield: Sheffield Academic Press, 1999), 280.

INTRODUCTION

1. George Keiser writes, "[a]s they came to enjoy the benefits of literacy
   (at least in the vernacular) and of a 'solid conservative prosperity,' many
   men and women from the middle classes sought an improvement in their
   spiritual welfare commensurate with the improvement in their material
   welfare." See " 'To Knawe God Almyghtyn': Robert Thornton's Devotional
   Book," *Analecta Cartusiana* 106 (1984): 123.

2. As Margaret Aston notes in reference to the foundation of intercessory
   institutions such as chantries, "The forms of spiritual self-help were
   multiplying." See "Popular Religious Movements," in *Faith and Fire:
   Popular and Unpopular Religion 1350–1600* (London: Hambledon Press,
   1993), 9. For the argument that confraternity was one of the dominant
   ways to participate in the "merit secured by spiritual good works," see R.
   N. Swanson, "Mendicants and Confraternity in Late Medieval England,"
   in *The Religious Orders in Pre-Reformation England*, ed. James G. Clark
   (Woodbridge: Boydell & Brewer, 2002), 123.

3. P. S. Jolliffe, *A Check-List of Middle English Prose Writings of Spiritual
   Guidance* (Toronto: Pontifical Institute of Medieval Studies, 1974), 21–22.

4. Theresa Coletti, "*Paupertas est donum Dei*: Hagiography, Lay Religion, and
   the Economics of Salvation in the Digby *Mary Magdalene*," *Speculum* 76.2
   (2001): 375.

5. I use the phrase "secular clerical life" in this sense throughout the study: cf.
   the following Middle English sense of "seculere" as attested in *MED*: "Of
   a member of the clergy: living in the world as opposed to living under a
   religious rule; not cloistered."

6. Pierre Bourdieu, *Outline of a Theory of Practice*, trans. Richard Nice
   (Cambridge: Cambridge University Press, 1977), 179. See Mark Addison
   Amos, "'For Manners Make the Man': Bourdieu, de Certeau, and the
   Common Appropriation of Noble Manners in the *Book of Courtesy*," in
   Medieval Conduct, ed. Kathleen Ashley and Robert L. A. Clark (Min-
   neapolis: University of Minnesota Press, 2001), 23–48. Amos reads Caxton's
   late fifteenth-century *Book of Courtesy* in light of Bourdieu's theories of
   "symbolic capital," "distinction," and *habitus*.

7. Bourdieu, *Outline of a Theory of Practice*, 181. For Bourdieu, "distinction" is
   a crucial byproduct of symbolic capital. He argues at 195, "[d]istinctions and
   lasting associations are founded in the circular circulation from which the
   legitimation of power arises as a symbolic surplus value." For an extended
   discussion of this concept, see Pierre Bourdieu, *Distinction: A Social Critique
   of the Judgement of Taste* (Cambridge, MA: Harvard University Press,
   1984).

8. Nancy Warren employs Bourdieu's notion of "symbolic capital" to study the ways in which late medieval English nuns "were enmeshed in material, symbolic, textual, political, and spiritual economies." *Spiritual Economies: Female Monasticism in Later Medieval England* (Philadelphia: University of Pennsylvania Press, 2001), vii.

9. Talal Asad, *Genealogies of Religion: Discipline and Reasons of Power in Christianity and Islam* (Baltimore: The Johns Hopkins University Press, 1993), 135.

10. The Fourth Lateran Council made this requirement definitive in Canon 21: "Every Christian of either sex, after attaining years of discretion, shall faithfully confess all his sins to his own priest at least once a year, and shall endeavor according to his ability to fulfill the penance enjoined him." Translation from John T. McNeill and Helena M. Gamer, eds., *Medieval Handbooks of Penance* (New York: Columbia University Press, 1938), 413. The Latin reads, "Omnis utriusque sexus fidelis, postquam ad annos discretionis pervenerit, omnia sua solus peccata confiteatur fideliter, saltem semel in anno, proprio sacerdoti, et injunctam sibi pænitentiam studeat pro viribus adimplere." C.-J. Hefele, *Histoires des conciles*, ed. and trans. Jean Leclercq, vol. 5, part 2 (Paris: Letouzey and Ane, 1913), 1350.

11. By the twelfth century, priestly absolution was given and then a penance was assigned; the idea that contrition should be the principal part of penance was elaborated by Abelard and Peter Lombard, among others. See Thomas Tentler, *Sin and Confession on the Eve of the Reformation* (Princeton: Princeton University Press, 1977), 19. After Lateran IV, Tentler argues, "the sacramental character of penance was emphasized... By the end of the century all the canonists and theologians agreed that sacramental confession was obligatory, divinely instituted, and necessary... for the remission of sins, even when the major part of them at the same time held that contrition was the most important and effective part of the Sacrament of Penance" (22).

12. *Genealogies of Religion*, 165. Asad continues, "it was a disciplinary technique for the self to create a desire for obedience to the law – but that was intrinsic to what the self was, not an instrument to be used by authority to keep an already constituted self in order."

13. H.-I. Marrou, "Doctrina et disciplina dans la langue des Pères de l'Église," *Bulletin du Cange* 9 (1934): 10.

14. *Ibid.*, 18. Emphasis in original.

15. *Ibid.*, 23.

16. *The Rule of Saint Benedict in Latin and English with Notes*, ed. Timothy Fry (Collegeville: The Liturgical Press, 1981), 157. The Latin reads, "Obsculta, o fili, praecepta magistri... et admonitionem pii patris libenter excipe et efficaciter comple, ut ad eum per oboedientiae laborem redeas, a quo per inoboedientiae desidiam recesseras. Ad te ergo nunc mihi sermo dirigitur, quisquis abrenuntians propriis voluntatibus, Domino Christo vero regi militaturus, oboedientiae fortissima atque praeclara arma sumis" (156).

This opening passage is borrowed, like much of Benedict's *Rule*, from the contemporary *Rule of the Master* (*Regula Magistri*). For details on Benedict's borrowings and his original contributions, see David Knowles, "The *Regula Magistri* and the *Rule* of St. Benedict," in *Great Historical Enterprises: Problems in Monastic History* (London: Thomas Nelson and Sons, 1963), 139–95.

17. Divided into seven rounds of day and night chant, the performance of praise is the monk's most important duty: Benedict orders that nothing should come before worship. Monks may pray privately any time after the Office is completed: "if at other times someone chooses to pray privately, he may simply go in and pray, not in a loud voice, but with tears and heartfelt devotion" (*The Rule of Saint Benedict*, 255). The Latin reads, "Sed et si aliter vult sibi forte secretius orare, simpliciter intret et oret, non in clamosa voce, sed in lacrimis et intentione cordis" (254).

18. Jean Leclercq, "Disciplina," in *Dictionnaire de spiritualité*, ed. Charles Baumgartner *et al.* (Paris: Beauchesne, 1957), 3:1296.

19. Hugh of St. Victor defines discipline as "the science of good living, [whose] principle is humility" (*ibid.*, 1300).

20. The friars argued for mendicancy as the key to their apostolic superiority over the rest of the clergy, both secular and monastic. In his *Protectarium Pauperis*, the Carmelite friar Richard Maidstone maintains that mendicancy was integral to the practice of the apostles. See Arnold Williams, ed., "*Protectarium Pauperis*, A Defense of the Begging Friars by Richard Maidstone, O. Carm. (d. 1396)," *Carmelus* 5 (1958): 132–80.

21. Gail McMurray Gibson, *The Theater of Devotion: East Anglian Drama and Society in the Late Middle Ages* (Chicago: University of Chicago Press, 1989), 128. Italics in original.

22. "*Speculum Christiani*": *A Middle English Religious Treatise of the 14th Century*, ed. Gustaf Holmstedt, EETS OS 182 (London: Humphrey Milford, 1933), 174.9–11.

23. See, for example, Peter of Celle's treatise *De Disciplina Claustri*, in which he equates the monastic life with the *vita apostolica*. Peter of Celle, *L'École du cloître*, ed. Gérard de Martel, Sources chrétiennes 240 (Paris: Éditions du Cerf, 1977), 122–30.

24. "[R]egula religionis quam Christus instituit est perfectissima possibilis, ergo si fuerit extranea superaddita, est prophana." John Wyclif, *De Civili Dominio*, vol. 3, ed. Johann Loserth (London: Wyclif Society, 1903), 20.3–5.

25. "Seculares sunt religiosi paupertatem, castitatem et obedienciam matri ecclesie et non conventuali preposito profitentes" (*ibid.*, 4.15–17).

26. "Those laboring like the apostles as the good knights of Jesus Christ among their enemies in the world deserve greater praise and reward than those retreating foolishly into the cloister." The Latin reads, "laborantes instar apostolorum sicut boni milites Christi Jesu inter hostes eius in seculo habent condicionem maioris laudis et meriti quam retrahentes vecorditer se in claustro" (*ibid.*, 35.10–12).

27. The Latin reads, "ne alicui professioni privata ligatus sit ab opere evangelii retardatus, dicente Gregorio: Fortis athleta Christi noluit includi infra claustrum ut magis lucrifaceret Deo suo" (*ibid.*, 36.14–17).

28. He remarks upon the danger of corruption for the priestly class, noting that there are more devout people now than ecclesiastics in the church and suggesting that the laity truly constitutes the church. See *ibid.*, 258.30–35.

29. Wyclif argues that for the man of religion, ideally "the act is more worthy, more useful and more significant than his habit": "actus est dignior, utilior et nocior quam suus habitus" (*ibid.*, 2.18–19). Observations added to the rules laid down by Christ in the gospels are proclaimed unlawful (*ibid.*, 13.18–20).

30. "Seminare autem verbum Dei ad edificacionem ecclesie est authonomatice christiana religio" (*ibid.*, 3.3–5).

31. As Michael Wilks notes, Wyclif had been deeply influenced by Robert Grosseteste, the thirteenth-century Dominican leader, on the importance of pastoral care, study of the Bible, and clerical poverty. Although he came later in life to criticize the mendicants, Wilks argues, "his own order was deliberately modelled on the friars." Michael Wilks, "Wyclif and the Great Persecution," in *Wyclif: Political Ideas and Practice* (Oxford: Oxbow Books, 2000), 197.

32. "[S]i autem pater carnalis et maiores utriusque testamenti tenentur docere filios legem suam, quanto magis patres spirituales, cuiusmodi debent esse omnes presbiteri! omnis enim fidelis ex vi seminis fidei habet potestatem gignendi spiritualiter natos ecclesie." John Wyclif, *De Veritate Sacrae Scripturae*, ed. Rudolf Buddensieg (London: Wyclif Society, 1906), 2:148.14–19.

33. He argues that holy scripture is "the first rule of all human perfection" (prima regula tocius perfeccionis humane). *De Veritate Sacrae Scripturae*, ed. Rudolf Buddensieg (London: Wyclif Society, 1905), 1:39.14.

34. Hudson, *The Premature Reformation*, 295.

35. André Vauchez, "'*Ordo Fraternitatis*': Confraternities and Lay Piety in the Middle Ages," in *The Laity in the Middle Ages: Religious Beliefs and Devotional Practices*, ed. Daniel E. Bornstein, trans. Margery J. Schneider (Notre Dame: University of Notre Dame Press, 1993), 111. The topic of semi-religious life in the high and later Middle Ages is vast: for a survey of developments in the definition of "religious" in canon law and lay practice, see John Van Engen, "Friar Johannes Nyder on Laypeople Living as Religious in the World," in *Vita Religiosa im Mittelalter*, ed. Franz J. Felten and Nikolas Jaspert (Berlin: Duncker & Humblot, 1999), 583–615. Van Engen notes that by the fourteenth century, the canonist Johannes Andreae (*c.* 1270–1349) defined "religious" more broadly than only those bound by a rule, "offering an inclusive vision of 'religious' as narrowing concentric circles: all baptized Europeans, the devoutly practicing, secular clergy in good standing, and the professed" (593).

36. These groups began as lay offshoots of the mendicant orders whose members followed modest rules of discipline in their own homes. The Franciscan third order, or Order of Penitents, received its first Rule in 1221; this Rule enjoins basic modesty, rules of tithing, fasting, and attendance at Communion, but there is no requirement of renunciation or specific works of charity beyond

the fellowship. See John Moorman, *The History of the Franciscan Order From its Origins to the Year 1517* (Oxford: Clarendon Press, 1968), 43.

37. D. W. Whitfield, "The Third Order of St. Francis in Mediaeval England," *Franciscan Studies* 13 (1953): 51. The survival in a single fifteenth-century manuscript of a Middle English rule for the Franciscan third order leaves open the possibility that at least one community of tertiaries existed. As Whitfield notes, though, the text might also have been copied for an individual tertiary or even for an antiquarian (*ibid.*, 53–55).

38. Norman Tanner, *The Church in Late Medieval Norwich 1370–1532*, Pontifical Institute Studies and Texts 66 (Toronto: Pontifical Institute of Mediaeval Studies, 1984), 65. He notes two groups of women living together described as "sisters" or "poor women" dedicated to chastity, as well as a third group of semi-religious women described as living under vow in a churchyard. Likewise, Roberta Gilchrist argues that *maisons dieu*, established to relieve the poor, may have overlapped in form and function with beguinages; if so, perhaps more urban Englishwomen lived semi-religious lives of poverty, chastity, and charity than historians have previously recognized. Gilchrist, *Gender and Material Culture: The Archaeology of Religious Women* (London: Routledge, 1994), 171–72.

39. Whitfield notes that in England "the Third Order was very largely by-passed by the practice of issuing letters of confraternity," adding, "it seems likely that a benefactor, who was assured of participation in the Order's masses and good works merely by making a donation and receiving in return a letter of fraternity, would not go to the extent of taking on the obligations of a tertiary Rule" ("The Third Order of St. Francis," 57).

40. Miri Rubin, *Charity and Community in Medieval Cambridge* (Cambridge: Cambridge University Press, 1987), 64–65.

41. Confraternity brought the promise of intercessory prayer as well as a "daily bond throughout this life with the prayers of the monks." H. E. J. Cowdrey, "Unions and Confraternity with Cluny," *The Journal of Ecclesiastical History* 16.2 (1965): 158–59. Although he is characterizing the practice of confraternity at Cluny earlier in the Middle Ages, Cowdrey's description also seems apt for the later English practice.

42. This is a quotation from the first known Franciscan letter of confraternity: the Latin reads, "vos ad universa et singula nostre religionis suffragia tam in vita quam in morte recipio, plenam vobis bonorum omnium tenore presentium participationem concedens, que per fratres nostros . . . operari dignabitur clementia salvatoris." A. G. Little, "Franciscan Letters of Fraternity," *Bodleian Library Record* 5 (1954): 13.

43. When a testator mentions at the beginning of a will that he/she wishes to be buried in the church of a particular religious order, this may be a sign of confraternity with that order.

44. The Latin reads, "volo quod corpus meum sepelliatur in habitu Fratrum Minorum, quia eorum frater sum in eodem ordine, et volo quod corpus meum tegatur nigro panno die sepulturæ meæ." See James Raine, ed.,

Testamenta Eboracensia, vol. 2, part 1, Surtees Society 4 (London: J. B. Nichols and Son, 1836), 100–01.

45. Barbara Harvey, *Living and Dying in England, 1100–1540: The Monastic Experience* (Oxford: Clarendon Press, 1993), 179.

46. R. N. Swanson observes that religious houses often sold large numbers of corrodies in order to shore up finances, but this strategy could be a risky proposition. Although the sale of corrodies could relieve short-term debt, the payment of annuities to all the corrodians "imposed a long-term burden. Annuities were worth while if their recipient died quickly, letting the house profit; but a long-lived annuitant was expensive." *Church and Society in Late Medieval England* (Oxford: Basil Blackwell, 1989), 237.

47. Bourdieu defines *habitus* as the systems of "regulated improvisation" that exist in the absence or in the interstices of express rules: "systems of durable, transposable dispositions, structured structures predisposed to function as structuring structures, that is, as principles which generate and organize practices and representations that can be objectively adapted to their outcomes without presupposing a conscious aiming at ends or an express mastery of the operations necessary in order to attain them. Objectively 'regulated' and 'regular' without being in any way the product of obedience to rules, they can be collectively orchestrated without being the product of the organizing action of a conductor." Pierre Bourdieu, *The Logic of Practice*, trans. Richard Nice (Stanford: Stanford University Press, 1990), 53.

48. Rubin, *Charity and Community in Medieval Cambridge*, 172.

49. "Concesserunt . . . dictis Thome et Johanne ad ecclesiam suam per medium claustri ad omnes horas divini officii." A. G. Little, ed. Eric Stone, "Corrodies at the Carmelite Friary of Lynn," *The Journal of Ecclesiastical History* 9.1 (1958): 20.

50. Bourdieu, *The Logic of Practice*, 75.

51. "The said prior and convent grant to the foresaid Thomas and Johanna that they will be participants of all the good things that shall be done through the brothers of the said convent in perpetuity, and that a chaplain of the foresaid convent shall forevermore celebrate [Mass] every day for the souls of the said Thomas and Johanna" (Little, "Corrodies at the Carmelite Priory of Lynn," 20–21). The Latin reads, "Concesserunt eciam dicti prior et conventus prefatis Thome et Johanne quod ipsi perticipes erunt omnium bonorum que per fratres dicti conventus fient imperpetuum, ac insuper unum capellanum inperpetuum de predicto conventu qui omni die ibidem celebrabit pro animabus dictorum Thome et Johanne."

52. *Fasciculi Zizaniorum Magistri Johannis Wyclif Cum Tritico, Ascribed to Thomas Netter of Walden*, ed. Walter W. Shirley (London: Her Majesty's Stationery Office, 1858), 277–82. The statements that material bread and wine remain after the consecration; that the accidents do not remain without the substance; and that Christ is not "identically, truly, and really" present in the sacrament, were declared heretical (277–78). The view that for the truly contrite penitent, confession was useless, was declared heretical (278);

and the view that all priests, regardless of their status, should be allowed to preach, was declared erroneous (280).

53. Virginia Bainbridge, *Gilds in the Medieval Countryside: Social and Religious Change in Cambridgeshire, c. 1350–58* (Woodbridge: The Boydell Press, 1996), 20. Extensive evidence of these guilds' ordinances exists as a result of a 1388 parliamentary demand that all such groups should account for themselves. This inquiry, probably undertaken with the intent of levying taxes on the guilds, required the masters and wardens of all guilds and brotherhoods to describe their foundations, forms of government, and possessions. For discussion of this parliamentary order and for texts of the London Middle English guild ordinances, see Caroline Barron and Laura Wright, "The London Middle English Guild Certificates of 1388–9," *Nottingham Medieval Studies* 39 (1995): 108–09. Over 500 of these returns survive, written mainly in Latin, but also in French and English.

54. See Bainbridge, *Gilds in the Medieval Countryside*, 125–28, for discussion of this complexity. Caroline Barron's influential article on London's religious fraternities surveys these groups with the assumption that each fraternity was associated with a given parish church. See Caroline Barron, "The Parish Fraternities of Medieval London," in *The Church in Pre-Reformation Society: Essays in Honour of F. R. H. Du Boulay*, ed. Caroline Barron and Christopher Harper-Bill (Woodbridge: The Boydell Press, 1985), 13–37. Scholars building on Barron's work have shown that some parish churches supported multiple guilds and that the administration of the parish and its guilds often overlapped. See Andrew Brown, *Popular Piety in Late Medieval England: The Diocese of Salisbury, 1250–1550* (Oxford: Clarendon Press, 1995), 142.

55. Barron, "The Parish Fraternities of Medieval London," 14.

56. Brown, *Popular Piety in Late Medieval England*, 148.

57. Barron notes, "the care of needy members was regarded as both a social and a Christian duty" ("The Parish Fraternities of Medieval London," 26). See also Ben R. McRee, "Charity and Gild Solidarity in Late Medieval England," *The Journal of British Studies* 32.3 (1993): 195–225.

58. Barbara Hanawalt in particular emphasizes the importance of the guilds' light-keeping function. See "Keepers of the Lights: Late Medieval English Parish Guilds," *Journal of Medieval and Renaissance Studies* 14.1 (1984): 21–37.

59. Barron and Wright, "The London Middle English Guild Certificates," 130. I have silently modernized punctuation from the extract.

60. Bainbridge, *Gilds in the Medieval Countryside*, 70.

61. *Ibid.*, 71.

62. Alan Kreider, *English Chantries: The Road to Dissolution* (Cambridge, MA: Harvard University Press, 1979), 5.

63. R. B. Dobson, "The Foundation of Perpetual Chantries by the Citizens of Medieval York," *Studies in Church History* 4, *The Province of York* (1967): 34. He cites a butcher and an ironmonger who founded chantries in York churches (at Holy Trinity, King's Court, and within All Saints' Pavement, respectively) in 1378. He notes, "from approximately 1330 to 1390, the

foundation of a perpetual chantry in a York church was emphatically not the exclusive privilege of the wealthy merchant and city oligarch."

64. Clive Burgess, "For the Increase of Divine Service: Chantries in Late Medieval Bristol," *The Journal of Ecclesiastical History* 36 (1985): 65.

65. Kreider, *English Chantries*, 40.

66. The Latin paragraph reads, "quatuordecim fidei articulos, decem mandata decalogi, duo precepta evangelii, scilicet gemine caritatis, septem etiam opera misericordie, septem peccata capitalia cum sua progenie, septem virtutes principales, ac septem gratie sacramenta." F. M. Powicke and C. R. Cheney, eds., *Councils and Synods, With Other Documents Relating to the English Church* (Oxford: Clarendon Press, 1964), 2:901.

67. W. A. Pantin, *The English Church in the Fourteenth Century* (Cambridge: Cambridge University Press, 1955), 189–219.

68. As Janet Coleman has noted, while the term "literatus" applied to a layman officially denoted grounding in Latin grammar, "[w]hen we add to this the ability to read in French and increasingly in English, then we have a situation in which the word 'literatus', the term 'literate,' takes on a multiplicity of meanings." Janet Coleman, *Medieval Readers and Writers 1350–1400* (London: Hutchinson, 1981), 24.

69. *The Lay Folks' Catechism*, ed. T. F. Simmons and H. E. Nolloth, EETS OS 118 (London: K. Paul, Trench, Trübner & Co, 1901), 20.

70. Eamon Duffy, *The Stripping of the Altars: Traditional Religion in Medieval England c.1400–c.1530* (New Haven: Yale University Press, 1992), 54. This work typically appears in manuscripts along with other free-standing works such as decalogue tracts, explanations of the seven deadly sins and/or the theological virtues, and discussions of the works of mercy. See Ralph Hanna III, *The Index of Middle English Prose Handlist XII: Smaller Bodleian Collections: English Miscellaneous, English Poetry, English Theology, Finch, Latin Theology, Lyell, Radcliffe Trust* (Cambridge: D. S. Brewer, 1997), xx. Also see Duffy, *The Stripping of the Altars*, Chapter 2, for further discussion of catechetical materials (54–75).

71. M. B. Parkes, "The Literacy of the Laity," in *Scribes, Scripts, and Readers: Studies in the Communication, Presentation, and Dissemination of Medieval Texts* (London: Hambledon Press, 1991), 283–84. In a similar vein, M. T. Clanchy asserts, "lay literacy grew out of bureaucracy rather than any abstract desire for education or literature." M. T. Clanchy, *From Memory to Written Record: England 1066–1307*, 2nd edn (Oxford: Basil Blackwell, 1993), 19.

72. As Clanchy asserts, the book of hours' "domestication of the liturgical book was the foundation on which the growing literacy of the later Middle Ages was built" (*From Memory*, 112). The first books of hours date from *c.* 1240–70 and were all designed for women (*ibid.*, 111).

73. Duffy, *The Stripping of the Altars*, 231.

74. The devotions of the book of hours, descended from accretions to the monastic breviary, did not vary with the liturgical year. They were not

obligatory, but voluntary and private, and their contents were not controlled by church authorities. The core of "essential" devotions tended to expand considerably in the fourteenth and fifteenth centuries to include "secondary elements" (gospel fragments, the Passion according to St. John, the prayers *Obsecro te* and *O Intemerata*, the fifteen joys of the Virgin, and the seven pleas to God) and "accessory elements," including the fifteen gradual psalms, hours in honor of various saints, prayers for the Christian day, prayers related to the Mass, the psalter of St. Jerome, the ten commandments, and others. Victor Leroquais, *Les Livres d'heures manuscrits de la Bibliothèque Nationale* (Macon: Protat Frères, 1927), xiv.

75. Christopher Wordsworth, ed., *Horae Eboracenses, the Prymer or Hours of the Blessed Virgin Mary according to the use of the illustrious church of York* (London: B. Quaritch, 1920), xxiv.

76. Duffy, *The Stripping of the Altars*, 220.

77. John Fisher, *English Works*, ed. J. E. B. Mayor, EETS ES 27 (London: N. Trübner & Co., 1876), 292.

78. Paul Saenger, "Books of Hours and the Reading Habits of the Later Middle Ages," in *The Culture of Print: Power and the Uses of Print in Early Modern Europe*, ed. Roger Chartier (Oxford: Basil Blackwell, 1989), 142.

79. *Ibid.*, 150.

80. Margaret Aston, "Devotional Literacy," in *Lollards and Reformers: Images and Literacy in Late Medieval Religion* (London: Hambledon Press, 1984), 106. (The article features an image of this window.)

81. Parkes, "The Literacy of the Laity," 284–85. Coleman views the expansion of English poetry and prose "as the reflection of a changing social structure and its changing ideals: a broadening of the middle range of society, its greater participation in government and its increasing demand for a literature read for information, for pleasure and for spiritual edification" (*Medieval Readers and Writers*, 24). Hilary Carey argues that the end of the fourteenth century was the historical moment at which English upper-class readers truly began to incorporate literature into their devotional lives. See "Devout Literate Laypeople and the Pursuit of the Mixed Life in Late Medieval England," *Journal of Religious History* 14 (1987): 361.

82. *The Prick of Conscience* was ascribed by some contemporaries to the hermit-mystic Richard Rolle (*d.* 1349), a legend discredited by Hope Emily Allen. See H. E. Allen, *Writings Ascribed to Richard Rolle, Hermit of Hampole, and Materials for His Biography* (New York: MLA, 1927), 372–97, for a detailed discussion of manuscript ascriptions to Rolle and other writers, including Grosseteste.

83. Lewis and McIntosh note that manuscripts of *The Prick of Conscience* begin to appear in large numbers after 1350, probably indicating that the work was composed not long before. Robert E. Lewis and Angus McIntosh, *A Descriptive Guide to the Manuscripts of the Prick of Conscience*, Medium Ævum Monographs New Series 12 (Oxford: The Society for the Study of Mediæval Languages and Literature, 1982), 4.

84. See Katherine C. Little, *Confession and Resistance: Defining the Self in Late Medieval England* (Notre Dame: University of Notre Dame Press, 2006), 7–12, on the importance of narrative in the process of lay subject formation in pastoral literature such as the *Fasciculus Morum* and *Handlyng Synne*.

85. Penance works in these two ways during one's life: "Ane es to clense here þe saule wele / Of dedly syn and of veniele; / Another to haf in heven mare mede; / Til þer twa may penaunce us lede." *The Prick of Conscience*, ed. Richard Morris (Berlin: Philological Society, 1863), 2776–79.

86. *The Prick of Conscience*, 9552–58.

87. Asad, *Genealogies of Religion*, 165.

88. Fiona Somerset, *Clerical Discourse and Lay Audience in Late Medieval England* (Cambridge: Cambridge University Press, 1998), 13.

89. Pantin, *The English Church in the Fourteenth Century*, 191.

90. Somerset, *Clerical Discourse and Lay Audience*, 13. In preparation for her study of "lewed clergie," or knowledge not specifically tied to clerical status and indeed often implying opposition to clerical authority, Somerset asserts that "lewed clergie," though a conceptual paradox, was not such an improbable concept in the late fourteenth century, since "the conventional linkage between learning and status did not hold fast in fourteenth century England, if indeed it ever had."

91. The work notes in its introduction that while laity ignorant of their Christian duties place their bodies and souls in danger, even more so do the priests who neglect their teaching duties: "And forthi that mikill folke now in this world / Ne is nought wele ynogh lered to knawe god almighten, / Ne loue him, ne serue him als thai suld do, / Als thaire dedis ofte sithe openly shewes, / In grete peril of thaime to lyue and to sawle, / And perauenture the defaitor in thaime, / That has thaire saules to kepe, and suld teche thame, / Als prelates, parsons, vikers, and prestes / That er halden be dette for to lere thame." *The Lay Folks' Catechism*, ed. Simmons and Nolloth, 4.33–41.

92. Somerset, *Clerical Discourse and Lay Audience*, 14. In a related vein, Moira Fitzgibbons shows that whereas Thoresby had a limited concept of spiritual instruction and emphasized simplicity and clarity above all, Gaytryge's translation includes changes in the order of the original text and subtle rhetorical shifts that emphasize laypeople's capacity to experience God more directly. See "Disruptive Simplicity: Gaytryge's Translation of Archbishop Thoresby's *Injunctions*," in *The Vernacular Spirit: Essays on Medieval Religious Literature*, ed. Renate Blumenfeld-Kosinski *et al.* (New York: Palgrave, 2002), 39–58.

93. Wendy Scase, *"Piers Plowman" and the New Anti-clericalism* (Cambridge: Cambridge University Press, 1989), 45.

94. Churchwardens acted as custodians of church furnishings as well as "possessors for the land of the parish" so that all land was accounted for. See Emma Mason, "The Role of the English Parishioner, 1100–1500," *The Journal of Ecclesiastical History* 27.1 (1976): 26.

95. For evidence of the exchange of books between laity and religious, see Mary C. Erler, "Exchange of Books Between Nuns and Laywomen:

Three Surviving Examples," in *New Science Out of Old Books: Studies in Manuscripts and Early Printed Books in Honour of A. I. Doyle*, ed. Richard Beadle *et al.* (Aldershot: Scolar, 1995), 360–73.

96. Jo Ann Hoeppner Moran, *The Growth of English Schooling, 1340–1548: Learning, Literacy, and Laicization in Pre-Reformation York Diocese* (Princeton: Princeton University Press, 1985), 208.

97. *Ibid.*, 197.

98. *Ibid.*, 206–07.

99. James G. Clark, *A Monastic Renaissance at St Albans: Thomas Walsingham and his Circle c.1350–1440* (Oxford: Clarendon Press, 2004), 31.

CHAPTER 1

1. Roger Ellis, "Figures of English Translation, 1382–1407," in *Translation and Nation: Towards a Cultural Politics of Englishness*, ed. Roger Ellis and Liz Oakley-Brown (Clevedon: Multilingual Matters, 2001), 5.

2. Vincent Gillespie's phrase, used in relating *Fervor Amoris* to *The Abbey of the Holy Ghost* on formal and conceptual grounds ("Anonymous Devotional Writings," 141). Shannon Gayk's term "regulatory aesthetic" describes a slightly later instance of literary-cultural translation which seems productively related in its methods and goals to those I consider in this chapter. Gayk argues that John Lydgate translates monastic techniques of *lectio* into English as a response to the period's prevailing "incarnational aesthetic," attempting to "reclaim monastic devotional practices and recapture a world in which lay piety was mediated by clerical authority." See "Images of Pity: The Regulatory Aesthetics of John Lydgate's Religious Lyrics," *Studies in the Age of Chaucer* 28 (2006): 179.

3. As Gillespie points out, clerical authors must contend with lay readers potentially "vulnerable to self-delusion and in danger of error and spiritual pride" ("Anonymous Devotional Writings," 131).

4. Pierre Bourdieu, *Outline of a Theory of Practice*, trans. Richard Nice (Cambridge: Cambridge University Press, 1977), 164. Emphasis in original.

5. Marjorie Curry Woods and Rita Copeland, "Classroom and Confession," in *The Cambridge History of Medieval Literature*, ed. David Wallace (Cambridge: Cambridge University Press, 1999), 392. They are characterizing the picture of the priest as described in Canon 21 of the Lateran Council of 1215: "prudent and cautious, so that in the manner of an expert physician he may pour wine and oil on the wounds of the injured person, enquiring diligently into the circumstances of the sin and the sinner, through which he may prudently discern what kind of counsel he should offer and what kind of remedy he should use."

6. Helen Barr, *Socioliterary Practice in Late Medieval England* (Oxford: Oxford University Press, 2001), 4.

7. *MED*, s.v. "reule" 2(a). See M. M. A. Schröer, ed., *Die Winteney-Version der Regula S. Benedicti Lateinische und Englisch mit Einleitung, Anmerkungen, Glossar und einem Facsimile zum erstenmale* (Halle: Max Niemeyer, 1888).

8. *MED*, s.v. "reulen" 2 (a): "To direct (sb., his heart, etc.) in moral or spiritual concerns, guide, influence."

9. Ann Warren, *Anchorites and their Patrons in Medieval England* (Berkeley: University of California Press, 1985), 8. The role was dominated by women in medieval England. These solitaries were supported by members of the community, often by one wealthy patron in particular (16).

10. *Ancrene Wisse* is related to the genre of the rule, but the use of "wisse," derived from Old English "wissian," meaning "rule, guide, direct, show," shows that the work is intended more as a "handbook" than a rule *per se*. See Anne Savage and Nicholas Watson, eds. and trans., *Anchoritic Spirituality: "Ancrene Wisse" and Associated Works* (New York: Paulist Press, 1991), 43.

11. *"Ancrene Wisse" Edited from MS Corpus Christi 402*, ed. J. R. R. Tolkien, EETS OS 249 (London: Oxford University Press, 1962), 5–6. In citations from this edition, I have changed tironian notae to "&" and expanded abbreviated words. "One rules the heart and makes it even and smooth . . . 'This rule is charity of a pure heart and a clean conscience and true belief' " (Savage and Watson, eds. and trans., *Anchoritic Spirituality*, 47).

12. *Ancrene Wisse*, ed. Tolkein, 7. "You should in all ways with all your might and strength guard well the inner, and the outer for her sake. The inner is always the same, the outer differs; for each should keep the outer according to the way she can best serve the inner using her" (Savage and Watson, eds. and trans., *Anchoritic Spirituality*, 48).

13. Nicholas Watson has shown that *Ancrene Wisse* was a complexly generative text for later Middle English writers, several of whom borrowed extensively from it to create new "guides to holy living" in the fourteenth century: these include *The Pore Caitif, Þe Holy Boke Gratia Dei, Þe Pater Noster of Richard Ermyte*, and *Book for a Simple and Devout Woman*. Watson argues, "*Ancrene Wisse* could function for later vernacular writers as a textual synecdoche for the life of holiness as it might be practiced by women and other notionally uneducated Christian people." See "*Ancrene Wisse*, Religious Reform and the Late Middle Ages," in *A Companion to "Ancrene Wisse,"* ed. Yoko Wada (Cambridge: D. S. Brewer, 2003), 199.

14. *MED*, s.v. "stable" 1a. (a) "Constant, steadfast; also, steadfast in virtue, virtuous . . . (b) of a lover: faithful, true; of love: durable, enduring; (c) resolute, unflinching; courageous . . . (d) of faith, piety, etc.: steadfastly maintained, unwavering, firm; (e) *eccl*. ~ dwellinge, the perseverance in monastic life avowed by members of the Benedictine order. 1b. (a) Unchanging, invariable; of God: immutable."

15. "[p]romittat de stabilitate sua et conversatione morum suorum et oboedientia" (*The Rule of Saint Benedict*, ed. Fry, 268).

16. See *ibid.*, 463.

17. New statutes relaxed some of the traditional focus on community life: "refectory meals, chapter meetings and even certain offices in the choir were no longer compulsory but minimum levels of attendance were recommended." James G. Clark, "The Religious Orders in Pre-Reformation England," in *The Religious Orders in Pre-Reformation England*, 11–12.

18. *General Prologue*, 173–74, in *The Riverside Chaucer*, ed. Larry D. Benson, 3rd edn (Boston: Houghton Mifflin, 1987). The figure of the monk who wanders beyond his cloister had been a commonplace in anti-monastic satire since the high Middle Ages. See Jill Mann, *Chaucer and Medieval Estates Satire: The Literature of Social Classes and the "General Prologue" to the "Canterbury Tales"* (Cambridge: Cambridge University Press, 1973), 29.

19. Nancy Bradley Warren draws attention to the importance of bridal identity in the rules and profession ceremonies of Franciscan and Bridgettine nuns: in clothing, construed as bridal in the Franciscan rule, and in the appellation "newe spouse" given the Bridgettine nun in the consecration service. *Spiritual Economies: Female Monasticism in Later Medieval England* (Philadelphia: University of Pennsylvania Press, 2001), 8.

20. In this way, Boniface wrote, nuns may "be able to serve God more freely, wholly separated from the public and worldly gaze and, occasions for lasciviousness having being removed, may most diligently safeguard their hearts and bodies in complete chastity." The Latin reads, "sic a publicis et mundanis conspectibus separatae omnino servire Deo valeant liberius, et, lasciviendi opportunitate sublata eidem corda sua et corpora in omni sanctimonia diligentius custodire." Translation by Elizabeth Makowski, *Canon Law and Cloistered Women: "Periculoso" and its Commentators 1298–1545* (Washington, DC: Catholic University Press, 1997), 135. Latin from Aemilius Friedberg, ed., *Corporis Iuris Canonici* (Leipzig: Bernhard Tauchnitz, 1881), 2:1054.

21. Although efforts were made to enforce strict enclosure, "the ideal of religious life contained in *Periculoso* was impracticable, because of the position of monastic houses in their society as landowners and providers of services." John Tillotson, "Visitation and Reform of the Yorkshire Nunneries in the Fourteenth Century," *Northern History* 30 (1994): 20.

22. *Ancrene Wisse*, ed. Tolkein, 8. The translation reads, "obedience, chastity and stability of abode, so that she will never change that abode again except only in case of need, such as force and fear of death" (Savage and Watson, eds. and trans., *Anchoritic Spirituality*, 49). This language anticipates that of the later *Periculoso* mandating strict enclosure of nuns, "so that none of them, tacitly or expressly professed, shall or may for whatever reason or cause (unless by chance any be found to be manifestly suffering from a disease of such a type and kind that it is not possible to remain with the others without grave danger or scandal), have permission hereafter to leave their monasteries" (Makowski, *Canon Law and Cloistered Women*, 135). The Latin reads, "sub perpetua in suis monasteriis debere de cetero permanere clausura ita, quod nulli earum, religionem tacite vel expresse professae, sit vel esse valeat quacunque ratione vel causa, (nisi forte tanto et tali morbo evidenter earum alique laborare constaret, quod non posset cum aliis absque gravi periculo seu scandalo commorari), monasteria ipsa deinceps egrediendi facultas" (Friedberg, ed., *Corporis Iuris Canonici*, 2:1054).

23. Barron and Wright, "The London Middle English Guild Certificates of 1388–9," 126.

24. *Ibid.*
25. *Ibid.*, 128. Emphasis added.
26. The earliest copy of *The Abbey of the Holy Ghost* appears in the compendious Vernon manuscript (Oxford, Bodleian Library, MS Engl.theol.a.1), copied in the late 1380s, probably for a women's religious house. The Vernon manuscript comprises five distinct sections containing I: legendary material; II: prayers and devotional material focused largely on the Virgin; III: didactic works including two poetic adaptations of *The Mirror of St Edmund* and a *Long Charter of Christ*; IV: more mystical and affective devotional works; and V: short lyrics, mainly on Christian tenets. The *Abbey* appears in part III, following *The Mirror of St. Edmund.* See N. F. Blake, "Vernon Manuscript: Contents and Organisation," in *Studies in the Vernon Manuscript*, ed. Derek Pearsall (Cambridge: D. S. Brewer, 1990), 46–59. Julia Boffey has made the most recent count of *Abbey* manuscripts: they total twenty-three, making it the most widely attested lay spiritual guide in my study. See "*The Charter of the Abbey of the Holy Ghost* and its Role in Manuscript Anthologies," *The Yearbook of English Studies* 33 (2003): 120, n.3.
27. Gillespie, "Anonymous Devotional Writings," 137.
28. This phrase is from the description of "habitus" in Pierre Bourdieu, *The Logic of Practice*, trans. Richard Nice (Stanford: Stanford University Press, 1990), 57.
29. With the later composition of the new, longer work *The Charter of the Abbey of the Holy Ghost*, by a slightly later English author, the *Abbey* was rendered even more accessible and explanatory for a lay audience. The *Charter* deploys the narrative of Christ's life to give lay readers more exact instructions for life in the world while shaping them as humble observers in the process of meditation. The composite *Abbey-Charter* text appears in eighteen manuscripts, the *Abbey* alone in an additional five, and the *Charter* alone in an additional six. For a discussion of the *Charter* as a disciplinary extension of the *Abbey*, see Nicole R. Rice, "Spiritual Ambition and the Translation of the Cloister: *The Abbey* and *Charter of the Holy Ghost*," *Viator* 33 (2002): 222–60.
30. As Nancy Warren notes, the *Abbey* uses "paradigms of female monasticism to suggest ways in which those in the world – men and women alike – might craft religious lives" (*Spiritual Economies*, 78).
31. *Ibid.*, 30.
32. Bourdieu's phrase, to refer to the role of "[s]chemes of thought and perception" in securing adherence to "established order." He writes, "The instruments of knowledge of the social world are . . . (objectively) political instruments which contribute to the reproduction of the social world by producing immediate adherence to the world, seen as self-evident and undisputed, of which they are the product and of which they reproduce the structures in a transformed form" (*Outline of a Theory of Practice*, 164).
33. The major structural model for these texts is the monastic building allegory, an ancient architectural form of *ars memorativa* revived in the thirteenth century, in which an imaginary building functions as a structure on which

to "hang" information. See Mary Carruthers, *The Book of Memory: A Study of Memory in Medieval Culture* (Cambridge: Cambridge University Press, 1990), 122. Hugh of St. Victor was particularly adept at creating this type of work, and the rubric announcing *L'Abbaye du Saint Esprit* in London, British Library, MS Additional 29986 attributes the text to him: "Cy comence le liure du cloistre de lame que hue de saint uictor fist" (fol. 149v).

34. Michel de Certeau offers a fundamental distinction between a "map" and a "tour": while a map offers a static description of a place, a tour describes movement of bodies through space. See *The Practice of Everyday Life*, trans. Steven Rendall (Berkeley: University of California Press, 1984), 119. For de Certeau, a "place" is ordered and static, while a "space" is "composed of intersections of mobile elements." In other words, "space is a practiced place" (117).

35. The author borrows from monastic norms when discussing officers such as the abbess (Charity), who in her loving authority closely resembles the Benedictine superior: "Madame Charity, who is the most worthy of all, will be abbess." ("Madame Charite qui est la plus vaillant de trestoutes si sera abbess.")

36. Ernest McDonnell, *The Beguines and Beghards in Medieval Culture, With Special Emphasis on the Belgian Scene* (New Brunswick, NJ: Rutgers University Press, 1954), 141–53. *L'Abbaye* borrows from the *Règle des fins amans* (*Rule of Courtly Lovers*), a late thirteenth-century text that reflects and constructs the practices of the semi-religious beguines. See Karl Christ, "*La Règle des fins amans*: Eine Beginenregel aus dem Ende des XIII. Jahrhunderts," in *Philologische Studien aus dem Romanisch-Germanischen Kulturkreise: Festgabe Karl Voretzsch*, ed. B. Schädel and W. Mulertt (Halle: Max Niemeyer, 1927), 173–213. For an excellent introduction to this work, see Barbara Newman, *From Virile Woman to WomanChrist* (Philadelphia: University of Pennsylvania Press, 1995), 139–43.

37. *Règle des fins amans*, 199: "que li cuer soient estable et joint ensanble en l'amour de Jhesucrist." Courtly conduct guides, featuring techniques for feminine self-discipline and containment in the secular realm, provided another resource for the author of *L'Abbaye*. The abbess Charity's realms of control – "thoughts, words, looks, comings, and goings" – recall those highlighted in such guides. See, for example, *Le Chastoiement des dames*, in *Die didaktischen und religiösen Dichtungen Robert's von Blois*, ed. Jacob Ulrich (Berlin: Mayer & Müller, 1895), 59.71–76.

38. Nicholas Watson has argued that the *Abbey* "purports to supply an equivalent of the monastic life for those who dwell in the world . . . such an interiorisation of the coenobitic ideal in practice fundamentally alters the Benedictine conception of the religious life as a communal affair, at the centre of which is the liturgy" ("The Methods and Objectives of Thirteenth-Century Anchoritic Devotion," in *The Medieval Mystical Tradition in England: Exeter Symposium IV*, ed. Marion Glasscoe [Cambridge: D. S. Brewer, 1987], 136).

39. For the early history of this concept, see Eric Jager, *The Book of the Heart* (Chicago: University of Chicago Press, 2000), 1–26.

40. Christiania Whitehead contends that the Middle English text "follows its French original closely, with the exception of several brief interpolations which adopt a more ecstatic and affectivist tone." *Castles of the Mind: A Study of Medieval Architectural Allegory* (Cardiff: University of Wales Press, 2003), 76.

41. "Mout de gent uoudroient entrer en religion et ne pueent ou pour pourete ou pour ce que il sont retenu par lian de mariage ou pour aucune reson. Pour ce si feis i liure que cil qui ne pueent entrer en religion temporele soient en religion esperituele" (London, British Library, MS Royal 16.E.XII, fol. 132v). This text is based on D. Peter Consacro's typescript transcription, checked against the manuscript. I thank him for providing me with this transcription.

42. D. Peter Consacro, "A Critical Edition of *The Abbey of the Holy Ghost* From All Known Extant English Manuscripts With Introduction, Notes, and Glossary" (Ph.D. diss., Fordham University, 1971), 1. Hereafter cited in the main text by page number.

43. *Ancrene Wisse*, ed. Tolkein, 5. "And you, my beloved sisters, have for a long time begged me for a rule" (Savage and Watson, *Anchoritic Spirituality*, 47). Stephanie Trigg notes of the anchoritic life, "The modern spirit has difficulty imagining itself in that situation, and wanting yet *more* discipline, but the request for a rule might reflect a need for structure, as much as further subjection." See "Learning to Live," in *Oxford Twenty-First Century Approaches to Literature: Middle English*, ed. Paul Strohm (Oxford: Oxford University Press, 2007), 462.

44. Anne Clark Bartlett, *Male Authors, Female Readers: Representation and Subjectivity in Middle English Devotional Literature* (Ithaca: Cornell University Press, 1995), 19. Bartlett draws upon Louis Althusser's theory of interpellation, whereby, he argues, individuals are transformed into "subjects" through the "*interpellation* or hailing" (emphasis in original). Althusser, "Ideology and Ideological State Apparatuses (Notes towards an Investigation)," in *Lenin and Philosophy and Other Essays*, trans. Ben Brewster (New York: Monthly Review Press, 1971), 118.

45. "Age" is rendered as "awe" in almost half of the manuscripts, removing a physical barrier and creating a double psychological one.

46. The early fifteenth-century poem dubbed "Why I Can't be a Nun" by its modern editor contains a contemporary example of familial opposition to religious profession. See James Dean, ed., *Six Ecclesiastical Satires* (Kalamazoo: Medieval Institute, 1991), 232. In its portrayal of a kind of anti-cloister, populated by allegorical figures including "Pride" and "Hypocrite," this short poem may well be a satirical response to *The Abbey of the Holy Ghost*, which would have been in circulation.

47. "seur bonne riuiere, cest de lermes et de pleurs. Vile et abaye qui est seur bonne riuiere si en mout ese et mout delicieuse. La Magdalainne fu fondee seur bonne riuiere donc grant bien len uint . . . Car, la bonne riuiere fet

la cite nete et liee et joieuse et seure et habundant de marchaundises"
(fol. 133r).

48. In the elaborate manuscript given to Marie de Bourbon (now London,
British Library, MS Additional 39843), *L'Abbaye*, which occupies fols. 2r–5v,
opens with a full-page illustration of the allegorical abbey and its inhabitants.

49. See Matthew 21:12: "And Jesus went into the temple of God, and cast out
all them that sold and bought in the temple."

50. Arguing for the important connection between Mary Magdalen and poverty
(as well as contemplation), Theresa Coletti observes, "*The Abbey of the
Holy Ghost* thus links the desires of the lay contemplative, the poor of the
Matthean text, and the ascetic Magdalene in the image of the spiritual abbey
built for those who possess earthly goods without excessive attachment to
them" ("*Paupertas est donum Dei*," 366).

51. Warren notes, "establishing an abbey of nuns, complete with a foundation
charter; staffing it with obedientiaries; and setting in motion the process
of visitation" are acts characteristic of female religious houses (*Spiritual
Economies*, 78).

52. In another illustrative passage, the *Abbey* adds *Ancrene Wisse*-inspired
touches to employ the virtue of Dread to "stabilize" and control the heart.
A spiritual version of "Drede" plays the role of monastic porter, the officer
who ensures the stability and enclosure of the "cloistre of þe herte and of þe
concience" (21). Ever-vigilant Drede "chaseþ out all vnþewes and clepeþ in
alle goode vertues, and, so stekeþ þe ȝates of þe cloistre and þe windouwes,
þat non vuel haþ entre into þe herte þorw þe ȝates of þe mouþ ne þorw þe
windouwes of þe eiȝen, ne of þe eren" (22).

53. "Fonding" also appears in *Ancrene Wisse*'s warnings against temptation:
"Understondeþ þenne on alre earst leoue sustren. þ[et] twa cunne
temptatiuns. twa cunne fondun ges beoð. uttre & inre. ant ba beoð
feoleualde. Vttre fondunge is hwer of kimeð licunge oþer mislicunge wið
uten oðer wið innen. mislicunge wið uten. ase secnesse. meoseise. scheome.
vnhap . . . wiðinnen heorte sar. grome. & wreaððe. Alswa onont þ[et] ha is
þine" (*Ancrene Wisse*, ed. Tolkein, 93). "Understand then first of all, dear sisters, that there are two kinds of temptations, two kinds of testing, outer and
inner; and both are of many different sorts. Temptation without is that from
which comes outer or inner pleasure or pain: outer pain such as sickness,
discomfort, humiliation, misfortune . . . inner, such as grief of heart, outrage,
and also anger at one's pain" (Savage and Watson, *Anchoritic Spirituality*,
114).

54. "Contemplation fera le dorteur" (fol. 134r).

55. H. E. Allen, *Writings Ascribed to Richard Rolle Hermit of Hampole and
Materials for his Biography* (New York: MLA, 1927), 340–41. As Rolle
writes in his anchoritic guide *The Form of Living*, "Þan may I say þat
contemplacioun is a wonderful ioy of Goddis loue . . . And þat wondreful
praisynge is in þe soule, and for aboundance of ioy and swetnese hit
ascendeth in to þe mouth, so þat þe hert and þe tonge accordeth in on,
and body and soule ioyeth in God lyuynge." *The Form of Living*, in *Richard

Rolle: Prose and Verse Edited from MS Longleat 29 and Related Manuscripts, ed. S. J. Ogilvie-Thomson, EETS OS 293 (Oxford: Oxford University Press, 1988), 24–25. Hereafter cited in the text by page number.

56. "Et aucune foiz la langue ne se puet tenir que ele ne chante . . . et li orteil quil ne dansent et senuoisent" (fol. 135v).

57. "Si puet bien estre auenu que aucunes ont estre si rauies la ou eles se seoient, que li fuisiaus lere cheoit dune part et la quenoil le dautre, u liure u sautier, et cheoient pasme" (fols. 135v–136r). Here the rapturous subject appears with spinning instruments in one hand, prayer books in the other. These items might be associated with the industrious, prayerful beguine, the wealthy lady of leisure, or even the Virgin Mary, often depicted spinning or reading just before the Annunciation.

58. In Rolle's *Form of Living*, the phrase "amore langueo" marks the beginning of the text's second part, providing the occasion for the mystic's dramatic ascent toward contemplation: "*Amore langueo.* These two wordes ben written in þe boke of loue þat is called þe songe of loue, or þe songe of songes. For he þat mych loueth, hym lust oft to synge of his loue, for ioy þat he or sho hath when þay þynke on þat þat þay loue" (15).

59. "Si y a i orloge de religion qui chiet au matinet; si y a orloge de contemplation et de saint beguignage; cest jelousie et amour de contemplation."

60. Allen offers the absence of beguinages in England as the only explanation for this change (*Writings Ascribed to Richard Rolle*, 340).

61. Christiania Whitehead, "Making a Cloister of the Soul in Medieval Religious Treatises," *Medium Ævum* 67.1 (1998): 18.

62. See, for example, the term as used in a Middle English *Pater Noster* tract written for a nun: "God, Lord, forȝyue me my synnes alle þat I haue trespasyde aȝeyns þee, as I forȝyue to þoo þat haue trespasid aȝens me." "*Þe Pater Noster of Richard Ermyte*": A Late Middle English Exposition of the Lord's Prayer, ed. F. G. A. M. Aarts (Nijmegen: Drukkerij Gebr. Janssen, 1967), 45.7–8.

63. For discussion of dating, see Margaret Connolly, ed., *Contemplations of the Dread and Love of God*, EETS OS 303 (London: Oxford University Press, 1993), xlii–xliii. Michael G. Sargent classifies the work as a compilation in "Minor Devotional Writings," in *Middle English Prose: A Critical Guide to Major Authors and Genres*, ed. A. S. G. Edwards (New Brunswick: Rutgers University Press, 1984), 160.

64. London, British Library, MS Arundel 197 and Oxford, Bodleian Library, MS Bodley 423. See Margaret Connolly, ed., *Contemplations of the Dread and Love of God*, 102. Arundel 197 concludes, "Here endethe this tretise that we calle ffervor amoris" (fol. 38v).

65. Connolly, ed., *Contemplations of the Dread and Love of God*, 102. London, British Library, MS Royal 17.A.xxv features an explicit reading, "Explicit tractatus amoris," and University of Pennsylvania Library MS Eng. 8 concludes, "Explicit tractatus qui vocatur amor dei." Oxford, Bodleian Library, MS Ashmole 1286 includes the phrase at the beginning (fol. 4r) and end of the work (fol. 32v).

66. Despite the title chosen for the recent critical edition, *Fervor Amoris* is listed as the alternate title in *The Index of Printed Middle English Prose*, ed. R. E. Lewis *et al.* (New York: Garland, 1985), 128. For other uses of the title *Fervor Amoris*, see Vincent Gillespie, "Lukynge in Haly Bukes: *Lectio* in Some Late Medieval Spiritual Miscellanies," *Analecta Cartusiana* 106 (1984): 25; Sargent, "Minor Devotional Writings," 160; Jolliffe, *A Check-List*, 97–98.

67. Text in Connolly, ed., *Contemplations of the Dread and Love of God*, 5. Hereafter cited (as *Fervor Amoris*) in the main text by page number.

68. Gillespie, "Anonymous Devotional Writings," 138.

69. Ralph Hanna draws attention to *Fervor Amoris* as one of the primary "Rolle-derived" texts in "Notes Toward a Future History of Middle English Literature: Two Copies of Richard Rolle's *Form of Living*," in *Chaucer in Perspective: Middle English Essays in Honour of Norman Blake*, ed. Geoffrey Lester (Sheffield: Sheffield Academic Press, 1999), 291.

70. The sensation of *fervor* is part of a triad followed in mystical intensity by *dulcor* and *canor*. See Nicholas Watson, *Richard Rolle and the Invention of Authority* (Cambridge: Cambridge University Press, 1991) for detailed discussion of this "passionate, and highly original, description of its author's own *experientia*" (113).

71. Rolle wrote three Middle English guides for religious women: *Ego Dormio*, *The Form of Living*, and *The Commandment*. *The Form of Living* is the only work that can be definitely associated with a particular reader: Margaret Kirkeby, an anchoress and former nun (*ibid.*, 223). *Ego Dormio*, a brief "epistolary homily" on the topic of love, may have been written for a nun (*ibid.*, 227). *The Commandment*, a more impersonal piece containing a greater amount of basic teaching partly borrowed from Rolle's own *Emendatio Vitae*, was probably also written for a nun (*ibid.*, 236). Like *The Form of Living*, *The Commandment* contains the exposition of the three degrees of love borrowed from Hugh of St. Victor, discussed further below.

72. Nicholas Watson, "Conceptions of the Word: The Mother Tongue and the Incarnation of God," *New Medieval Literatures* 1 (1997): 103–04.

73. Although the engagement with Rolle is more sustained and significant for this study, *Fervor Amoris*'s four degrees ("ordeine," "clene," "stedefast," and "parfit") may find their source in the *Revelationes* of St. Bridget (*d.* 1370), the Swedish mystic and monastic founder. Bridget's *Revelationes*, which may have been circulating in Latin in England by the 1380s, contains a passage envisioning a "city of joy" that may only be entered by those who "haue a iii-fold cherite: þat is to sey, ordinat, clene, trewe, and perfite." The categories and subheadings enumerated here provide a skeletal scheme that *Fervor Amoris* elaborates. See Roger Ellis, ed., *The Liber Celestis of St. Bridget of Sweden: The Middle English Version in British Library MS Claudius B i, Together with a Life of the Saint from the Same Manuscript*, EETS OS 291 (Oxford: Oxford University Press, 1987), 240.

74. Watson, *Richard Rolle and the Invention of Authority*, 1.

75. The other use of the term comes later in *The Form of Living*, after an inset love lyric to Jesus. Rolle exhorts Margaret to meditate on the Name of Jesus: "If þou wil be wel with God, and haue grace to reul þi life right, and cum to þe ioy of loue, þis name Iesus, fest hit so faste in þi herte þat hit cum neuer out of þi þoght" (18).

76. Richard of St. Victor's four degrees, discussed in *De Quatuor Gradibus Violentiae Caritatis (On the Four Degrees of Violent Charity)*, are adapted and rearranged from an earlier twelfth-century epistle written by an unnamed Ivo to another monk. They include: *insuperabilis, inseparabilis, incessabilis,* and *insatiabilis*. See Gervais Dumeige, ed., *Ives: Épître à Séverin sur la charité, Richard de Saint-Victor: Les quatres degrés de la violente charité* (Paris: J. Vrin, 1955). The degrees of love posited in *Ego Dormio* do not follow this scheme but instead correspond roughly with the movement from active to contemplative life, beginning with observing the commandments and avoiding sin, proceeding to "forsake al þe world . . . and . . . stody how clene þou may be in herte, and how chaste in body," and culminating finally in perfect love: "þan shal þou be in rest within, and lightly cum to gostly lif, þat þou shalt fynd swetter þan eny erthly þynge" (Ogilvie-Thomson, ed., *Richard Rolle: Prose and Verse,* 28).

77. This scheme also appears in an abbreviated form in *The Commandment* (*ibid.,* 34–35).

78. The conservatism of *Fervor Amoris*'s adaptation of Rolle is illuminated by contrast with two Wycliffite responses to *The Form of Living* that Fiona Somerset has brought to light. In *De Amore*, a Latin text attributed to Wyclif, and in *Five Questions on Love*, an English translation and adaptation thereof, Somerset finds elaborated a "Wycliffite spirituality" that responds to Rolle's pronouncements on the fire of love and the hierarchy of degrees of love to "present an alternative Wycliffite model of relation to God, deliberately distinct from Rolle's, and pointedly illustrating its own foundation in the Bible . . . aiming to confirm them in active Lollardy rather than contemplative anchoritism." Fiona Somerset, "Wycliffite Spirituality," in *Text and Controversy From Wyclif to Bale: Essays in Honour of Anne Hudson*, ed. Helen Barr and Ann M. Hutchison (Turnhout: Brepols, 2005), 381.

79. Manuscript disposition of the text frequently emphasizes the monumental quality of the "kalender" and of the text itself, its alphabetically ordered chapters set off with rubrics.

80. Gillespie notes, "one of the major innovations in vernacular works of this type is the apparatus which is found with the *Fervor Amoris* in all manuscripts and which appears to be a design feature of the work" ("Lukynge in Haly Bukes," 25). See Margaret Connolly's comments on the use of this apparatus to appeal to a "mixed market" of readers: "The 'Eight Points of Charity' in John Rylands University Library MS English 85," in *"And gladly wolde he lerne and gladly teche": Essays on Medieval English Presented to Professor Matsuji Tajima on His Sixtieth Birthday*, ed. Yoko Iyeiri and Margaret Connolly (Tokyo: Kaibunsha, 2002), 195–96. The organization of *Fervor Amoris* into chapters made

the work easy to excerpt: the "Eight Points of Charity" is a series of excerpts, with new material added, forming a short treatise on charity and the love of God.

81. Hans Robert Jauss's comments are useful for a consideration of *Fervor Amoris's* strategic beginnings. He writes of the literary work, "[i]t awakens memories of that which was already read, brings the reader to a specific emotional attitude, and with its beginning arouses expectations for the 'middle and end,' which can then be maintained intact or altered, reoriented, or even fulfilled ironically in the course of the reading according to specific rules of the genre or type of text." *Toward an Aesthetic of Reception*, trans. Timothy Bahti (Minneapolis: University of Minnesota Press, 1982), 23.

82. As Gillespie notes of another contemporary reference to Rolle in a manuscript colophon, *Fervor Amoris* acknowledges Rolle's "status . . . as a spiritual teacher" but then draws attention to "the worth of the text in its new context" ("Anonymous Devotional Writings," 135).

83. This observation about pronouns has also been made by Anthony Annunziata, "*Contemplations of the Dread and Love of God*, Morgan MS 861" (Ph.D. diss., New York University, 1966), xxxiv. He argues that this change encourages readers to "focus more clearly on the way of the active life."

84. See, for example, the discussion of confession in Chaucer's *Parson's Tale*: "I seye, Seint Augustyn seith, / 'Synne is every word and every dede, and al that men coveiten, agayn the lawe of Jhesu Crist; and this is for to synne in herte, in mouth, and in dede.'" Benson, ed., *The Riverside Chaucer*, X.957–58.

85. Rolle expresses this concern several times in the text. For commentary, see Watson, *Richard Rolle and the Invention of Authority*, 251.

86. This sentiment is a common one in monastic writings. Bernard of Clairvaux warns, "How often does he not suggest that fasts be prolonged, until a man is so weak that he is useless for the service of God!" "Quoties, produci jejunia, ut divinies obsequiis eo inutilem redderet, quo imbecilem!" Bernard of Clairvaux, *On the Song of Songs*, trans. Kilian Walsh, OCSO, Cistercian Fathers Series 7 (Kalamazoo: Cistercian Publications, 1983), 2:152–53.

87. This is an idea expressed in *The Prick of Conscience,* which notes, in its discussion of the joys of heaven, that "whasa wille tak þe way þider-ward, / Behoves in gud werkes travaille hard, / Ffor tylle þe kyngdom of heven may no man com / Bot he ga bi þe way of wisdom" (7539–42).

88. Barron and Wright, "The London Middle English Guild Certificates," 142.

89. Gillespie notes in reference to another passage the connection that *Fervor Amoris* creates between "social stability" and "spiritual mobility" ("Anonymous Devotional Writings," 139).

90. In the short treatise on "Eight Points of Charity," warnings about the dangers of worldly pride are expanded. Just before the section cited above, this work adds some new comments directed particularly at readers who possess "gouernail" over others. It adds, "wite þou wel þat þi staat or þi richesse or þi greet kyn makiþ not þee greet bifore God. But to gouerne þi staat wel aftir Goddis lawe and in þin owne reputacioun holde þee more vnworþi

bifore God þan þe leeste of hem that doen reuerence to þee" (Connolly, "The 'Eight Points of Charity' in John Rylands Library MS 85," 208–09).

91. See Proverbs 1:7, Psalm 110:10, and Ecclesiasticus 1:16.

92. Curry Woods and Copeland, "Classroom and Confession," 377.

93. *The Chastising of God's Children*, a contemporary compilation written for the guidance of nuns at Barking, has a quite similar reference to "drede" in conjunction with confession to one's spiritual father: "good it is to drede, and as openli as he can ofte declare his conscience to his goostli fadir, in special if he kan, or ellis in general wordis; and þis is a souereyn remedie to al temptacions." *The Chastising of God's Children and the Treatise of Perfection of the Sons of God*, ed. Joyce Bazire and Eric Colledge (Oxford: Basil Blackwell, 1957), 111.

94. See Rolle: "when þei han suffre[d] many temptaciouns, and þe foul noyes of thoghtes þat ben ydel, and of vanytees þe which wil comber ham þat can nat destroi ham, is passynge away, he maketh ham gaddre to ham har hert and fest [hit] only in hym; and openeth to þe eigh of har soule þe yate of heuyn, so þat þat eigh loke in to heuyn" (*The Form of Living*, 25).

95. For this phrase, see Allen J. Frantzen, "Spirituality and Devotion in the Anglo-Saxon Penitentials," *Essays in Medieval Studies* 22 (2005): 125. John Hirsh notes on the basis of manuscript evidence that this type of prayer originated in a monastic setting. "The Origin of Affective Devotion," in *The Boundaries of Faith: The Development and Transmission of Medieval Spirituality* (Leiden: E. J. Brill, 1996), 15.

96. Rolle's *Form* also exhorts the reader, if she wishes to achieve contemplative "þoght of þe loue of Ihesu Criste," to "secheth reste withouten, þat hit be nat letted with comers and goers and ocupaciouns of worldes þynges" (23).

97. *Meditationes Vitae Christi* contain these insights on the function of meditation: "To him who searches for it [the mysteries of the Passion] from the bottom of the heart and with the marrow of his being, many unhoped-for steps would take place by which he would receive new compassion, new love, new solace, and then a new condition of sweetness that would seem to him a promise of glory." Isa Ragusa and Rosalie Green, eds., *Meditations on the Life of Christ: An Illustrated Manuscript of the Fourteenth Century* (Princeton: Princeton University Press, 1961), 317. The Latin reads, "Nam profundo corde et totis viscerum medullis eam perscrutanti, multi adsunt passus insperati, ex quibus novam compassionem, novum amorem, novas consolationes, et per consequens novum quemdam statum susciperet, quæsibi præsagium et participatio gloriæviderentur." *Sancti Bonaventuræ Opera Omnia*, ed. A. C. Peltier (Paris: Ludovicus Vives, 1868), 12:599.

98. See Rolle: "And also soon as thou mayist, comme to thi confessioun, and rise oute þereof and than say 'Lord, I haue this day and al my life falsly and wickedly despended aȝeyns thi louynge and the helthe of my soule'" (*Meditation A*, in Ogilvie-Thomson, ed., *Richard Rolle: Prose and Verse*, 67). The passage is reminiscent of the typical Middle English "devotional confession." One such text appears in the first part of London, British

Library, MS Harley 1706, a compilation whose second part contains *Fervor Amoris*. This work, the Middle English *St Brendan's Confession*, leads readers through a confession according to the seven deadly sins, the ten commandments, the five bodily wits, and the seven works of bodily and spiritual mercy. Its section on the five wits begins thus: "O þow hiʒe excellent lorde God: lowly to þe I knowleche þat my fyue wittis I haue mysspendid..." R. H. Bowers, "The Middle English *St. Brendan's Confession*," *Archiv für das Studium der Neueren Sprachen* 175 (1939): 46.

99. *Fervor Amoris* earlier expressed a rather pessimistic view of contemporary religious life, lamenting, "bicause mankinde is now and euer þe lengur more fieble, or percas more unstable, þerfore unneþis schuld we finde now a sad contemplatif man or woman" (6).

100. Lynn Staley, "Chaucer and the Postures of Sanctity," in Aers and Staley, *The Powers of the Holy*, 181.

101. Some of the many studies that employ such strategies include Gail McMurray Gibson, "Resurrection as Dramatic Icon in the *Shipman's Tale*," in *Signs and Symbols in Chaucer's Poetry*, ed. J. P. Hermann and J. J. Burke (University: University of Alabama Press, 1981), 102–12; R. H. Winnick, "Luke 12 and Chaucer's *Shipman's Tale*," *The Chaucer Review* 30.2 (1995): 164–90.

102. Lee Patterson, *Chaucer and the Subject of History* (Madison: University of Wisconsin Press, 1991), 363.

103. *Ibid.*, 366.

104. John C. McGalliard, "Characterization in Chaucer's *Shipman's Tale*," *Philological Quarterly* 54.1 (1975): 17.

105. This phrase is Janette Richardson's. As part of her argument about the "spiritual blindness or obtuseness" that causes characters to "utilize the material symbols of spiritual existence for purely earthly purposes without realizing the incongruity," Richardson takes the merchant's discourse on the transitoriness of life (lines 230–34) as a sign of his "spiritual longings, and to this extent he demonstrates impulses worthy of man's elevation above the animal." Janette Richardson, *Blameth Nat Me: A Study of Imagery in Chaucer's Fabliaux* (The Hague: Mouton, 1970), 118–19.

106. Patterson, *Chaucer and the Subject of History*, 361. He argues, "the *Tale* stimulates in its readers an unnatural alertness to the possibility of ambiguity; insecure in our grasp of such unstable linguistic material, and fearing an embarrassing revelation of our own naivete, we interrogate each element of the text in order to discover the playful or mocking meaning it conceals" (360).

107. By juxtaposing Chaucer with devotional prose, I propose to consider in its complexity the idea of monastic "lyf" as a contested version of religious discipline rather than having immediate recourse to the contingent category of "mysticism." For a study that argues for the Middle English "mystics" as sources for Chaucer, see Robert Boenig, *Chaucer and the Mystics: The Canterbury Tales and the Genre of Devotional Prose* (Lewisburg: Bucknell University Press, 1995).

108. Much has been made of the fact that the *Tale* concerns a merchant and a monk; most studies have focused on its extension of mercantile exchange relations to sexual matters, and thus on the monk's imitation of the merchant. See William F. Woods, "A Professional Thyng: The Wife as Merchant's Apprentice in The *Shipman's Tale,*" *The Chaucer Review* 24.2 (1989): 139–49.

109. Geoffrey Chaucer, *The Shipman's Tale,* in *The Riverside Chaucer,* ed. David Benson, VII.25, 31–32. Cited hereafter in the main text by line number.

110. See Paul Strohm for a discussion of this language of sworn "bretherhede" in a secular vein: he views the *Shipman's Tale* as an example, along with those of Friar, Summoner, and Pardoner, of "the debasement of sworn brotherhood" in a post-feudal world. Paul Strohm, *Social Chaucer* (Cambridge, MA: Harvard University Press, 1989), 96–102. Steven Kruger considers the *Shipman's Tale* as a work demonstrating the typically "unstable" nature of male bonding in Chaucer due to its "competition with heterosexual attraction." Steven Kruger, "Claiming the Pardoner: Toward a Gay Reading of Chaucer's *Pardoner's Tale,*" in *Critical Essays on Geoffrey Chaucer,* ed. Thomas C. Stillinger (New York: G. K. Hall, 1998), 159.

111. Richardson, *Blameth Nat Me,* 119–20.

112. *Ibid.,* 121.

113. Woods, "A Professional Thyng," 143.

114. These lines from *The Prick of Conscience* describe individuals' responsibilities at the day of judgment: "[O]f þair awen saules þai sal reken þar, / And of þair bodys þat þam obout bar" (5978–79).

115. For this phrase see Margaret Aston, "Popular Religious Movements," in *Faith and Fire: Popular and Unpopular Religion 1350–1600,* 9.

116. Remarking the "religious and moral *potential* of this passage," David Aers argues that this scene ruthlessly transforms spiritual potential into material profit. But while Aers generalizes this view to suggest that in the *Tale* at large, "[r]eligion thus sanctifies a life centred on the individualistic and socially irresponsible pursuit of economic profit," I would argue that this reversal is only a partial translation. David Aers, *Chaucer* (Brighton: Harvester Press, 1986), 22–23. Emphasis in original.

117. Quoted phrase from Patterson, *Chaucer and the Subject of History,* 356.

118. St. Augustine, author of the other rule that the Monk of the *General Prologue* scornfully rejects, for "What sholde he studie and make hymselven wood, / Upon a book in cloystre alwey to poure, / Or swynken with his handes, and laboure, / As Austyn bit? How shal the world be served?" (184–87).

119. Sylvia Thrupp notes an "acute fear of the temptation of gambling" among the London merchant class. Sylvia Thrupp, *The Merchant Class of Medieval London* (Ann Arbor: University of Michigan Press, 1948), 167. As Scattergood notes, the merchant is shown to be "typical of the best of his class, the epitome of the successful merchant." V. J. Scattergood, "The Originality of the *Shipman's Tale,*" *The Chaucer Review* 11.3 (1977): 214.

120. In a remark that seems apt for this tale, Nicholas Watson observes, "Even where every possible religious outlook on life is made irrelevant by a given

tale's genre, as with the fabliaux, this irrelevance can sometimes be part of the point." Nicholas Watson, "Christian Ideologies," in *A Companion to Chaucer*, ed. Peter Brown (Oxford: Basil Blackwell, 2000), 86–87.

121. The term is used in a similar sense in the *Man of Law's Tale*, 523: "She kneleth doun and thanketh Goddes sonde."

122. Winnick notes that one might hear "God speaking through the wife" in this scene ("Luke 12 and Chaucer's *Shipman's Tale*," 172).

CHAPTER 2

1. Although the dates of the three versions of *Piers Plowman* (A-Text, B-Text, and C-Text) remain disputed, they are generally agreed to have been finished *c.* 1370, *c.* 1379, and *c.* 1385–86, respectively. I shall cite primarily from the B-Text, the most widely surviving version, which may be close in date with the guides treated in this chapter. For discussion of the three versions and controversies surrounding their order, see Ralph Hanna III, "On the Versions of *Piers Plowman*," in *Pursuing History: Middle English Manuscripts and Their Texts* (Stanford: Stanford University Press, 1996), 203–43.

2. William Langland, *"Piers Plowman": The B Version*, ed. George Kane and Talbot Donaldson (London: The Athlone Press, 1975), Passus 12, lines 98–112. Citations will appear hereafter in the main text by passus and line number.

3. Somerset, *Clerical Discourse and Lay Audience in Late Medieval England*, 42.

4. These should all be considered, in Elizabeth Schirmer's phrase, as texts that are "diverse, multi-generic, and theologically distinctive." See "Reading Lessons at Syon Abbey," in *Voices in Dialogue*, ed. Linda Olson and Kathryn Kerby-Fulton (Notre Dame: Notre Dame University Press, 2005), 350.

5. M. M. Bakhtin, "Discourse in the Novel," in *The Dialogic Imagination*, ed. Michael Holquist, trans. Caryl Emerson and Michael Holquist (Austin: University of Texas Press, 1981), 346.

6. See Nicholas Watson, "Fashioning the Puritan Gentry-Woman: Devotion and Dissent in *Book to a Mother*," in *Medieval Women: Texts and Contexts in Late Medieval Britain: Essays for Felicity Riddy*, ed. Jocelyn Wogan-Browne *et al.* (Turnhout: Brepols, 2000), 170–71.

7. James Simpson groups Hilton's *Mixed Life* with *The Abbey of the Holy Ghost* as works that "cultivate and constrain lay spirituality by restricting the lay eye to the image, and by prohibiting the lay mind from abstract reflection" (*Reform and Cultural Revolution*, 435). In his introductory remarks about Hilton, Barry Windeatt calls Hilton "orthodox and conservative" despite acknowledging the innovative approach taken in the *Mixed Life* (*English Mystics of the Middle Ages* [Cambridge: Cambridge University Press, 1994], 109).

8. See Vincent Gillespie's recent call to attend to the importance of dialogue in orthodox contexts ("Vernacular Theology," 419). In a departure from the more widespread view of Hilton, Nicholas Watson has suggested that Hilton, despite his appearance of conservatism, may be seen to share concerns with

writers "more radical than himself." See Nicholas Watson, "'Et que est huius ydoli materia? Tuipse': Idols and Images in Walter Hilton," in *Images, Idolatry, and Iconoclasm in Late Medieval England: Textuality and the Visual Image*, ed. Jeremy Dimmick *et al.* (Oxford: Oxford University Press, 2002), 97.

9. Bakhtin, "Discourse in the Novel," 279.

10. *MED*, s.v. "clerc."

11. Steven Justice, "Inquisition, Speech, and Writing: A Case from Late-Medieval Norwich," *Representations* 48 (Autumn 1994): 20.

12. Watson finds that several works drawing upon *Ancrene Wisse* encourage laypeople to imagine themselves superior to fellow Christians and to become the "spiritual equivalents of solitaries." Nicholas Watson, "*Ancrene Wisse*, Religious Reform, and the Late Middle Ages," in *A Companion to "Ancrene Wisse,"* ed. Yoko Wada (Cambridge: D. S. Brewer, 2003), 209.

13. Rita Copeland, *Pedagogy, Intellectuals, and Dissent in the Later Middle Ages: Lollardy and Ideas of Learning* (Cambridge: Cambridge University Press, 2001), 22.

14. Ralph Hanna, *London Literature, 1300–1380* (Cambridge: Cambridge University Press, 2005), 185. He is citing from Cambridge, Magdalene College, MS Pepys 2498, fol. 48a.

15. Moira Fitzgibbons, "Jacob's Well and Penitential Pedagogy," *Studies in the Age of Chaucer* 27 (2005): 226.

16. *Jacob's Well: An Englisht Treatise on the Cleansing of Man's Conscience*, ed. Arthur Brandeis, EETS OS 115 (London: Kegan Paul, Trench, Trübner & Co., 1900), Part 1, 276.

17. David Lawton stresses the dialogic nature of *Piers Plowman* in contrast to the monologism of the other discourses it encompasses ("social, political, theological, and academic"). See "The Subject of *Piers Plowman*," *The Yearbook of Langland Studies* 1 (1987): 4.

18. G. R. Evans notes the paradox in medieval theological study between "the urge to explore and the need to guard very carefully a precious body of truth entrusted to the Church to preserve and transmit." See "Theology: The Vocabulary of Teaching and Research 1300–1600: Words and Concepts," in *Vocabulary of Teaching and Research Between Middle Ages and Renaissance: Proceedings of the Colloquium, London, Warburg Institute, 11–12 March 1994*, ed. Olga Weijers (Turnhout: Brepols, 1995), 120.

19. The quoted phrase is from Kantik Ghosh, *The Wycliffite Heresy: Authority and the Interpretation of Texts* (Cambridge: Cambridge University Press, 2002), 149.

20. Simpson, *Reform and Cultural Revolution*, 462.

21. Simpson, "Desire and the Scriptural Text," 234.

22. Katherine Little contends that *Piers Plowman* and the Lollards testify to similar "frustration with traditional discourses" and dismay at the corruption of sacramental practice and "pastoral instruction." Little, "'Bokes Ynowe': Vernacular Theology and Fourteenth-Century Exhaustion," *English Language*

Notes 44.1 (Spring 2006): 110–11. The spiritual guides in question here propose to re-energize those discourses by giving lay readers newly participatory roles in the process of pastoral and spiritual education.

23. Bakhtin, "Discourse in the Novel," 280–81.

24. Somerset, *Clerical Discourse and Lay Audience*, 65.

25. *Ibid.*, 80–91. See A. J. Perry, ed., *Dialogus inter Militem et Clericum, Richard FitzRalph's Sermon: "Defensio Curatorum" and Methodius: "þe Bygynnyng of þe World and þe Ende of Worldes" by John Trevisa, vicar of Berkeley*, EETS OS 167 (London: Oxford University Press, 1925), 2.12–4.2, 20.1–23.7.

26. Somerset, *Clerical Discourse and Lay Audience*, 87.

27. Copeland, *Pedagogy, Intellectuals, and Dissent in the Later Middle Ages*, 127.

28. For this text see Anne Hudson, ed., *Selections from English Wycliffite Writings* (Toronto: Medieval Academy, 1997, reprint of Cambridge: Cambridge University Press, 1978), 96.

29. As Moira Fitzgibbons has argued, the fifteenth-century work *Dives and Pauper*, *c.* 1405–10, also uses dialogue form to emphasize the interpretive abilities of lay readers. This work incorporates certain aspects of Lollard thought, such as the laity's right to study scripture, while holding orthodox positions on matters such as ecclesiastical wealth and auricular confession. See Moira Fitzgibbons, "Knowing Believers: Pastoralia, the Laity, and Interpretive Christianity" (Ph.D. diss., Rutgers University, 2001), 127–91. Also see Hudson, *The Premature Reformation*, 418–21.

30. For example Boethius's *Consolation of Philosophy* and Augustine's *Soliloquium*. See Seth Lerer, *Boethius and Dialogue: Literary Method in "The Consolation of Philosophy"* (Princeton: Princeton University Press, 1985) for an introduction to both, particularly 45–47.

31. For this phrase see W. A. Davenport, "Patterns in Middle English Dialogues," in *Medieval English Studies Presented to George Kane*, ed. Edward Kennedy *et al.* (Wolfeboro, NH: D. S. Brewer, 1988), 139.

32. E. C. Ronquist, "Learning and Teaching in Twelfth-Century Dialogues," *Res Publica Litterarum* 13 (1990): 239. For example, Anselm of Canterbury's dialogues offer an active role to the student figure, who proposes questions and offers evidence (241). Asad shows that Bernard of Clairvaux's sermons propose forms of "ritual dialogue" in which monks may relate to superiors "in terms of authority rather than of domination" (*Genealogies of Religion*, 144).

33. Helen M. Moon, ed., *"þe Lyfe of Soule": An Edition with Commentary*, Salzburg Studies in English Literature, Elizabethan and Renaissance Studies 75 (Salzburg: Institut für Englische Sprache und Literatur, 1978), li. The text is extant in three fifteenth-century devotional anthologies: Oxford, Bodleian Library, MS Laud Misc. 210; London, British Library, MS Arundel 286; and San Marino, Huntington Library, MS 502. Moon discusses the manuscripts at v–xxv; her descriptions should be supplemented by the following. For MS Laud Misc. 210, see Elisabeth Dutton, "Compiling Julian: The *Revelation of Love* and Late-Medieval Devotional Compilation" (Ph.D. diss., Oxford

University, 2002), 95–105; for MS Arundel 286, see Domenico Pezzini, "How Resoun Schal Be Keper of þe Soule: Una Traduzione del Quattrocento Inglese Dalle Rivelazioni (VII, 5) Di S. Brigida Di Svezia," *Aevum* 60 (1986): 265; for MS Huntington 502, see Consuelo Dutschke, *Guide to Medieval and Renaissance Manuscripts in the Huntington Library* (San Marino: Huntington Library, 1989), 1:237–39. *The Life of Soul* is also included in the anthology *Cultures of Piety: Medieval English Devotional Literature in Translation*, ed. Anne Clark Bartlett and Thomas H. Bestul (Ithaca: Cornell University Press, 1999). See Paul F. Schaffner's translation of part of the work, based on MS Laud Misc. 210 (118–40) and his transcription of the Middle English text (217–31).

34. See Moon, lxxiv–lxxvii, for comparison with the more controversial biblical translation found in A. C. Paues, ed., *A Fourteenth Century Biblical Version* (Cambridge: Cambridge University Press, 1904). Moon notes that *The Life of Soul* expresses some views similar to those of the early Lollards, advocating the importance of grace and knowledge of the Bible, and opposing the taking of oaths.

35. Despite Moon's suggestion that the text was written for "a religious group" (i), no evidence other than these titles proves that the work was composed for a monk or nun. MS Laud Misc. 210, which may be the oldest and is textually the most reliable manuscript, is the one whose *personae* are almost certainly not monastic figures.

36. Moon, ed., *Þe Lyfe of Soule*, 1.1–8 (hereafter cited in main text by page and line number).

37. Hebrews 13:14 reads: "For we have not a lasting city, but we seek one that is to come."

38. In MS Arundel 286, the teacher figure ("Fader") addresses the learner as "Sone"; in MS Huntington 502, the teacher figure ("Broþer") addresses the learner as "Sustir."

39. As positive evidence for his dating, McCarthy offers the author's reference to "Heroud" near the end of the text, probably an allusion to Edward III, who had been called "Herod" by the Carmelite friar John of Kenyngham, or to his son John of Gaunt, leader of Edward's council from 1371 to 1377, who fit the description of "false reynynge of wommenliche men . . . ouercome wiþ Heredias" in that he lived with Catherine Swynford for almost twenty years. See Adrian James McCarthy, ed., *"Book to a Mother": An Edition with Commentary*, Salzburg Studies in English Literature: Elizabethan and Renaissance Studies 92.1 (Salzburg: Institut für Anglistik und Amerikanistik, 1981), xxxii–xxxiii.

40. Schirmer, "Reading Lessons at Syon Abbey," 353.

41. See Watson, "Fashioning the Puritan Gentry-Woman," 170. *Book to a Mother* is extant in four south-west Midlands manuscripts, in varying states of completeness: MS Laud Misc. 210 (together with *The Life of Soul*); London, British Library, MS Additional 30897; London, British Library, MS Egerton 826; and Oxford, Bodleian Library, MS Bodley 416. Brief discussion of

manuscripts appears in McCarthy, iii–xviii. For more detailed discussion of MS Laud Misc. 210, see Dutton, "Compiling Julian," 95–105; for discussion of the other manuscripts, with particular attention to MS Bodley 416, see Dutton, "Textual Disunities and Ambiguities of *mise-en-page* in the Manuscripts Containing *Book to a Mother*," *Journal of the Early Book Society* 6 (2003): 149–59.

42. Watson notes, "the only viable form of religious life is one of radical holiness, in which sin is remedied only by perfect living . . . the only remedy for sin is the rigorous imitation of Christ" ("Fashioning the Puritan Gentry-Woman," 180). Nancy Bradley Warren has offered a different assessment of the *Book*, arguing that it retools monastic paradigms to exert social control over female readers (see *Spiritual Economies*, 77–92).

43. Watson, "Fashioning the Puritan Gentry-Woman," 183.

44. See Moon, *Þe Lyfe of Soule*, lxxvii–lxxx, for discussion of the similarity of their respective discussions of the ten commandments ("hestes"). *The Pore Caitif*, which opens by comparing the reader to "a childe willynge to be a clerk," also contains an extended explanatory "Prologue of the Ten Hestes." See Brady, ed., "*The Pore Caitif*," 24–91.

45. In Chapter 4, I return to *Book to a Mother*'s anti-fraternal stance. Given the south-west Midlands provenance of all four surviving manuscripts of *Book to a Mother*, this author's advice to his mother can be located in the context of economic, social, and educational hardships associated with rural clerical life in the late fourteenth century.

46. McCarthy, ed., *Book to a Mother*, 71.7–10 (hereafter cited in the main text by page and line number).

47. Elisabeth Dutton considers the *Book*'s multivocality in connection with principles of compilation ("Christ the Codex," 83).

48. See *MED*, s.v. "comelynge."

49. See the comparable moment in the Prologue to *Pore Caitif*, which contends, "as a child willynge to be a clerk, bigynneþ first at þe ground, þat is his abice: so he þis desiringe to spede þe beter, bigynneþ at þe ground of helþe: þat is cristen mannes bileeue" (1.6–10).

50. F. J. Furnivall, ed., *Political, Religious, and Love Poems*, EETS OS 15 (London: Oxford University Press, 1866), 271. Also see Fitzgibbons, "*Jacob's Well* and Penitential Pedagogy," 222–23, for an invocation of schoolroom imagery to enforce lay meekness.

51. For the history of the charter of Christ as a devotional image and for printed texts of these works, see Mary Caroline Spalding, *The Middle English Charters of Christ* (Bryn Mawr: Bryn Mawr College, 1914). Also see Emily Steiner, *Documentary Culture and the Making of Medieval English Literature* (Cambridge: Cambridge University Press, 2003), 49–90, for discussion of the "documentary poetics" of the charters and related works.

52. See Helen Barr, ed., *The "Piers Plowman" Tradition: A Critical Edition of "Pierce the Ploughman's Crede," "Richard the Redeless," "Mum the Sothsegger," and "The Crowned King"* (London: J. M. Dent, 1993), 61. These lines are

cited in abbreviated form in Copeland, *Pedagogy, Intellectuals, and Dissent in the Later Middle Ages*, 134–35.

53. *Ibid.*, 135.
54. *Ibid.*, 136.
55. See Dutton, "Christ the Codex," 91–92, for a discussion of the passage just following this one, in which the author reorders passages from the Book of Baruch to focus on the image of the Book as Christ.
56. Perhaps due to Hilton's fame as the author of the *Scale*, his *Mixed Life* survives in many more manuscripts than do *Book to a Mother* or *The Life of Soul*. The earliest extant copy of the *Mixed Life* appears in the Vernon manuscript (Oxford, Bodleian Library, MS eng. theol. a.1): the work is extant in seventeen manuscripts in total and was printed as the "third book" of the *Scale* in Wynkyn de Worde's edition of 1494. See S. J. Ogilvie-Thomson, ed., *Walter Hilton's "Mixed Life,"* xii–xxvi, for summary discussion of manuscripts.
57. The two guides were probably written relatively close in time as well. Although the dating of Hilton's *Mixed Life* is uncertain, verbal echoes among his *Mixed Life*, *Scale of Perfection* Book I, and his Latin letters *De Imagine Peccati* and *Epistola de Utilitate et Prerogativis Religionis* suggest that these works may have been written relatively close in time. These four share a remarkable similarity in their exposition of Leviticus 6:12 ("Ignis in altari meo semper ardebit, et sacerdos surgens mane subiciet ligna ut ignis non extinguatur"). See *Mixed Life* 37.427–39.-39.449 and *Scale of Perfection* Book I, chapter 32 (the critical edition of Book I by A. J. Bliss is being completed for EETS by Michael Sargent). *De Imagine* and *De Utilitate* are printed in *Walter Hilton's Latin Writings*, ed. J. P. H. Clark and Cheryl Taylor, Analecta Cartusiana 124 (Salzburg: Institut für Anglistik und Amerikanistik, 1987), 2 vols. For the relevant passage in *De Imagine*, see 1:77.80; for *Epistola de Utilitate*, see *ibid.*, 168.843. Hilton wrote the latter for his friend Adam Horsley, encouraging him to join the Carthusian order, which Horsley did in 1386; thus, the work can be dated to *c.* 1385. If, as Sargent speculates in a private communication, *Scale* I, the *Mixed Life*, and *De Imagine Peccati* slightly precede *Epistola de Utilitate*, they may be roughly dated to the first half of the 1380s. I thank Michael Sargent for bringing these connections to my attention.
58. I treat this passage as the beginning of the work, but the critical edition prints a longer version of the *Mixed Life*, attested in six manuscripts and one print, which features an additional opening passage and a closing letter. The opening passage posits a division between "bodili" and "goostli" estates in the church and argues that those in former estate may use "bodili werkes" to cleanse themselves from sin and be "abled to gosteli werk" (4.28–32). I agree with Michael Sargent that this passage, which resembles some of Hilton's comments in the *Scale of Perfection*, seems to have been added by a later writer attempting to create a transitional passage from the *Scale* to the *Mixed Life*. Sargent argues that "the unsophisticated division between 'physical' and 'spiritual' rather than 'active' and 'contemplative' does not

seem . . . appropriate for Hilton," and he lays out a persuasive textual case against considering the longer version as authorial. See Michael G. Sargent, ed., *The Mirror of the Blessed Life of Jesus Christ: A Full Critical Edition, based on Cambridge University Library Additional MSS 6578 and 6686 with Introduction, Notes and Glossary* (Exeter: Exeter University Press, 2004), 82–83.

59. Copeland, *Pedagogy, Intellectuals, and Dissent*, 134.

60. Although Ogilvie-Thomson includes the phrase "warnynge and wissynge" in the critical edition and I find it supports my arguments about Hilton's didactic strategies, it should be noted that the word "warnynge" appears in only seven of the seventeen *Mixed Life* manuscripts.

61. See Nicholas Watson, "'Et que est huius ydoli materia? Tuipse': Idols and Images in Walter Hilton," 96.

62. See Lesley Smith, "The Theology of the Twelfth- and Thirteenth-Century Bible," in *The Early Medieval Bible*, ed. Richard Gameson (Cambridge: Cambridge University Press, 1994), 223.

63. "Et haec quidem sapientia scripta est in Christo Iesu tanquam in libro vitae, in quo *omnes thesauros sapientiae et scientiae* recondidit Deus Pater." Bonaventure, *Decem Opuscula ad theologiam mysticam spectantia*, ed. Patres Collegii S. Bonaventurae (Quaracchi: Collegium S. Bonaventurae, 1949), 202. The phrase "in quo sunt omnes thesauros sapientiae et scientiae recondidit" quotes Colossians 2:3. See McCarthy xxxviii–xliii for discussion of the tradition of the "Christ Book" image.

64. Wyclif describes how his anxiety about the incongruity between the physical Bible and its status as God's word culminated in his understanding of Christ as book in four senses: formal, essential, according to its intelligible and its existent being: "It is by means of these distinctions I have understood Scripture to be indestructibly true according to the literal sense." *On the Truth of Holy Scripture*, trans. Ian Christopher Levy (Kalamazoo: Medieval Institute Publications, 2001), 102. The Latin reads: "per istas distincciones intellexi scripturam infringibiliter veram ad literam." *De Veritate Sacrae Scripturae*, ed. Rudolf Buddensieg (London: Wyclif Society, 1905), 1:114.18–19. Also see Mary Dove, *The First English Bible* (Cambridge: Cambridge University Press, 2007), 29. I thank Dr. Dove for allowing me to see this book prior to publication.

65. *On the Truth of Holy Scripture*, 98–99. The Latin reads: "iste liber non potest solvi, cum deitas ac humanitas septiformi gracia copulantur insolubiliter in eadem persona. illum librum debet omnis cristianus adiscere, cum sit omnis veritas. unde ut doceamur in hoc dicto intelligere illum librum et non opera hominum ordinavit spiritus sanctus in correctis codicibus hoc relativum 'quem' et non 'quam' . . . et patet ex fide scripture, quod oportet esse scripturam summe autenticam preter signa sensibilia." *De Veritate Sacrae Scripturae*, 1:109.21–110.20.

66. Ghosh, *The Wycliffite Heresy*, 55.

67. See *De Veritate Sacrae Scripturae*, ed. Buddensieg, 2:167.18–22.

68. "Cristus est dei virtus et dei sapiencia, quod nullus cristianus potest efficaciter cognoscere, nisi ex sciencia scripturarum, igitur omnis cristianus tenetur scripturas cognoscere. ignorare namque scripturas est ignorare Cristum, cum Cristus sit scriptura, quam debemus cognoscere, et fides, quam debemus credere" (*ibid.*, 169.30–170.5).

69. In rejecting these ecclesiastical aids, Wyclif was not arguing for a *sola scriptura* position: even as he decried what he considered to be human traditions supplanting the Bible's centrality, he often appealed to the Church Fathers and ancient creeds for support of his positions (Levy, *On the Truth of Holy Scripture*, Introduction, 19).

70. See Watson, "Fashioning the Puritan Gentry-Woman," for a brief discussion of parallels between the *Book* and Wyclif's thought: he notes that Wyclif's *De Civili Dominio* resembles *Book to a Mother* in describing Christ's life as the "exemplar and ground" for all Christians and "the text's emphasis on poverty could be taken to echo Wyclif's narrower call for the clergy to imitate Christ's poverty" (183). See also McCarthy's discussion of "The Problem of Orthodoxy," xlvi–lvii.

71. Watson, "Fashioning the Puritan Gentry-Woman," 177.

72. Schirmer, "Reading Lessons at Syon Abbey," 352.

73. At the top of the page that includes this passage, MS Egerton 826, fol. 36v, features the red heading "Crist is trewe bok" (visible under ultra-violet light).

74. The allegorization of the book as a record of the conscience, which can be scraped and written upon as a parchment, is a venerable one. This image is elaborated in a twelfth-century monastic sermon from Durham Cathedral that exhorts listeners to become "scribes of the Lord": the sermon is discussed, edited, and translated by Richard H. and Mary A. Rouse, "From Flax to Parchment: A Monastic Sermon from Twelfth-Century Durham," in *New Science out of Old Books: Studies in Manuscripts and Early Printed Books in Honour of A. I. Doyle*, ed. Richard Beadle and A. J. Piper (London: Scolar, 1995), 1–13. The passage is also discussed in Jager, *The Book of the Heart*, 51–52.

75. 2 Corinthians 3:3 declares Christians to be "the epistle of Christ ministered by us, and written not with ink, but with the Spirit of the living God; not in tables of stone, but in fleshly tables of the heart." For a similar image in the Hebrew Bible, see Jeremiah 31:33: "I will give my law into their bowels, and I will write it in their heart: and I will be their God, and they shall be my people." Steven Justice shows that the fifteenth-century Lollard work *The Lantern of Liȝt* invokes the image from Jeremiah to critique Arundel's Constitutions for outlawing biblical translation, flaunting the prohibition in the process by quoting directly from the Bible ("Inquisition, Speech, and Writing," 21).

76. See *Regula Pastoralis* 2.5. *S. Gregorii Magni Regulae Pastoralis Liber*, trans. H. R. Bramley (Oxford: James Parker, 1874), 70–71. I discuss Hilton's adaptation of the Gregorian pastoral model further in Chapter 3 below.

77. See *MED*, s.v. "accorden" 5: "Of things: (a) to be compatible or harmonious . . . (b) to correspond, be proportionate; be related or refer (to sth.); (c) to be comparable, similar, or alike (in some respect); be the same; (d) to compare (one word with another), play on words."

78. In his skepticism about the true piety of the "maister of diuinite," the author's comments take on an anti-mendicant aspect, for the university friar's insistence upon being called "master" was a detail familiar from contemporary anti-fraternal satire. See Scase, *"Piers Plowman" and the New Anticlericalism*, 42.

79. Watson, "Fashioning the Puritan Gentry-Woman," 178, notes, "[i]t also follows that to serve as an effective pointer the book must, as a structure always in danger of substituting for the reality it represents, seek to disappear."

80. See Simpson, *Reform and Cultural Revolution*, 435. Simpson argues that Hilton insists upon "prohibiting the lay mind from abstract reflection" by advising that his reader "meditate in 'the ymaginacioun of the manheed of oure Lord' but not to 'seke knowynge or feelynge more goosteli of the Godhede.'"

81. *Ibid.*, 489.

82. I borrow these terms from Watson, who suggests in "'Et que est huius ydoli materia? Tuipse'" (103, n.23) that these tend to be viewed as two separate literary camps.

83. See David Lawton, "Englishing the Bible," in *The Cambridge History of Medieval English Literature*, ed. David Wallace (Cambridge: Cambridge University Press, 1999), 454–82. In addition to translation strictly speaking, a great variety of biblically based texts were produced in later medieval England, including prose summary of Old Testament episodes, metrical versions of individual books, and lives of Christ in prose and verse (see 477–82). Lawton argues persuasively that translations, commentaries and paraphrases should be considered "in a continuum that links private devotion with public teaching" (477).

84. See *De Veritate Sacrae Scripturae*, 1:79.17–80.7.

85. Shepherd writes, "Medieval liturgies are bewildering mosaics cut and shaped for a purpose out of the Scriptures." Geoffrey Shepherd, "English Versions of the Scriptures Before Wyclif," in *The Cambridge History of the Bible*, vol. 2, ed. G. W. H. Lampe (Cambridge: Cambridge University Press, 1969), 363.

86. Wyclif first called for scripture to be available in the "common tongue" in his late work *Trialogus* (1382–83). See *Trialogus*, ed. Gotthard Lechler (Oxford: Clarendon Press, 1869), 240.12–13.

87. Ralph Hanna notes, "This condemnation, like Arundel's later one, was surely abortive, and failed to stem the composition and the later encroachment into nonheterodox circles of Lollard vernacular scripture." Ralph Hanna, "English Biblical Texts before Lollardy and their Fate," in *Lollards and Their Influence in Late Medieval England*, ed. Fiona Somerset et al. (Woodbridge: The Boydell Press, 2003), 152.

88. Mary Dove, *The First English Bible*, offers a full account of the complex relations between the Earlier Version, a very literal translation, and the more idiomatic Later Version. The translators probably did not intend to produce two distinct versions, but the text began to circulate before this process was complete, and thirty-six manuscripts survive of the complete Bible in the Earlier Version (139). Dove speculates that planning began in the early 1370s (80). The English Bible began to be copied *c.* 1390, by which time work on the Later Version was already well underway. Also see Hudson, *The Premature Reformation*, 238–39.

89. This debate pitted those in favor of translation as a means of promoting lay comprehension of the Bible's lessons against those fearing its consequences would be anticlericalism or evasion of priestly authority. The debate survives in three determinations: two against translation by the Dominican Thomas Palmer and the Franciscan William Butler, one in favor by Richard Ullerston, a secular cleric. See Dove, *The First English Bible*, 6–22, for details of the debate. For Butler's and Palmer's determinations, see Margaret Deanesly, *The Lollard Bible and Other Medieval Biblical Versions* (Cambridge: Cambridge University Press, 1920), 401–37. Ullerston's tract has not been printed but is discussed in Anne Hudson, "The Debate on Bible Translation, Oxford 1401," *The English Historical Review* 90.354 (January 1975): 1–18.

90. Article Seven reads, "nobody [may] hereafter translate any text of sacred scripture into the English language or another language by his own authority, by way of book, pamphlet, or tract, nor may anyone read any such book, pamphlet, or tract now newly composed in the time of the said John Wycliff, or since, or to be composed hereafter, in part or in whole, publicly or in private, under pain of greater excommunication, unless the said translation be approved by the ordinary of the place, or if the matter should require it, by the provincial council; whoever acts against this [ruling] will be punished as a promoter of heresy and error." The Latin reads: "nemo deinceps aliquem textum sacrae scripturae auctoritate sua in linguam Anglicanam vel aliam transferat, per viam libri, libelli, aut tractatus, nec legatur aliquis hujusmodi liber, libellus, aut tractatus jam noviter tempore dicti Johannis Wycliff, sive citra, compositus, aut inposterum componendus, in parte vel in toto, publice, vel occulte, sub majoris excommunicatis poena, quousque per loci dioecesanum, seu, si res exegerit, per concilium provinciale ipsa translatio fuerit approbata: qui contra fecerit, ut fautor haeresis et erroris similiter puniatur." David Wilkins, ed., *Concilia Magnae Britanniae et Hiberniae* (London: R. Gosling, 1737), 3:317.

91. As Simpson puts it, "the acid text of a good reading is not that the reader has perceived the original intention of the biblical text, but rather that the reader has become a better person for having read" (*Reform and Cultural Revolution*, 478).

92. Although previous scholarship had dated the Prologue to *c.* 1395–97 (e.g. Hudson, *The Premature Reformation*, 247; Deanesly, *The Lollard Bible*, 257), Dove argues for the earlier date on the grounds that connections the Prologue

draws between Oxford clerics and sodomy should be associated not with accusations in the *Twelve Conclusions of the Lollards* (posted at Westminster in 1395) but with those brought against John Bloxham of Merton College in the mid-1380s (see *The First English Bible*, 110–13).

93. Dove, *The First English Bible*, 4.

94. See *ibid.*, 145, on explanations of translation practices geared toward achieving "open" sense and 170–71 on glossing as a means to making the "sentence" of the Bible as "open" as the Latin original.

95. Ghosh, *The Wycliffite Heresy*, 160.

96. From the Prologue to the Prophets. Josiah Forshall and Sir Frederic Madden, eds., *The Holy Bible, Containing the Old and New Testaments, with the Apocryphal books, in the Earliest English Versions Made from the Latin Vulgate by John Wycliffe and his Followers* (Oxford: Oxford University Press, 1850), 3:226.17.

97. *Ibid.*, 1:2.31–3.2.

98. Hanna notes of this passage, "[i]n this interpretation, Lollard reading is governed by the same rules as Lollard ownership or dominion: it comes only by grace, not by grammar and Donatus." Ralph Hanna III, "The Difficulty of Ricardian Prose Translation: The Case of the Lollards," *MLQ* 51 (1990): 337.

99. In MS Arundel 286 (fol. 121v), this is one of three passages marked with a pointing hand, probably that of the scribe. The other pointing hands appear at fol. 121r (pointing to the sentence "For trewe beleue in Crist wiþ trewe werkis doynge is boþe brede and flesche to oure soule and þe kepynge of his techynge is þe dringe of oure soule, for it is boþe water and bloode") and fol. 126v (pointing to the word "mekenes").

100. Simpson, *Reform and Cultural Revolution*, 489.

101. For Rachel and Leah as representing the contemplative and active lives, respectively, see, for example, Augustine's *Contra Faustum*, Book 22, Chapter 52 (Sancti Aureli Augustini, *De Utilitate Credendi, De Duabus Animabus Contra Fortunatum, Contra Adimantum, Contra Epistulam Fundamenti, Contra Faustum*, ed. Joseph Zycha [Prague: F. Tempsky, 1891], 645–46).

102. Also see Schirmer, "Reading Lessons at Syon Abbey," 352.

103. Deanesly, *The Lollard Bible*, 219. Deanesly argues that Hilton is referring to Latin Bibles because the *Mixed Life* predates the earliest Wycliffite Bible translations.

104. I interpret this passage differently from Nancy Warren, who understands this eucharistic model of incorporation as eliding the mother's agency. Warren argues that here, "the reader does not make something of the text by incorporating it; rather, the incorporated text makes something of the reader" (*Spiritual Economies*, 92).

105. For an edition of this text, see Anna Paues, *A Fourteenth Century English Biblical Version*. For discussion of manuscripts, see *ibid.*, xi–xxiii. Citations from this edition will appear in the main text by page and line number.

106. Deanesly, *The Lollard Bible*, 309.

107. *Ibid.*, 308. Deanesly speculates, based on the author's apparent anxiety about the danger of death he incurs by making a biblical translation, that the work was written after Arundel's Constitutions were published.

1. S. S. Hussey, "Langland, Hilton, and the Three Lives," *Review of English Studies* New Series 7.26 (1956): 145.
2. Anne Middleton, "The Audience and Public of 'Piers Plowman,'" in *Middle English Alliterative Poetry and its Literary Background: Seven Essays*, ed. David Lawton (Woodbridge: D. S. Brewer, 1982), 104.
3. See Hudson, *The Premature Reformation*, 314 and 338. On Wyclif's anti-prelatical preaching of 1377 (reported in Thomas Walsingham's *Chronicle*), see 65–66.
4. Thomas J. Heffernan, "Orthodoxies' *Redux*: The *Northern Homily Cycle* in the Vernon Manuscript and its Textual Affiliations," in *Studies in the Vernon Manuscript*, ed. Derek Pearsall (Cambridge: D. S. Brewer, 1990), 79. Scribal dialect and textual associations with London, British Library, MS Additional MS 37787 (the Simeon manuscript) have led most scholars to link the Vernon manuscript to Bordesley Abbey in northern Worcestershire. See Ralph Hanna, "Introduction," in *The Index of Middle English Prose Handlist XII*, xii.
5. As in Chapter 2, *Piers Plowman* will be cited from the Kane and Donaldson edition of the B-Text. Both A- and B-Texts would have been in circulation by the time Hilton wrote the *Mixed Life*, while the C-Text likely post-dates Hilton's guide. On the early readership of *Piers Plowman*, see Kathryn Kerby-Fulton and Steven Justice, "Langlandian Reading Circles and the Civil Service in London and Dublin, 1380–1427," *New Medieval Literatures* 1 (1997): 59–83. They note, "*Piers* was, arguably, the most *immediately* influential literary work of the late fourteenth century, rapidly disseminated and frequently cited within the poet's own lifetime" (62).
6. For this debate, see Henry W. Wells, "The Construction of Piers Plowman," *PMLA* 44 (1929): 123–40, and Nevill K. Coghill, "The Character of Piers Plowman Considered From the B Text," *Medium Ævum* 2 (1933): 108–35. Wells originated the identification, while Coghill argued for Piers Plowman as a symbol of each of these lives, modifying the third to stress the episcopal life. Wells subsequently argued that the three lives were "not vocational callings but mental states" in "The Philosophy of *Piers Plowman*," *PMLA* 53 (1938): 349. See Hussey, "Langland, Hilton, and the Three Lives," 132–33, for a summary of the debate and a discussion which convincingly puts it to rest. As he notes, it is unlikely that Langland knew the sources on which Hilton drew for his theory.
7. D. N. Lepine notes that, by the fifteenth century, "priests were sometimes considered gentlemen by virtue of their office and called spiritual gentlemen." "The Origins and Careers of the Canons of Exeter Cathedral 1300–1455,"

in *Religious Belief and Ecclesiastical Careers in Late Medieval England*, ed. Christopher Harper-Bill (Woodbridge: The Boydell Press, 1991), 97.

8. See Hussey, "The Three Lives," 136; George R. Keiser, "'To Knawe God Almyghtyn': Robert Thornton's Devotional Book," *Analecta Cartusiana* 106.2 (1984): 118–19; Ruth Nisse, *Defining Acts: Drama and the Politics of Interpretation in Late Medieval England* (Notre Dame: University of Notre Dame Press, 2005), 128–29. Nisse is mainly concerned with the uses of the *Mixed Life* in the fifteenth-century East Anglian play *Wisdom*.

9. *Ibid.*, 129.

10. See Roger Dymmok, *Liber Contra XII Errores et Hereses Lollardorum*, ed. H. S. Cronin (London: Wyclif Society, 1922).

11. Somerset, *Clerical Discourse and Lay Audience*, 114.

12. Hudson, ed., *Selections from English Wycliffite Writings*, 26.

13. John Wyclif, *Tractatus de Officio Regis*, ed. Alfred W. Pollard and Charles Sayle (London: Wyclif Society, 1887), 28.16–18. The Latin reads, "Quamvis autem tale officium in laico foret laudabile, est tamen in clerico propter repugnaticiam legis dei et professionis facte ordini nimium monstruosum." For an examination of these arguments in relation to contemporary political events, particularly concern about clerical dominance in royal administration, see Anne Hudson, "*Hermofodrita or Ambidexter*: Wycliffite Views on Clerks in Secular Office," in *Lollardy and the Gentry in the Later Middle Ages*, ed. Margaret Aston and Colin Richmond (Stroud: Sutton Publishing, 1997), 41–51.

14. Somerset, *Clerical Discourse and Lay Audience*, 119.

15. The fourteenth-century *Book of Vices and Virtues* attributes the "mene staate" to those who "gouernen hemself wel and oþere and lyuen after þe comaundementes": *The Book of Vices and Virtues*, ed. W. Nelson Francis, EETS OS 217 (London: Oxford University Press, 1942), 120.35–36. The *Book* later describes the way in which "man and wommen þat leden aungeles lif in erþe bi here holynesse" may ascend temporarily to contemplation but must always return to earth "for here owne profiȝt gostliche and for oþeres also" (273.34–274.14).

16. Hilton's "medled lif" may be a translation of "vita mixta," a phrase used by the thirteenth-century canonist Henry of Segusio. See F. J. Steele, *Towards a Spirituality for Lay-Folk: The Active Life in Middle English Religious Literature from the Thirteenth Century to the Fifteenth*, Salzburg University Studies in English Literature: Elizabethan & Renaissance Studies 92.23 (Lewiston, NY: The Edwin Mellen Press, 1995), 155–56. Steele briefly notes Hilton's strategy of constructing the addressee as a "lay prelate" (158).

17. For a speculative biography of Hilton, see J. P. H. Clark, "Walter Hilton in Defence of the Religious Life and the Veneration of Images," *The Downside Review* 103.350 (January 1985): 19–20.

18. John P. H. Clark and Cheryl Taylor, eds., *Walter Hilton's Latin Writings*, Analecta Cartusiana 124 (Salzburg: Institut für Anglistik und Amerikanistik, 1987), 2:256.146–49.

19. Nisse, *Defining Acts*, 132.
20. "Dicit enim Apostolus: Vnusquisque habet donum suum a Deo, alius sic, alius vero sic. Nam quosdam dedit Apostolos, quosdam Prophetas, quosdam vero Doctores, in edificacionem corporis Christi mistici . . . Et hoc sicut in primitiva ecclesia, ita et modo. Alios facit actiuos, alios contemplatiuos, alios rectores, alios simplices sacerdotes, alios religiosos, alios heremitas" (Clark and Taylor, eds., *Walter Hilton's Latin Writings*, 2:289.851–56). This epistle has several elements in common with *The Scale of Perfection* I and II: see J. P. H. Clark, "Action and Contemplation in Walter Hilton," *The Downside Review* 97 (October 1979): 268.
21. Though he may conclude too much from very limited biographical evidence, Jonathan Hughes usefully associates Hilton with a northern movement of pastoral education and literature in the latter half of the fourteenth century. See *Pastors and Visionaries: Religion and Secular Life in Late Medieval Yorkshire* (Woodbridge: The Boydell Press, 1988), 174–97.
22. See *Epistola de Utilitate et Prerogativis Religionis*, in Clark and Taylor, eds., *Walter Hilton's Latin Writings*, 1:124.89–99. Also see 170.892–171.894 for his statement that the "dogmas of the heretics" ("dogmata hereticorum") will do nothing to shake the security of a religious life founded "on the firm rock, Christ" ("super firmam petram, Christum").
23. The condemned proposition to which Hilton may be responding is number 20: "anyone who enters into private religion is rendered more unfit and less suited to the observance of God's commandments" ("aliquis ingreditur religionem privatam quamcunque, redditur ineptior et inhabilior ad observantiam mandatorum Dei"). See *Fasciculi Zizaniorum Magistri Johannis Wyclif Cum Tritico, Ascribed to Thomas Netter of Walden*, ed. Walter W. Shirley (London: Rolls Series, 1858), 281–82.
24. As with the Latin letters, there are significant parallels between the guidance of the *Mixed Life* and Hilton's most famous vernacular work, *The Scale of Perfection*. At various points *Scale* II, while offering advice exclusively on contemplation, addresses the problem of balancing desire for contemplation with the demands of the outside world. See S. S. Hussey, "Walter Hilton: Traditionalist?" in *The Medieval Mystical Tradition in England*, ed. Marion Glasscoe (Exeter: University of Exeter Press, 1980), 10–11.
25. Somerset, *Clerical Discourse and Lay Audience*, 24.
26. *Ibid.*, 52; see *Piers Plowman*, 15.322–32.
27. English translation from *S. Gregorii Magni Regulae Pastoralis Liber*, trans. H. R. Bramley, 27. Hereafter cited in the main text by page number. The Latin reads: "En ab utrisque exterius diuersa uox prodiit, sed non a diuerso fonte dilectionis emanauit. Duo quippe sunt praecepta caritatis, Dei uidelicet amor et proximi." Latin text from *Règle pastorale*, ed. and trans. Bruno Judic, Floribert Rommel, and Charles Morel (Paris: Les Éditions du Cerf, 1992), 1:150.
28. See Augustine's remarks on Varro's three lives in *The City of God*, 19.19. Augustine approves of the leisured and active lives and the life combining

both ("ex utroque composito") but stipulates, "no one ought to be so leisured as to take no thought in that leisure for the interest of his neighbour, nor so active as to feel no need for the contemplation of God." *The City of God*, trans. Henry Bettenson (New York: Penguin Books, 1972), 880. The Latin reads, "Nec sic esse quisque debet otiosus, ut in eodem otio utilitatem non cogitet proximi, nec sic actuosus, ut contemplationem non requirat Dei." *Aurelii Augustini Opera*, Part 14, vol. 2, Corpus Christianorum Series Latina 48 (Turnhout: Brepols, 1955), 686.

29. See *The Scale of Perfection*, ed. and trans. John P. H. Clark and Rosemary Dorward (New York: Paulist Press, 1991), 137–39.

30. For the early fourteenth-century origins of the debate over dominion and grace, see Aubrey Gwynn, S. J., *The English Austin Friars in the Time of Wyclif* (Oxford: Oxford University Press, 1940), 59–73. Gwynn traces the progress of the idea that "only the faithful can have just and righteous lordship" (60) from Giles of Rome's curialist position to John Wyclif's arguments for ecclesiastical disendowment. Also see Michael Wilks, "Predestination, Property, and Power: Wyclif's Theory of Dominion and Grace," *Studies in Church History* 2 (1965): 220–36.

31. For discussion of the philosophical bases and implications of Wyclif's theory of dominion, see Stephen E. Lahey, *Philosophy and Politics in the Thought of John Wyclif* (Cambridge: Cambridge University Press, 2003), 68–107.

32. Hudson, *The Premature Reformation*, 328. She remarks further, "[d]isendowment was the logical outcome of Wyclif's exaltation of the gospels and epistles to the status of sole legitimate guide to christian behaviour" (340).

33. Wyclif owed some aspects of his formulation to Richard FitzRalph, who built upon earlier fourteenth-century pro-papal developments of the tradition that divine righteousness (*iustitia*) must ground all human institutions. See *De Civili Dominio*, 1:1.9–2.12. Wyclif's own version of the theory entailed that *dominium* ultimately belonged to the *predestinati* alone. On the relationship between FitzRalph's and Wyclif's positions, see Lahey, *Philosophy and Politics*, 49–63.

34. "Illud autem unum est corpus Christi misticum, ex omnibus predestinatis aggregatum" (*De Civili Dominio*, 1:360.8–9).

35. Quotation from Wilks, "Predestination, Property and Power," 235. See *De Civili Dominio*, 1:134.8–9.

36. See Pamela Gradon, "Langland and the Ideology of Dissent," *Proceedings of the British Academy* 66 (1980): 185–88, on the demand for disendowment in earlier theologians including Marsilius of Padua, for whom it was a necessary consequence of the church's subjection to temporal power.

37. The Latin reads, "nunquam tantum scidissent christianorum imperium temporale in civile dominium monstruose atque preposter surrepentes. Abhinc quidem obliti sunt regule Baptiste 1 Thym. VI, 8" (*De Civili Dominio*, 2:21.17–22).

38. *Ibid.*, 21.37–22.6. Wilks argues, "The practical significance of Wyclif's doctrine of dominion and grace was therefore the reverse of revolutionary. Behind a smokescreen of predestinarian speculation it enabled him to reconstruct the old lay ideal of a theocratic monarchy and a proprietary church" ("Predestination, Property and Power," 235). David Aers shows that despite Wyclif's remarks in earlier works, such as *De Ecclesia*, exhorting all Christians to a life of apostolic purity, the clergy are in his later writings held to a radical standard of renunciation while laity are allowed to continue with "business as usual." See "John Wyclif's Understanding of Christian Discipleship," in *Faith, Ethics and Church: Writing in England, 1360–1409* (Cambridge: D. S. Brewer, 2000), 132.

39. *De Civili Dominio*, 3:217.25–29.

40. "To have civil [dominion] should be forbidden entirely to clerics, because it requires care about temporal things and about following the laws of men" ("Nam habere civiliter, cum necessitat ad sollicitudinem circa temporalia et leges hominum observandas, debet omnino clericis interdici"). Wyclif, *Trialogus*, 306.

41. *Ibid.*, 311.

42. A broad critical consensus has developed that Langland should be considered a basically orthodox reformer rather than a Wycliffite. The essential study of *Piers Plowman* in relation to Wyclif is Gradon's "Langland and the Ideology of Dissent." Also see Simpson, *Piers Plowman: An Introduction to the B-Text*, 180. On relations between *Piers Plowman* and vernacular Wycliffism, see Christina von Nolcken, "*Piers Plowman*, the Wycliffites, and *Pierce the Plowman's Creed*," *The Yearbook of Langland Studies* 2 (1988): 71–102, and the special section on "Langland and Lollardy" in *The Yearbook of Langland Studies* 17 (2003).

43. Traugott Lawler, "The Secular Clergy in *Piers Plowman*," *The Yearbook of Langland Studies* 16 (2002): 98. For reservations with some aspects of Lawler's argument, see Míceál Vaughan's "Response" (118–29).

44. Kathryn Kerby-Fulton expresses this view: see "*Piers Plowman*," in *The Cambridge History of Medieval English Literature*, 527.

45. This passage is absent in the A-Text: instead there is support for the endowment of secular clergy (see 11.195–203). It appears in the C-Text spoken by Liberum Arbitrium (17.217–32).

46. This moment of prophecy was often cited in the period: not only by Wyclif and Langland, but also by Uthred of Boldon and John Gower, among others (see Scase, *"Piers Plowman" and the New Anticlericalism*, 90–91).

47. In keeping with their belief that Langland revised from B to C using a corrupt B manuscript, Kane and Donaldson argue that the majority reading "good" was introduced into the B-Text by scribes. They restore the C reading "charite" as authorial based on its superior alliterative effect. See "Editing the B Version," in *"Piers Plowman": The B Version*, 152. "Charite" also seems preferable as the *lectio difficilior*.

48. Derek Pearsall calls it "shockingly direct" in "Langland and Lollardy: From B to C," *The Yearbook of Langland Studies* 17 (2003): 21. As he notes, orthodox doctrine held that priests should live on tithes, although Wyclif objected to them as extrabiblical.

49. Scase contends that the term "charite" emphasizes the movement, fundamental to the "new anticlericalism" for which she argues, of the critique of possession (civil dominion) from the friars to all clergy (*"Piers Plowman" and the New Anticlericalism*, 97).

50. I depart from Hughes, who suggests that the *Mixed Life* was originally "partly directed at secular clergy" (*Pastors and Visionaries*, 211). Hilton's addressee was clearly a layman, as Carey notes in "Devout Literate Laypeople," 374.

51. Song of Songs 2:4: "He brought me into the cellar of wine, he set in order charity in me."

52. Similar terms coalesce, though in a negative way, in what may be Hilton's earliest extant work, *De Imagine Peccati*. In this work Hilton laments to another solitary their collective lack of "order" and "rule": "Quid ergo facimus tu et ego, nostrique similes, homines pigri et inutiles, tota die stantes ociosi? . . . nusquam ocupamus locum alicuius ministri eciam minimi in ecclesia ordinati, sed quasi liberi, relicti nostro sensui nostreque voluntati, quasi in nullo ordine sumus. Timendum est nobis ne proiciamur vbi nullus est ordo, sed sempiternus orror" (Clark and Taylor, eds., *Walter Hilton's Latin Writings* 1:90.319–91.328). Jonathan Hughes's translation reads, "What do we do, your and our like, lazy useless men standing all day idle? . . . In no way do we fill the place of any servant, even the least appointed in the church, but we are as it were left freely to our own feeling and our own free will as if in no order. We must be fearful lest we are cast away where there is no order but eternal confusion" (*Pastors and Visionaries*, 255).

53. "Sit rector singulis compassione proximus, prae cunctis contemplatione suspensus, ut . . . ne aut alta petens proximorum infirma despiciat, aut infirmis proximorum congruens, appetere alta derelinquat" (*Règle pastorale*, 196).

54. "quia dum per animarum praesulem terreni exercetur officium iudicis, a gregis custodia uacat cura pastoris" (*Règle pastorale*, 220).

55. Carey, "Devout Literate Laypeople," 373.

56. I have emended Bramley's "manhood" to "humanity."

57. "Hinc ipsa Veritas per susceptionem nobis nostrae humanitatis ostensa, in monte orationi inhaeret, miracula in urbibus exercet, imitationis uidelicet uiam bonis rectoribus sternens; ut etsi iam summa contemplando appetunt, necessitatibus tamen infirmantium compatiendo misceantur" (*Règle pastorale*, 200).

58. The phrase "prelates & curatis" appears in Vernon, Simeon, and Plimpton (New York, Columbia University Library, MS 271), which on account of their age and northern provenance, should probably be considered more authoritative than Ogilvie-Thomson's base text, London, Lambeth Palace, MS 472.

59. Scase, *"Piers Plowman" and the New Anticlericalism*, 22.

60. *Ibid.* On 182, n.36, Scase notes, "[i]n MS F [Cambridge University Library Ff.5.35, a copy of the C-Text] the ambiguity is removed with rewriting; a few other MSS have 'ac' or 'and' for 'As'."

61. "Nam cum quilibet post sanctitatis habitum terrenis se actibus inserit, quasi colore permutato ante humanos oculos eius reuerentia despecta pallescit" (*Règle pastorale*, 224).

62. In line 497, Conscience cites John 10:11: "bonus pastor animam suam ponit."

63. See James M. Powell, "*Pastor Bonus*: Some Evidence of Honorius III's Use of the Sermons of Pope Innocent III," *Speculum* 52.3 (1977): 527–28, on Gregory's use of the *pastor bonus* image in sermons.

64. See Lawrence Warner, "Becket and the Hopping Bishops," *The Yearbook of Langland Studies* 17 (2003): 107–34, for Langland's emphasis on "episcopal martyrdom" in connection to an anti-fraternal ethic.

65. See Gratian's *Decretum*, Part 1, Distinctio 42, in Emil Friedberg, ed., *Corpus Iuris Canonici* (Graz: Akademische Druk-u. Verlaganstalt, 1959), 151–52.

66. The term "withdrawen" is varied and complex in later Middle English: in the above passage, in addition to the primary sense of "refrain, desist, stop," one might also detect the sense of "withdraw from" as used in the phrase "withdraw into the sete of thought." Definitions from *MED*, s.v. "withdrauen" 3(a) and 1(a) c.

67. *Speculum Christiani*, ed. Holmstedt, 30–32. This work survives in over sixty manuscripts, primarily in Latin with English prose and verse throughout. The Latin reads, "O lucra dampnosa! inuenis pecuniam & perdis iusticiam, quam non deberet homo uelle perdere pro aliquo precio sub celo" (31–33).

68. *Ibid.*, 222. Ecclesiasticus 31:8 is cited as follows in the Latin manuscript: "Beatus diues, qui inuentus est sine macula, et qui post aurum non abiit, nec sperauit in thesauris pecunia" (223).

69. The instances of the term and its verb form "covet" are too many to enumerate here. For the critically important issue of the term in relation to the conflict between secular clergy and friars, see Scase, *"Piers Plowman" and the New Anticlericalism*, 23–32, and Lawrence M. Clopper, *"Songes of Rechelesnesse": Langland and the Franciscans* (Ann Arbor: University of Michigan Press, 1999), 87–93. As these critics and others have shown, the friars are central to understanding the problem of covetise in all its social complexity.

70. While the verb "winnen" might often mean simply profiteering, its range of denotations also includes this less common sense listed as 5 (a) in *MED*: "To derive a nonmaterial benefit, profit morally, spiritually, or psychologically." In a recuperation of covetise related to his wider argument for disendowment, Wyclif views the renovation of this desire in terms of clerical disendowment, arguing in *De Civili Dominio* that coveting, normally to be deplored in accordance with the commandment not to covet the neighbor's goods, may be considered righteous if temporal lords covet the misused possessions of the clergy in order to distribute them to the poor (*De Civili Dominio*, 2:23.35–24.17).

71. "The Secular Clergy in *Piers Plowman*," 107.

72. In giving very selective consideration to the character of Piers, I acknowledge that his status, in David Aers's term, as a constantly evolving "focal figure in a visionary process," renders any such treatment exceedingly partial. This phrase from Aers, *Piers Plowman and Christian Allegory* (London: Edward Arnold, 1975), 131 n.123.

73. As Simpson glosses, noting the changing subject of the verb, "Will will only know charity, or Christ, by seeking out the principle by which he, as the human will, is known. This principle is provisionally Piers, and ultimately Christ" (*Introduction*, 186).

74. Clopper's phrase, in *"Songes of Rechelesnesse,"* 184. Although he is referring to the pardon scene in Passus 6, the appellation seems fitting for Piers here too.

75. Aers, *Piers Plowman and Christian Allegory*, 88.

76. See Scase, *"Piers Plowman" and the New Anticlericalism*, 23–32, for discussion of restitution in connection with controversy over the friars' rights to pastoral care. The friars are of course central to this passus and the apocalyptic scenario of Passus 20.

77. Quoted phrase from Frank, *"Piers Plowman" and the Scheme of Salvation*, 107 (cf. Romans 13). David Aers has drawn attention to the conjunction of just payment and charity in Augustine, who defines "just souls" are those who will "live justly and be rooted in justice by assigning to everyone his due, so that they may owe no man anything except to love one another" ("uiuant iusteque morati sint sua cuique distribuendo ut nemini quidquam debeant nisi ut inuicem diligant"). *On the Trinity, Books 8–15*, ed. Gareth B. Mathews, trans. Stephen McKenna (Cambridge: Cambridge University Press, 2002), 17. Latin from *Sancti Aurelii Augustini De Trinitate Libri XV*, ed. W. J. Mountain, Corpus Christianorum Series Latina 50 (Turnhout: Brepols, 1968), 283 (italics in original). See David Aers, "Justice and Wage-labor after the Black Death: Some Perplexities for William Langland," in *Faith, Ethics, and Church*, 58.

78. See Aers, "Justice and Wage-labor," 66.

79. See Simpson, *Introduction*, 243.

80. Aers, "Langland and the Church: Affirmation and Negation," in *Chaucer, Langland, and the Creative Imagination* (London: Routledge & Kegan Paul, 1980), 51.

81. *The Abbey of the Holy Ghost* uses similar language in its discussion of poverty: "Pouerte . . . casteþ out of þe herte al þat is of eorþliche þinges and worldliche þouhtes, þat þei þat haue erþliche goodes, with loue, þei ne faste not heore hertes þeron. And þeose ben cleped pore in spirit."

82. Cf. Matthew 19:28: "when the Son of man shall sit on the seat of his majesty, you also shall sit on twelve seats judging the twelve tribes of Israel."

83. This phrase, included in *Speculum Christiani* 14.11–12, appears to derive from Chrysostom's Homily 63 on Matthew 19:16, a section of which reads, "Therefore that we may not have superfluous sorrows, let us forsake the love of money that is ever paining, and never endures to hold its peace, and let us remove ourselves to another love, which both makes us happy, and hath

great facility, and let us long after the treasures above. For neither is the labour here so great, and the gain is unspeakable, and it is not possible for him to fail of them who is but in any wise watchful and sober, and despises the things present." John Chrysostom, *The Homilies of S. John Chrysostom on the Gospel of St. Matthew* (Oxford: John Henry Parker, 1851), 3:858. The Latin reads, "Ne itaque in cassura doleamus, perpetuo furentem, pecuniarum amorem, qui numquam reprimi potest, rejicientes, ad alium appellamus, qui nos possit beatos efficere, quique multam habeat facilitatem, supernosque thesauros concupiscamus. Neque enim hic labor tantus, et lucrum ineffabile est, nec potest qui vigilat et praesentia despicit." *Patrologiae Graecae*, ed. J.-P. Migne (Paris: J.-P. Migne, 1828–33), vol. 58, col. 607.

CHAPTER 4

1. Geoffrey Chaucer, *The Friar's Prologue*, in Benson, ed., *The Riverside Chaucer*, III.1271–79.
2. Susan Signe Morrison, "Don't Ask, Don't Tell: The Wife of Bath and Vernacular Translations," *Exemplaria* 8.1 (1996): 97–98.
3. Andrew Galloway, "Marriage Sermons, Polemical Sermons, and *The Wife of Bath's Prologue*: A Generic Excursus," *Studies in the Age of Chaucer* 14 (1992): 29. A similar point is made by Ralph Hanna in "The Difficulty of Ricardian Prose Translation," *MLQ* 51 (1990): 329.
4. Making the laywoman reader stand in for a larger lay public was not a novel strategy: as Vincent Gillespie has noted, some works written principally for religious women were also offered to readers living in the world: as for example a treatise "aȝence fleshly affecciouns" in whose preface the author says, "þouȝ þis tretis and writyng after þe maner of spech be made to women allonly and þat for certeyn causys yet every man havying discrecioun þat redis þerin may also take well hys lernyng and spirituall availe þerby as it had ben written to hem also specially as it is written to women." See "Vernacular Books of Religion," in *Book Production and Publishing in Britain, 1375–1475*, ed. Jeremy Griffiths and Derek Pearsall (Cambridge: Cambridge University Press, 1989), 321.
5. For the quoted phrases, see Rita Copeland, "Why Women Can't Read: Medieval Hermeneutics, Statutory Law, and the Lollard Heresy Trials," in *Representing Women: Law, Literature, and Feminism*, ed. Susan Sage Heinzelman and Zipporah Batshaw Wiseman (Durham, NC: Duke University Press, 1994), 260, 262.
6. On the complex subject of women's relation to clerical authority in the medieval period, see Gary Macy, *The Hidden History of Women's Ordination: Female Clergy in the Medieval West* (Oxford: Oxford University Press, 2008). Macy shows that prior to the twelfth century, the term "ordination" covered a much wider range of ministries, some reserved to women, than subsequently: during the early Middle Ages, "ordination was not limited to only those ministries that served at the altar, that is, the priesthood and the diaconate" (35).

7. See Christine Ryan Hilary's Explanatory Notes to the *Wife of Bath's Prologue* (*The Riverside Chaucer*, 864).
8. McCarthy, ed., *Book to a Mother*, xxxiv.
9. See the Conclusion for a study of Oxford, Bodleian Library, MS Laud misc. 210, one such manuscript.
10. As Elisabeth Dutton notes ("Textual Disunities and Ambiguities," 155), it is impossible to tell why the work ends here. Although the text concludes at the end of a sentence and thus is not obviously broken off, the final folio (fol. 58v) is filled by text, making it seem likely that the book originally contained additional quires.
11. Alan J. Fletcher, "A Hive of Industry or a Hornet's Nest? MS Sidney Sussex 74 and its Scribes," in *Late-Medieval Religious Texts and Their Transmission: Essays in Honour of A. I. Doyle*, ed. A. J. Minnis (Cambridge: D. S. Brewer, 1994), 154–55. MS Egerton 826 Scribe A has been located in north-west Warwickshire.
12. Cambridge, Sidney Sussex College, MS 74, and Dublin, Trinity College, MS 74, respectively. In addition to the Wycliffite sermons, Sidney Sussex MS 74 also features several quite orthodox items, including *The Pater Noster of Richard Ermyte* and Thomas Wimbledon's sermon *Redde Racionem Villicacionis Tue*, copied by two other scribes (see Fletcher, "Hive of Industry," 143–44, for a description of contents and scribal stints).
13. Claire Waters, *Angels and Earthly Creatures: Preaching, Performance, and Gender in the Later Middle Ages* (Philadelphia: University of Pennsylvania Press, 2004), 19.
14. This is Morenzoni's phrase ("expliquer publiquement le texte sacré") from his introduction to Thomas of Chobham, *Summa de Arte Praedicandi*, ed. Franco Morenzoni, CCCM 82 (Turnhout: Brepols, 1988), xli. Translated by Waters, *Angels and Earthly Creatures*, 21.
15. Thomas of Chobham, *Summa de Arte Praedicandi*, 57. The Latin reads, "uitia reprehendere et fidem et bonos mores astruere."
16. *Speculum Christiani*, ed. Holmstedt, 2.
17. Alastair Minnis, "Chaucer's Pardoner and the 'Office of Preacher,'" in *Intellectuals and Writers in Fourteenth-Century Europe*, ed. Piero Boitani and Anna Torti (Tübingen: Gunter Narr, 1986), 99.
18. Translation by Leopold Krul, in *Three Medieval Rhetorical Arts*, ed. J. J. Murphy (Berkeley: University of California Press, 1971), 124. The Latin reads: "Nullus laicus vel religiosus, nisi per Episcopum vel Papam licentiatus, nec mulier quantumcumque docta et sancta, praedicare debet. Nec sufficit alicui dicere quod sit a Deo missus, nisi hoc manifeste ostendate quia hoc solent haeretici dicere . . . Ex isto videtur quod sacerdotes parochiales praedicare non possunt, nisi licentietur ab Episcopis vel Papa, nec sufficit quod licentietur a rectoribus." Thomas-Marie Charland, ed., *Artes Praedicandi* (Ottawa: Publications de l'Institut d'études médiévales d'Ottawa, 1936), 241–42.
19. H. Leith Spencer, *English Preaching in the Late Middle Ages* (Oxford: Oxford University Press, 1993), 173.

20. "Seminare autem verbum Dei ad edificacionem ecclesie est authonomatice christiana religio" (*De Civili Dominio*, 3:3.3–4).
21. For the fifteenth conclusion see *Fasciculi Zizaniorum*, 280. See Romans 10:15: "And how shall they preach unless they be sent, as it is written: How beautiful are the feet of them that preach the gospel of peace, of them that bring glad tidings of good things?" See *Fasciculi Zizaniorum*, 277–79, for the propositions condemned as heretical, and 279–82 for those considered erroneous.
22. ". . . ad bene vivendum, et bene docendum suum evangelium, et ministrandum populo suo necessaria sacramenta. Et quilibet homo sanctus, qui est membrum Christi, et erit salvatus, est verus presbyter ordinatus a Deo" (*Fasciculi Zizaniorum*, 388–89). This list of eleven errors, of which this is the third, appears in the manuscript just before the list of views that Purvey publicly abjured in 1401 (see 400–07). Anne Hudson notes that although most of the statements made are common to Wycliffite belief, "Purvey went a good deal further than Wyclif in his assertions about the priesthood of all believers." See "John Purvey: A Reconsideration of the Evidence for his Life and Writings," in *Lollards and Their Books* (London: Hambledon Press, 1985), 88. The errors were reportedly recorded by the Carmelite friar Richard Lavenham and are preserved solely in the *Fasciculi Zizaniorum* manuscript. They correspond in many points to the abjured propositions listed afterward, but it is unclear whether Lavenham's work dates from before or after Purvey's trial (92).
23. For the 1382 persecutions of Wycliffites at Oxford, see K. B. McFarlane, *John Wycliffe and the Beginnings of English Nonconformity* (New York: MacMillan, 1953), 107–20, and for the trials of such prominent Lollards as Swinderby, see 121–34.
24. See "Confessio et Revocatio Ejusdem Johannis Purvey," in *Fasciculi Zizaniorum*, 400–07. His abjuration of views on unlicensed preaching appears at 404.
25. See Alastair Minnis, "'Respondet Waltherus Bryth . . .': Walter Brut in Debate on Women Priests," in *Text and Controversy From Wyclif to Bale: Essays in Honour of Anne Hudson*, ed. Helen Barr and Ann M. Hutchison (Turnhout: Brepols, 2005), 229, n.2.
26. See I Timothy 2:11–12.
27. Translation beginning at "Paul teaches . . ." by Alcuin Blamires, in "Women and Preaching in Medieval Orthodoxy, Heresy, and Saints' Lives," *Viator* 26 (1995): 136–37. Emphasis in original. The Latin reads, "Docere et predicare verbum Dei competit sacerdotibus et ad hoc tam a Cristo quam ab apostolis sunt in ecclesia ordinati, et Paulus docet mulieres in silencio discere cum omni subieccione et docere mulieri non permittit neque dominari in virum. Quod tamen non possunt docere neque in virum dominari non dicit Paulus, nec ego audeo affirmare, cum mulieres, sancte virgines, constanter predicarunt verbum Dei et multos ad fidem converterunt sacerdotibus tunc non audentibus loqui verbum." *Registrum Johannis Trefnant, Episcopi Herefordensis*, ed. William W. Capes (London: Canterbury and York Society, 1916), 345.
28. Brut's apparent belief in the spiritual equality of men and women seems to undergird his view on women's preaching capacity: this idea of equality

is expressed secondhand in the refutation of his views that appears in the London, British Library, MS Harley 31 *quaestio* entitled "Utrum mulieres sunt ministri ydonei ad conficiendum eukaristie sacramentum." It reads in part, "The bodies of men and women are of the same most special species, and so are their souls and also their composites [i.e., the combinations of body and soul which constitute persons]. Therefore, a woman is able to exercise whatever spiritual power a man can . . . Nothing more is required for someone to become a priest except that he be admitted by God." The Latin reads, "Item, corpora virorum et mulierum sunt eiusdem speciei specialissime, similiter et anime et eciam conposita. Ergo, mulier cuiuscumque potestatis spiritualis est capax cuius vir est capax . . . Item non plus requiritur ad hoc quod aliquis sit sacerdos nisi quod sit a Deo admissus." English translation and Latin text from Minnis, "'Respondet Walterus Bryth . . . ,'" 230.

29. Waters, *Angels and Earthly Creatures*, 22.

30. At his trial, Brut reportedly said that he would retract anything not proven "by the authority of sacred scripture or by probable reason founded in sacred scripture" ("ex auctoritate scripture sacre aut racione probabili in scriptura sacra fundata"). See *Registrum*, 358.

31. Thomas of Chobham notes that women may only preach in time of necessity (*Summa de Arte Praedicandi*, 71–72). In his *Summa confessorum* Thomas exhorts wives to be "predicatrices" to their husbands, but as Alastair Minnis notes, Thomas is using the language of preaching "in a loose and metaphorical sense, and private rather than public instruction is assumed." *Fallible Authors: Chaucer's Pardoner and Wife of Bath* (Philadelphia: University of Pennsylvania Press, 2008), 332.

32. This manuscript is described and the *quaestio* "Utrum liceat mulieribus docere viros publice congregatos" printed, along with the earlier *quaestio* by Henry of Ghent upon which it draws, in Alcuin Blamires and C. W. Marx, "Woman Not to Preach: A Disputation in British Library MS Harley 31," *The Journal of Medieval Latin* 3 (1993): 50–63. Minnis has recently noted that, while it is impossible to know precisely what Brut said, the elaborate arguments for women's ministry included in London, British Library, MS Harley 31 may, ironically, have been generated by those seeking to refute him (*Fallible Authors*, 222). See 231–45 for further discussion of this question.

33. See 55, section 4, for teaching as a work of mercy ("de operibus spiritualibus"). At 58, section 12, under "Rationes Sancti Thome," part of the argument reads, "to teach and persuade publicly in the church does not belong to subjects but to prelates, but the woman, on account of her female status, is naturally subject to the man" ("quia docere et persuadere publice in ecclesia non pertinet ad subditos sed ad prelatos; sed mulier, propter condicionem feminei status est naturaliter subdita viro").

34. See 61, item 16: "It is permitted to women having sound doctrine to teach women and children in silence" ("Licet mulieribus sanam doctrinam habentibus in silencio docere mulieres et paruulos"). See Minnis, *Fallible*

Authors, 189–99, for discussion of this distinction in Aquinas and Henry of Ghent in connection with biblical precedents.

35. See 62, item 19, which argues that "father," not "mother," is the subject of "taught" (*docebat*). As Blamires and Marx note ("Women Not to Preach," 53, n.72), this solution, taken from Henry of Ghent, is adopted from the interlinear *Glossa Ordinaria*, which supplies *pater* as a subject rather than *mater*, an interpretation perpetuated in both the King James and Douai/Rheims translations: "For I was also my father's son, tender and as an only son in the sight of my mother: And he taught me . . . "

36. See 62, item 19: "Alternatively it is said that the mother taught him separately; she did not teach people publicly." The Latin reads: "aliter dicitur quod mulier docuit eum ad partem; non tamen publice docuit populum."

37. Blamires, "Women and Preaching," 151.

38. See Patterson, *Chaucer and the Subject of History*, 290–96, for a discussion of "male fear of vidual sexuality" and its representations in antifeminist literature.

39. Barbara Hanawalt notes that in London after the Black Death, as guilds became increasingly powerful economic entities, a high percentage of guild widows ensured the continuity of their lives and the retention of their property by remarrying to a member of the deceased husband's guild. Barbara Hanawalt, "Remarriage as an Option for Urban and Rural Widows in Late Medieval England," in *Wife and Widow in Medieval England*, ed. Sue Sheridan Walker (Ann Arbor: University of Michigan Press, 1993), 153–54.

40. *Ibid.*, 159.

41. *Ibid.*, 145, 148.

42. Mary Erler, "English Vowed Women at the End of the Middle Ages," *Mediaeval Studies* 57 (1995): 172. In a number of cases, husbands left testamentary provisions granting wives more property if they remained single (see 173).

43. *Ibid.*, 157.

44. *Ibid.*, 165.

45. One aristocratic vowess, Maud, Countess of Oxford, lived in two separate women's communities: she joined Campsey Ash as a vowess in 1347 and in 1369 went to live at her son-in-law's foundation, Bruisyard Abbey. See Marilyn Oliva, *The Convent and the Community in Late Medieval England: Female Monasteries in the Diocese of Norwich, 1350–1540* (Woodbridge: The Boydell Press, 1998), 48.

46. Erler, "English Vowed Women," 182.

47. *Ibid.*, 181.

48. See Warren, *Spiritual Economies*, 87–91.

49. For example, he finds "maumetrie" particularly rampant among "religiouse men and wommen [who] trauelen bisiliche wiþ gret cost to make hem semliche to cursed proude folk þat haue lore here tast of God þorw lustes and likinges" (113.3–5).

50. Warren, *Spiritual Economies*, 84. See for example the further warning against "maumetrie," where the author laments "hou monye men and wommen

haue be lost and dampned seþ Eue bigan to teche þis lessoun, wiþ suche maumetrie sturinge hem to lecherie" (113.19–21).

51. *MED* includes the following relevant definitions of "proprete": 1 (b): "private or individual ownership" and 2 (a): "Land or goods owned, property; a piece of land, a possession."

52. The Franciscans rejected property based on Christ's command to "take nothing for your journey" (Luke 9:3) and (at least in theory) lived communally based on the model of the primitive church of Acts 4:32. See James Doyne Dawson, "Richard FitzRalph and the Fourteenth-Century Poverty Controversies," *The Journal of Ecclesiastical History* 34.3 (1983): 317.

53. *De Civili Dominio*, 3:77.16–35.

54. Clerics who subsisted on salaries received lower wages when they were fixed at pre-plague levels. See William J. Dohar, *The Black Death and Pastoral Leadership: The Diocese of Hereford in the Fourteenth Century* (Philadelphia: University of Pennsylvania Press, 1995), 72–74.

55. Invoking the story of Christ's temptation in order to warn his mother against the allures of the world, he cites clerics as a case in point. The devil tempts "men of Holi Chirche and wommen to desiren benefices and dignitees, prelacies and such oþere, þe whuche þei schulde raþur forsake þan desire, for moni perelis þat fallen bi hem" (56.15–18). Above this discussion MS Egerton 826 features the heading "Aȝens religyious."

56. By 1419 in Hereford, half of the churches in the diocese were "subject to some form of monastic control either in the outright possession of revenues by appropriation, parish advowsons or annual pensions owed them by churches" (Dohar, *The Black Death and Pastoral Leadership*, 28).

57. *Ibid.*, 114.

58. For example, in his discussion of the mother's baptism the author shows detailed knowledge of sacramental procedure: "þenk what couenaunt þou madest whanne þou were baptized bifore witnesses – þat is before þe prest and þi godfadir and þi godmoderis – to forsake þe deuel and alle his werkis and alle his pompes" (42.3–6).

59. Although the Rule of St. Francis has a complicated history, existing in at least three successive forms, its inspiration is indisputably the gospel, its founding value absolute poverty. The *Legenda Major* reports that Francis, seeking guidance, opened the scriptures three times. First he read Matthew 19:21 ("if thou wilt be perfect, go sell all that thou hast . . . "); then he opened the pages to two other passages with the same emphasis: Luke 9:3 ("Take nothing for your journey"), and Matthew 16:24 ("if any man will come after me, let him deny himself." See Clopper, *"Songes of Rechelesnesse,"* 36.

60. In an early, well-documented incident of tension between secular clergy and the friars, the rectors of London churches presented a petition to the Provincial Council in 1309, complaining that the friars were abusing their privileges of preaching, confessions, and burial, as well as lamenting the danger that the friars presented to laymen who sought them out for confession. See W. A. Pantin, *The English Church in the Fourteenth Century*, 157.

61. See Norman P. Tanner, S. J., ed., *Decrees of the Ecumenical Councils*, for a description of the limited privileges of the friars to hear confession, impose penances, and offer absolution to penitents (1:366–67).

62. The passage at the end of these directives in particular seems to favor the friars. It directs that even if the prelates "issue a general refusal" of confession rights to friars, they can still "freely and lawfully hear the confessions of those wishing to confess to them and impose salutary penances, and then impart absolution. The Latin reads, "nos exnunc ipsis, ut confessiones sibi confiteri volentium libere liciteque audire valeant et eisdem poenitentias imponere salutares, atque eisdem beneficium absolutionis impertiri, gratiose concedimus de plenitudine apostolicae potestatis" (*ibid.*, 1:367).

63. Dohar, *The Black Plague and Pastoral Leadership*, 76.

64. See Pantin, *The English Church*, 159, for this suggestion.

65. Dohar, *The Black Plague and Pastoral Leadership*, 76.

66. Pantin, *The English Church*, 160. Pantin's translation. The Latin reads, "huiusmodi dominorum et dominarum nobilium confessores, quin pocius proditores et animarum deceptores notorii, emendaciones peccatorum soli et poli iure lesis restituendas convertunt eisdem in predam." See 267, from Public Record Office, D.L., 42/8 (Selby Register). This volume is the letter-book of Geoffrey de Gaddesby, Abbot of Selby, 1342–64.

67. Alcuin Blamires, "The Wife of Bath and Lollardy," *Medium Ævum* 58.2 (1989): 232.

68. Hudson, ed., *Selections From English Wycliffite Writings*, 24.

69. There was not a consistent Lollard position on this question, however. The Wycliffite treatise *Of Wedded Men and Wifis and of Here Children Also* defends clerical marriage yet argues that "clene virginité" is "moche betre" than marriage. This treatise is included in Eve Salisbury, ed., *The Trials and Joys of Marriage* (Kalamazoo: Medieval Institute Publications, 2002), 191–201 (see 192–93).

70. These female saints are the sorts of models that Lollards would attempt to extirpate as part of a rejection of the cult of saints, in the process removing an aspect of religious practice historically important to women in particular. See Shannon McSheffrey, *Gender and Heresy: Women and Men in Lollard Communities, 1420–1530* (Philadelphia: University of Pennsylvania Press, 1995), 148.

71. Minnis describes this passage in " 'Respondet Waltherus Bryth . . . ,' " 233. The Latin trial transcript reads, "modicum loquitur Cristus expresso sermone ut distinguat sacerdotes a reliquo populo nec utitur hoc nomine, sacerdos, aut hoc nomine, presbiter, in evangelio sed aliquos vocat discipulos aliquos vero apostolos quos misit ad baptizandum predicandum" (Capes, ed., *Registrum*, 343).

72. Waters, *Angels and Earthly Creatures*, 123.

73. For this phrase, see Nicholas Watson, "Fashioning the Puritan Gentry-Woman," 182.

74. Waters argues, "The Wife's – and Chaucer's – success in undermining the clerical voice's authoritative claims is suggested by the fact that the Parson,

the only figure with the kind of moral qualifications to preach that the church would recognize, never once uses the term [preacher] to refer to himself" (*Angels and Earthly Creatures*, 165).

75. *Ibid.*, 144.

76. For the quoted phrase, see Elaine Tuttle Hansen, *Chaucer and the Fictions of Gender* (Berkeley: University of California Press, 1992), 27: she offers several sources that espouse what she calls this "majority view," including Mary Carruthers, "The Wife of Bath and the Painting of Lions," *PMLA* 94 (1979): 209–22.

77. We can attribute opposition to the Parson's preaching to the Wife of Bath if we grant that she speaks the following words, from the Epilogue to the *Man of Law's Tale*: "Heer schal he nat preche; / He schal no gospel glosen here ne teche . . . My joly body schal a tale telle" (II.1179–85). The uncertainty of who speaks these lines turns on the textual instability of the Epilogue to the *Man of Law's Tale*, in which these lines are attributed to the Shipman, while the *Wife of Bath's Prologue* follows in most manuscripts. Hanna observes in his Textual Notes to the Epilogue, "Given such phraseology as 1185 *My joly body*, the Epilogue probably goes back to a point in the development of the Tales when the Wife of Bath was still assigned the Shipman's fabliau" (Benson, ed., *The Riverside Chaucer*, 1126).

78. Blamires, "The Wife of Bath and Lollardy," 226. See Minnis, *Fallible Authors*, 259–96, for discussion of why the term "expres" does not necessarily impute a Lollard vocabulary to the Wife of Bath.

79. Patterson, *Chaucer and the Subject of History*, 307.

80. "Si autem acceperis uxorem, non peccasti. Et si nupserit virgo, non peccavit, tribulationem tamen carnis habebunt huiusmodi."

81. Blamires, "The Wife of Bath and Lollardy," 234.

82. Patterson, *Chaucer and the Subject of History*, 308.

83. See Chapter 2 above for discussion of the *Book*'s focus on using the Bible to teach the reader "to iugge for to destroye sinne."

84. See Waters, *Angels and Earthly Creatures*, 23. Waters notes that St. Birgitta uses this image of conception and prophecy to connect herself to Mary and the Apostles simultaneously. In one of her Old Swedish meditations, Birgitta prays to the apostles and evangelists that "by your prayer the same spirit [may deign] to visit my heart and come alight in it . . . Then I would receive words and deeds to do and speak according to his blessed will" (*ibid.*, 137). Waters observes, "Like Mary, like the Apostles, Birgitta is the body that 'receives' the Holy Spirit and so receives the gift of prophecy *and* the right and duty to speak it."

85. Warren, *Spiritual Economies*, 90.

86. The "couenaunt of fullouȝt" is a theme to which the MS Egerton 826 scribe draws particular attention: this heading appears four consecutive times over an earlier sequence discussing baptism (fols. 39v–41r).

87. "Vre deore wurðe leafdi seinte Marie þe ah to alle wummen to beo forbisne. wes of se lutel speche. þat nohwer in hali writ ne finde we þat ha spec but

fowr siðen. ah for se selt speche hire wordes weren heuie & hefden muche mihte" (*Ancrene Wisse*, ed. Tolkien, 41). "Our precious St. Mary, who ought to be an example for all women, was of so few words that nowhere in Holy Writ do we find that she spoke, except for four times: but because of this rarity of speech, her words were heavy and full of power" (Savage and Watson, eds. and trans., *Anchoritic Spirituality*, 76).

88. Despite the Virgin Mary's traditionally powerful, even quasi-priestly, position in the church, authorities such as Albert the Great insisted that she could not be understood to be ordained, for that was beneath her dignity and her conformity to the requirement that women be excluded from the sacrament of ordination (see Minnis, *Fallible Authors*, 189–91).

89. Galloway, "Marriage Sermons, Polemical Sermons, and *The Wife of Bath's Prologue*," 22.

90. For this term, see Nicholas Watson, "Chaucer's Public Christianity," *Religion and Literature* 37.2 (2005): 112. With attention to the same passage, Watson argues that the Wife of Bath "repudiates even the desire for perfection, and in the process the entire ethos of *imitatio Christi* as variously expressed in all the perfectionist religiosities of Chaucer's time" (109).

91. Dutton, "Christ the Codex," 88.

92. Both father and son are called "Tobie" in the Wycliffite Bible. See *The Wycliffite Bible*, ed. Forshall and Madden, 2:576.

93. Tobias 7:15 reads, "The God of Abraham, and the God of Isaac, and the God of Jacob be with you, and may he join you together, and fulfil his blessing in you." See Jean-Baptiste Molin and Protais Mutembe, *Le Rituel du mariage en France du XIIe au XVIe siècle*, Théologie historique 26 (Paris: Beauchesne, 1974), 323.

94. For a brief description of this volume, see A. I. Doyle, "Books Belonging to the Vere Family and Barking Abbey," *Transactions of the Essex Archaeological Society* New Series 25.2 (1958): 241–42. The Tobit and Susannah texts in the codex both derive from the later Wycliffite Bible.

95. For discussion of the *Tobias* as schooltext, see John Fleming, "Muses of the Monastery," *Speculum* 78.4 (2003): 1085–86. For the *Tobias* in translation, see Ian Thomson and Louis Perraud, eds. and trans., *Ten Latin Schooltexts of the Later Middle Ages*, Mediaeval Studies 6 (Lewiston, NY: The Edwin Mellen Press, 1990).

96. As Chaucer's Parson puts it more directly, "[t]he seconde manere of chastitee is for to been a clene wydewe, and eschue the embracynges of man, and desiren the embracynge of Jhesu Crist. Thise been tho that han been wyves and han forgoon hire housbondes" (Benson, ed., *The Riverside Chaucer*, X.943–44).

97. In another contemporary parallel, *The Pore Caitif* connects the story of Tobias to the explanation of God's "hestes," including the story of Tobias and Sara when discussing the prohibitions on lechery. See Brady, ed., *The Pore Caitif*, 62.

98. Hudson, *The Premature Reformation*, 325. Also see John Wyclif, *Tractatus de Potestate Pape*, ed. Johann Loserth (London: Wyclif Society, 1907), 312.
99. For this phrase, see Lawler, "The Secular Clergy in *Piers Plowman*," 95.
100. Patterson, *Chaucer and the Subject of History*, 286.
101. Marshall Leicester, *The Disenchanted Self: Representing the Subject in the Canterbury Tales* (Berkeley: University of California Press, 1990), 25.

CONCLUSION

1. Little, *Confession and Resistance*, 12.
2. See Chapter 2 above for the text of Article Seven of the Constitutions.
3. While Ullerston finds the laity to be "populus sapiens et intelligens gens magnus," he notes that his opponents approvingly call the English people "populus stultus et ignarus." Quoted in Watson, "Censorship and Cultural Change," 845 (from Vienna, Hofbibliothek, MS 4133, fol. 203r).
4. Vincent Gillespie argues persuasively that Ullerston represents "the voice of moderate reform." See "Vernacular Theology," in *Oxford Twenty-First Century Approaches to Literature: Middle English*, ed. Paul Strohm, 413.
5. Hilton represents a bridge between these two groups: see J. P. H. Clark, "Late Fourteenth-Century Cambridge Theology and the English Contemplative Tradition," in *The Medieval Mystical Tradition in England: Exeter Symposium V*, ed. Marion Glasscoe (Cambridge: D. S. Brewer, 1992), 1–16.
6. Watson suggests that in an atmosphere of "self-censorship," new vernacular writings tended to avoid difficult theological questions and were in general "simpler, more cautious, and less numerous than fourteenth-century theological writings" ("Censorship and Cultural Change," 831 and 834).
7. For a discussion of the changes Love made in his translation and adaptation of the pseudo-Bonaventuran text, see Sargent, "The Transformation of the *Meditationes Vitae Christi*," in *The Mirror of the Blessed Life of Jesus Christ: A Full Critical Edition*, 38–54. Also see "The Anti-Wycliffite Stance of *The Mirror of the Blessed Life of Jesus Christ*," in *ibid.*, 54–75.
8. *The Mirror*, 10.9–16 (hereafter cited in the main text by page and line number). Although Love thus seems to have intended the *Mirror* for a primarily lay audience, his references to aspects of Carthusian life in several instances suggest he may also have envisioned Carthusian readers (see *The Mirror*, 50–51).
9. However, see Simpson: "[c]loser inspection reveals, however, an unexpectedly liberal reading practice, and an implicit invitation to transgress the bounds that the work apparently wishes to preserve" (*Reform and Cultural Revolution*, 434).
10. A contemporary compiler seems to have found these texts complementary as well, for there is a copy of *Fervor Amoris* immediately following Love's *Mirror* in Cambridge, University Library, MS Additional 6686.
11. Quoted phrases from Watson, "Censorship and Cultural Change," 835; also see 856–58.

12. Shannon McSheffrey's recent work on Lollards in the later fifteenth century has added new evidence to the picture of how heterodox readers used devotional texts and how Arundel's Constitutions were enforced. She argues that the later Lollards were avid users of orthodox religious works, albeit in unanticipated ways, and contends that "advocacy of vernacular prayer and possession of English books" were not used as grounds for the accusation of heresy unless the suspect also openly challenged the church's authority. See "Heresy, Orthodoxy and Vernacular Religion 1480–1525," *Past and Present* 186 (February 2005): 59–60.

13. On questions of manuscript evidence, dating, and the critical privileging of "challenging" religious literature, see Sargent, "The *Mirror* and Vernacular Theology in Fifteenth-Century England," in *The Mirror*, 75–96. Simpson concurs with Watson about the authorial anxiety caused by the Constitutions but argues that many fifteenth-century devotional works, including saints' lives, "actively exploit the secondary status of ostensibly naïve devotional writing to express complex notions of geography, history, textuality, and selfhood" (*Reform and Cultural Revolution*, 391). Gillespie contends that the long episcopate of Thomas Chichele (1414–43) encouraged a movement of "orthodox reform" manifest not only in Latin sermons but also in the vernacular poetry of writers including Hoccleve, Audelay, and Lydgate. See "Vernacular Theology," 416–19.

14. Several recent accounts of the Constitutions have further investigated the extent of their application and effects. Steven Justice argues for the legislation's "minimal effect" outside a small group of Lollard texts and individuals already suspected of Lollardy. See " 'General Words': Response to Elizabeth Schirmer," in *Voices in Dialogue: Reading Women in the Middle Ages*, ed. Linda Olson and Kathryn Kerby-Fulton (Notre Dame: University of Notre Dame Press, 2005), 387. Kathryn Kerby-Fulton considers the reception, before and after Arundel, of a varied body of visionary theological works in England. Using extensive case studies, she shows how many demonstrate "the diversity of medieval intellectual and spiritual experience and the tolerance accorded it by a host of authorities: ecclesiastical, secular, authorial, scribal, personal." *Books Under Suspicion: Censorship and Tolerance of Revelatory Writing in Late Medieval England* (Notre Dame: University of Notre Dame Press, 2006), 15.

15. As Seth Lerer has recently observed, "[b]asic to medieval literary circulation was the miscellany or anthology." Seth Lerer, "Medieval English Literature and the Idea of the Anthology," *PMLA* 118.5 (2003): 1253. Julia Boffey and John Thompson helpfully define an anthology as a book in which "items (and groups of items) from many different sources were copied together, in planned sections, to make up large volumes which could have served both individual and corporate needs." Julia Boffey and John J. Thompson, "Anthologies and Miscellanies: Production and Choice of Texts," in *Book Production and Publishing in Britain 1375–1475*, 279. They argue that "miscellanies," which could overlap in form and function with "commonplace books," are in general not governed by a single logic, having

perhaps been compiled in stages by individuals with different aims. For Ralph Hanna, "miscellaneity" is a crucial principle of Middle English literary culture, involving "the oscillation between the planned and the random." Ralph Hanna III, "Miscellaneity and Vernacularity: Conditions of Literary Production in Late Medieval England," in *The Whole Book: Cultural Perspectives on the Medieval Miscellany*, ed. Stephen G. Nichols and Siegfried Wenzel (Ann Arbor: University of Michigan Press, 1996), 37–38.

16. Nichols and Wenzel write, "[a]rguing that the individual manuscript contextualizes the text(s) it contains in specific ways, materialist philology seeks to analyze the consequences of this relationship on the way these texts may be read and interpreted" (*The Whole Book*, 2).

17. Two notable examples are London, British Library, MS Additional 36983 and Lincoln Cathedral MS 91. The former is a paper collection of devotional and didactic works, many of them narrative: the book was copied by a series of scribes, probably for a lay household, and also includes saints' lives, *The Prick of Conscience*, and *The Three Kings of Cologne*, among many other contents. For discussion of this manuscript, see Rice, "Spiritual Ambition and the Translation of the Cloister," 253–56.

18. The same is true for *Fervor Amoris*, which survives in fewer copies, most of whose inscriptions and/or contents suggest association with religious houses (Gillespie, "Vernacular Books of Religion," in *Book Production and Publishing in Britain 1375–1475*, 342–43). A few of Gillespie's examples include Cambridge, Trinity College, MS B.15.42, which may have been owned by a friar; London, British Library, MS Harley 2409, given by one Cistercian nun to another; London, British Library, MS Royal 17.A.xxv, owned by a sixteenth-century friar; and Oxford, Bodleian Library, MS Ashmole 1286. (For a different view of MS Ashmole 1286, see Trivedi, "'The Pore Caitif': *Lectio* through *Compilatio*," 134–40.) Another such volume, Oxford, Bodleian Library, MS Bodley 423, is a composite book of which sections B and C were copied by a Carthusian scribe. These sections begin with *Fervor Amoris* and feature other texts including extracts from St. Bridget's *Revelations* and the Middle English translation of Aelred's rule for an anchoress, *A Tretyse þat is a rule and form of lyuynge perteynyng to a Recluse*. For description see *The Book of Tribulation*, ed. Alexandra Barratt (Heidelberg: Carl Winter, 1983), 7–9.

19. A. I. Doyle, "A Survey of the Origins and Circulation of Theological Writings in English in the 14th, 15th, and Early 16th Centuries with Special Consideration of the Part of the Clergy Therein" (Ph.D. diss., University of Cambridge, 1953), 1:218.

20. Sargent, ed., *The Mirror*, 75.

21. See Julia Boffey, "*The Charter of the Holy Ghost* and its Role in Manuscript Anthologies," *The Yearbook of English Studies* 33 (2003): 127. Boffey notes that Cambridge, Trinity College, MS O.1.29 and London, British Library, MS Harley 2406, both "anthologies designed for spiritual instruction," each contain "at least one tract seemingly aimed at enclosed religious." London, British Library, MS Stowe 39, which features a large illustration of nuns

working in an abbey, changes the first lines of the *Abbey* text to address "my
dere systres" (fol. 1r).

22. Several manuscripts feature the *Abbey* and *Charter* either separately or in
    sequence, together with female saints' lives and Marian material. Boffey
    provides a complete list of manuscripts whose contents suggest an effort
    to appeal to women readers: they include Cambridge, University Library,
    MS Ll.5.18, in which the *Abbey* and *Charter* appear with prose lives of St.
    Margaret and St. Dorothy; Stonyhurst College MS 43, which includes the
    Charter and a prose life of St. Katherine; London, Lambeth Palace, MS
    432, which contains *Abbey* and *Charter*, lives of St. Dorothy and St. Jerome,
    Bridgettine texts, and miracles of the Virgin; Tokyo, Takamiya MS 65 (*olim*
    Bradfer-Lawrence MS 8), featuring a conflated version of *Abbey* and *Charter*
    along with Marian miracles; and London, British Library, MS Harley 5272,
    with its *Life of our Lady*, Life of St. Dorothy, *Abbey*, and *Charter*. See Boffey,
    "*The Charter of the Holy Ghost*," 127–30.

23. Unfortunately this scribe has not been identified. I am grateful to George
    Keiser for helping me to date this book. In notes that he kindly shared with
    me, Keiser dates the manuscript to 1440–60 and records that the entire book
    was copied by this one scribe in a mixed anglicana/secretary bookhand. This
    book is briefly discussed in A. S. G. Edwards, "Fifteenth-Century English
    Collections of Female Saints' Lives," *The Yearbook of English Studies* 33
    (2002): 135.

24. Roberta Gilchrist, *Gender and Material Culture: The Archaeology of Religious
    Women* (London: Routledge, 1994), 123. See Warren, *Spiritual Economies*, 20–
    25, on the importance of *familiae* to fifteenth-century female monastic life.

25. Felicity Riddy, "'Women Talking About the Things of God': A Late
    Medieval Sub-Culture," in *Women and Literature in Britain, 1150–1500*, ed.
    Carole M. Meale (Cambridge: Cambridge University Press, 1993), 110. Riddy
    documents numerous instances of laywomen bequeathing their devotional
    books to nuns. She notes at 108 one particularly lavish example: in 1448,
    Dame Agnes Stapleton bequeathed copies of "Bonaventura" (perhaps Love's
    Mirror), *The Prick of Conscience*, *The Chastising of God's Children*, and her
    "Vice and vertues" to four separate houses of nuns. See also Mary Erler,
    "Exchange of Books Between Nuns and Laywomen," *passim*.

26. George Keiser, "Piety and Patronage in Fifteenth-Century England:
    Margaret, Duchess of Clarence, Symon Wynter and Beinecke MS 317," *The
    Yale University Library Gazette* 60.1–2 (1984): 43. The only ownership marks
    that remain in MS Harley 5272 date from the sixteenth century: one reads
    "Iohanni Mellowes" (fol. 18v), another "Iohn Cradock" (fol. 33r). Another
    note on fol. 42r testifies to female ownership: "Thys ys Elsabeth danes book
    / he that stelhyn / Shall be hangyd by a croke."

27. David Bell, *What Nuns Read: Books and Libraries in Medieval English Nunner-
    ies*, Cistercian Studies Series 158 (Kalamazoo: Medieval Institute, 1995), 105.

28. As Carole Meale notes, Margaret, Lady Hungerford (*d.* 1478) cultivated a
    particular devotion to the Virgin and was known to have owned a copy of

the *Lives of the Saints* in French. Carole M. Meale, "'. . . alle the bokes that I haue of latyn, englisch, and frensch': Laywomen and Their Books in Late Medieval England," in *Women and Literature in Britain, 1150–1500*, 128.

29. For these lines, see Joseph E. Lauritis, ed., *A Critical Edition of John Lydgate's Life of Our Lady*, Duquesne Studies Philological Series 2 (Louvain: Editions E. Nauwaelaerts, 1961), Book II, 540–43.

30. *Ibid.*, Book I, 855–59.

31. Other virgins who receive angelic ministrations while imprisoned include St. Margaret and St. Katherine, whose Middle English lives appear together, along with the Life of St. Julian, in London, British Library, MS Royal 17.A.xxvii.

32. This *Abbey* text is closely related to the one copied in Cambridge, Jesus College, MS 46. Consacro speculates that this small textual group may be descended from London, British Library, MS Harley 2406, which may have connections to the Gilbertine order. If so, it is possible that all three manuscripts are of monastic provenance. See Consacro, ed., *The Abbey of the Holy Ghost*, cxiii.

33. For an aristocratic woman's regulated devotional life, see C. A. J. Armstrong, "The Piety of Cicely, Duchess of York: A Study in Late Mediaeval Culture," in *England, France, and Burgundy in the Fifteenth Century* (London: Hambledon Press, 1983), 135–56.

34. Doyle, "A Survey," 1:268.

35. In MS Royal 17.C.xviii, the *Mixed Life* addresses "Brethyrne and sustren." Doyle has argued that this address is "not only a further generalisation, but also possibly a sign of communal reading, which the construction of the treatise, and some of the copies, would suit in favorable conditions" (*ibid.*, 200).

36. Lincoln Cathedral MS 91 and MS Ashmole 751 have several similar contents, of which only one is identical: a short instructive story on contrition. Other similar contents include Middle English explications of the ten commandments, the *Mirror of St. Edmund* (Thornton's in English, MS Ashmole 751's in Latin), and sections of the *Mixed Life*. Both compilations feature extracts from Rolle's Latin works, and texts attributed to Rolle, although not the same ones. For details on Thornton's Rolle extracts, see John J. Thompson, "Another Look at the Religious Texts in Lincoln, Cathedral Library, MS 91," in *Late Medieval Religious Texts and Their Transmission: Essays in Honour of A. I. Doyle*, ed. A. J. Minnis (Cambridge: D. S. Brewer, 1994), 180–81. For MS Ashmole 751's, see William Henry Black, ed., *A Descriptive, Analytical, and Critical Catalogue of the Manuscripts Bequeathed unto the University of Oxford by Elias Ashmole, Esq., M.D., F.R.S., Also of some Additional MSS. Contributed by Kingsley, Lhuyd, Borlase, and Others* (Oxford: Oxford University Press, 1845), 362–65. Also see Hope Emily Allen, *Writings Ascribed to Richard Rolle*, 94, 130, 192, 347.

37. London, Lambeth Palace, MS 472 contains a collection of Hilton's English works, including the *Scale of Perfection*, I and II. See Ogilvie-Thomson, ed., *Walter Hilton's "Mixed Life,"* xii–xiv, for detailed discussion of the volume.

38. This phrase is coined by George Keiser, in "'To Knawe God Almyghtyn': Robert Thornton's Devotional Book," *Analecta Cartusiana* 106.2 (1984): 103–29. He argues that the "devotional book" should be considered an intentionally compiled religious volume, separate from the other parts of Lincoln Cathedral MS 91, which also features a volume of secular romances and a book of medical recipes. He notes that it is not clear whether Thornton himself, or a later owner, brought the three books together into the present large volume (104).

39. According to Keiser, Thornton was "a member of the minor gentry who in 1418 became lord of East Newton, in the wapentake of Ryedale, North Riding of Yorkshire." George Keiser, "Lincoln Cathedral MS 91: The Life and Milieu of the Scribe," *Studies in Bibliography* 32 (1979): 159.

40. Thornton seems to have gathered and copied his texts over a long period of time, *c.* 1420–50 (*ibid.*). Keiser notes in "'To Knawe God Almyghtyn'" that "whatever unity and coherence the book has derives not from the ordering of the texts, but from the fact that clearly discernable tastes and preferences governed the compiler's choice of texts" (*ibid.*, 112).

41. Cited from *English Prose Treatises of Richard Rolle of Hampole, Edited from Robert Thornton's MS in the Library of Lincoln Cathedral*, ed. George G. Perry, EETS OS 20, rev. edn. (London: Oxford University Press, 1921), 27. Although Thornton's source for this incomplete copy of the *Mixed Life* is not known, Keiser has speculated, based on family connections and records, that some of Thornton's texts, including possibly the text of the *Mixed Life*, which contains some female forms of address, were borrowed from the local nunnery of Nun Monkton ("More Light on the Life and Milieu of Robert Thornton," 116–17).

42. Keiser, "To Knawe God Almyghtyn," 123.

43. These short catechetical items are included on fol. 196r–v, and the sermon covers fols. 213v–218v. See *ibid.*, 112–14.

44. *Ibid.*, 117.

45. *St. Edmund's Mirror*, in *Religious Pieces in Prose and Verse from the Thornton Manuscript*, ed. George G. Perry, EETS OS 26 (London: Oxford University Press, 1914), 46.

46. Doyle notes that the end of the manuscript features a note reading "'de clericis cuius ordines sint in congregacione terrenorum', and on the alienation of the goods of churches; some rough jottings seem to relate to cows and sheep and various payments, including one to or from 'Archidiacon. Ebor.', but they are hardly legible. The volume shows clear pastoral but also strong devotional interests; in view of the accounts last mentioned, probably not a mendicant but possibly either a secular or monastic compilation" ("A Survey," 2:77).

47. This lyric is divided into two parts in the manuscript, with these two separate headings, although it is represented as a single work in the modern edition. See *Medieval English Lyrics: A Critical Anthology*, ed. R. T. Davies (London: Faber and Faber, 1963), 146–48 (text) and 332–32 (notes). For descriptions of the English prose, see *The Index of Printed Middle English Prose*, ed. R. E. Lewis *et al.* (New York: Garland, 1985), items 58, 126, 233, 564. Also see *The*

Index of Middle English Prose Handlist IX: Manuscripts Containing Middle English Prose in the Ashmole Collection, Bodleian Library, Oxford, ed. L. M. Eldredge (Cambridge: D. S. Brewer, 1992), 27. For printed editions of the stories from Caesarius of Heisterbach, see "De inperfecta contricione," in *English Prose Treatises*, 6–7, and Carl Horstmann, ed., *Yorkshire Writers: Richard Rolle of Hampole, An English Father of the Church and His Followers* (London: Swan Sonnenschein, 1895), 1:157. For the Mandeville extracts, see M. C. Seymour, "Secundum Iohannem Maundvyle," *English Studies in Africa* 4 (1961): 148–58.

48. See Ralph Hanna III, "Booklets in Medieval Manuscripts: Further Considerations," in *Pursuing History: Middle English Manuscripts and Their Texts* (Stanford: Stanford University Press, 1996), 28.

49. *Ibid.*, 29.

50. I have silently expanded abbreviations and modernized punctuation in these citations from the manuscript.

51. Lines 178–80 in the critical edition. Ogilvie-Thomson notes that the reading "persones" as opposed to "persoone" occurs in nine manuscripts (more than half), but "prelates and curates" is an uncommon reading, present in only three other witnesses: Vernon, Simeon, and Plimpton (Columbia University MS 271).

52. Hanna, "Booklets in Medieval Manuscripts," 29.

53. Love writes, "Whereof & oþer vertuese exercise þat longeþ to contemplatif lyuyng, & specialy to a recluse, & also of medelet life, þat is to sey sumtyme actife & sumtyme contemplatif, as it longeþ to diuerse persones þat in worldly astate hauen grace of gostly loue; who so wole more pleynly [be] enformed & tauht in english tonge; lete him loke þe tretees þat þe worþi clerk & holi lyuere Maister Hilton þe Chanon of Thurgarton wrote in english by grete grace & hye discrecion" (Sargent, ed., *The Mirror*, 122.34–41).

54. Compare Hilton's statement that the mixed life belongs "speciali to men of holi chirche, as to prelates and oþire curates whiche haue cure and souereynte ouer oþere men for to [kepe] and for to rule hem, boþe here bodies and principali heer soules, in fulfillynge of þe deedes of mercy bodili and gostli" (*Mixed Life*, ed. Ogilvie-Thomson, 14.144–48).

55. Sargent, ed., *The Mirror*, 372.

56. Thompson, "Another Look," 180.

57. This story from Caesarius also appears in the moral treatise *Jacob's Well*, to illustrate the discussion of the sentence of excommunication. Here the story leads directly into an exhortation to obey one's confessor. See *Jacob's Well*, ed. Brandeis, 12–13.

58. This manuscript was probably a clerical collection, according to Doyle, who suggests "it may be either mendicant or monastic, some pastoral interest being almost inevitable in the case of the former, and not uncommon in the latter" ("A Survey," 2:118). The story is printed as the first of the selection of English texts from London, British Library, MS Harley 1022, in Horstmann, ed., *Yorkshire Writers*, 1:157.

59. Of the other fifteenth-century volumes featuring *Book to a Mother*, Oxford, Bodleian Library, MS Bodley 416 may also be considered to register the *Book*'s impulse to complaint and religious reform in a few of its other contents. These include religious poems attacking vanity in dress and bemoaning contemporary abuses. For description and discussion, see Dutton, "Disunities and Ambiguities," 150–51.

60. Hanna, "English Biblical Texts before Lollardy and Their Fate," 150–53; McSheffrey, "Heresy, Orthodoxy and English Vernacular Religion, 1480–1525," 65–67.

61. Vincent Gillespie has noted that the book might have been made for either lay or clerical readers. See Gillespie, "'Lukynge in Haly Bukes': *Lectio* in Some Medieval Spiritual Miscellanies," *Analecta Cartusiana* 106 (1984): 20.

62. Elisabeth Dutton, "Compiling Julian: The *Revelation of Love* and Late-Medieval Devotional Compilation" (Ph.D. diss., Oxford University, 2002), 105. For a more detailed discussion of the manuscript's codicology and a more complete discussion of its contents, see *ibid.*, 95–105. Gillespie has suggested a degree of thematic cohesion in the book, arguing that the inclusion of *Book to a Mother*, *The Life of Soul*, *The Abbey*, and *The Charter of the Holy Ghost* might lead one to read the volume "as a collection of 'forms of living'" ("Vernacular Books of Religion," 326).

63. Hudson, *The Premature Reformation*, 424. Although Jill C. Havens called MS Laud Misc. 210 a Wycliffite compilation "put together by individual heretics compelled by a collective desire to gather up any and all vernacular materials that reinforced their fundamentalist agenda," I would argue that the manuscript might be considered reformist and even "fundamentalist" in some respects, without necessarily being heretical. See Jill C. Havens, "A Narrative of Faith: Middle English Devotional Anthologies and Religious Practice," *The Journal of the Early Book Society* 7 (2004): 68. Recently Havens has taken a more cautious stance toward the book, briefly mentioning it in connection with the circulation of Wycliffite tracts as "an anthology of popular orthodox devotional texts . . . together with distinctly Lollard items." See "Shading the Grey Area: Determining Heresy in Middle English Texts," in *Text and Controversy from Wyclif to Bale*, 350.

64. The text of the *Form of Living* ends with a blank page, which may indicate that it was not originally intended for placement in this particular book (see Dutton, "Compiling Julian," 97).

65. Dutton notes that this treatise on "Diliges Dominum Deum tuum," even though ink color and spacing suggest that it may have been copied later, was placed immediately after *Book to a Mother* "by design" (*ibid.*, 98). The *Diliges dominum* is item G.26 in P. S. Jolliffe, *A Check-List*, 90. For a printed version, see Horstmann, ed., *Yorkshire Writers*, 2:454–55.

66. In transcribing from the manuscript, I have silently modernized punctuation and expanded abbreviations.

67. This codicological observation is made by Dutton, "Compiling Julian," 59.

68. *Visitacio Infirmorum* is entry L.5(b) in Jolliffe, *A Check-List*, 124. According to Jolliffe, the work is attested in thirteen other manuscripts. For a printed version, see Horstmann, ed., *Yorkshire Writers*, 2:45–60. *De Utilitatibus Tribulationis* is J.3(c): it is extant in only one other manuscript, London, British Library, MS Royal.B.xvii (Jolliffe, *A Check-List*, 116). For a printed version, see Horstmann, ed., *Yorkshire Writers*, 2:449–58.

69. The treatise on preaching is of a type that typically circulated individually as *quaterni*: see Anne Hudson, "Some Aspects of Lollard Book Production," in *Lollards and Their Books* (London: Hambledon Press, 1985), 184.

70. Hudson, *The Premature Reformation*, 425.

Bibliography

MANUSCRIPTS

Lincoln
Lincoln Cathedral Library MS 91

London
British Library Harley MS 5272
British Library Egerton MS 826
British Library Additional MS 39843

Oxford
Bodleian Library Ashmole MS 751
Bodleian Library Laud Miscellaneous MS 210

PRINTED PRIMARY SOURCES

"Ancrene Wisse" Edited from MS Corpus Christi 402. Ed. J. R. R. Tolkein. EETS OS 249. London: Oxford University Press, 1962.

Augustine of Hippo. *De Utilitate Credendi, De Duabus Animabus Contra Fortunatum, Contra Adimantum, Contra Epistulam Fundamenti, Contra Faustum*. Ed. Joseph Zycha. Prague: F. Tempsky, 1891.

The City of God. Trans. Henry Bettenson. New York: Penguin Books, 1972.

Aurelii Augustini Opera, Part 14, vol. 2. Corpus Christianorum Series Latina 48. Turnhout: Brepols, 1955.

Sancti Aurelii Augustini De Trinitate Libri XV. Ed. W. J. Mountain. Corpus Christianorum Series Latina 50. Turnhout: Brepols, 1968.

On the Trinity Books 8–15. Ed. Gareth B. Mathews, trans. Stephen McKenna. Cambridge: Cambridge University Press, 2002.

Barr, Helen, ed. *The "Piers Plowman" Tradition: A Critical Edition of "Pierce the Ploughman's Crede," "Richard the Redeless," "Mum the Sothsegger," and "The Crowned King."* London: J. M. Dent, 1993.

Bartlett, Anne Clark, and Thomas H. Bestul, eds. *Cultures of Piety: Medieval English Devotional Literature in Translation*. Ithaca: Cornell University Press, 1999.

Benedict of Nursia. *The Rule of Saint Benedict in Latin and English with Notes.* Ed. Timothy Fry. Collegeville: The Liturgical Press, 1981.

Bernard of Clairvaux. *On the Song of Songs.* Trans. Kilian Walsh, OCSO. 4 vols. Kalamazoo: Cistercian Publications, 1983.

The Book of Tribulation. Ed. Alexandra Barratt. Heidelberg: Carl Winter, 1983.

The Book of Vices and Virtues. Ed. W. Nelson Francis. EETS OS 217. London: Oxford University Press, 1942.

"Book to a Mother": An Edition with Commentary. Ed. Adrian James McCarthy. Salzburg Studies in English Literature: Studies in the English Mystics 92.1. Salzburg: Institut für Anglistik und Amerikanistik, 1981.

Bonaventure. *S. Bonaventuræ Opera Omnia.* Vol. 12. Ed. A. C. Peltier. Paris: Ludovicus Vives, 1868.

  Decem Opuscula ad Theologia Mysticam Spectantia. Ed. Patres Collegii S. Bonaventura. Quaracchi: Collegium S. Bonaventuræ, 1949.

Brady, Mary Teresa, ed. *"The Pore Caitif:* Edited from MS Harley 2336 with Introduction and Notes." Ph.D. diss., Fordham University, 1954.

Bridget of Sweden. *The Liber Celestis of St. Bridget of Sweden: The Middle English Version in British Library MS Claudius B i, Together With a Life of the Saint From the Same Manuscript.* Ed. Roger Ellis. EETS OS 291. Oxford: Oxford University Press, 1987.

Chaucer, Geoffrey. *The Riverside Chaucer.* Gen. ed. David Benson. 3rd edn. Boston: Houghton Mifflin, 1987.

Christ, Karl, ed. *"La Règle des fins amans:* Eine Beginenregel aus dem Ende des XIII. Jahrhunderts." *Philologische Studien aus dem Romanisch-Germanischen Kulturkreise: Festgabe Karl Voretzsch.* Ed. B. Schädel and W. Mulertt. Halle: Max Niemeyer, 1927. 173–213.

John Chrysostom. Homily 63 on the Gospel of Matthew. In *Patrologiae Graecae.* Ed. J.-P. Migne. Vol. 58. Paris: J.-P. Migne, 1857–66.

  The Homilies of John Chrysostom on the Gospel of Matthew. Oxford: John Henry Parker, 1851.

Consacro, Peter D., ed. "A Critical Edition of *The Abbey of the Holy Ghost* From All Known Extant English Manuscripts With Introduction, Notes and Glossary." Ph.D. diss., Fordham University, 1971.

Contemplations of the Dread and Love of God. Ed. Margaret Connelly. EETS OS 303. London: Oxford University Press, 1993.

Davies, R. T., ed. *Medieval English Lyrics: A Critical Anthology.* London: Faber and Faber, 1963.

Dean, James, ed. *Six Ecclesiastical Satires.* Kalamazoo: Medieval Institute, 1991.

Dumeige, Gervais, ed. *Ives: Épître à Séverin sur la charité, Richard de Saint-Victor: Les quatres degrés de la violente charité.* Paris: J. Vrin, 1955.

Dymmok, Roger. *Liber Contra XII Errores et Hereses Lollardorum.* Ed. H. S. Cronin. London: Wyclif Society, 1922.

Fasciculi Zizaniorum Magistri Johannis Wyclif Cum Tritico, Ascribed to Thomas Netter of Walden. Ed. Walter W. Shirley. London: Her Majesty's Stationery Office, 1858.

Friedberg, Aemilius, ed. *Corporis Iuris Canonici.* 2 vols. Graz: Akademische Druck-u. Verlagsanstalt, 1959.

Forshall, Josiah, and Sir Frederic Madden, eds. *The Holy Bible, Containing the Old and New Testaments, With the Apocryphal books, in the Earliest English Versions Made From the Latin Vulgate by John Wycliffe and His Followers.* 4 vols. Oxford: Oxford University Press, 1850.

Furnivall, F. J., ed. *Political, Religious, and Love Poems.* EETS OS 15. London: Oxford University Press, 1866.

Gregory, Saint. *S. Gregorii Magni Regulae Pastoralis Liber.* Trans. R. H. Bramley. Oxford: James Parker, 1874.

Règle pastorale. Ed. Bruno Judic and Floribert Rommel, trans. Charles Morel. 2 vols. Sources Chrétiennes 381. Paris: Éditions du Cerf, 1992.

Hefele, C.-J. *Histoires des conciles.* Ed. and trans. Jean Leclercq. Vol. 5, Part 2. Paris: Letouzey and Ane, 1913.

Hilton, Walter. *Walter Hilton's "Mixed Life" Edited From Lambeth Palace MS 472.* Ed. S. J. Ogilvie-Thomson. Salzburg Studies in English Literature: Elizabethan & Renaissance Studies 92.15. Salzburg: Institut für Anglistik und Amerikanistik, 1986.

Walter Hilton's Latin Writings. 2 vols. Ed. J. P. H. Clark and Cheryl Taylor. Analecta Cartusiana 124. Salzburg: Institut für Anglistik und Amerikanistik, 1987.

Horstmann, Carl, ed. *Yorkshire Writers: Richard Rolle of Hampole, an English Father of the Church, and His Followers.* 2 vols. London: Swan Sonnenschein & Co., 1895–96.

Hudson, Anne, ed. *Selections From English Wycliffite Writings.* Cambridge: Cambridge University Press, 1978. Reprint Toronto: Medieval Academy, 1997.

Jacob's Well: An Englisht Treatise on the Cleansing of Man's Conscience. Ed. Arthur Brandeis. EETS OS 115. London: Kegan Paul, Trench, Trübner & Co., 1900.

Langland, William. *"Piers Plowman": The B Version.* Ed. George Kane and Talbot Donaldson. London: The Athlone Press, 1975.

The Lay Folks' Catechism. Ed. T. F. Simmons and H. E. Nolloth. EETS OS 118. London: Oxford University Press, 1901.

The Lay Folks' Mass Book. Ed. T. F. Simmons. EETS OS 71. London: Oxford University Press, 1879.

Leroquais, Victor, ed. *Les Livres d'heures manuscrits de la Bibliothèque Nationale.* Macon: Protat Frères, 1927.

Love, Nicholas. *The Mirror of the Blessed Life of Jesus Christ: A Full Critical Edition, Based on Cambridge University Library Additional MSS 6578 and 6686 with Introduction, Notes and Glossary.* Ed. Michael G. Sargent. Exeter: Exeter University Press, 2004.

Lydgate, John. *A Critical Edition of John Lydgate's Life of Our Lady.* Ed. Joseph A. Lauritis. Duquesne Studies Philological Series 2. Louvain: Editions E. Nauwelaerts, 1961.

"Þe Lyfe of Soule": An Edition with Commentary. Ed. Helen M. Moon. Salzburg Studies in English Literature, Elizabethan and Renaissance Studies 75. Salzburg: Institut für Englische Sprache und Literatur, 1978.

McNeill, John T., and Helena M. Gamer, eds. *Medieval Handbooks of Penance.* New York: Columbia University Press, 1938.

Murphy, J. J., ed. *Three Medieval Rhetorical Arts.* Berkeley: University of California Press, 1971.

"Þe Pater Noster of Richard Ermyte": A Late Middle English Exposition of the Lord's Prayer. Ed. F. G. A. M. Aarts. Nijmegen: Drukkerij Gebr. Janssen, 1967.

Paues, Anna, ed. *A Fourteenth Century English Biblical Version.* Cambridge: Cambridge University Press, 1904.

Perry, George G., ed. *English Prose Treatises of Richard Rolle of Hampole, Edited from Robert Thornton's MS in the Library of Lincoln Cathedral.* EETS OS 20, rev. edn. London: Oxford University Press, 1921.

Religious Pieces in Prose and Verse from the Thornton Manuscript. EETS OS 26. London: Oxford University Press, 1914.

Peter of Celle. *L'École du cloître.* Ed. Gérard de Martel. Sources Chrétiennes 240. Paris: Éditions du Cerf, 1977.

Powicke, F. M., and C. R. Cheney, eds. *Councils and Synods, With Other Documents Relating to the English Church.* 2 vols. Oxford: Clarendon Press, 1964.

The Prick of Conscience. Ed. Richard Morris. Berlin: Philological Society, 1863.

Ragusa, Isa, and Rosalie Green, eds. *Meditations on the Life of Christ: An Illustrated Manuscript of the Fourteenth Century.* Princeton: Princeton University Press, 1961.

Raine, James, ed. *Testamenta Eboracensia.* Vol. 2, Part 1. Surtees Society 4. London: J. B. Nichols and Son, 1836.

Registrum Johannis Trefnant, Episcopi Herefordensis. Ed. William A. Capes. London: Canterbury and York Society, 1916.

Robert of Blois. "Le Chastoiement des Dames." In *Die didactischen und religiösen dichtungen Robert's von Blois.* Ed. Jacob Ulrich. Berlin: Mayer & Müller, 1895. 57–78.

Rolle, Richard. *Richard Rolle: Prose and Verse Edited From MS Longleat 29 and Related Manuscripts.* Ed. S. J. Ogilvie-Thomson. EETS OS 293. London: Oxford University Press, 1988.

Salisbury, Eve, ed. *The Trials and Joys of Marriage.* Kalamazoo: Medieval Institute Publications, 2002.

Savage, Ann, and Nicholas Watson, eds. and trans. *Anchoritic Spirituality: "Ancrene Wisse" and Associated Works.* New York: Paulist Press, 1991.

Spalding, Mary Caroline, ed. *The Middle English Charters of Christ.* Bryn Mawr: Bryn Mawr Press, 1914.

"Speculum Christiani": A Middle English Religious Treatise of the 14th Century. Ed. Gustaf Holmstedt. EETS OS 182. London: Humphrey Milford, 1933.

Tanner, Norman, P. S. J., ed. *Decrees of the Ecumenical Councils.* 2 vols. Washington, DC: Sheed & Ward, 1990.

Thomas of Chobham. *Summa de Arte Praedicandi*. Ed. Franco Morenzoni. Corpus Christianorum Continuatio Mediaevalis 82. Turnhout: Brepols, 1988.

Thomson, Ian, and Louis Perraud, eds. *Ten Latin Schooltexts of the Middle Ages*. Mediaeval Studies 6. Lewiston: The Edwin Mellen Press, 1990.

Wilkins, David, ed. *Concilia Magnae Britanniae*. 4 vols. London: R. Gosling, 1737.

Windeatt, Barry, ed. *English Mystics of the Middle Ages*. Cambridge: Cambridge University Press, 1994.

Wordsworth, Christopher, ed. *Horae Eboracenses, the Prymer or Hours of the Blessed Virgin Mary According to the Use of the Illustrious Church of York*. London: B. Quaritch, 1920.

Wyclif, John. *De Civili Dominio*. Vol. 1. Ed. Reginald Poole. London: Wyclif Society, 1900–04.

De Civili Dominio. Vols. 2–3. Ed. Iohann Loserth. London: Wyclif Society, 1885.

Tractatus De Officio Regis. Ed. Alfred W. Pollard and Charles Sayle. London: Wyclif Society, 1887.

De Veritate Sacrae Scripturae. 3 vols. Ed. Rudolf Buddensieg. London: Wyclif Society, 1905–07.

On the Truth of Holy Scripture. Trans. Christopher Ian Levy. Kalamazoo: Medieval Institute Publications, 2001.

Trialogus et Supplementum Trialogi. Ed. Gotthard Lechler. Oxford: Clarendon Press, 1869.

SECONDARY SOURCES

Aers, David. *Piers Plowman and Christian Allegory*. London: Edward Arnold, 1975.

Chaucer, Langland and the Creative Imagination. London: Routledge & Kegan Paul, 1980.

Chaucer. Brighton: Harvester Press, 1986.

Faith, Ethics and Church: Writing in England, 1360–1409. Cambridge: D. S. Brewer, 2000.

✶Aers, David, and Lynn Staley. *The Powers of the Holy: Religion, Politics, and Gender in Late Medieval English Culture*. University Park: The Pennsylvania State University Press, 1996.

Allen, H. E. *Writings Ascribed to Richard Rolle Hermit of Hampole and Materials for His Biography*. New York: MLA 1927.

Althusser, Louis. "Ideology and Ideological State Apparatuses (Notes towards an Investigation)." In *Lenin and Philosophy and Other Essays*. Trans. Ben Brewster. New York: Monthly Review Press, 1971.

Amos, Mark Addison. "'For Manners Make the Man': Bourdieu, De Certeau, and the Common Appropriation of Noble Manners in the *Book of Courtesy*." In *Medieval Conduct*, ed. Kathleen Ashley and Robert L. A. Clark. Minneapolis: University of Minnesota Press, 2001. 23–48.

Annunziata, Anthony William. "Contemplations of the Dread and Love of God, Morgan MS. 861." Ph.D. diss., New York University, 1966.

Armstrong, C. A. J. "The Piety of Cicely, Duchess of York: A Study in Late Mediaeval Culture." In *England, France, and Burgundy in the Fifteenth Century*.
London: Hambledon Press, 1983. 135–56.

Asad, Talal. *Genealogies of Religion: Disciplines and Reasons of Power in Christianity
and Islam*. Baltimore: The Johns Hopkins University Press, 1993.

Aston, Margaret. *Lollards and Reformers: Images and Literacy in Late Medieval
Religion*. London: Hambledon Press, 1984.

"Popular Religious Movements." In *Faith and Fire: Popular and Unpopular
Religion 1350–1600*. London: Hambledon Press, 1993. 1–26.

✦ Bainbridge, Virginia. *Gilds in the Medieval Countryside: Social and Religious Change
in Cambridgeshire, c. 1350–1558*. Woodbridge: The Boydell Press, 1996.

Bakhtin, M. M. *The Dialogic Imagination*. Ed. Michael Holquist and trans.
Caryl Emerson and Michael Holquist. Austin: University of Texas Press,
1981.

Barr, Helen. *Socioliterary Practice in Late Medieval England*. Oxford: Oxford University Press, 2001.

Barron, Caroline. "The Parish Fraternities of Medieval London." In *The Church in
Pre-Reformation Society: Essays in Honour of F. R. H. Du Boulay*, ed. Caroline
Barron and Christopher Harper-Bill. Woodbridge: The Boydell Press, 1985.
13–37.

Barron, Caroline, and Laura Wright. "The London Middle English Guild Certificates of 1388–9." *Nottingham Medieval Studies* 39 (1995): 108–45.

✦ Bartlett, Anne Clark. *Male Authors, Female Readers: Representation and Subjectivity
in Middle English Devotional Literature*. Ithaca: Cornell University Press,
1995.

★ Bell, David. *What Nuns Read: Books and Libraries in Medieval English Nunneries*.
Cistercian Studies Series 158. Kalamazoo: Cistercian Publications, 1995.

Black, William Henry, ed. *A Descriptive, Analytical, and Critical Catalogue of the
Manuscripts Bequeathed unto the University of Oxford by Elias Ashmole, Esq.,
M.D., F.R.S., Also of Some Additional MSS. Contributed by Kingsley, Lhuyd,
Borlase, and Others*. Oxford: Oxford University Press, 1845.

Blake, N. F. "Vernon Manuscript: Contents and Organisation." In *Studies in
the Vernon Manuscript*, ed. Derek Pearsall. Cambridge: D. S. Brewer, 1990.
45–59.

Blamires, Alcuin. "The Wife of Bath and Lollardy." *Medium Aevum* 58.2 (1989):
224–42.

"Women and Preaching in Medieval Orthodoxy, Heresy, and Saints' Lives."
Viator 26 (1995): 135–52.

Blamires, Alcuin, and C. W. Marx, "'Woman Not to Preach': A Disputation in
British Library MS Harley 31." *The Journal of Medieval Latin* 3 (1993): 50–63.

Boenig, Robert. "The Middle English *Contemplations of the Dread and Love of
God*." *Studia Mystica* 9.2 (1986): 27–36.

Chaucer and the Mystics: The Canterbury Tales and the Genre of Devotional Prose.
Lewisburg: Bucknell University Press, 1995.

✦ Boffey, Julia. "*The Charter of the Abbey of the Holy Ghost* and its Role in Manuscript
Anthologies." *The Yearbook of English Studies* 33 (2003): 120–30.

Boffey, Julia, and John J. Thompson. "Anthologies and Miscellanies: Production and Choice of Texts." In *Book Production and Publishing in Britain 1375–1475*, ed. Jeremy Griffiths and Derek Pearsall. Cambridge: Cambridge University Press, 1989. 279–315.

Bourdieu, Pierre. *Outline of a Theory of Practice*. Trans. Richard Nice. Cambridge: Cambridge University Press, 1977.

—— *The Logic of Practice*. Trans. Richard Nice. Stanford: Stanford University Press, 1990.

Bowers, R. H. "The Middle English *St. Brendan's Confession*." *Archiv für das Studium der Neueren Sprachen* 175 (1939): 40–49.

Brown, Andrew. *Popular Piety in Late Medieval England: The Diocese of Salisbury 1250–1550*. Oxford: Clarendon Press, 1995.

Burgess, Clive. "For the Increase of Divine Service: Chantries in Late Medieval Bristol." *The Journal of Ecclesiastical History* 36 (1985): 46–65.

Carey, Hilary M. "Devout Literate Laypeople and the Pursuit of the Mixed Life in Later Medieval England." *Journal of Religious History* 14 (1987): 361–81.

Carruthers, Mary. "The Wife of Bath and the Painting of Lions." *PMLA* 94 (1979): 209–22.

—— *The Book of Memory: A Study of Memory in Medieval Culture*. Cambridge: Cambridge University Press, 1990.

—— *The Craft of Thought: Meditation, Rhetoric, and the Making of Images, 400–1200*. Cambridge: Cambridge University Press, 1998.

Charland, Thomas-Marie. *Artes Praedicandi*. Ottawa: Publications de l'Institut d'études médiévales d'Ottawa, 1936.

Clanchy, M. T. *From Memory to Written Record: England 1066–1307*. 2nd edn. Oxford: Basil Blackwell, 1993.

Clark, James G., ed. *The Religious Orders in Pre-Reformation England*. Woodbridge: The Boydell Press, 2002.

—— *A Monastic Renaissance at St Albans: Thomas Walsingham and His Circle c.1350–1440*. Oxford: Clarendon Press, 2004.

Clark, J. P. H. "Action and Contemplation in Walter Hilton." *Downside Review* 97 (1979): 204–20.

—— "Walter Hilton in Defence of the Religious Life and the Veneration of Images." *The Downside Review* 103.350 (January 1985): 1–25.

—— "Late Fourteenth-Century Cambridge Theology and the English Contemplative Tradition." In *The Medieval Mystical Tradition in England: Exeter Symposium V*, ed. Marion Glasscoe. Cambridge: Boydell and Brewer, 1992. 1–16.

Clopper, Lawrence M. *"Songes of Rechelesnesse": Langland and the Franciscans*. Ann Arbor: University of Michigan Press, 1997.

Coghill, Nevill K. "The Character of Piers Plowman Considered from the B Text." *Medium Ævum* 2 (1933): 108–35.

Coleman, Janet. *Medieval Readers and Writers 1350–1400*. London: Hutchinson, 1981.

Coletti, Theresa. "*Paupertas Est Donum Dei*: Hagiography, Lay Religion, and the Economics of Salvation in the Digby *Mary Magdalene*." *Speculum* 76.2 (2001): 337–78.

Connolly, Margaret. "The 'Eight Points of Charity' in John Rylands University Library MS English 85." In *"And Gladly wolde he lerne and gladly teche":* *Essays on Medieval English Presented to Professor Matsuji Tajima on His Sixtieth Birthday*, ed. Yoko Iyeiri and Margaret Connolly. Tokyo: Kaibunsha, 2002. 195–215.

"Public Revisions or Private Responses? The Oddities of BL, Arundel MS 197, with Special Reference to *Contemplations of the Dread and Love of God.*" *British Library Journal* 20.1 (1994): 55–64.

Copeland, Rita. "Why Women Can't Read: Medieval Hermeneutics, Statutory Law, and the Lollard Heresy Trials." In *Representing Women: Law, Literature, and Feminism*, ed. Susan Sage Heinzelman and Zipporah Batshaw Wiseman. Durham, NC: Duke University Press, 1994. 253–86.

Pedagogy, Intellectuals, and Dissent in the Later Middle Ages: Lollardy and Ideas of Learning. Cambridge: Cambridge University Press, 2001.

Cowdrey, H. E. J. "Unions and Confraternity with Cluny." *The Journal of Ecclesiastical History* 16.2 (1965): 152–62.

Curry Woods, Marjorie, and Rita Copeland. "Classroom and Confession." In *The Cambridge History of Medieval Literature*, ed. David Wallace. Cambridge: Cambridge University Press, 1999. 376–406.

Davenport, W. A. "Patterns in Middle English Dialogues." In *Medieval English Studies Presented to George Kane*, ed. Edward Kennedy *et al.* Wolfeboro, NH: D. S. Brewer, 1988. 127–45.

Dawson, James Doyne. "Richard FitzRalph and the Fourteenth-Century Poverty Controversies." *Journal of Ecclesiastical History* 34.3 (1983): 315–44.

Deanesly, Margaret. *The Lollard Bible and Other Medieval Biblical Versions.* Cambridge: Cambridge University Press, 1920.

De Certeau, Michel. *The Practice of Everyday Life.* Trans. Steven Rendall. Berkeley: University of California Press, 1984.

Dobson, R. B. "The Foundation of Perpetual Chantries by the Citizens of Medieval York." *Studies in Church History* 4: *The Province of York* (1967): 22–38.

Dohar, William J. *The Black Death and Pastoral Leadership: The Diocese of Hereford in the Fourteenth Century.* Philadelphia: University of Pennsylvania Press, 1995.

Dove, Mary. *The First English Bible.* Cambridge: Cambridge University Press, 2007.

Doyle, A. I. "A Survey of the Origins and Circulation of Theological Writings in English in the 14th, 15th, and Early 16th Centuries, with Special Consideration of the Part of the Clergy Therein." 2 vols. Ph.D. diss., University of Cambridge, 1953.

"Books Belonging to the Vere Family and Barking Abbey." *Transactions of the Essex Archaeological Society* New Series 25.2 (1958): 222–43.

"The Shaping of the Vernon and Simeon Manuscripts." In *Studies in the Vernon Manuscript*, ed. Derek Pearsall. Woodbridge: D. S. Brewer, 1990. 1–14.

Duffy, Eamon. *The Stripping of the Altars: Traditional Religion in Medieval England c.1400–c.1530.* New Haven: Yale University Press, 1992.

Dutschke, Consuelo W., ed. *Guide to Medieval Manuscripts in the Huntington Library*. 2 vols. San Marino: Huntington Library, 1989.

Dutton, Elisabeth. "Compiling Julian: The *Revelation of Love* and Late-Medieval Devotional Compilation." Ph.D. diss., Oxford University, 2002.

———. "Textual Disunities and Ambiguities of *mise-en-page* in the Manuscripts Containing *Book to a Mother*." *Journal of the Early Book Society* 6 (2003): 149–59.

———. "Christ the Codex: Compilation as Literary Device in *Book to a Mother*." *Leeds Studies in English* New Series 35 (2004): 81–100.

Edwards, A. S. G. "Fifteenth-Century English Collections of Female Saints' Lives." *The Yearbook of English Studies* 33 (2002): 131–41.

Ellis, Roger. "Figures of English Translation, 1382–1407." In *Translation and Nation: Toward a Cultural Politics of Englishness*, ed. Roger Ellis and Liz Oakley-Brown. Clevedon: Multilingual Matters, 2001. 7–47.

Erler, Mary C. "English Vowed Women at the End of the Middle Ages." *Mediaeval Studies* 57 (1995): 156–203.

———. "Exchange of Books Between Nuns and Laywomen: Three Surviving Examples." In *New Science Out of Old Books: Studies in Manuscripts and Early Printed Books in Honour of A. I. Doyle*, ed. Richard Beadle and A. J. Piper. Aldershot: Scolar Press, 1995. 360–73.

———. *Women, Reading and Piety in Late Medieval England*. Cambridge: Cambridge University Press, 2002.

Evans, G. R. "Theology: The Vocabulary of Teaching and Research 1300–1600: Words and Concepts." In *Vocabulary of Teaching and Research Between Middle Ages and Renaissance: Proceedings of the Colloquium, London, Warburg Institute, 11–12 March 1994*, ed. Olga Weijers. Turnhout: Brepols, 1995. 118–33.

Farnhill, Ken. *Guilds and the Parish Community in Late Medieval East Anglia, c. 1470–1550*. York: York Medieval Press, 2001.

Fitzgibbons, Moira. "Knowing Believers: Pastoralia, the Laity, and Interpretive Christianity." Ph.D. diss., Rutgers University, 2001.

———. "Disruptive Simplicity: Gaytryge's Translation of Archbishop Thoresby's *Injunctions*." In *The Vernacular Spirit: Essays on Medieval Religious Literature*, ed. Renate Blumenfeld-Kosinski *et al.* New York: Palgrave, 2002. 39–58.

———. "*Jacob's Well* and Penitential Pedagogy." *Studies in the Age of Chaucer* 27 (2005): 213–37.

Fleming, John. "Muses of the Monastery." *Speculum* 78.4 (2003): 1071–1106.

Fletcher, Alan J. "A Hive of Industry or a Hornet's Nest? MS Sidney Sussex 74 and its Scribes." In *Late-Medieval Religious Texts and Their Transmission: Essays in Honour of A. I. Doyle*, ed. A. J. Minnis. Cambridge: D. S. Brewer, 1994. 131–55.

Frantzen, Allen J. "Spirituality and Devotion in the Anglo-Saxon Penitentials." *Essays in Medieval Studies* 22 (2005): 117–28.

Galloway, Andrew. "Langland and the Schools." *The Yearbook of Langland Studies* 6 (1992): 89–107.

"Marriage Sermons, Polemical Sermons, and *The Wife of Bath's Prologue*: A Generic Excursus." *Studies in the Age of Chaucer* 14 (1992): 3–30.

Gayk, Shannon. "Images of Pity: The Regulatory Aesthetics of John Lydgate's Religious Lyrics." *Studies in the Age of Chaucer* 28 (2006): 175–203.

Gibson, Gail McMurray. "Resurrection as Dramatic Icon in the *Shipman's Tale*." In *Signs and Symbols in Chaucer's Poetry*, ed. J. P. Herman and J. J. Burke. University: University of Alabama Press, 1981. 102–12.

The Theater of Devotion: East Anglian Drama and Society in the Late Middle Ages. Chicago: University of Chicago Press, 1989.

Gilchrist, Roberta. *Gender and Material Culture: The Archaeology of Religious Women*. London: Routledge, 1994.

Gillespie, Vincent. "Lukynge in Haly Bukes: *Lectio* in Some Medieval Spiritual Miscellanies." *Analecta Cartusiana* 106 (1984): 1–27.

"Vernacular Books of Religion." In *Book Production and Publishing in Britain 1375–1475*, ed. Derek Pearsall and Jeremy Griffiths. Cambridge: Cambridge University Press, 1989. 317–44.

"Anonymous Devotional Writings." In *A Companion to Middle English Prose*, ed. A. S. G. Edwards. Cambridge: D. S. Brewer, 2004. 127–49.

"Vernacular Theology." In *Oxford Twenty-First Century Approaches to Literature: Middle English*, ed. Paul Strohm. Oxford: Oxford University Press, 2007. 401–20.

Ghosh, Kantik. *The Wycliffite Heresy: Authority and the Interpretation of Texts.* Cambridge: Cambridge University Press, 2002.

Gradon, Pamela. "Langland and the Ideology of Dissent." *Proceedings of the British Academy* 66 (1980): 179–205.

Gwynn, Aubrey, S. J. *The English Austin Friars in the Time of Wyclif.* Oxford: Oxford University Press, 1940.

Hanawalt, Barbara. "Keepers of the Lights: Late Medieval English Parish Gilds." *Speculum* 14.1 (1984): 21–37.

"Remarriage As an Option for Urban and Rural Widows in Late Medieval England." In *Wife and Widow in Medieval England*, ed. Sue Sheridan Walker. Ann Arbor: University of Michigan Press, 1993. 141–64.

Hanna, Ralph III. "The Difficulty of Ricardian Prose Translation: The Case of the Lollards." *MLQ* 51 (1990): 319–40.

Pursuing History: Middle English Manuscripts and Their Texts. Stanford: Stanford University Press, 1996.

"Miscellaneity and Vernacularity: Conditions of Literary Production in Late Medieval England." In *The Whole Book: Cultural Perspectives on the Medieval Miscellany*, ed. Stephen G. Nichols and Siegfried Wenzel. Ann Arbor: University of Michigan Press, 1996. 37–51.

The Index of Middle English Prose Handlist XII: Smaller Bodleian Collections: English Miscellaneous, English Poetry, English Theology, Finch, Latin Theology, Radcliffe Trust. Cambridge: D. S. Brewer, 1997.

"Notes Toward a Future History of Middle English Literature: Two Copies of Richard Rolle's *Form of Living*." In *Chaucer in Perspective: Middle English

Essays in Honour of Norman Blake, ed. Geoffrey Lester. Sheffield: Sheffield Academic Press, 1999. 270–300.

"English Biblical Texts before Lollardy and Their Fate." In *Lollards and Their Influence in Late Medieval England*, ed. Fiona Somerset *et al.* Woodbridge: The Boydell Press, 2003. 141–53.

London Literature, 1300–1380. Cambridge: Cambridge University Press, 2005.

⚹Hansen, Elaine Tuttle. *Chaucer and the Fictions of Gender.* Berkeley: University of California Press, 1992.

Harvey, Barbara. *Living and Dying in England 1100–1540: The Monastic Experience.* Oxford: Clarendon Press, 1993.

Havens, Jill C. "A Narrative of Faith: Middle English Devotional Anthologies and Religious Practice." *Journal of the Early Book Society* 7 (2004): 67–84.

"Shading the Grey Area: Determining Heresy in Middle English Texts." In *Text and Controversy From Wyclif to Bale*, ed. Helen Barr and Ann M. Hutchison. Turnhout: Brepols, 2005. 337–52.

Heffernan, Thomas. "Orthodoxies' *Redux*: *The Northern Homily Cycle* in the Vernon Manuscript and its Textual Affiliations." In *Studies in the Vernon Manuscript*, ed. Derek Pearsall. Cambridge: D. S. Brewer, 1990. 75–88.

Hirsh, John. "The Origins of Affective Devotion." In *The Boundaries of Faith: The Development and Transmission of Medieval Spirituality.* Leiden: E. J. Brill, 1996. 11–30.

Hudson, Anne. "The Debate on Bible Translation, Oxford 1401." *The English Historical Review* 90.354 (January 1975): 1–18.

Lollards and Their Books. London: Hambledon Press, 1985.

The Premature Reformation: Wycliffite Texts and Lollard History. Oxford: Clarendon Press, 1988.

"*Hermofodrita or Ambidexter*: Wycliffite Views on Clerks in Secular Office." In *Lollardy and the Gentry in the Later Middle Ages*, ed. Margaret Aston and Colin Richmond. Stroud: Sutton Publishing, 1997. 41–50.

Hughes, Jonathan. *Pastors and Visionaries: Religion and Secular Life in Late Medieval Yorkshire.* Woodbridge: The Boydell Press, 1988.

Hussey, S. S. "Langland, Hilton, and the Three Lives." *Review of English Studies New Series* 7.26 (1956): 132–50.

"Walter Hilton: Traditionalist?" In *The Medieval Mystical Tradition in England*, ed. Marion Glasscoe. Exeter: University of Exeter Press, 1980. 1–16.

Jager, Eric. *The Book of the Heart.* Chicago: University of Chicago Press, 2000.

Jauss, Hans Robert. *Toward an Aesthetic of Reception.* Trans. Timothy Bahti. Minneapolis: University of Minnesota Press, 1982.

Jolliffe, P. S. *A Check-List of Middle English Prose Writings of Spiritual Guidance.* Toronto: Pontifical Institute of Medieval Studies, 1974.

Justice, Steven. "Inquisition, Speech, and Writing: A Case from Late-Medieval Norwich." *Representations* 48 (Autumn 1994): 1–29.

"'General Words': Response to Elizabeth Schirmer." In *Voices in Dialogue: Reading Women in the Middle Ages*, ed. Linda Olson and Kathryn Kerby-Fulton. Notre Dame: University of Notre Dame Press, 2005. 377–94.

Keiser, George. "Lincoln Cathedral MS 91: The Life and Milieu of the Scribe." *Studies in Bibliography* 32 (1979): 159–65.

"The Holy Boke Gratia Dei." *Viator* 12 (1981): 289–317.

"More Light on the Life and Milieu of Robert Thornton." *Studies in Bibliography* 36 (1983): 111–19.

"'To Knawe God Almyghtyn': Robert Thornton's Devotional Book." *Analecta Cartusiana* 106 (1984): 103–29.

"Patronage and Piety in Fifteenth-Century England: Margaret, Duchess of Clarence, Symon Wynter and Beinecke MS 317." *The Yale University Library Gazette* 60.1–2 (1985): 32–46.

Kerby-Fulton, Kathryn. "*Piers Plowman*." In *The Cambridge History of Medieval English Literature*, ed. David Wallace. Cambridge: Cambridge University Press, 1999. 513–38.

Books Under Suspicion: Censorship and Tolerance of Revelatory Writing in Late Medieval England. Notre Dame: University of Notre Dame Press, 2006. 513–38.

Kerby-Fulton, Kathryn, and Steven Justice. "Langlandian Reading Circles and the Civil Service in London and Dublin, 1380–1427." *New Medieval Literatures* 1 (1997): 59–83.

Knowles, David. "The *Regula Magistri* and the *Rule* of St. Benedict." *Great Historical Enterprises and Problems in Monastic History*. London: Thomas Nelson and Sons, 1963. 139–95.

Kreider, Alan. *English Chantries: The Road to Dissolution*. Cambridge, MA: Harvard University Press, 1979.

Krug, Rebecca. "The Comfort of Form: Prayer and Lay Women's Devotion in the Fifteenth Century." Paper presented at the International Congress on Medieval Studies, Kalamazoo, MI, May 2007.

Kruger, Steven. "Claiming the Pardoner: Toward a Gay Reading of Chaucer's *Pardoner's Tale*." In *Critical Essays on Geoffrey Chaucer*, ed. Thomas C. Stillinger. New York: G. K. Hall, 1998. 150–72.

Lahey, Stephen E. *Philosophy and Politics in the Thought of John Wyclif*. Cambridge: Cambridge University Press, 2003.

Lawler, Traugott. "The Secular Clergy in *Piers Plowman*." *The Yearbook of Langland Studies* 16 (2002): 85–117.

Lawton, David. "The Subject of *Piers Plowman*." *The Yearbook of Langland Studies* 1 (1987): 1–30.

"Englishing the Bible." In *The Cambridge History of Medieval English Literature*, ed. David Wallace. Cambridge: Cambridge University Press, 1999. 454–82.

Leclercq, Jean. "Disciplina." In *Dictionnaire de spiritualité, ascétique et mystique, doctrine et histoire*, ed. Charles Baumgartner *et al.* Vol. 3. Paris: Beauchesne, 1957. 1291–1302.

Leicester, Marshall. *The Disenchanted Self: Representing the Subject in "The Canterbury Tales."* Berkeley: University of California Press, 1990.

Lepine, D. N. "The Origins and Careers of the Canons of Exeter Cathedral 1300–1455." In *Religious Belief and Ecclesiastical Careers in Late Medieval England,* ed. Christopher Harper-Bill. Woodbridge: The Boydell Press, 1991. 87–120.

Lerer, Seth. *Boethius and Dialogue: Literary Method in "The Consolation of Philosophy."* Princeton: Princeton University Press, 1985.

✹ "Medieval English Literature and the Idea of the Anthology." *PMLA* 118.5 (2003): 1251–67.

Lewis, Robert E., and Angus McIntosh. *A Descriptive Guide to the Manuscripts of the Prick of Conscience.* Medium Ævum Monographs New Series 12. Oxford: The Society for the Study of Mediaeval Languages and Literature, 1982.

Little, A. G., ed. Eric Stone. "Franciscan Letters of Fraternity." *Bodleian Library Record* 5 (1954): 13–25.

Little, A. G. "Corrodies at the Carmelite Priory of Lynn." *Journal of Ecclesiastical History* 9.1 (1958): 8–29.

Little, Katherine C. *Confession and Resistance: Defining the Self in Late Medieval England.* Notre Dame: University of Notre Dame Press, 2006.

"'Bokes Ynowe': Vernacular Theology and Fourteenth-Century Exhaustion." *English Language Notes* 44.1 (Spring 2006): 109–13.

Macy, Gary. *The Hidden History of Women's Ordination: Female Clergy in the Medieval West.* Oxford: Oxford University Press, 2008.

Makowski, Elizabeth. *Canon Law and Cloistered Women: "Periculoso" and its Commentators 1298–1545.* Washington, DC: Catholic University Press, 1997.

Mann, Jill. *Chaucer and Medieval Estates Satire: The Literature of Social Classes and the "General Prologue" to the "Canterbury Tales."* Cambridge: Cambridge University Press, 1973.

Marrou, H.-I. "'Doctrina' et 'Disciplina' dans la langue des Pères de L'Église." *Bulletin du Cange* 9 (1934): 5–25.

Mason, Emma. "The Role of the English Parishioner, 1100–1500." *The Journal of Ecclesiastical History* 27.1 (1976): 17–29.

McDonnell, Ernest. *The Beguines and Beghards in Medieval Culture, With Special Emphasis on the Belgian Scene.* New Brunswick, NJ: Rutgers University Press, 1954.

McFarlane, K. B. *John Wycliffe and the Beginnings of English Nonconformity.* New York: MacMillan, 1953.

McGalliard, John C. "Characterization in Chaucer's *Shipman's Tale*." *Philological Quarterly* 54.1 (1975): 1–18.

McRee, Ben R. "Charity and Gild Solidarity in Late Medieval England." *The Journal of British Studies* 32.3 (1993): 195–225.

McSheffrey, Shannon. *Gender and Heresy: Women and Men in Lollard Communities 1420–1530.* Philadelphia: University of Pennsylvania, 1995.

"Heresy, Orthodoxy and Vernacular Religion 1480–1525." *Past and Present* 186 (February 2005): 47–80.

Meale, Carole M. "'. . . alle the bokes that I haue of latyn, englisch, and frensch': Laywomen and Their Books in Late Medieval England." In *Women and*

Literature in Britain, 1150–1500, ed. Carole M. Meale. Cambridge: Cambridge University Press, 1993. 128–58.

Middleton, Anne. "The Audience and Public of *Piers Plowman*." In *Middle English Alliterative Poetry and its Literary Background: Seven Essays*, ed. David Lawton, Cambridge: D. S. Brewer, 1982. 101–54.

Minnis, A. J. *Medieval Theory of Authorship: Scholastic Literary Attitudes in the Later Middle Ages*. London: Scolar Press, 1984.

———. "Chaucer's Pardoner and the 'Office of Preacher.'" In *Intellectuals and Writers in Fourteenth-Century Europe*, ed. Piero Boitani and Anna Torti. Tübingen: Gunter Narr, 1984. 88–119.

———. "'Respondet Waltherus Bryth . . .' Walter Brut in Debate on Women Priests." In *Text and Controversy From Wyclif to Bale: Essays in Honour of Anne Hudson*, ed. Helen Barr and Ann M. Hutchison. Turnhout: Brepols, 2005. 229–50.

———. *Fallible Authors: Chaucer's Pardoner and Wife of Bath*. Philadelphia: University of Pennsylvania Press, 2008.

Molin, Jean-Baptiste, and Protais Mutembe. *Le Rituel du mariage en France du XIIe au XVIe siècle*. Théologie historique 26. Paris: Beauchesne, 1974.

Moorman, John. *The History of the Franciscan Order From its Origins to the Year 1517*. Oxford: Clarendon Press, 1968.

Moran, Jo Ann Hoeppner. *The Growth of English Schooling, 1340–1548: Learning, Literacy, and Laicization in Pre-Reformation York Diocese*. Princeton: Princeton University Press, 1985.

Morrison, Susan Signe. "Don't Ask, Don't Tell: The Wife of Bath and Vernacular Translations." *Exemplaria* 8.1 (1996): 97–123.

Newman, Barbara. *From Virile Woman to WomanChrist: Studies in Medieval Religion and Literature*. Pennsylvania: University of Pennsylvania Press, 1995. 137–67.

➤ Nichols, Steven J., and Siegfried Wenzel, eds. *The Whole Book: Cultural Perspectives on the Medieval Miscellany*. Ann Arbor: University of Michigan Press, 1996.

Nisse, Ruth. *Defining Acts: Drama and the Politics of Interpretation in Late Medieval England*. Notre Dame: University of Notre Dame Press, 2005.

Oliva, Marilyn. *The Convent and the Community in Late Medieval England: Female Monasteries in the Diocese of Norwich 1350–1540*. Woodbridge: The Boydell Press, 1998.

Pantin, W. A. *The English Church in the Fourteenth Century*. Cambridge: Cambridge University Press, 1955.

———. "Instructions for a Devout and Literate Layman." In *Medieval Learning and Literature: Essays Presented to Richard William Hunt*, ed. J. J. G. Alexander and M. T. Gibson. Oxford: Clarendon Press, 1976. 398–422.

Parkes, M. B. "The Literacy of the Laity." In *Scribes, Scripts and Readers: Studies in the Communication, Presentation and Dissemination of Medieval Texts*. London: Hambledon Press, 1991. 275–98.

Patterson, Lee. *Chaucer and the Subject of History*. Madison: University of Wisconsin Press, 1991.

Pearsall, Derek. "Langland and Lollardy: From B to C." *The Yearbook of Langland Studies* 17 (2003): 7–23.

Pezzini, Domenico. "How Resoun Schal Be Keper of þe Soule: una traduzione del quattrocento inglese dalle *Rivelazioni* (VII, 5) di S. Brigida di Svezia." *Aevum* 60 (1986): 253–81.

Powell, James M. "*Pastor Bonus*: Some Evidence of Honorius III's Use of the Sermons of Pope Innocent III." *Speculum* 52.3 (1977): 522–37.

Rhodes, Jim. *Poetry Does Theology: Chaucer, Grosseteste, and the "Pearl"-Poet*. Notre Dame: University of Notre Dame Press, 2001.

✦ Rice, Nicole R. "Spiritual Ambition and the Translation of the Cloister: *The Abbey* and *Charter of the Holy Ghost*." *Viator* 33 (2002): 222–60.

Richardson, Janette. *Blameth Nat Me: A Study of Imagery in Chaucer's Fabliaux*. The Hague: Mouton, 1970.

✱ Riddy, Felicity. "'Women Talking about the Things of God': A Late Medieval Sub-Culture." In *Women and Religion in Britain, c. 1100–1500*, ed. Carol M. Meale. Cambridge: Cambridge University Press, 1993. 104–27.

Ronquist, E. C. "Learning and Teaching in Twelfth-Century Dialogues." *Res Publica Litterarum* 13 (1990): 239–56.

Rouse, Richard H., and Mary A. "From Flax to Parchment: A Monastic Sermon from Twelfth-Century Durham." In *New Science Out of Old Books: Studies in Manuscripts and Early Printed Books in Honour of A. I. Doyle*, ed. Richard Beadle and A. J. Piper. London: Scolar, 1995. 1–13.

Rubin, Miri. *Charity and Community in Medieval Cambridge*. Cambridge: Cambridge University Press, 1987.

Saenger, Paul. "Books of Hours and the Reading Habits of the Later Middle Ages." In *The Culture of Print: Power and the Uses of Print in Early Modern Europe*, ed. Roger Chartier. Oxford: Basil Blackwell, 1989. 141–73.

Sargent, Michael G. "Minor Devotional Writings." In *Middle English Prose: A Critical Guide to Major Authors and Genres*, ed. A. S. G. Edwards. New Brunswick: Rutgers University Press, 1984. 147–75.

Scase, Wendy. *"Piers Plowman" and the New Anticlericalism*. Cambridge: Cambridge University Press, 1989.

Scattergood, V. J. "The Originality of the *Shipman's Tale*." *The Chaucer Review* 11 (1977): 210–31.

✱ Schirmer, Elizabeth. "Reading Lessons at Syon Abbey." In *Voices in Dialogue: Reading Women in the Middle Ages*. Ed. Linda Olson and Kathryn Kerby-Fulton. Notre Dame: Notre Dame University Press, 2005. 345–76.

Shepherd, Geoffrey. "English Versions of the Scriptures Before Wyclif." In *The Cambridge History of the Bible*, vol. 2, ed. G. W. H. Lampe. Cambridge: Cambridge University Press, 1969. 362–87.

Simpson, James. *"Piers Plowman"*: An Introduction to the B-Text. London: Longman, 1990.

"Desire and the Scriptural Text: Will as Reader in *Piers Plowman*." In *Criticism and Dissent in the Middle Ages*, ed. Rita Copeland. Cambridge: Cambridge University Press, 1996. 215–43.

Reform and Cultural Revolution. Vol. 2 of *The Oxford English Literary History.* Oxford: Oxford University Press, 2002.

Smith, Lesley. "The Theology of the Twelfth- and Thirteenth-Century Bible." In *The Early Medieval Bible*, ed. Richard Gameson. Cambridge: Cambridge University Press, 1994. 223–32.

Somerset, Fiona. *Clerical Discourse and Lay Audience in Late Medieval England.* Cambridge: Cambridge University Press, 1998.

———. "Wycliffite Spirituality." In *Text and Controversy From Wyclif to Bale: Essays in Honour of Anne Hudson*, ed. Helen Barr and Ann M. Hutchison. Turnhout: Brepols, 2005. 375–86.

Spencer, H. L. *English Preaching in the Late Middle Ages.* Oxford: Oxford University Press, 1993.

Steele, F. J. *Towards a Spirituality for Lay-Folk: The Active Life in Middle English Religious Literature From the Thirteenth Century to the Fifteenth.* Salzburg University Studies in English Literature: Elizabethan & Renaissance Studies 92:23. Lewiston, NY: The Edwin Mellen Press, 1995.

Steiner, Emily. *Documentary Culture and the Making of Medieval English Literature.* Cambridge: Cambridge University Press, 2003.

Strohm, Paul. *Social Chaucer.* Cambridge, MA: Harvard University Press, 1989.

Swanson, R. N. *Church and Society in Late Medieval England.* Oxford: Basil Blackwell, 1989.

———. "Mendicants and Confraternity in Late Medieval England." In *The Religious Orders in Pre-Reformation England*, ed. James G. Clark. Woodbridge: Boydell & Brewer, 2002. 121–41.

Szittya, Penn R. *The Antifraternal Tradition in Medieval Literature.* Princeton: Princeton University Press, 1986.

Tanner, Norman. *The Church in Late Medieval Norwich.* Pontifical Institute Studies and Texts 66. Toronto: Pontifical Institute of Mediaeval Studies, 1984.

Tentler, Thomas. *Sin and Confession on the Eve of the Reformation.* Princeton: Princeton University Press, 1977.

Thompson, John J. "Another Look at the Religious Texts in Lincoln, Cathedral Library, MS 91." In *Late Medieval Religious Texts and Their Transmission: Essays in Honour of A. I. Doyle*, ed. A. J. Minnis. Cambridge: D. S. Brewer, 1994. 169–87.

Thomson, Williel R. *The Latin Writings of John Wyclyf: An Annotated Catalog.* Toronto: Pontifical Institute of Medieval Studies, 1983.

Thrupp, Sylvia. *The Merchant Class of Medieval London.* Ann Arbor: University of Michigan Press, 1948.

Tillotson, John. "Visitation and Reform of the Yorkshire Nunneries in the Fourteenth Century." *Northern History* 30 (1994): 1–21.

Trigg, Stephanie. "Learning to Live." In *Oxford Twenty-First Century Approaches to Literature: Middle English*, ed. Paul Strohm. Oxford: Oxford University Press, 2007. 459–71.

Trivedi, Kalpen. "The 'Pore Caitif': *Lectio* through *Compilatio*: Some Manuscript Contexts." *Mediaevalia* 20 (2001): 129–52.

Van Engen, John. "Friar Johannes Nyder on Laypeople Living as Religious in the World," in *Vita Religiosa im Mittelalter*, ed. Franz J. Felten and Nikolas Jaspert. Berlin: Duncker & Humblot, 1999. 583–615.

Vauchez, André. "'*Ordo Fraternitatis*': Confraternities and Lay Piety." In *The Laity in the Middle Ages: Religious Practices and Experiences*, ed. Daniel E. Bornstein and trans. Margery J. Schneider. Notre Dame: University of Notre Dame Press, 1993. 107–17.

Walsh, Katherine. *A Fourteenth-Century Scholar and Primate: Richard FitzRalph in Oxford, Avignon and Armagh*. Oxford: Clarendon Press, 1981.

Warner, Lawrence. "Becket and the Hopping Bishops." *The Yearbook of Langland Studies* 17 (2003): 107–34.

Warren, Ann K. *Anchorites and Their Patrons in Medieval England*. Berkeley: University of California Press, 1985.

Warren, Nancy Bradley. *Spiritual Economies: Female Monasticism in Late Medieval England*. Philadelphia: University of Pennsylvania Press, 2001.

Waters, Claire. *Angels and Earthly Creatures: Preaching, Performance and Gender in the Later Middle Ages*. Philadelphia: University of Pennsylvania Press, 2004.

Watson, Nicholas. "The Methods and Objectives of Thirteenth-Century Anchoritic Devotion." In *The Medieval Mystical Tradition in England: Exeter Symposium IV*, ed. Marion Glasscoe. Cambridge: D. S. Brewer, 1987. 132–53.

Richard Rolle and the Invention of Authority. Cambridge: Cambridge University Press, 1991.

"Censorship and Cultural Change in Late-Medieval England: Vernacular Theology, the Oxford Translation Debate, and Arundel's Constitutions of 1409." *Speculum* 70 (1995): 822–64.

"Conceptions of the Word: The Mother Tongue and the Incarnation of God." *New Medieval Literatures* 1 (1997): 85–124.

"The *Gawain*-Poet as a Vernacular Theologian." In *A Companion to the "Gawain"-Poet*, ed. Derek Brewer and Jonathan Gibson. Cambridge: D. S. Brewer, 1997. 293–313.

"Visions of Inclusion: Universal Salvation and Vernacular Theology in Pre-Reformation England." *Journal of Medieval and Early Modern Studies* 27 (1997): 145–87.

"Christian Ideologies." In *A Companion to Chaucer*, ed. Peter Brown. Oxford: Basil Blackwell, 2000. 75–89.

"The Middle English Mystics." In *The Cambridge History of Medieval English Literature*, ed. David Wallace. Cambridge: Cambridge University Press, 1999. 539–65.

"Fashioning the Puritan Gentry-Woman: Devotion and Dissent in *Book to a Mother*." In *Medieval Women: Texts and Contexts in Late Medieval Britain: Essays for Felicity Riddy*, ed. Jocelyn Wogan-Browne *et al*. Turnhout: Brepols, 2000. 169–84.

"'Et que est huius ydoli materia? Tuipse': Idols and Images in Walter Hilton." In *Images, Idolatry, and Iconoclasm in Late Medieval England: Textuality and the Visual Image*, ed. Jeremy Dimmick *et al.* Oxford: Oxford University Press, 2002. 95–111.

"*Ancrene Wisse*, Religious Reform and the Late Middle Ages." In *A Companion to Ancrene Wisse*, ed. Yoko Wada. Cambridge: D. S. Brewer, 2003. 197–226.

"Chaucer's Public Christianity." *Religion and Literature* 37.2 (2005): 99–114.

Wells, Henry W. "The Construction of Piers Plowman." *PMLA* 44 (1929): 123–40.

Whitehead, Christiania. "Making a Cloister of the Soul in Medieval Religious Treatises." *Medium Ævum* 67.1 (1998): 2–29.

Castles of the Mind: A Study of Medieval Architectural Allegory. Cardiff: University of Wales Press, 2003.

Whitfield, D. W. "The Third Order of St. Francis in Medieval England." *Franciscan Studies* 13 (1953): 50–59.

Wilks, Michael. "Predestination, Property, and Power: Wyclif's Theory of Dominion and Grace." *Studies in Church History* 2 (1965): 220–36.

"Wyclif and the Great Persecution," in *Wyclif: Political Ideas and Practice.* Oxford: Oxbow Books, 2000. 179–203.

Williams, Arnold. "Relations Between the Mendicant Friars and the Secular Clergy in England in the Later Fourteenth Century." *Duquesne Studies Annuale Mediaevale* 1 (1960): 22–95.

Winnick, R. H. "Luke 12 and Chaucer's *Shipman's Tale*." *The Chaucer Review* 30.2 (1995): 164–90.

Wogan-Browne, Jocelyn, *et al.*, eds. *The Idea of the Vernacular.* University Park: The Pennsylvania State University Press, 1999.

Woods, William F. "A Professional Thyng: The Wife as Merchant's Apprentice in The *Shipman's Tale*." *The Chaucer Review* 24.2 (1989): 139–49.

Index

CAMBRIDGE STUDIES IN MEDIEVAL LITERATURE

Made in the USA
Monee, IL
13 June 2023

35730977R00157